THE RUSSO-UKRAINIAN WAR

ALSO BY SERHII PLOKHY

Chernobyl Roulette: War in the Nuclear Disaster Zone

Atoms and Ashes: A Global History of Nuclear Disasters

The Frontline: Essays on Ukraine's Past and Present

Nuclear Folly: A History of the Cuban Missile Crisis

*Forgotten Bastards of the Eastern Front:
American Airmen Behind the Soviet Lines and
the Collapse of the Grand Alliance*

Chernobyl: The History of a Nuclear Catastrophe

Lost Kingdom: The Quest for Empire and the Making of the Russian Nation

The Man with the Poison Gun: A Cold War Spy Story

The Gates of Europe: A History of Ukraine

The Last Empire: The Final Days of the Soviet Union

The Cossack Myth: History and Nationhood in the Age of Empires

Yalta: The Price of Peace

Ukraine and Russia: Representations of the Past

*The Origins of the Slavic Nations:
Premodern Identities in Russia, Ukraine, and Belarus*

*Unmaking Imperial Russia:
Mykhailo Hrushevsky and the Writing of Ukrainian History*

Tsars and Cossacks: A Study in Iconography

The Cossacks and Religion in Early Modern Ukraine

THE RUSSO-UKRAINIAN WAR

THE RETURN OF HISTORY

Serhii Plokhy

W. W. NORTON & COMPANY
Independent Publishers Since 1923

In memory of all those who died defending freedom, theirs and ours

For information about permission to reproduce selections from this book,
write to Permissions, W. W. Norton & Company, Inc.,
500 Fifth Avenue, New York, NY 10110

For information about special discounts for bulk purchases, please contact
W. W. Norton Special Sales at specialsales@wwnorton.com or 800-233-4830

Manufacturing by Lakeside Book Company
Production manager: Anna Oler

Library of Congress Control Number: 2023933126

ISBN 978-1-324-07892-0 pbk.

W. W. Norton & Company, Inc., 500 Fifth Avenue, New York, N.Y. 10110
www.wwnorton.com

W. W. Norton & Company Ltd., 15 Carlisle Street, London W1D 3BS

1 2 3 4 5 6 7 8 9 0

CONTENTS

Maps   vi

Preface: Making Sense of War   xv

1.   Imperial Collapse   1

2.   Democracy and Autocracy   34

3.   Nuclear Implosion   63

4.   The New Eastern Europe   81

5.   The Crimean Gambit   100

6.   The Rise and Fall of the New Russia   118

7.   Putin's War   135

8.   The Gates of Kyiv   155

9.   Eastern Front   176

10. The Black Sea   199

11. The Counteroffensive   219

12. The Return of the West   243

13. The Pivot to Asia   269

Afterword: The New World Order   293

Acknowledgments   305

Notes   309

Index   367

The Russian Empire and the USSR

ARCTIC

GREAT BRITAIN

NETH.

BEL

DEN.

NORWAY

SWEDEN

FINLAND

GERMANY

Baltic Sea

Murmansk

Novaya Zemlya

Barents Sea

Kara Sea

AUSTRIA-HUNGARY

POLAND

BALTIC STATES

St. Petersburg

Archangelsk

Dnieper R.

Kyiv

Moscow

UKRAINE

Don R.

Kazan

Volga R.

Ekaterinburg

Ural Mountains

Ob R.

Yenisei R.

ROM.

BUL.

Crimea

Black Sea

Caucasus

Trans-Siberian Railroad

Tomsk

OTTOMAN EMPIRE

Baku

Caspian Sea

TURKESTAN

Aral Sea

KAZAKHS

Syr Darya R.

Irtysh R.

Lake Balkhash

ARABIA

IRAN

Amu Darya R.

UZBEKS

Bukhara

Toshkent

Persian Gulf

AFGHANISTAN

INDIA

TIBET

U.A.E.

OMAN

NEPAL

0   250   500 mi

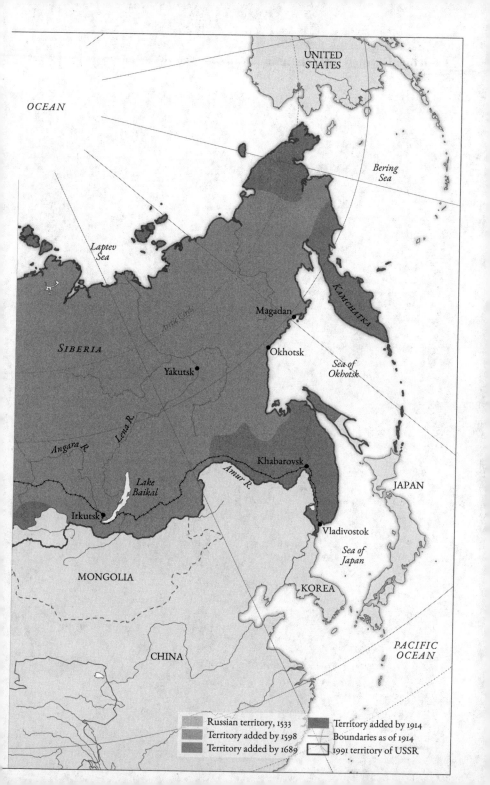

OCEAN

UNITED
STATES

Bering
Sea

Laptev
Sea

КAMCHATKA

SIBERIA

Magadan

Arctic Circle

Okhotsk

Yakutsk

Sea of
Okhotsk

Lena R.

Angara R.

Khabarovsk

Amur R.

Lake
Baikal

JAPAN

Irkutsk

Vladivostok

MONGOLIA

Sea of
Japan

KOREA

CHINA

PACIFIC
OCEAN

Russian territory, 1533	Territory added by 1914
Territory added by 1598	Boundaries as of 1914
Territory added by 1689	1991 territory of USSR

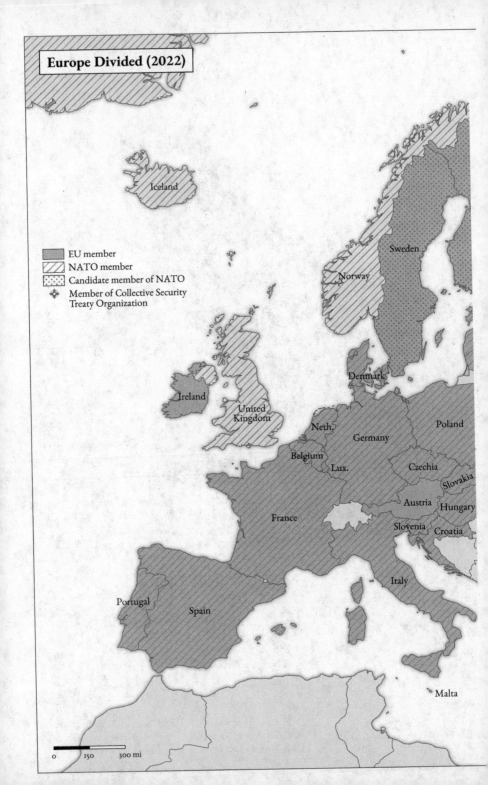

Europe Divided (2022)

- EU member
- NATO member
- Candidate member of NATO
- Member of Collective Security Treaty Organization

Iceland

Sweden

Norway

Denmark

Ireland

United Kingdom

Neth.

Germany

Poland

Belgium

Lux.

Czechia

Slovakia

Austria

Hungary

France

Slovenia

Croatia

Italy

Portugal

Spain

Malta

0   150   300 mi

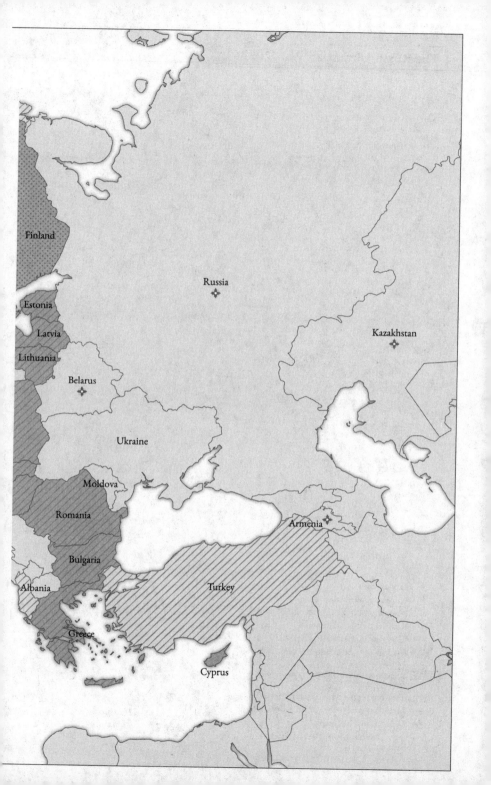

Finland

Russia

Estonia

Kazakhstan

Latvia

Lithuania

Belarus

Ukraine

Moldova

Romania

Armenia

Bulgaria

Albania

Turkey

Greece

Cyprus

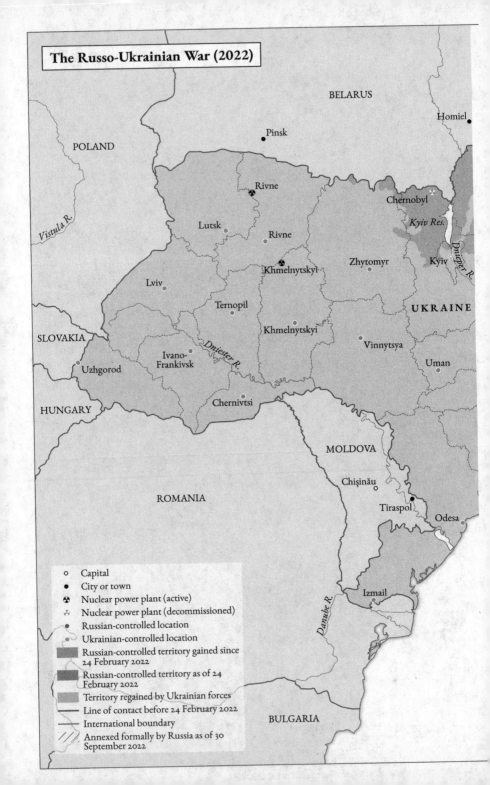

The Russo-Ukrainian War (2022)

BELARUS

Homiel

Pinsk

POLAND

Rivne

Chernobyl

Kyiv Res.

Lutsk

Rivne

Zhytomyr

Kyiv

Dnieper R.

Khmelnytskyi

Lviv

UKRAINE

Ternopil

Khmelnytskyi

SLOVAKIA

Ivano-
Frankivsk

Dniester R.

Vinnytsya

Uman

Uzhgorod

HUNGARY

Chernivtsi

MOLDOVA

Chișinău

ROMANIA

Tiraspol

Odesa

Izmail

Danube R.

BULGARIA

○ Capital
● City or town
☢ Nuclear power plant (active)
☢ Nuclear power plant (decommissioned)
● Russian-controlled location
● Ukrainian-controlled location
Russian-controlled territory gained since
24 February 2022
Russian-controlled territory as of 24
February 2022
Territory regained by Ukrainian forces
— Line of contact before 24 February 2022
— International boundary
/// Annexed formally by Russia as of 30
September 2022

Chernihiv

Kursk

Voronezh

RUSSIA

Konotop

Sumy

Belgorod

Kharkiv

Kremenchuk Res.

Poltava

Cherkasy

Izyum

Siverodonetsk

Kremenchuk

Kramatorsk

Donbas

Luhansk

Kropyvnytskyi

Dnipro

Pavlohrad

Horlivka

Kryvyi Rih

Zaporizhia

Donetsk

South Ukraine

Kakhovka Res.

Zaporizhia

Rostov

Don R.

Mykolaiv

Mariupol

Melitopol

Nova Kakhovka

Berdyansk

Kherson

Henichesk

Sea of Azov

Crimea

Kerch

Krasnodar

Simferopol

Kerch Strait

Novorossiysk

Sevastopol

Black Sea

0   50   100 mi

The World Divided (2022)

Cuba

Venezuela

Nicaragua

Condemns Russia
West-leaning

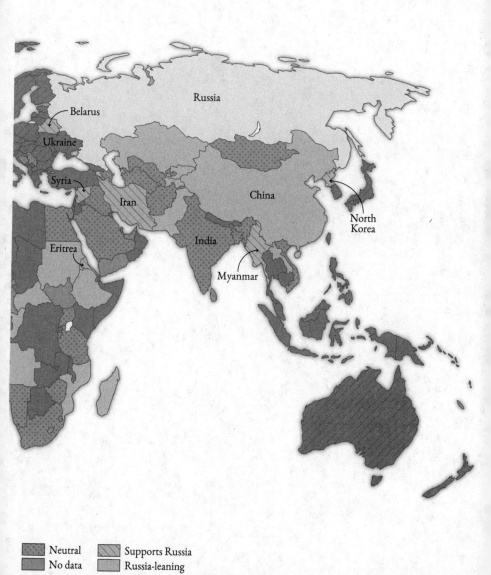

Russia

Belarus

Ukraine

Syria

Iran

Eritrea

China

India

Myanmar

North
Korea

Neutral

No data

Supports Russia

Russia-leaning

Preface

MAKING SENSE OF WAR

The start of the Russian invasion caught me in Vienna, the capital of the former empire whose actions triggered World War I and the city whose takeover by Nazi Germany as part of the Anschluss of Austria in 1938 led the way to the outbreak of World War II. A new war was in the air when the citizens of Vienna went to bed on the evening of February 23, 2022. After watching disturbing news on CNN, I hoped for a better outcome, but the presentiment of trouble was there. The next morning I woke up earlier than usual, around 6:00 a.m. I reached for my phone to check the news but instead somehow got to my email.

My heart sank once I read the subject line of an email: "My goodness." The message came from a colleague at Harvard with whom I had been discussing the chances of a new war since October, when he first alerted me to the possibility of a major conflict. Russian troops were massing close to the Ukrainian borders, and the American media had begun reporting on them almost in real time. I hoped that the troop movement was part of Russian blackmail. My colleague believed that it could be for real. Now, even before opening the email, I knew that it had happened—the invasion he warned about. I opened the email. The concluding lines read: "Nothing good will come of it. Every day gives a different message. Tonight U.S. intelligence predicts a blitz, but let's see tomorrow. I hope you are OK in Vienna."

I was not OK. Something had begun, but I did not know what it was. My guess was that Putin and the Russians had invaded eastern Ukraine, the battleground of 2014–15. With those thoughts, I opened another email. Its subject line was empty, but it came from a colleague in Dnipro, which had been far behind the front lines of the 2014–15 war. The email made it clear that there would be no territory behind the lines in this war. "I'm getting my things together to leave Dnipro; maybe I'll send 'fragments' of my books to your e-mail address, because I don't know what comes next, and my computer may be lost somewhere in these events," wrote my colleague, adding: "We are well acquainted with the fate of manuscripts in wartime." I sent a positive response and thanked him for trusting me with his unfinished work.

It was only then that I checked the news: an all-out invasion of Ukraine had begun, with cities from Kyiv to Dnipro to my native Zaporizhia attacked by Russian missiles. It was surreal. I called my sister in Zaporizhia. She was awake. Explosions were being heard in part of the city, thankfully distant from the quarter where she lived in our parents' house. She was calm. The previous night I had called and advised her to buy enough gasoline for her car. She did not follow my advice, believing, like almost everyone in Ukraine, that a large-scale war was an impossibility. Now war had begun, and neither of us was prepared for it. We would have to take one day at a time. I would be calling her twice daily, morning and evening. Always the same questions: How was last night? How was your day? The meaning of "good night" and "good day" had suddenly changed. Any day or night with sirens but no missile attacks or bombings was good.

On that first morning I put on a white shirt and a blazer. Since I was going to the archives of the International Atomic Energy Agency, where I was researching the international history of the Chernobyl nuclear disaster of 1986, the choice of outfit was unusual, if not down-right strange. But I overdressed on purpose to show by my appearance that I was collected and prepared to carry out my duties, whatever they might be in wartime conditions, no matter the news from the front lines. My inspiration was the diary of George F. Kennan, the renowned American diplomat and international relations expert. On waking up to the news of Hitler's attack on Czechoslovakia in March 1939, he shaved meticulously not to give an impression of a "harried appearance." He was determined to perform his functions as a diplomat, no matter what.

At the archives, people looked at me with evident sympathy. "I am sorry about what is happening to your country," one of the archivists told me. The words implied that the end was near: the country would be taken over, if not today, then tomorrow. Had I dressed up for its funeral? I hoped not but did not know what to expect. Later that day, a photographer from the *Neue Zürcher Zeitung* showed up in my office at the Vienna Institut für die Wissenschaften vom Menschen to take a photo of me for an interview conducted a few days earlier. The image that appeared in the newspaper showed me disheveled, my hair blown by the wind in every direction, but wearing my white shirt and looking sad but determined. In the interview that I had given *The New Yorker* a few days earlier, I predicted that the Ukrainians would fight. "I don't know when and how," I told the reporter, "but I have no doubt that there will be resistance."[1]

The events of the subsequent days and weeks showed that I had guessed right in predicting resistance, but I could not have imagined its scope, or the scope of the coming war itself. The invasion, which Putin called a "military operation" that was supposed to last a few days, or a few weeks at most, turned into the greatest conventional war in Europe since 1945. It has claimed tens of thousands of lives of men and women, many of them innocent civilians, and created the largest refugee crisis in Europe, once again since the end of World War II. In the following months, the number of women, children, and elderly who fled the fighting in Ukraine reached a total of twelve million people, and those who found refuge in the countries of Eastern and Central Europe exceeded five million. Nuclear sites like Chernobyl and the nuclear power plants in Zaporizhia, the largest in Europe, became new battlegrounds, and there were veiled threats of the use of nuclear weapons.

How did all this happen? Neither emotionally nor professionally was I ready to think through and explain to myself and others what was going on as a result of Russia's unprovoked aggression. Madness and criminality seemed the only rational explanations. But as the media kept reaching out to me for commentary, I felt that I could not refuse, as my words might actually have some impact on the course of events. I realized that as a historian I could offer something that others lacked when it came to understanding the largest military conflict in Europe since World War II. Eventually I convinced myself that, to rephrase Winston Churchill, historians are the worst interpreters of current events except everyone else.

As a historian, I did my best to put the developments unfolding in front of me and the world at large in historical and comparative perspective. What made such a war of aggression possible? What made the Ukrainians resist as they did and are continuing to do? Finally, what will be the most important consequences of the war for Ukraine, Russia, Europe, and the world? These were the questions that I asked myself as I slowly recovered from the shock of the first days of the aggression and began relearning to think analytically. I also tried to identify signs of the coming Russo-Ukrainian war that we had failed to recognize at the time, engaging in wishful thinking instead.

In the minds of many of us, history had reached its end with the fall of the Berlin Wall, if not in Francis Fukuyama's understanding of that fall as the ultimate victory of liberal democracy as a form of political order, then in the conviction that despite continuing rivalry between great powers, unprovoked invasions followed by territorial annexations and large-scale military actions had been relegated to the past. There had been clear signs to the contrary—the wars in Chechnya, the former Yugoslavia, and then Afghanistan and Iraq—but we preferred to ignore them. The rise of populism and authoritarian regimes, as well as authoritarian tendencies in democratic nations, suggested parallels with the 1930s, but most of us brushed them aside.

History is now back with a vengeance, displaying its worst features and opening its most fearsome pages, filled with scenes of violence and destruction. We know what happened as a result of the rise of dictatorships in Europe on the eve of World War II, and we can now easily imagine where the rise of authoritarianism in Europe, Eurasia, and elsewhere may lead today. It is time to learn from history by putting current events into context, both historical and geopolitical, to understand their roots, predict outcomes, and try to end the violence.

In this book I take a *longue durée* approach to understanding the current war. I decline the temptation to identify the date of February 24, 2022, as its beginning, no matter the shock and drama of the all-out Russian assault on Ukraine, for the simple reason that the war began eight years earlier, on February 27, 2014, when Russian armed forces seized the building of the Crimean parliament. Two sets of agreements, called Minsk I and Minsk II, ended that stage of the war in diplomatic terms a year later, in February 2015. Nevertheless, an undeclared war involving shelling and shooting across the demarcation line in Ukraine's Donbas region continued for the next seven years, killing more than 14,000 Ukrainians but attracting little international attention. That phase ended with Russia's formal withdrawal from the Minsk agreements and the start of its all-out invasion of Ukraine in February 2022.

In the pages that follow I discuss the current war, its origins, course, and the already apparent and possible future consequences. As I show here, the roots of the current war are to be found in the history of imperial collapse in the nineteenth and twentieth centuries, which also produced the key ideas that have fueled the current conflict. My basic argument is that what we see today is not an entirely new phenomenon. In many ways, the current conflict is an old-fashioned imperial war conducted by Russian elites who see themselves as heirs and continuators of the great-power expansionist traditions of the Russian Empire and the Soviet Union. On Ukraine's part it is first and foremost a war of independence, a desperate attempt on behalf of a new nation that emerged from the ruins of the Soviet collapse to defend its right to existence.

Despite its imperial roots, the current war is being waged in a new international environment defined by the proliferation of nuclear weapons, the disintegration of the post–Cold War international order, and an unprecedented resurgence of populist nationalism, last seen in the 1930s, throughout the world. The war clearly indicates that Europe and the world have all but spent the peace dividend resulting from the collapse of the Berlin Wall in 1989 and are entering a new, as yet undetermined, era. A new world order, possibly replicating the bipolar world of the Cold War era, is being forged in the flames of the current war. At the time of writing that war is not over, and we do not yet know what its end will bring. But it is quite clear even today that the future of the world in which we and our children and grandchildren will be living depends greatly on its outcome.

1

IMPERIAL COLLAPSE

It was 7:00 p.m. Moscow time on Christmas Day, December 25, 1991. Mikhail Gorbachev, the former general secretary of the Communist Party of the USSR and soon to be the former president of the Soviet Union, sat at the desk in his Kremlin office and read a prepared statement in front of television cameras.

Gorbachev addressed his listeners as "dear compatriots and fellow citizens." In fact, he was speaking to the entire world: CNN was broadcasting his brief address live. The Soviet leader was stepping down as president of the USSR. At 7:12 p.m., when Gorbachev finished speaking, the Soviet Union officially ceased to exist. The communist regime, which had managed to save the Russian empire of the tsars from collapse, grown into a superpower, and threatened the world with nuclear annihilation, was no more. The red banner over the Kremlin was lowered less than half an hour later, to be replaced with the white, blue, and red banner of the Russian Federation, similar to the tricolor flag of the Russian Empire before its collapse in the Revolution of 1917.[1]

In his twelve-minute speech, the president of the Union of the Soviet

Socialist Republics, known all over the world as the USSR, declared that he was resigning for "reasons of principle." He had striven to maintain "the Union state and integrity of the country" but was unable to do so. "Events took another course. What prevailed was the tendency to divide the country and dismember the state, with which I cannot agree." Gorbachev was resigning as president of a country whose legal existence was already at an end. It had been dissolved by the leaders of the fifteen Union republics constituting the USSR earlier that month.[2]

While the disintegration of the Soviet Union had been underway for some time, it became irreversible on December 1, 1991, when the citizens of Ukraine, the Union's second-largest republic after Russia, went to the polls to decide whether they wanted their country to become independent. The turnout exceeded 84 percent of eligible voters, and more than 92 percent of them chose independence. Even residents of the Ukrainian Donbas (Donets Basin), adjoining Russia's western border, voted for independence by a margin of almost 84 percent. In the Crimea, the only region of Ukraine with a majority Russian population, 54 percent supported independence. Sevastopol, the home port of the Black Sea Fleet, did even better, registering 57 percent support for Ukrainian independence.[3]

The vote came as a shock to Gorbachev but not to President Boris Yeltsin of Russia, Gorbachev's onetime protégé and then his challenger and rival. Yeltsin had been briefed on the likely outcome a few days earlier by his adviser Galina Starovoitova, an anthropologist and pro-democracy activist. On hearing the projections, Yeltsin was incredulous. "It cannot be true!" was his first reaction. "This is our fraternal Slavic republic! There are 30 percent Russians there. The Crimea is Russian! All the people living east of the Dnieper gravitate toward Russia!" It took close to 40 minutes for Starovoitova to convince her boss that the polling data were pointing in one direction and one direction only, an overwhelming vote for independence. Yeltsin made his decision on the spot: he would recognize Ukrainian independence and meet with the soon-to-be-elected president of Ukraine, Leonid Kravchuk, to forge an alliance and a new union different from the one led by Mikhail Gorbachev.[4]

The meeting took place on December 7 and continued into the next day at the Belavezha hunting grounds on the Belarusian-Polish border. The Belarusian leaders, including the head of the republic's parliament, Stanislav Shushkevich, hosted the Russian and Ukrainian presidents, who decided the fate of the USSR. Once Kravchuk refused to join the reformed Union proposed by Gorbachev, Yeltsin's aide Gennadii Burbulis proposed to dissolve the USSR altogether. Frightened by this, the head of the Belarusian KGB reported the treasonous proposal to his bosses in Moscow, but there was no active response—by that time, Gorbachev had few remaining supporters in the Soviet capital. The Soviet Union was replaced by the Commonwealth of Independent States, a regional international organization rather than a new state. Less than two weeks later, the leaders of the Central Asian republics joined the Commonwealth as its founding members. Now Gorbachev had no allies in the republics either. Bowing to the inevitable, he resigned on December 25, 1991.[5]

Gorbachev's foreign-policy aide, Anatolii Cherniaev, who was also the principal drafter of his superior's resignation speech, later wrote in his assessment of the Soviet Union's last year of existence: "What actually went on with the USSR that year was what happened 'at the appointed time' to other empires when the potential allotted to them by history expired." The fall of empires was very much on Cherniaev's mind when he introduced such phrases as "What is most ruinous in this crisis is the disintegration of statehood" and "We are heirs to a great civilization" into the draft of Gorbachev's speech. But he also admitted the futility of any attempt to save the failing empire. "Gorbachev's efforts to rescue the Union are hopeless spasms," wrote Cherniaev in his diary in November 1991, going on to observe: "And yet it would all have blown over were it not for Ukraine, for the Crimea, which cannot be given away."[6]

The Soviet Union fell on account of the Ukrainian referendum, when after some hesitation the Ukrainians decided to put the question of their independence to a vote. Gorbachev argued in favor of an all-Union referendum on the fate of the USSR, but there was no referendum in any other republic. Most of them, including Russia, simply accepted the results of the Ukrainian referendum as a verdict not only on the independence of the Ukrainian republic but also on the future of the USSR. Neither Gorbachev nor Yeltsin imagined the Soviet Union without its second-largest republic, a key element of Russian imperial and Soviet history and mythology. Restoring the imperial project in any form would depend on Russia's ability to bring Ukraine back into the fold. "Without Ukraine, Russia ceases to be an empire, but with Ukraine suborned and then subordinated, Russia automatically becomes an empire," remarked Zbigniew Brzezinski a few years later.[7]

The Myth of Origins

Most Russians believe today, as they have believed for centuries, that their state and nation originated in Kyiv (in the Russian version, "Kiev"), the center of the medieval polity that historians call Kyivan Rus'. Centered on today's Ukrainian capital, it encompassed a good part of what is now Ukraine, Belarus, and European Russia. Kyivan Rus', formed in the tenth century, fell under the blows of the Mongols in the thirteenth century, but not before giving birth to numerous semi-independent polities. The most powerful of them were Galicia-Volhynia in present-day Ukraine and southern Belarus; Great Novgorod or the Novgorodian republic in the northwestern lands of the former Kyivan realm; and the principality of Vladimir—later Moscow in its northeastern part—the historical core of modern Russia.[8]

The Russians can indeed trace back to Kyiv the origins of their religion, written language, literature, arts, law code, and—extremely important in the premodern era—their ruling dynasty. Their attempts to claim Kyiv as the source of their ethnicity, language, and popular culture turned out to be more problematic. Travelers from Moscow and St. Petersburg found that the locals in Kyiv and environs spoke a language different from theirs, sang different songs, and had a distinct culture. But that did not matter too much, as the myth of Russia's Kyivan origins had already embedded itself in the consciousness of the Russian elites by the late fifteenth century.[9]

The origins of that myth go back to the mid-fifteenth century, the earliest years of the Grand Principality of Moscow, later known as Muscovy, as an independent state. Its founder was Ivan the Great, the ruler of Moscow and one of the many descendants of the Kyivan princes who established Moscow's rule over a huge realm extending from Nizhnii Novgorod in the east to Great Novgorod, or simply Novgorod, in the west. It was in the midst of Ivan's war against Novgorod, one of the heirs of Kyivan Rus', that the myth of Russia's Kyivan origins was born, originally as a dynastic claim. Ivan declared himself the heir of the Kyivan princes, claiming the right to rule Novgorod on that basis. He defeated the Novgorodians at the Battle of Shelon in 1471 and absorbed the republic into his realm in 1478. The independent Russian state, born of the struggle between Moscow and Novgorod, resulted from the victory of authoritarianism over democracy.

Ivan's military victory over the Novgorodians also made him completely independent of the Tatar khans, descendants of the Mongol Empire, whose rule over Muscovy gradually became ever more nominal. The Tatars tried to prevent Ivan from taking Novgorod—ironically enough, protecting Russian democracy—but failed and had to retreat. The conquest of Novgorod also symbolized the victory of Ivan's dynastic claim to be the sole legitimate heir of the Kyivan princes. In the coming years he would use that status again and again to claim more Russian, Ukrainian, and Belarusian lands. The powerful historical myth of the Russian dynasty's Kyivan origins underlay the policy of newly independent Muscovy—a policy of conquest.[10]

Ivan III was the first ruler of Muscovy who tried to call himself "tsar," a European word meaning "emperor," or ruler of rulers, derived from the name of Julius Caesar. But the first ruler actually to be crowned tsar was his grandson, Ivan the Terrible. Ivan III passed on to his heir not only the authoritarian institution of princely power, which the grandson successfully turned into a form of tyranny, but also the myth of Kyivan origins. Ivan IV (the Terrible) claimed to be a descendant of Emperor Augustus, a genealogical link that he tried to trace back through the princes of Kyiv to the emperors of Byzantium and their Roman predecessors. He also sought to increase the Muscovite realm beyond his grandfather's possessions.

In the 1550s Ivan IV conquered the khanates of Kazan and Astrakhan, which, like Muscovy itself, were successor states of the once mighty Mongol empire. He would count the years of his rule as master of the khanates of Muscovy, Kazan, and Astrakhan separately, indicating his conquest of these Volga khanates as the key achievement justifying his claim to the title of tsar. Having subdued those khanates, he turned west, trying to reach the Baltic Sea and fighting a ground war against the Grand Duchy of Lithuania on the territory of today's Baltic states and Belarus—other parts of the once mighty Kyivan Rus'. But Ivan's attempt to extend Muscovy's rule westward failed in the midst of the Livonian War (1558–83) in which Muscovy was confronted by the coalition of the states that included Poland-Lithuania, Sweden, and Denmark.[11]

The seventeenth century began with the capture of Moscow by Polish troops and their allies, the Ukrainian Cossacks. During this "Time of Troubles" and in its aftermath, Muscovy separated itself from Kyiv and the Ukrainian and Belarusian lands not only politically but also in religion. The Muscovites no longer regarded the Kyivans as fellow Orthodox believers, claiming that they had been corrupted by accepting the rule of Catholic kings and becoming open to the West. Defeated on the battlefield and undermined by internal strife, Muscovy paused in its obsession with Kyiv, its history, and the justification it provided for further conquest. But this was a relatively short intermission rather than the end of the imperial show.[12]

One of the outcomes of the sixteenth-century Livonian War, lost by Ivan the Terrible, had been the union of the Kingdom of Poland with the Grand Duchy of Lithuania, comprising the latter's Ukrainian and Belarusian lands, in the face of the Muscovite threat. The Union of Lublin (1569) established the Polish-Lithuanian Commonwealth, an early modern state with limited royal power and strong central and local parliaments or diets. As part of the Commonwealth deal, Poland established its control over Ukraine and Kyiv, while the Belarusian lands remained within the Grand Duchy of Lithuania. This division would play a key role in the development of modern Ukrainians and Belarusians as separate nationalities.[13]

The leading role in the formation of modern Ukraine was played by the Cossacks—freemen and runaway serfs who emerged by the late sixteenth century as a powerful military force on the lower Dnieper in the "no-man's land" between the Kingdom of Poland and the Crimean Khanate, one more distant relative of the Mongol Empire. Under the leadership of their commander, Hetman Bohdan Khmelnytsky, the Cossacks rebelled against Polish rule in 1648, seeking to establish their political freedoms as a social estate and practice their Orthodox religion unhindered. This bloody revolt, among whose victims were the Jews of Ukraine, culminated in the establishment of a Cossack state.

The new state needed allies if it was to hold out against the overwhelming Polish and Lithuanian forces arrayed against it. After more than five years of warfare, Khmelnytsky entered into an alliance with Muscovy, recognizing the sovereignty of the tsar in exchange for his military protection against Ukraine's enemies. The deal was struck between Khmelnytsky and the tsar's plenipotentiaries in the Ukrainian city of Pereiaslav in January 1654. Muscovy's immediate goal in entering the war against the Polish-Lithuanian Commonwealth was the recovery of lands lost to Poland during the Time of Troubles. But memories of the Kyivan inheritance were soon revived, and the Ukrainian Orthodox were once again considered co-religionists. The protection of Orthodox brethren against the Polish Catholic kings and the revival of the Muscovite dynasty's Kyivan roots became the legitimizing watchwords of the new westward drive.[14]

In the nineteenth century the Russian historians, including the most influential of them, Vasilii Kliuchevsky, claimed that the "gathering of the Russian lands," or the "reunification of Rus'" after the Mongol invasion by the Moscow princes and then the tsars, was the quintessential feature of the Russian historical process. That interpretation of history, rooted in the myth of Russia's Kyivan origins, was supposed to culminate in the triumphal reunification of the Rus' lands in one Russian state, or "Russia, one and indivisible." According to Kliuchevsky, that process had been largely completed by the mid-nineteenth century.[15]

No element of the reunification saga was considered more important by the imperial historians than the establishment of Muscovy's control over eastern Ukraine in the mid-seventeenth century. Their Soviet successors hailed it as the "reunification of Ukraine with Russia"—in effect, the culmination of Ukrainian history with its complete assimilation by Russia. Many Ukrainian historians, for their part, referred to the "reunification" as a military alliance, personal union, or even outright subjugation.

The Poles were soon defeated. The Muscovites then moved into Belarus and established their garrisons in Cossack Ukraine, including the city of Kyiv. The lengthy incorporation of the Ukrainian Cossack state into the Tsardom of Moscow, and the encroachment on what the Cossacks called their "rights and freedoms"—the elements of their democratic political culture—had begun. The Ukrainian Cossack elites found the new conditions unacceptable, and in 1708 their new hetman, Ivan Mazepa, led a revolt against the Muscovite tsar, subsequently emperor, Peter I. It was Peter who would change his country's name from Muscovy to Russia, a name derived from Byzantine Greek, and proclaim the establishment of the Russian Empire in 1721.

Mazepa joined the advancing forces of King Charles XII of Sweden, only to be defeated along with his new protector in the Battle of Poltava (1709), fought in the heart of the Ukrainian Cossack lands. Moscow's victory in that battle led to triumph in the Northern War (1721), catapulting the Russian Empire into the position of a European power with holdings in the Baltics and Central Europe, where it reduced the Polish-Lithuanian Commonwealth to its de facto protectorate. In Ukraine, Peter curtailed Cossack autonomy by abolishing the office of hetman and placing the Cossack state, known to historians as the Hetmanate, under the jurisdiction of a Russian administrative body called the Little Russian Collegium.[16]

Empress Catherine II, who ruled from 1762 to 1796, completed the destruction of the Hetmanate and the integration of the Cossack polity into the Russian Empire, which she inherited from Peter I. This was completed in the midst of the Russo-Turkish wars of the late eighteenth century, which brought huge swaths of territory in what is today southern Ukraine under Russian control. The Crimea was annexed, and with the threat of Crimean Tatar incursions gone, there was no longer any point in tolerating the Ukrainian Cossacks and their democratic institutions. The Cossack regiments were integrated into the Russian imperial army, and the last of the Cossack institutions were eliminated with the Russian assault on the Zaporizhian Host (Army) in the lower Dnipro region (1775).

In the three partitions of Poland, Catherine claimed all of Belarus and most of the Ukrainian lands. She struck a medal on the occasion of the second partition of 1793, its inscription reading *Ottorzhennaia vozvratikh* (I returned what was torn away). The reference was once again to the lands that had once belonged to the Kyivan state. The Ukrainian territories, whether previously ruled by the Cossacks or the Poles, with the exception of western Ukrainian lands that fell to the Habsburg monarchy, were now brought into the Russian Empire as mere provinces with no particular rights or privileges.

The Cossacks, with their state and institutions, were gone. But not their memory. In the nineteenth century that memory would become a powerful instrument in the hands of those who created the modern Ukrainian nation. They would produce a new Ukrainian anthem beginning with the words "Ukraine has not yet perished." The reference was to the continuing existence of the nation in spite of the destruction of its spiritual temple, the Cossack state.[17]

The Ascent of a Nation

Not until the nineteenth century did the Russian Empire encounter an enemy that it could not defeat. The name of the enemy was nationalism.

It came first in two Polish uprisings that rocked the Russian Empire. In the long run, however, it was Ukrainian nationalism, awakened by the imperial campaigns to suppress Polish mobilization, that posed the main threat to imperial Russian statehood. If the Poles resisted imperial rule, the Ukrainians threatened the unity of the "reunified" Catherinian empire by claiming an identity distinct from the Russian.

The Russian Empire was confronted with the national question by the first Polish uprising in 1830–31. The Poles, whose multiethnic state of Poland-Lithuania had been partitioned by Russia, Prussia, and Habsburg Austria in the second half of the eighteenth century, raised the flag of modern nationalism against all the partitioning empires in the early nineteenth century. They were the first to come up with the idea that a nation could strive for political sovereignty even if it lacked a state apparatus. That idea was expressed in the opening words of the Polish anthem, which served as a model for the Ukrainian hymn: "Poland has not yet perished."[18]

The empire struck back by forging a model of Russian nationalism closely allied with its empire. In 1832, in the aftermath of the first Polish uprising, the newly appointed deputy minister of education, Count Sergei Uvarov, proposed a tripartite formula to Emperor Nicholas I that could serve as the keystone of a new Russian identity to be forged by the educational system. It consisted of three concepts to which a loyal subject of the tsar would have to subscribe: Orthodoxy, Autocracy, and Nationality. In the past, Russian subjects had been obliged to be loyal to God, the Sovereign, and the Fatherland. Nationality, which replaced the "fatherland," was as much a reaction to rising Polish nationalism as it was an attempt to emulate German nation-building. Uvarov was particularly influenced by the ideas of the German historian and philologist Karl Wilhelm Friedrich Schlegel, a follower of Johann Gottfried von Herder, who envisioned a unified German state to be based on the German nation united by language and customs.[19]

For Uvarov, the envisioned nationality was to be indisputably Russian, but it would include the other East Slavic heirs of Kyivan Rus', the Ukrainians and Belarusians. The population of the two lesser branches was mainly Orthodox in religion, but a significant minority belonged to the Uniate Church, which had been established in the late sixteenth century. Its adherents, who lived in the eastern borderlands of partitioned Poland, followed Orthodox ritual but acknowledged the supremacy of the Roman pope. In Uvarov's eyes they were Russian but not Orthodox, and many believed them susceptible to Polish insurgent propaganda. The "problem" was solved before the end of the 1830s, when the Uniates were forcibly "reunited" with the Russian Orthodox Church. The Russian nation, integrated by loyalty to the tsar, was now united by religion as well.

The history textbooks written under Uvarov's supervision legitimized the creation of one Russian nation, now united within imperial borders and subject to the scepter of the tsar. The imperial narrative envisioned the origins of the Russian nation in medieval Kyiv of the princely era. That nation had been divided by foreign invaders ranging from the Mongols to the Poles but reunited by the Russian tsars to become once again consolidated and invincible.[20]

The model of a united Russian nation did not remain unchallenged for long. Taking a cue from the Poles, the Ukrainians soon raised the banner of their own national movement. The empire encountered a challenge from the ranks of the Russian nation that it was trying to build in opposition to Poland. In the 1840s, Kyivan intellectuals led by a professor of history at the local university, Mykola Kostomarov, and a drawing instructor at the same university, Taras Shevchenko, formed a clandestine organization that claimed the existence of a distinct Ukrainian nation. Drawing on traditions of Cossack history and historical chronicles, they were fascinated with the Ukrainian language and the lore and culture of the common people. According to Herder and his followers, that was the taproot of national identity.

The modern Ukrainian national project was born, and it was much more threatening to the Russian Empire than the Polish revolt. Kostomarov envisioned a Slavic federation to replace the Romanov and Habsburg monarchies and empires. The empire felt compelled to adjust the model of the unified Russian nation. It did so in the aftermath of the second Polish uprising (1863–64), which once again put the loyalty not only of the Poles but also of the Ukrainians and Belarusians into question. The new model of the unified Russian nation was tripartite, postulating the existence of separate "tribes" of Great Russians, Little Russians (Ukrainians), and White Russians (Belarusians). They spoke different "dialects" of Russian, went the argument, put forward by the conservative Russian journalist Mikhail Katkov, among others, but that was no reason to doubt the unity of the tripartite nation.[21]

To ensure that it would remain united, the authorities decided to arrest the development of distinct Ukrainian and Belarusian languages. The first ban on the publication in Ukrainian of anything other than folklore—including the Bible, religious texts, and language primers, along with school textbooks—was introduced in 1863 and remained in effect, with some modifications, until the first decade of the twentieth century. It was then abolished in the turmoil caused by the Revolution of 1905 in the Russian Empire. The ban on Ukrainian-language pub-lications delayed the development of the modern Ukrainian national project but failed to suppress it. The Ukrainians of Galicia, a part of Ukraine taken over by Austria as a result of the partitions of Poland, continued to publish in Ukrainian not only their own works but also the writings of their counterparts from Russian-ruled Ukraine.[22]

The Russian imperial authorities regarded developments in the Slavic lands of one of its key rivals, the Habsburg monarchy (refash-ioned into a dual Austro-Hungarian monarchy after Austria's defeat by Germany in 1866), with utmost suspicion. Of particular concern were the Ukrainians of three provinces, Galicia, Bukovyna, and what is known today as Transcarpathia, settled by ethnic Ukrainians. They called themselves Rusyns and, in the course of the nineteenth cen-tury, developed not one but three nation-building projects. The one that emerged from the Revolution of 1848 conceived them as a distinct Rusyn or Ruthenian nationality, loyal to the Habsburgs and maintain-ing few ties with the rest of Ukraine.

The Habsburgs supported the Ruthenian movement as a counter-weight to the much more active Polish one, but, weakened vis-à-vis the

Hungarians, with whom they now had to share power, they made the Poles their favorites at the expense of the Ruthenians. In response, some Ruthenian leaders and followers looked for support to St. Petersburg, declaring themselves members of the Russian nation. The so-called Russophile movement was born. But the new generation of Ruthenian activists renounced both the Habsburg and the Russian projects, defining the Ruthenians of Austria-Hungary as Ukrainians and building bridges with the Ukrainian movement in the Russian Empire.[23]

The imperial Russian authorities made numerous attempts to support the Russophile movement in Galicia and other Habsburg provinces. They even subsidized the leading Russophile newspaper and accepted the leaders of the movement prosecuted by the Austrian authorities as refugees (the Austrians suspected them of being tsarist agents). Despite this imperial support, the Russophiles were largely sidelined politically by proponents of the Ukrainian project as the nineteenth century came to an end. The Galician Ukrainians made it possible for Ukrainian authors from the Russian Empire to publish their Ukrainian-language works and welcomed key Ukrainian intellectuals who wished to move to Galicia. The most prominent of them, the historian Mykhailo Hrushevsky, moved to Lviv (Austrian Lemberg) to become a professor at the local university. He created a new master narrative of Ukrainian history and after the fall of the Russian Empire became the first head of an independent Ukrainian state.[24]

The Fall of the Empire

While the Russian Empire failed to use ethno-nationalism to undermine the rival Habsburg monarchy and protect itself from the rise of the Ukrainian movement, St. Petersburg's efforts to use nationality and religion against its other rival, the Ottoman Porte, proved much more successful.

The decline of the Ottoman Empire can be traced back to the last decades of the seventeenth century, but it was the rise of nationalism among the subjugated peoples in the nineteenth century that delivered

the death blow to the empire. That century witnessed numerous uprisings of Orthodox and Slavic subjects in the Balkan peninsula against
Ottoman rule. The Serbs and Greeks were the first to rebel, establishing independent states in the first decades of the century. The Russians
were there to help, motivated more by geopolitics and religious affinity
than by ideas of nationality. The recognition of both countries came in
the aftermath of a Russo-Turkish war (1828–29) that all but turned the
Ottoman Empire into a Russian dependency.

The rise of pan-Slavism in Russia and the Orthodox religion of the
Ottoman subjects in the Balkans became important factors in justifying Russian involvement in Ottoman affairs, which continued throughout the nineteenth century and the early twentieth. In 1875 the Slavs
of Herzegovina rebelled against Ottoman rule, as did the Bulgarians.
They were followed by the Serbs in parts of Serbia and Montenegro
still controlled by the Ottomans. Although the Ottomans crushed the
revolts, by 1877 the Russians had moved their troops into the Ottoman
possessions, defeating the sultan's army. The peace settlement signed
at the Congress of Berlin in 1878 included international recognition of
the independence of Romania, Serbia, and Montenegro, as well as the
autonomy of Bulgaria, a state that included only a fraction of Bulgar-
ian territory.[25]

Russia's support for Serbia, this time not against the Ottomans but
against Austria-Hungary, became one of the immediate causes of World
War I, underlining the importance of nationalism and the threat that it
posed to empires. In all the belligerent countries, including the Russian
Empire, the world war began with a surge of nationalism and chauvin-
ism on the part of the ruling nations. In Austria-Hungary there was a
crackdown on Slavic nationalism, including the Russophile movement
among the Ukrainians in Austrian Galicia. In the Russian Empire, the
authorities shut down Ukrainian institutions and organizations.

While crushing minority nationalism at home, the warring parties did their best to play the nationality card against one another to
mobilize national movements behind the front lines. The Russians
promised statehood and autonomy to the Poles within the German and

Austrian borders; the Austrians promised a state to the Ukrainians. As the war dragged on, the belligerent empires sought to undermine their enemies by recognizing the claims of national minorities on their territories or even by creating nation-states on such territories. The Germans led the charge, together with the Austrians, declaring the creation of the Kingdom of Poland in 1916.[26]

The fall of the Romanov dynasty in March 1917 as a result of the February Revolution opened the floodgates for the creation of autonomous polities on the territory of the Russian Empire. The Bolshevik coup in October of that year led to the further destruction of the imperial institutions and formation of independent states on the foundations of new autonomies. But the Bolsheviks managed to reinstate the unity of the former imperial lands by combining their military strength with cultural concessions to the nationalities, recruitment of supporters among their intelligentsias, and recognition of their right of political autonomy and use of their national languages in the conduct of public affairs.

The Bolsheviks' main competitors were White Army generals dedicated to the idea of Russia, one and indivisible. Since they conceived the Russian republic-to-be as a Russian nation-state, they could not hope to appeal to the non-Russian nationalities, and their prewar model of social relations alienated the peasants and workers. The Bolsheviks, for their part, sought unsuccessfully to regain control of Finland, Poland, and the Baltics under the banner of world revolution. They also lost parts of Ukraine and Belarus to Poland and the former Russian province of Bessarabia (the future Moldova) to Romania. But they conquered and kept most of the rest of the empire.[27]

On the eve of his all-out invasion of Ukraine in February 2022, Vladimir Putin would claim that it was the Bolsheviks, Vladimir Lenin in particular, who had created a Ukrainian state and, indeed, modern Ukraine itself. Even a cursory acquaintance with the history of the Russian Revolution and the concomitant fall of the Russian Empire indicates that the modern Ukrainian state came into existence not thanks to Lenin but against his wishes.[28]

In June 1917, soon after the fall of monarchy, the Central Rada

(Council), the revolutionary Ukrainian parliament, created in Kyiv and led by historian Mykhailo Hrushevsky, proclaimed Ukraine's autonomy within a future Russian republic. But it was only after the Bolshevik coup in Petrograd in the fall of 1917 that the Central Rada declared the creation of the Ukrainian People's Republic, which encompassed most of present-day Ukrainian territory within the borders of the Russian Empire, including the mining region of the Donbas. The new state wanted to maintain federal ties with Russia, but the Bolshevik invasion of January 1918 made that impossible.

The Central Rada declared the independence of Ukraine and entered in the anti-Bolshevik alliance with Germany and Austria-Hungary. The Bolsheviks waged war on the Ukrainian government under the banner of their own Ukrainian People's Republic—a fiction created to provide a degree of legitimacy for the Bolshevik takeover of Ukraine. Bolshevik troops massacred the population of Kyiv, killing hundreds if not thousands of its citizens, including Metropolitan Vladimir (Bogoiavlensky) of the Orthodox Church. The Bolshevik commander in Kyiv, Mikhail Muraviev, sent Lenin a telegram: "Order has been restored in Kyiv."[29]

The Central Rada had to leave Kyiv but soon returned, having signed an agreement with Germany and Austria-Hungary, whose troops moved into Ukraine in the spring of 1918 and drove the Bolsheviks out of its territory, including the Donbas. The Germans soon replaced the democratic Central Rada with the authoritarian regime of hetman Pavlo Skoropadsky, but the democratic Ukrainian People's Republic was restored when the Germans withdrew from Ukraine late in 1918. The Bolsheviks moved in once again, this time under the banner of their adversary Ukrainian People's Republic, formally independent of Russia.[30]

By the time the Bolsheviks reemerged in Ukraine and launched their military campaign to bring the Ukrainian provinces of the former Russian Empire back under central control, Ukrainian national consciousness was so widespread that Vladimir Lenin felt compelled to change his strategy. He concluded that Ukrainian aspirations to independence were so strong, not only among Ukrainians in general but even among the Ukrainian Bolsheviks themselves, as to require the granting of a degree of autonomy and a status equal to that of Russia.[31] Not only were the Ukrainians recognized as a distinct nationality (as were the Belarusians), no longer a "tribe" of a tripartite Russian nation as in tsarist times, but pro forma recognition of independence was given to a puppet Soviet Ukrainian state, and Ukrainian became its official language.

Realizing that the national movements brought to power by the effects of World War I and the Revolution of 1917 would have to be accommodated, the Bolsheviks strove to gain the cooperation of Ukraine's new political and cultural elites. This accommodation eventually went beyond issues of language, culture, and the recruitment of local cadres into de facto occupation administrations. It also included the creation of state institutions and recognition of the formal independence of the Bolshevik-controlled puppet states formed to delegitimize the new truly independent states and governments established by the national minorities in the borderlands of the former empire.

The Communist Union

Vladimir Lenin's main contribution to the history of Russo-Ukrainian relations was not the formation of a modern Ukrainian state. It was, rather, the endowment of Russia, or the Russian Federation—the name under which it entered the Soviet Union—with a territory and institutions of its own, distinct for the first time in centuries from the territory and institutions of the empire that the Bolsheviks were seeking to preserve. If anything, Lenin laid the foundations for the formation of modern Russia, not Ukraine.

In 1922 Lenin clashed with Joseph Stalin over the structure of the Soviet state then in the making. How were its constituent republics— formally independent states actually controlled by the Bolshevik Party—to be integrated into a Soviet Union led by Russia? The non-Russian polities involved were the Ukrainian Soviet Socialist Republic, the Belarusian Soviet Socialist Republic, and the Transcaucasian Soviet

Federative Socialist Republic, including Georgia, Armenia, and Azerbaijan. Stalin proposed to bring them all into the Russian Federation as autonomous regions, but the Ukrainian and Georgian Bolsheviks were opposed, since that would significantly limit their prerogatives as rulers of de jure independent republics.

Lenin sided with the Ukrainians and Georgians, proposing a Union of Socialist Soviet Republics that the Russian Federation would join on equal terms with the others. He won the day, and the treaty formally establishing the Union of Soviet Socialist Republics was signed on December 30, 1922. Stalin went along. For the future of Russo-Ukrainian relations, as well as Russia's relations with all the other peoples and nationalities of the former empire, the creation of the USSR would prove fateful. For the first time in its history, Russia had acquired a territory and institutions separate from the tsarist imperial governing bodies. The imperial function would now be exercised by all-Union rather than Russian republican institutions.

Despite the formation of the USSR, the Russian Bolsheviks retained control over the other republics through the organization that mattered most—the Communist Party. Known initially as the Russian and then the all-Union Communist Party of Bolsheviks, it remained highly centralized, gradually turning the federal structure of the Soviet Union into a mere formality. Unlike the other republics, Russia did not have a communist party of its own but controlled the all-Union party, in which the parties of the republics were given no more rights than the provincial communist organizations of the Russian Federation. Although the federal façade was maintained, the Soviet Union got a centralized system of government in the form of the all-Union party.[32]

The USSR began its life with massive affirmative action for the non-Russian cultures outside the Russian Federation. But cultural Russification of the borderlands returned in the late 1920s and early 1930s, when Stalin emerged as Lenin's sole successor and began preparing the country for war. One reason for the change was industrialization, which, given Russian control of the all-Union party, came with the advance of Russian as the language of administration, science, and technology. Another reason was accommodation of the Russians as the largest nationality in the now Soviet empire, along with concern to integrate the non-Russian nationalities culturally so that they would not switch sides in the coming war.

In Ukraine, the largest non-Russian republic of the USSR, the change of nationality policy was signaled by show trials against the Ukrainian intelligentsia. The first such trial, which took place in 1929, was followed by an attack on the Ukrainian party cadres and the peasantry, which reached its peak during the Holodomor, or the Great Ukrainian Famine of 1932–33. A number of key Ukrainian communists committed suicide, while others were dismissed from their positions and jailed. As many as four million people were starved to death as part of a concerted campaign to crush the peasant resistance to the collectivization and maximize grain delivery for Soviet industrialization. In the month leading up to the start of the famine, Stalin warned his associates that such measures were needed to prevent loss of control over Ukraine. The Holodomor turned Ukraine, previously known as the breadbasket of Europe, into a land devastated by famine.[33]

World War II led to another shift in Moscow's policy toward the nationalities. Although Russocentrism was not abandoned, more manifestations of Ukrainian and other non-Russian patriotism were allowed. The Soviet takeover of Poland's eastern provinces following the Molotov-Ribbentrop Pact of 1939 was justified as liberation of fellow Ukrainians and Russians from Polish capitalist oppression. It was also celebrated in ethnic terms as the reunion of western Ukraine and western Belarus with the corresponding Soviet republics. The old imperial reunification paradigm was back, dressed this time in Ukrainian and Belarusian clothing.

After Hitler attacked the USSR in June 1941, non-Russian nationalism was mobilized once again, especially in Ukraine, to encourage patriotic resistance to the German invasion. Once German forces occupied all of Ukraine with the assistance of their Romanian and Hungarian allies, Moscow did not mind promoting the Ukrainian language, culture, and history to mobilize resistance and inspire the loyalty of more than six million Ukrainians drafted into the Red Army. The Ukrainian card was also played at home and abroad to justify the military takeover and annexation of western Ukrainian lands ruled by Poland, Czechoslovakia, and Romania during the interwar period.[34]

In 1914 the Russian army had captured the city of Lviv, then under Austrian rule, justifying it as liberation of fellow Russians—that was the tsarist authorities' official term for the local population. As World War II drew to an end, the Soviets played not the Russian but the Ukrainian national card when they integrated Lviv into the Ukrainian SSR, although the city was largely Polish in ethnic composition, with Jews (largely exterminated during the Holocaust) as the second-largest ethnic group.

While the authorities were eager to exploit Ukrainian ethnicity to justify Soviet westward expansion, they did not welcome or tolerate every expression of Ukrainian patriotism and nationalism. The radical Organization of Ukrainian Nationalists (OUN), formed in the western Ukrainian lands during the interwar period, was considered particularly dangerous. Its members were known to the Soviets as Banderites: their leader, Stepan Bandera, and some of his followers were imprisoned in German concentration camps after a failed attempt to declare an independent Ukrainian state in alliance with Germany and against the USSR in the summer of 1941. The Nazi occupiers, who regarded Slavs as subhuman, deported more than two million Ukrainians to Germany as slave laborers and persecuted Ukrainian patriots of every description.

The two branches of the OUN, one led by Bandera, the other by his less-known rival Andrii Melnyk, turned against the Germans by the end of 1941. In 1943 the Bandera faction assumed leadership of the 40,000-strong Ukrainian Insurgent Army, a guerrilla force that fought against the Polish Home Army and the Nazis and, later, against the Red Army for control of western Ukraine. The Ukrainian nationalist insurgency was not completely crushed until the early 1950s, the last years of Stalin's rule, earning the designation of the strongest and longest-lasting movement of resistance to the Soviets anywhere in east-central Europe.

The Soviets did their best to discredit the Ukrainian nationalists by condemning their early collaboration with the Germans and exposing the participation of some OUN members in the Holocaust and the ethnic cleansing of Poles during the German occupation of Ukraine. They also made major concessions to the Ukrainian language, which became dominant in western Ukrainian government institutions, replacing Polish. But the Sovietization of western Ukraine was carried out mainly by repression. Not only the captured fighters of the Ukrainian Insurgent Army but also civilians suspected of helping the insurgents were resettled or deported en masse to gulag camps in the Russian SFSR, making Ukrainians the largest ethnic group of political prisoners in the Soviet Union—a phenomenon documented by Aleksandr Solzhenitsyn in his *Gulag Archipelago*.[35]

The Russo-Ukrainian Condominium

After Stalin's death in 1953, the fortunes of the Ukrainian communist elite, which had been fully subordinated to Moscow during the Holodomor and then purged during the Great Terror of the late 1930s, improved dramatically. The agent of change was Stalin's top man in Ukraine, Nikita Khrushchev, who had headed the Communist Party of Ukraine from 1938 to 1949. He now used the support of his Ukrainian clients to outmaneuver his competitors in Moscow and become the supreme leader of the USSR. The Ukrainian cadres formed the core of Khrushchev's pyramid of power: since there was no separate Russian Communist Party, they constituted the largest voting bloc in the all-Union party's Central Committee, which had the power to elect and remove party leaders.[36]

Under Khrushchev, the Ukrainian party elite emerged as the junior partner of its Russian counterparts in running the Soviet Union, which evolved into a Russo-Ukrainian condominium at the leadership level.

A sign of the new prominence of Ukraine and its rise in the symbolic hierarchy of Soviet nations was the transfer of the Crimean Peninsula from Russia to Ukraine in 1954, orchestrated by Khrushchev. Officially, the "gift" marked the tercentenary of the Pereiaslav Agreement of 1654, which had brought Cossack Ukraine under Muscovite control, constituting the "reunification of Ukraine and Russia," as it was hailed in Soviet propaganda. This was presented to the general public as proof of the trust that Russia now reposed in Ukraine.

In reality, the Crimean Peninsula was attached to the mainland Ukrainian administration in order to accelerate its postwar recovery, which was proceeding more slowly than in other regions of the European USSR. This was due in part to Stalin's forcible deportation of the peninsula's indigenous population, the Crimean Tatars, who were accused of wartime collaboration with the Germans.[37]

The rise of Ukraine's symbolic importance as the second most important Soviet republic and of the Ukrainian party elite as the junior partner of the Russian party bosses continued into the 1960s and 1970s under Khrushchev's successor, Leonid Brezhnev. The Russian-born Khrushchev had spent much of his career in Ukraine, while Brezhnev, also an ethnic Russian, was a native of Ukraine. Brezhnev became the leader of a political clan known as the "Dnipropetrovsk mafia," named for the industrial city in Ukraine where he began his political career and recruited cadres personally loyal to him, appointing them to key positions in Moscow and Kyiv. The prominence that Ukrainian party and managerial elites acquired in the central government was partly a reflection of Ukraine's importance in the Soviet economy. It was, after all, the second most populous and economically productive republic of the USSR.[38]

In 1967, when the Soviet government celebrated the fiftieth anniversary of the 1917 Revolution, official reports stressed the economic leadership of the Russian Federation. "The industry of the RSFSR," it was claimed at the time, "accounts for about half the all-Union production of pig iron, steel, rolled iron, coal, gas, mineral fertilizer, sulphuric acid, and metal-cutting machinery, two-thirds of electrical energy and chemical equipment, more than 80 percent of oil production and production of automobiles, paper, and textiles; three-quarters of chemical fiber, more than 60 percent of cement, and more than 90 percent of wood pulp for export."[39]

But immediately after the Russian Federation in terms of contribution to the all-Union coffers came Ukraine. "The Ukrainian SSR produces half the all-Union production of pig iron, more than 40 percent of its steel and rolled iron, more than half its iron ore, and one-third of its coal and gas," read the same economic report. "Almost all the all-Union production of diesel locomotives is concentrated in Ukraine, all the production of sugar-beet harvesting combines, and about half the production of metallurgical machinery, the production of large quantities of metal-cutting machinery, tractors, and automobiles, as well as machinery for the energy industry, electrotechnical, chemical, transport and lifting equipment, and other machinery."[40]

In the 1960s the Russian Federation had a population of approximately 118 million, while the Ukrainian SSR had 42 million. If Russia accounted for 57 percent of the all-Union population, which stood at 208 million, Soviet Ukraine claimed 20 percent. Ukraine's contribution to the Soviet economy was thus comparable to its share of the Soviet population: it accounted for some 18 percent of the workforce and roughly the same percentage of Soviet economic output. There were more than 7 million ethnic Russians living in Ukraine at the time, and approximately 3.4 million Ukrainians in the Russian Federation. Without exception, Ukrainians in Russia spoke not only their native language but also Russian; some of them spoke only Russian. Russians in Ukraine overwhelmingly spoke Russian, as did a good many ethnic Ukrainians, especially those residing in the large industrial centers of Ukraine's east and south.[41]

Brezhnev clamped down on the Ukrainian cultural revival that had begun as part of Khrushchev's de-Stalinization effort in the late 1950s. In 1972 the Kremlin removed from power the independently minded party boss of Ukraine, Petro Shelest, a national communist by conviction, and launched a campaign against the Ukrainian intelligentsia that led to numerous arrests and blacklisting of major Ukrainian cultural figures, including the prominent poet Lina Kostenko. Among those arrested were members of the Ukrainian Helsinki Group, the second such organization established in the USSR to monitor human-rights abuses perpetrated by the Soviet authorities in violation of the Helsinki Final Act—an agreement, signed by the representatives of thirty-five mostly European states, including the United States and the USSR in 1975.[42]

By the time Mikhail Gorbachev came to power in 1985, the Ukrainian national revival was long exhausted, and the Ukrainian cultural elites had little ability to challenge the policies coming from Moscow. With the progress of Russification in Ukraine, which hit the country's east and south particularly hard, Soviet officialdom's dream of turning Russians and Ukrainians into one people, in linguistic and cultural terms at least, seemed closer to realization than ever.

Gorbachev was so convinced that the Soviet "nationality question" had been resolved once and for all that he decided to ignore an unwritten rule established soon after Stalin's death: the leader of a party organization in every republic had to be a representative of the local nationality. In December 1986 he replaced the long-serving head of the Communist Party of Kazakhstan, Dinmukhamed Kunaev, with his own loyalist Gennadii Kolbin, an ethnic Russian from the Urals. Unexpectedly for Moscow, young Kazakhs met Kolbin with protests and riots—the first case of nationality-driven mass action in the Soviet Union in decades. Gorbachev backed down and eventually allowed the local Kazakh leader Nursultan Nazarbaev to replace Kolbin.

That was just the beginning. In 1988 an Azeri-Armenian conflict exploded into riots over the fate of Nagorno-Karabakh, an Armenian enclave in Azerbaijan. But no matter how challenging the central authorities found interethnic and interrepublican clashes in the Caucasus and Central Asia, they paled in comparison to the pro-independence movement that would soon gain strength in the Baltic republics and then in Ukraine, the USSR's second most important republic. National mobilization in Ukraine would threaten the unity not only of the USSR but also of its Slavic core, as the rise of the Ukrainian movement had done in the Russian Empire of the nineteenth century.[43]

The Fall of the USSR

The downfall of the Soviet Union began in the most recent additions to the Soviet territory—the lands annexed in the course of World War II, first in the wake of the Molotov-Ribbentrop Pact and then recaptured from Nazi Germany in 1944–45 as a result of the Yalta agreements. There the power of Moscow was the weakest. In the forefront of mobilization against the Soviet center were the Baltic states, especially Estonia and Lithuania. In November 1988 Estonia became the first Soviet republic to declare its sovereignty, meaning that its laws took precedence over those of the Union.

Lithuania, for its part, was the first republic to declare itself completely independent of the Soviet Union. It did so in March 1990 at the first session of the freely elected Lithuanian parliament. Even the Communist Party of Lithuania abandoned the USSR, proclaiming its secession from the Communist Party of the Soviet Union. Leadership passed to representatives of an alternative elite from the ranks of intellectuals and technocrats, not unlike the process in Eastern Europe a few years later. The Baltic drive to regain independence lost in the flames of World War II had a ripple effect throughout the Soviet Union. To oppose the Baltic "Popular Fronts"—pro-independence organizations that sent hundreds of thousands of people into the streets to achieve their goal—Moscow and local party elites organized "International Fronts" that sought to mobilize Russian and Russian-speaking minorities in the republics.[44]

Russian mobilization in the western borderlands of the USSR soon spilled over into Russia itself. The "Russia first" approach united Russian nationalists and democrats, propelling Gorbachev's former protégé and later sworn enemy, Boris Yeltsin, first to the position of head of the Russian parliament and then to that of Russian president. Yeltsin's victory resulted from several mobilizations, including those of Russian nationalists and democratic activists in the major cities. Finally, there was the backing of newly organized workers who went on strike over economic conditions, expecting that Russian authorities could help them when Union officials failed to do so.

By June 1991 Moscow had two presidents, one of Russia and the other of the USSR. But in Russia, unlike in the Baltic republics, opposition to the center was led by a former party boss, not by an intellectual, as was the case in Lithuania, where the former music professor Vytautas Landsbergis played roughly the same role as Yeltsin. Even though Yeltsin publicly abandoned the Communist Party and then suspended its activities, the new Russian elite never made a clean break with the communist past, as did its counterparts in the Baltics. That was a consequential difference.

In Ukraine, the mobilization began in earnest in 1989, when Gorbachev managed to unseat the Communist Party leader, Volodymyr Shcherbytsky, Brezhnev's protégé and a key member of the "Dnipropetrovsk mafia." It combined elements of the Baltic and Russian mobilizations. In the parts of western Ukraine annexed by the Soviet Union on the basis of the Molotov-Ribbentrop Pact, it followed the Baltic model, focusing on issues of history, language, culture, and national sovereignty. Ukraine's declaration of independence from the Soviet Union in the wake of the failed August 1991 coup in Moscow came not only as a result of the alliance between nationalists, democrats, and striking workers in the Donbas region but also thanks to the support of the party apparatus, which had been threatened by Yeltsin's suspension of Communist Party activity.[45]

On December 1, 1991, Ukrainians delivered the final blow to the Soviet Union by voting overwhelmingly for independence. The Baltics were effectively gone by that time, as was Moldova and a good part of the Caucasus. But the Belarusians and Central Asians, who counted on a continuing supply of subsidized gas and oil from Russia, were in no hurry to leave. Even resource-rich Kazakhstan was hesitant about independence, partly because of its large Russian and Slavic population. But the Russian leadership decided to end the existence of the USSR because it did not want to bear the economic burden of the Union without Ukraine's substantial human and economic resources. Boris Yeltsin had one more explanation for his decision to recognize the Ukrainian vote for independence: nationality and culture. He told the US president George H. W. Bush more than once that without Ukraine, Russia would be outgunned in a union consisting largely of the non-Slavic Muslim republics. Ukraine's overwhelming vote for independence and Russia's decision to recognize it spelled the end of the USSR, compelling the Belarusians and Central Asians to leave as well, willingly or not.[46]

On December 25, 1991, when Mikhail Gorbachev announced his resignation as president of the Soviet Union, the disintegration of the USSR did not come to an end. In fact, it entered the most challenging and dangerous part of the process. The Commonwealth of Independent States, established by the USSR's political successors in December 1991, created a mechanism to negotiate the numerous issues related to the disintegration of the Soviet Union. But it proved unable to solve the most crucial of them—the role of Russia in the post-Soviet space and the degree of sovereignty that Russia was prepared to concede to its former subjects.

Many of the Russian leaders regarded the Commonwealth as a temporary compromise. As Yeltsin put it in his speech to the Russian parliament after the Belavezha summit, "In today's conditions only the Commonwealth of Independent States can ensure the preservation of political, legal and economic space built up over the centuries but now almost lost." Gennadii Burbulis, Yeltsin's key adviser at Belavezha, envisioned the new era that began in Russian history after the failed August coup as a transitional stage in which Russia would manage to rebuild itself by monopolizing proceeds from the sale of oil and natural gas instead of sharing them with other CIS members. "We must save Russia and strengthen its independence, separating ourselves from the rest," argued Yeltsin's advisers soon after the failed coup. "After that, when it [Russia] is back on its feet, everyone will rally to it and the question [of the Union] can be resolved again."[47]

Immediately after the formal dissolution of the USSR, tensions developed between its two largest successor states, Russia and Ukraine. Would CIS members be fully independent and free to conduct their own domestic and foreign policies, or would their sovereignty be limited? Russia never ceded its role as the dominant member of the Commonwealth, striving to turn it into a Russia-led political, economic, and military union. Ukraine, though a founding member of the Commonwealth, never joined it formally, participating in some programs but not in others. Russo-Ukrainian tensions continued throughout the 1990s, leading to a tug of war and then outright military conflict in the opening decades of the twenty-first century. If the collapse of the USSR was sudden and largely bloodless, growing strains between its two largest successors would develop into limited fighting in the Donbas in 2014 and then into all-out warfare in 2022, causing death, destruction, and a refugee crisis on a scale not seen in Europe since the Second World War.

Deceiving Peace

Why did they not fight in 1991? Why did Russia forgo war to preserve the Soviet Union in the late 1980s and early 1990s? These questions are best considered in the context of the often dramatic and bloody efforts on the part of European and Eurasian imperial powers to save their territorial possessions in the course of the nineteenth and twentieth centuries.

As noted at the beginning of this chapter, the collapse of the Soviet Union was perceived by contemporaries and participants as basically similar to the fall of previous world empires. One such observer was Gorbachev's close adviser, Anatolii Cherniaev. Another participant who made similar comparisons was Boris Yeltsin's chief economic adviser and handpicked acting prime minister, Yegor Gaidar. Outside Russia, such comparisons were drawn by Jack F. Matlock, a former US ambassador to the USSR, and by the doyen of American Sovietology, George F. Kennan.[48]

In 1995, in his review of Matlock's memoir, titled *Autopsy on an*

Empire, Kennan wrote: "I find it hard to think of any event more strange and startling, and at first glance more inexplicable, than the sudden and total disintegration and disappearance from the international scene, primarily in the years 1987 through 1991, of the great power known successively as the Russian Empire and the Soviet Union." Kennan referred to the fall of previous empires as gradual. That of the Soviet Union was not. "How then to explain the extreme abruptness, the sharp quick ending, and not least the relative bloodlessness with which the great Soviet Empire came to an end in the four years in question, bearing with it those attributes of the earlier Russian Empire which it had contrived to incorporate into itself?" Kennan asked himself and his readers.[49]

Was the Soviet experience unique? We can start by considering the British Empire, the most powerful such institution of the modern era, which offered the Russians a Commonwealth model for opting out of a traditional imperial project. British imperial disentanglement was gradual indeed. It began, arguably, with the eighteenth-century American Revolution, followed by slowly developing autonomism in the dominions of Canada, Australia, and New Zealand in the nineteenth and twentieth centuries. Attempts to crush South African and Irish movements for independence proved unsuccessful in the wake of World War I; in the decades after World War II Britain withdrew from India and subsequently from its African colonies.[50]

The end of the French Empire was more rapid and partially because of that more bloody. The French colonies in Indochina were seized by the Japanese almost immediately after Nazi Germany's defeat of France in 1940. Recovering their colonies after the war became a matter of national pride for the French, who conducted brutal wars in Vietnam and Indochina but were defeated and had to withdraw. Their withdrawal from Africa, especially the divisive war in Algeria, added another sanguinary page to France's imperial collapse, almost causing the demise of the French republic itself. It survived only by giving up its colonies.

The Dutch Empire, with its possessions in the East Indies, had been in decline since the late eighteenth century before it actually collapsed. The Netherlands' withdrawal from their colonies, which ended with the independence of Indonesia, Suriname, and autonomy of the Netherlands Antilles, can be compared to the decline of the British Empire. Belgium's brutal rule in the Congo, followed by its withdrawal after the crisis in that country during the early 1960s, places the Belgian Empire more in the French than in the British camp. The Portuguese, founders of one of the first global empires, were the last to withdraw from their African territories in the mid-1970s. They did so after a fight, and their withdrawal caused one of the bloodiest and longest wars in Africa's postcolonial history—the Angolan Civil War lasted for more than quarter of a century, from 1975 to 2002.[51]

Finally, there was the Ottoman Porte, whose decline began earlier than that of other empires, culminating in the loss of its possessions as a result of defeat in World War I. The Turks shared the same experience as Austria-Hungary, another Russian rival in the region. The Ottoman case seems especially comparable to the Soviet collapse because its consequences played out for a long time. If the Balkan Wars of 1912–13 and World War I spelled the end of the Porte as an imperial power, its former Balkan possessions were the scene of the Yugoslav wars of 1991–2001, which coincided with the disintegration of the USSR.

Yugoslavia, a federative south Slavic state formed on the ruins of the Habsburg and Ottoman Empires and reconstituted after World War II in 1945, ceased to exist in the 1990s with the secession of its key republics. Like the Russians in the USSR, the Serbs in Yugoslavia constituted the most populous nationality and ran the largest republic of the federation. The efforts of their leader, the former communist functionary Slobodan Milošević, first to keep the federation together and then to build Greater Serbia by adding Serbian-dominated enclaves in other parts of the former Yugoslavia, resulted in lengthy and destructive warfare, involving war crimes and genocide. In 1999 this prompted NATO to bomb Serbian-controlled parts of the defunct federation.

The military conflict in Yugoslavia began in June 1991 with the secession of Slovenia and efforts of the Serb-dominated Yugoslav armed forces to stop the Slovenian bid for independence. By August the war had engulfed Croatia, with the Yugoslav army besieging first the city of Vukovar and then Dubrovnik on Croatia's Adriatic coast. War in Bosnia began in 1992, followed in 1998 by war in Kosovo. The last chapter, in 2001, involved armed conflict between the Macedonian armed forces and military detachments of local Albanians, who made up close to a quarter of the population of the new state of Macedonia. But the final disintegration of the former Yugoslavia did not occur until the first decade of the twenty-first century. Montenegro declared itself independent of the defunct Federal Republic of Yugoslavia—in fact, of Serbia—in 2006, and Kosovo did the same in 2008. The disintegration of the Ottoman imperial legacy in the Balkans, following almost a century of unstable federalism, was finally complete.

To the surprise and relief of many, the Russians, led by Boris Yeltsin, refused to follow in the footsteps of the Serbs, who turned the former Yugoslav army into an instrument of Serbian aggrandizement and then of genocide. Nor did the Russians cling to the Soviet republics that Russia had dominated, as the French and Belgians did to their former colonies. Instead, the Russians seem to have taken a page from the dissolution of the Portuguese empire. Both empires ceased to exist as a result of relatively peaceful revolutions that took place in their capitals, where reformers tried to dismantle authoritarian government and initiate political, economic, and social reforms. In both countries, the existence of empire was an obstacle to such reforms.[52]

Boris Yeltsin and his advisers sought to implement their reforms in Russia, not in the Soviet Union, where Gorbachev's efforts to democratize the system were opposed by the conservatively minded communist elites that controlled most of the Soviet republics. To free his Russian reformers from the limitations imposed on them by Gorbachev's vacillating political center, which was stymied by competing pro- and anti-reform factions, Yeltsin allied himself with pro-democratic reformers in the Baltic states and pro–status quo elites in Central Asia, all in an effort to undermine existing Union institutions. Yeltsin did not intend to subvert the Soviet Union in the process, but once the disintegration that he helped to set off developed a momentum of its own, he went along. His main political rival, Mikhail Gorbachev, and the Soviet Union itself were swept away as a result.

Keeping the secessionist republics under Russian control by military force was an unlikely policy choice for other reasons as well. One of them was the enormous political, ideological, and economic influence that the United States wielded over the Soviet Union at this time, as well as the place that America occupied in the imagination of Soviet-era reformers, from Gorbachev to Yeltsin and beyond. Washington did not want the republics to fight one another, fearing the possibility of a "Yugoslavia with nukes"—a scenario that Gorbachev never tired of raising in his conversations with President George H. W. Bush.

The Russian president was prepared to use force against autonomous republics within the Russian Federation if they should attempt to secede, but not against similar aspirations of Union republics such as Ukraine. Moreover, the Soviet Army was short of resources, and Russians serving in it were not eager to fight. Yeltsin's ill-fated attempt to deploy the army against Chechnya in the fall of 1991 resulted in the complete encirclement of the demoralized Russian troops mobilized for the conflict.

A major factor was the rivalry between Gorbachev, who represented the Union center and wanted to save the Soviet empire, and Yeltsin, who had rebelled against Gorbachev and, by extension, against the empire that he represented. In the case of Chechnya, Gorbachev refused to authorize the use of force, and there was little that Yeltsin could do as long as Gorbachev held supreme command of the Soviet armed forces. In the battle between Gorbachev and Yeltsin for the loyalty of the Soviet military, there was no clear winner. Nor was there any prospect of Russia's effectively projecting force beyond its borders unless the two rivals managed to act in concert. With reformist Russia rebelling against the imperial center, there was a deadlock not only between the leaders but also between the political and social forces supporting them. If the reformists were to prevail, then the empire had to go.

The role of Ukraine in bringing about the Soviet collapse can hardly be exaggerated. Not only was it a key political actor pushing for the dissolution of the USSR, but it also helped to ensure a peaceful disintegration. By declaring independence, rallying overwhelming voter support for it, and insisting on nothing less, Ukraine killed not only Gorbachev's project of a reformed Union but also Yeltsin's more modest plan of a confederation of republics under Russian control. At the same time, by going out of its way to adopt a demonstratively tolerant attitude toward its Russian minority—the largest outside Russia—Ukraine made it much easier for Yeltsin to ignore pressures to protect the formerly dominant nationality in the peripheries of the empire. The Ukrainian Russians were not apprehensive about an independent Ukrainian state and gave it their majority support, making the collapse of the USSR not only inevitable but also largely peaceful.

2

DEMOCRACY AND AUTOCRACY

I t was the largest armed conflict to break out on the streets of Moscow since the Russian Revolution of 1917. On the morning of October 4, 1993, six T-80 tanks of the elite Taman Guards Motor Rifle Division took positions on the New Arbat Bridge spanning the Moskva River across from the Russian parliament building known as the White House. Sometime after 9:00 a.m. the tanks opened fire, aiming at the floors housing the offices of the parliamentary leadership. The conference room was hit first, then the office of the speaker of Parliament, Professor Ruslan Khasbulatov, and then the office of the vice president, General Aleksandr Rutskoi, who had opposed Boris Yeltsin and made the rebel parliament his new home.

"I was in my office when the shell went through the glass and exploded in the righthand corner," Rutskoi recalled later. "Fortunately, my desk was on the left side of the room. I rushed outside in complete shock. I don't know what saved me." The tanks fired twelve rounds, setting the building on fire. Dozens of people were killed on the spot. "When I opened the door where a shell had recently exploded, I couldn't enter," recalled a survivor of the attack who had been on the sixth floor. "It was a bloody mess in there."[1]

By midday troops were entering the parliament building, taking over one floor after another. The survivors, including Rutskoi and Khasbulatov, were detained and arrested. The battle for the White House, which had started a few days earlier between defenders of parliament and government troops, left more than a hundred dead—77 civilians and 24 servicemen. On that day alone, according to official reports, 158 individuals were taken to hospitals, where 19 died. The Russian parliament ceased to function for the next few months, and the building was turned over to the executive branch of government, led by the president.[2]

For Yeltsin, this was the second battle for the White House in slightly more than two years. During the hard-line coup against Mikhail Gorbachev in August 1991, Yeltsin had led the defense of the building, which had become a symbol of Russian democracy. Now he led the government troops in their assault on the very same parliament, which was being protected by his top lieutenants of August 1991. Yeltsin prevailed in both struggles; Russian democracy did not. Saved from destruction by Soviet tanks in August 1991, it was all but destroyed by Russian tanks in October 1993.

Toward the end of 1993, Yeltsin held a referendum on a new Russian constitution that significantly enhanced the powers of the presidential office. Russian voters supported the president. In two years, one month, and two weeks, Russia all but ended its experiment with parliamentary democracy and laid the constitutional foundations for a strong presidential regime. In fact, that calculation exaggerates the length of the experiment: throughout most of 1992 and 1993, President Yeltsin ruled the country by decree.[3]

Born of the collapse of the USSR, Russian democracy foundered on the rocks of Russian statehood, which punched a huge hole in its side. This was a disappointment to many who had seen Russia as a beacon of democracy in 1990–91. But the Gorbachev-era democratic experiment survived in the former USSR's second-largest republic, Ukraine. The year 1993 proved difficult for Ukraine as for Russia, and the economic downturn produced a real threat of communist restoration in both countries. But Ukraine found a different way out of the political crisis.[4]

The mid-1990s saw Russia and Ukraine part ways in political development: Russia became more authoritarian with each passing year, while Ukraine stayed democratic despite repeated efforts of the presidential office to follow the Russian model and subordinate parliament to itself. Numerous factors contributed to these different outcomes, which would strongly affect relations between the two former senior partners of the Soviet project.

Ukrainian democracy presented a major threat to the Russian political regime, as it provided an example of a functioning political system with a strong parliament, which encouraged and empowered Russian liberal opposition to the increasingly authoritarian regime in Moscow. Apart from that, the Ukrainian democratic tradition and parliamentary system made it much more difficult for Russia to regain control over Ukraine. Furthermore, Western insistence on democratic rule as a prerequisite for good relations with the post-Soviet states privileged Ukraine in building long-term political ties with Europe and the United States.

The clash between Ukrainian democracy and Russian authoritarianism turned into an international crisis during Ukraine's Orange Revolution of 2004, when voters refused to accept falsified results of the presidential elections that gave victory to the Russian-backed candidate, Viktor Yanukovych. The Western powers took a strong stand in support of Ukrainian democracy and the candidate who was ultimately declared the winner, Viktor Yushchenko. The Orange Revolution put Ukraine and Russia and, subsequently, Russia and the West on a collision course that would eventually lead to war.[5]

Reform vs. Democracy

Russia's road to autocracy began in earnest on September 21, 1993, when the popularly elected president, Boris Yeltsin, signed decree number 1400, dissolving the country's two legislative bodies, the Congress of People's Deputies, a super-parliament that had the right to amend the constitution and impeach the president, and a smaller parliament, called the Supreme Soviet, which adopted laws and could veto presidential decrees.

Yeltsin had no power under the existing constitution to dissolve either of the legislative bodies, but that is what he did in September 1993. The reason was simple: as he saw it, the parliamentarians were not only challenging his power but also making it all but impossible for him to continue the economic reforms that he had been determined to implement since his election to supreme political office in the summer of 1991. The reforms, known as "shock therapy," began on January 2, 1992. The government freed prices and cut subsidies to state-run enterprises, which constituted the entire Russian economy at the time. Prices rose drastically, enterprises found themselves on the verge of bankruptcy, and average income was halved almost overnight, only to keep falling. Almost half the population found itself below the poverty line, defined as an income of US $21.00 per month.[6]

Popular discontent with "shock therapy" led to political turmoil. Late in 1991, reformists and Russian nationalists came together in parliament to "save Russia" from looming economic collapse by granting Yeltsin extraordinary powers to rule by decree for one full year. The economic miracle that Yeltsin promised parliament did not happen. Russia's GDP, which fell by 5 percent in 1991, plummeted three times as much in 1992. Proponents of radical reform were in retreat, while former communists and nationalists went on the offensive. They believed that Yeltsin had lost his way, becoming a hostage of Western-backed liberal young economists such as Yegor Gaidar, whom Yeltsin had appointed as Russia's prime minister at the age of thirty-five.

In December 1992, with Yeltsin's one-year grace period running out, the Russian parliament refused to extend his emergency powers and reappoint Gaidar as prime minister. Yeltsin, who had never ruled in any other way, rebelled in turn. He wanted a new constitution. The crisis was resolved by a compromise: Yeltsin agreed to a different prime minister, and parliament agreed to extend his rule by decree until April 1993, when a referendum on the new constitution was to take place. But in March the Congress of People's Deputies—the super-parliament controlled by Yeltsin's opponents—amended the constitution, rescinding some of Yeltsin's powers. Yeltsin shot back by declaring a "special regime" that not only extended his rule by decree but gave him even more powers.

A constitutional crisis hit Russia sixteen months after the country became fully independent. The Constitutional Court and the attorney general's office protested Yeltsin's move as unconstitutional, and the Congress of People's Deputies attempted to impeach Yeltsin but could not muster the two-thirds majority required to force him out of office. The referendum on support for the president and his reforms took place in late April, with most voters backing the president and mandating early parliamentary elections. Both the Congress and the Supreme Soviet were defeated, but the crisis was far from over.[7]

Summer was spent on a futile war of decrees in which parliament sought to regain lost ground by issuing resolutions on foreign policy and confirming the election of local governments. In September 1993 Yeltsin decided to dissolve both the Congress and the Supreme Soviet, resorting once again to a plebiscite in order to adopt a new constitution with enhanced presidential powers. On September 21 he signed a decree dissolving both bodies. The decree was in direct violation of the existing constitution, which provided that any president attempting to dissolve an "elected organ of state power" would immediately become illegitimate.

De jure, by signing the decree, Yeltsin automatically lost all his powers. So said not only the leaders of parliament but also Yeltsin's own vice president, Aleksandr Rutskoi, calling the decree a coup d'état. The Supreme Soviet annulled the decree, and the Congress impeached the president. Rutskoi took his place as interim president and appointed his own government, including a new defense minister. Armed supporters of parliament attempted to take over the Ostankino television center but were driven back by government forces supporting Yeltsin.[8]

The minister of defense, General Pavel Grachev, and the top brass remained loyal to Yeltsin. After demanding a written order from the president to enter the capital and receiving it in the early hours of October 3, Grachev gave orders to his troops in Moscow. He personally instructed a captain in charge of one of the tanks stationed on the Moskva River bridge to aim at the office of the head of parliament, Ruslan Khasbulatov. "That must be Khasbulatov's office—they are all there. You must hit that window. Can you do that?" asked Grachev. The captain assured the minister that he could. Parliament was fired at, its defenders overpowered, and its leaders arrested. Yeltsin shut down dozens of political organizations and prohibited the publication of numerous newspapers, including the communist mouthpiece, *Pravda*.[9]

In a telephone conversation with President Bill Clinton the next day, Yeltsin presented what had happened as a victory for democracy. In the tradition of Soviet political discourse, he called his opponents "fascists." "Now that these events are over, we have no more obstacles to Russia's democratic elections and our transition to democracy and a market economy," Yeltsin assured Clinton. "The fascist organizations that had been active in these events have now been banned, so now I feel that all will be fine." Clinton was eager to support his Russian ally. "You did everything exactly as you had to, and I congratulate you for the way you handled it," declared the American president.[10]

The assault on democracy took place in full view of Washington and with its publicly expressed approval. In private, some US officials raised questions about the lack of freedom of speech during the electoral campaign and the "half-baked constitution," which ensured the "preponderance of authority in the hands of the chief executive." But in public, representatives of the administration praised Yeltsin. For Clinton and many others in the United States, Russia, and beyond, Yeltsin was not only the symbol of Russian democracy but also its last hope. What was good for Yeltsin was good for Russia, the United States, and democracy itself, went the thinking at the time.[11]

In December 1993, Russian citizens voted on the new constitution drafted by Yeltsin's aides. "I won't deny it, the powers of the president in the draft are considerable indeed," Yeltsin told a reporter in November 1993. "And what would you want? In a country that has got used to tsars or chiefs; a country in which well-defined interest groups have not coalesced, and their leaders have not been determined, in which normal parties are barely embryonic; a country in which executive discipline is exceedingly weak, where nihilism with regard to the law is completely rampant—in such a country, could one bet only or mainly on parliament? In half a year, if not sooner, the people are sure to demand a dictator. Such a dictator will be found quickly, I assure you. And perhaps in that very parliament."[12]

Yeltsin was declaring, in effect, that Russia was not ready for democracy and presenting himself as its savior from an even worse evil—dictatorship. He won the referendum with 58 percent support for the new constitution. It was a vote of confidence in Yeltsin: most of those who voted in favor of the constitution did not read the draft. The parliamentary elections held simultaneously with the referendum showed that Russians wanted strong presidential power without reform. Yegor Gaidar's reformists, backed by Yeltsin, got only 15 percent of the vote. The winner, with 23 percent, was the radical nationalist—indeed, neofascist—politician Vladimir Zhirinovsky, who led the Liberal Democratic Party. The communists, now all but banned, garnered 12 percent.[13]

The new constitution drastically reduced the power of the legislative branch and increased the powers of the president and the executive, with negative consequences for Russia's political life. Parliament, never very influential in the country's post-Soviet politics and marginalized because of Yeltsin's rule by decree, was now pushed off to the margins of the political process not only de facto but also de jure. Boris Yeltsin and his aides believed that by enhancing presidential powers they were saving not just the reform program but democracy itself from what Yeltsin had characterized as an imminent dictatorship. But the new constitution established a precedent for authoritarian rule.[14]

Democracy vs. Reform

The Russian turn toward authoritarianism took place against the background of a dramatic economic downturn and was explained by a variety of factors ranging from the resource curse linked to the oil and gas riches of Russia to its "super-presidential" system of government.[15]

Considered historically, the authoritarian turn was preconditioned by the imperial collapse of the late 1980s and 1990s and informed by the long association of the Russian masses and elites with a strong state. The resentment produced on both the popular and the elite levels by Russia's loss of superpower status as a consequence of de facto defeat in the Cold War made that turn more likely. It was further strengthened by the humiliation produced by the loss of the outer empire in Eastern Europe and the inner empire within the borders of the USSR. Occupation troops were now recalled from Eastern Europe, and many ethnic Russians living in the former Soviet republics fled to the Russian Federation. Finally, Moscow's attempts to stop the disintegration of the Russian Federation produced two wars against Chechnya (1994–96 and 1999–2009), creating a highly militarized Russian state that delivered the final blow to the country's democratic development.

The economic downturn was even more pronounced in Ukraine, which lacked an equivalent of the rich oil and gas deposits that the Russian authorities could use to mitigate the effects of the recession. Sixty-two percent of Ukrainians found themselves below the poverty line of US $21.00 per month in 1995, as compared to less than 50 percent of Russians in 1993. But democracy survived in Ukraine despite numerous difficulties common to the post-Soviet states, societies, and economies. One reason for this was Ukraine's regional diversity and the weakness of Ukrainian nationalism, which had limited regional appeal in the 1990s, leading some scholars to call it a "minority faith."[16]

"Ukraine became the most competitive and democratic country in the Commonwealth of Independent States (CIS) over the post–Cold War era—experiencing four electoral turnovers, a vibrant media, and repeated mass movements for political change," wrote the political scientist Lucan Way in 2015, characterizing Ukrainian politics as "pluralism by default." According to him, "Ukraine's surprising pluralism was rooted in underdeveloped ruling parties, a weak authoritarian state, and national divisions between eastern and western Ukraine." "Overall," continued Way, "leaders had little capacity to keep allies in line, manipulate the electoral process, starve opponents of resources, and violently suppress opposition challenge."[17]

If in the eyes of the Russian public and a good part of the elite the fall of the USSR as a superpower and empire was a loss for Russia, the Ukrainian elite and much of the public considered it a gain for their country. Historically, Ukraine had been ruled from foreign capitals, so its population and political elite felt little nostalgia for their previous subordination to Moscow. With no recent tradition of national statehood, the country was unlikely to coalesce quickly around a political center of its own: instead, there was a strong regionalism that fragmented Ukrainian political space and made politics much more competitive than they had ever been in Russia. The weakness of Ukrainian nationalism prevented the country's political elite from accepting a single national narrative, as had happened in Russia. And yet Ukraine never fragmented completely, as the regional elites competed for primacy in the newly independent country, where they could play much more prominent roles than those assigned to them under the Soviet regime.[18]

Leonid Kravchuk, Yeltsin's Ukrainian counterpart, was elected president of his country in 1991 and, like Yeltsin, advanced to the presidential office from that of speaker of parliament. Kravchuk had his own problems with the legislative body that he had used as a power base to ascend to the highest office in the land. His political instincts were rather similar to those of his Russian counterpart. Kravchuk did not like the rebellious Ukrainian parliament—the Verkhovna Rada—and wanted to hold a referendum in order to increase the powers of his new office. But the Ukrainian political elite and society at large had little appetite for such a scenario.

In Ukraine, as in Russia, the economy and public reaction to the dissolution of the USSR were the two key issues that turned national politics into a never-ending drama, casting president and parliament in opposing roles. But those issues played out differently in Ukraine, where, most importantly, the political elite enhanced rather than undermined the democratic institutions born out of the chaos of Gorbachev's political and economic reforms. Russia's "democratic moment" became an "era of democracy" in Ukraine.

Leonid Kravchuk was never the revolutionary that Yeltsin had become during the late Soviet period. If Yeltsin had served in the course of his party career as a regional boss responsible for administering large administrative and economic entities such as Sverdlovsk oblast (province) and Moscow, Kravchuk was a quintessential apparatchik, running the propaganda department of the Ukrainian Central Committee. While Yeltsin left the Communist Party early, protesting the slow pace of Gorbachev's reforms, Kravchuk remained loyal to the end. If Yeltsin was elected to parliament and then became its chairman against the will of the party leadership, then Kravchuk took the helm of the Ukrainian parliament thanks to the support of the party bosses. And while Yeltsin ran for the Russian presidency against a communist candidate supported by the Kremlin, Kravchuk competed successfully against a pro-democratic candidate who also happened to be a former prisoner of the Gulag.

The differences between Yeltsin and Kravchuk extended to their styles of presidential leadership. If Yeltsin was a charismatic populist, highly voluntarist in his attitude to power, Kravchuk was a cunning apparatchik and consensus builder. He would need those skills in office, as he led a country very different from Russia and faced a very different parliament. Ukraine was divided by history, culture, and the political orientations and instincts of its people as the Russian Federation never was.[19]

The east and south of Ukraine had been the industrial heartland of the Soviet Union, was highly Russified in culture, and had millions of ethnic Russians among its inhabitants. The center was largely rural and Ukrainian-speaking, a product of the Soviet Ukrainian national project of the 1920s, which tolerated Ukrainian cultural but not political identity. Then there was the west, which had long been part of central European states and empires. Its strongly exclusivist national identity had been strengthened by the interwar nationalist movement and the lengthy guerrilla war against Soviet rule waged by the Ukrainian Insurgent Army in the late 1940s and early 1950s.[20]

As in Russia, the Ukrainian "democrats" emerged as the most dynamic force in late Soviet and early post-Soviet politics. Their principal concern was not economic reform but state-building. By the end of 1991 Yeltsin had established control over all-Union managerial cadres and institutions that had plenty of experience in running an independent state; in Ukraine such institutions had to be built almost from scratch on the basis of ministries that in Soviet times had merely relayed orders from Moscow to the periphery, ensuring that production quotas and directives from the top were fulfilled in a timely manner.[21]

When it came to market reforms, the Ukrainian parliament lacked a strong lobby to advocate or adopt them, and the public was not ready to support them. Economic reform meant hardship, which might very well split the country and scupper its independence. A poll conducted in 1993 suggested that only 19 percent of Ukrainians were prepared to endure economic reforms in order to strengthen and maintain independence, while 44 percent were not. Most of the former resided in the west, while most of the latter lived in the east and south. Thus, Ukraine found itself first resisting, then delaying, and finally emulating reforms.[22]

That postponement of economic reform held off an economic downturn but ultimately made it more severe. If the Russian economy lost 15 percent of GDP in 1992, 9 percent in 1993, and 13 percent in 1994, in Ukraine the respective figures were 10 percent in 1992, 14 percent in 1993, and 23 percent in 1994. The Ukrainian parliament printed money that steadily lost value; Yeltsin did not allow the Russian parliament to do so. The Ukrainian karbovanets began to fall almost immediately after it was introduced. On October 1, 1992, its official value was 340 karbovanets to the US dollar; two months later, it was 715 karbovanets to the dollar. In 1993 the karbovanets fell from 740 to 40,000 to the dollar, and inflation reached 10,256 percent. The state budget reached a deficit of 40 percent.[23]

In Ukraine, as in Russia, economic crisis produced or exacerbated political crisis. Unlike Yeltsin, Kravchuk never wrested from parliament the right to rule by decree. Instead, parliament granted that right temporarily to the prime minister, whose survival depended on a parliamentary vote. The main tension in Ukrainian politics emerged not between president and parliament but between president and prime minister. That confrontation paralyzed the executive branch, worsening the economic crisis that engulfed the country and provoking massive strikes among the Donbas miners, who marched on Kyiv to present their demands.

To resolve the conflict, Kravchuk took a page from Yeltsin's book and proposed a referendum to determine whether the president should be empowered to run the government, to serve as an expression of confidence in the incumbent. The referendum was scheduled for late September 1993, the month in which Yeltsin undertook his own coup against the Russian parliament. But mass protests in Kyiv prevented Kravchuk from carrying out his referendum. Instead, new elections, both parliamentary and presidential, were scheduled for the following year.[24]

The Ukrainian Constitution

Leonid Kravchuk did his best to turn the elections into a referendum on Ukrainian independence, presenting himself as its creator and defender. His opponent, the former director of Europe's largest missile factory and former prime minister of Ukraine, Leonid Kuchma, campaigned on a platform of rebuilding economic ties with Russia. The Ukrainian electorate split along the east-west axis, with Kravchuk supported mostly by the rural and Ukrainian-speaking west and center of the country and Kuchma by the predominantly urban and Russian-speaking east and south. No candidate crossed the 50-percent mark in the first round of the elections. In the second round, Kuchma prevailed by 52 percent over Kravchuk's 45. Kravchuk left office, making no attempt to challenge the results. Ukraine had managed to do what Russia was never able to achieve, handling a transfer of presidential power through free and fair elections.[25]

The parliamentary elections in Ukraine ended very much like those in Russia, with a de facto win of communist candidates and their allies, brought to parliament by a wave of popular discontent produced by the economic crisis. The new president, Leonid Kuchma, was oriented toward economic reforms, including mass privatization of state enterprises: Ukraine had postponed it too long and was now in a worse economic situation than Russia. But the leftist parliament wanted to return to state regulation. In Russia, the new constitution empowered the president to act on his own with regard to economic reforms, but in Ukraine, the president could do little without the consent of parliament.

Leonid Kuchma wanted a new constitution, but parliamentary leaders wanted the old one. Following in Yeltsin's footsteps, Kuchma threatened to put his own draft constitution to a referendum. Knowing from Russian experience where that could lead, parliament decided to compromise. Urgency was added by the 1996 presidential elections in Russia, in which a communist candidate had a good chance of beating Yeltsin. Fears grew in Kyiv that with a communist at the helm in Russia and communists making up the largest faction in the Ukrainian parliament, they might try to resurrect the Soviet Union.

In June 1996 the Ukrainian parliament adopted the text of Kuchma's new constitution, creating a mixed presidential-parliamentary system of government. In this power-sharing arrangement the president acquired the right to veto laws adopted by parliament and even to dissolve parliament under certain circumstances. But parliament gained a decisive role in appointing the prime minister and key cabinet members, including the head of the national bank. Parliament also placed its representatives on the constitutional court and the board of the national

bank. Furthermore, it reserved for itself the right to amend the constitution and conduct referendums.[26]

The Ukrainian parliament thus survived the economic and political crisis of the mid-1990s as an independent and powerful political
institution, capable of limiting presidential prerogatives. No less importantly, parliament remained very diverse in political representation. No
political party or regional elite was strong enough to capture parliament
and impose its will or political vision on the entire country. Compromise emerged as the only viable way for the elites to sort out their differences and accommodate one another's interests. That unwritten law
of Ukrainian politics would not change with the succession of power
brokers. Whether they were Communist Party bosses, "red directors"
who benefited from Kuchma's privatization of enterprises that they had
been managing, or representatives of the new economic elites and oligarchs, the political rules remained the same: one had to look for allies
and be ready for compromises.

The key issue contested in Ukrainian politics became not economic reform but nation-building and relations with the former imperial master, Russia. In Ukraine, unlike in Russia, communists and
nationalists were divided and at each other's throats, the nationalists
being pro-Western and pro-reform, the communists anti-reform and
pro-Russian. The country's regional and cultural diversity, inherited
from its long history of rule by foreign empires and states, contributed
enormously to the political pluralism of Ukrainian society.

The national democrats, based largely in western Ukraine, insisted
on ending dependence on Russia in political, economic, and cultural
terms as soon as possible and at any price. The former Communist
Party and industrial bosses elected in the east for their part pushed for
closer ties with Russia, on whose energy supplies the regional economy
depended, and whose language and culture were shared by a good part
of the population of eastern and southern Ukraine. The center emerged
as the battleground in this undeclared cultural and economic war
between east and west, making each side reluctant to resort to extremes,

promoting compromise, and helping to keep the country together. The same role was performed by the millions of Russified ethnic Ukrainians, who served as both buffer and glue linking the Russian-speaking ethnic Russians in the east and south and Ukrainian-speaking ethnic Ukrainians in the west and center of the country.[27]

Despite its political, economic, and cultural diversity, the country stayed together. If in Russia the fall of the USSR brought a sense of defeat and resentment, the Ukrainian elites saw themselves as beneficiaries of imperial collapse and had numerous incentives to unite around the idea of Ukrainian sovereignty, despite the different ways in which they imagined it. There was more optimism in the corridors of power in Kyiv than there was in Moscow, notwithstanding Ukraine's disastrous economic performance.

The Russian Presidency

The Russian presidential elections of 1996, which frightened Ukrainian parliamentarians into adopting a compromise constitution to prevent the communist restoration of the USSR, set Russia on a path toward an authoritarian form of government that subsequently became known as "managed" or "sovereign" democracy—the use and abuse of the electoral system to maintain and solidify authoritarian rule.

The first step was taken on March 15, 1996, when the Russian communists who had won the previous year's parliamentary elections sponsored a vote in the Duma renouncing the ratification of the Belavezha agreements between Russia, Ukraine, and Belarus that had dissolved the Soviet Union in December 1991. The communist resolution was supported by 250 deputies, with only 98 voting against it. The resolution was nonbinding, and under the new constitution parliament had no power to implement it, but it was a direct challenge to Yeltsin and his legitimacy as president of post-Soviet Russia. Yeltsin immediately denounced the vote as an attack on Russia—"an attempt to liquidate our statehood."[28]

Whether the communist leaders of the Duma were indeed preparing to restore the Soviet Union or not, they left no doubt that they wanted to unseat Yeltsin in the forthcoming presidential elections. His opponents during the constitutional crisis of 1994, vice president Aleksandr Rutskoi and the speaker of parliament, Ruslan Khasbulatov, who had been arrested after Yeltsin's assault on parliament, were now free, released from custody by the Duma's vote. But the strongest candidate for the presidency was not Rutskoi or Khasbulatov. They were overshadowed by the head of the Russian Communist Party, Gennadii Ziuganov, who enjoyed the support of more than 20 percent of the Russian electorate, while support for Yeltsin had dropped to somewhere between 5 and 8 percent of eligible voters.[29]

Yeltsin's inner circle, including his trusted bodyguard Aleksandr Korzhakov, who also served as gatekeeper to the president, argued that Yeltsin should ban the Communist Party, dissolve the Duma, postpone the elections until 1998, and rule by decree. Yeltsin agreed and ordered his aides to prepare decrees introducing all those measures. Russian democracy was about to suffer another blow, once again at the hands of Yeltsin and once again, ostensibly, with the noble goal of preserving it. But the reformers in Yeltsin's government, led by the author of the Russian privatization reform, Anatolii Chubais, rebelled against the plan proposed by the president's security team.

Chubais enlisted the support of Yeltsin's daughter, Tatiana Diachenko, who convinced her father to meet him. He all but accused Yeltsin of betraying the principles for which he had fought all those years. According to his own recollections, Yeltsin felt ashamed. The plans to postpone the elections were scrapped; Korzhakov and his group lost power and were banned from the Kremlin. Yeltsin decided to face the electorate, and Chubais became the head of his electoral campaign. Democracy seemed to be pushing back against the authoritarian instincts.

It was a gamble, Yeltsin-style. As in 1991, he was once again putting his political career, if not his life, on the line. Again he presented himself as Russia's savior from communism, this time from a communist resurgence. The budget was oriented toward the payment of pensions and salaries, while government officials were mobilized to get out the pro-Yeltsin vote. Yeltsin's shock therapy had cost him popular support but also produced a new class of the super-rich prepared to back him. In the fall and early winter of 1995, a group of Russian bankers made an informal deal with the president's office, offering their media resources and money to fuel his electoral campaign and bribe voters and regional elites by offering construction projects. In exchange, they were promised shares in government-owned enterprises at a bargain price.[30]

Boris Yeltsin plunged into the frenzy of the electoral campaign. Having been in poor health for quite some time and prone to depression, which he treated with alcohol, Yeltsin suffered a heart attack in mid-campaign but managed to cross the finish line. Thanks to the support of the state apparatus and the bankers, he prevailed. His strategy of presenting himself as the only force capable of stopping the return of communism worked. Yeltsin finished ahead of the communist candidate, Ziuganov, in the first round, gaining 36 percent of the vote to Ziuganov's 32 percent, and then beat him 54 to 41 percent in the second round. By that time the third-place finisher in the first round, General Aleksandr Lebed, had already joined Yeltsin's government, being appointed secretary of the Security Council.[31]

Yeltsin won, the communists and nationalists were stopped, and some semblance of democracy had been preserved. The bankers who financed Yeltsin's presidential campaign and already owned the media now became industrialists as well. A new oligarchic class had been born. Its members were not looking forward either to a communist revanche or to the establishment of a dictatorship in Russia. The best way to keep their assets was to maintain some form of electoral democracy. Yeltsin saw his victory as a mandate to continue, indeed to accelerate, market reforms. Hopes for such acceleration were dashed by the Asian financial crisis of 1997, which caused a Russian default on ruble-denominated bonds by August 1998. Within a few weeks the currency tumbled from 6.3 to 21 rubles to the US dollar. Inflation would soon reach 87 percent.[32]

The financial collapse of 1998 presented a new challenge to the Russian political system. Presidential elections were scheduled for the year 2000, but neither Yeltsin's health nor the Russian constitution would allow him to run for another term. Who would succeed the president was an open question. Yeltsin believed that he had the right and, indeed, the responsibility to choose his successor. The rest would be done by the method employed in the 1996 elections, pulling together the resources of the state and friendly oligarchs, who had united around Yeltsin and become known as "the family." The steppingstone to the presidency was the office of prime minister. Getting there as speaker of parliament, as Yeltsin himself had done, was now out of the question—the Duma was in the hands of the president's opponents.[33]

The tryouts for president in what had become known as Operation "Successor" began with the appointment of Sergei Stepashin, the forty-seven-year-old former minister of the interior, as prime minister. His task, as far as Yeltsin was concerned, was to prove loyal to Yeltsin himself and gain popularity with voters. Stepashin achieved neither. On the first count, he sought compromises with Yeltsin's opponents, suggesting that the future president would do nothing to protect Yeltsin from his enemies once his term in office was up. Stepashin was also unable to deal with the security situation in and around Chechnya, the Russian Federation's main internal problem and an open wound since the early 1990s.

Stepashin was out of office by August, to be replaced by another representative of the government's security bloc, the former director of the Federal Security Service and secretary of the Security Council, Vladimir Putin. A former KGB officer and aide to Yeltsin's key ally of the early 1990s, the mayor of St. Petersburg, Anatolii Sobchak, Putin had moved to Moscow after Sobchak lost the elections of 1996. He joined the presidential administration and was then appointed to head the Federal Security Service. Putin established equally good relations with the reformers, oligarchs, and Yeltsin apparatchiks, in particular Valentin Yumashev, the head of the presidential administration after

Chubais, like Yeltsin a native of the Urals, and subsequently his son-in-law. It was the family that picked Putin as Yeltsin's prime minister and successor.[34]

Like Stepashin, Putin was expected to protect Yeltsin from the attacks of his political opponents and prove his ability to win elections. Putin was successful in both tasks. Even before his appointment to the prime ministerial office, he proved his loyalty to Yeltsin by going after his foes. As head of the Federal Security Service, he provided videotape of a rendezvous that Yeltsin's critic Attorney General Yurii Skuratov had with prostitutes in a Moscow apartment. Skuratov had informally coordinated security services on behalf of Yeltsin's political opponents. Now his career was all but finished, while Putin's prospects improved: he was soon appointed secretary of the Security Council and was on the way to becoming prime minister.[35]

Putin, a colorless apparatchik whose name was not well known even among the government elite, to say nothing of the general public, performed a miracle after his appointment, becoming the most popular Russian politician in a few short months. In August, a mere 2 percent of Russian voters were prepared to favor him, yet by the end of the year he had the support of 51 percent of the potential electorate. How could that happen? Two key advantages were full control of government media and the help of oligarchs friendly to the Kremlin, along with their media resources. But even more important was the image of the new prime minister that the media brought to the general public. He came across as a young, energetic, and decisive leader who could protect Russia from enemies foreign and domestic.

Yeltsin placed Putin in charge of waging war against Chechen rebels who broke out of Chechnya into neighboring Dagestan in August 1999, the month of Putin's appointment as prime minister, and declared the formation there of the Islamic State of Dagestan. Putin took control of the war effort in the most public way possible, appearing on television again and again to threaten the rebels and demonstrate his and Russia's resolve to defeat the insurrection. Many observers argued that both the Chechen raid into Dagestan and terrorist acts in Russian cities attributed to the Chechens were in fact provoked or staged by the Russian security services, all in an effort to showcase the ability of Russia's top security official to deal with the crisis and gain the trust of the public, which would be voting in presidential elections a year later.

The Chechen War

Chechnya had emerged as a key factor in Russian politics even before the fall of the USSR. Chechens led by General Dzhokhar Dudaev supported Boris Yeltsin during the coup of August 1991 in Moscow in the hope that the new democratic leadership of Russia would recognize their right to self-determination. Their goal was the independence of Chechnya. But Yeltsin and his advisers made a clear distinction between Union republics such as Ukraine and Estonia, which they allowed to leave without a fight, and autonomous republics and regions within the borders of the Russian Federation, which they wanted to retain, treating the inviolability of the borders of the Union republics as the founding principle of their own statehood.

In the fall of 1991 Yeltsin sent Russian troops to Chechnya but failed to check its drive for independence. His troops were demoralized, not ready to fight, and Mikhail Gorbachev, who still controlled the all-Union military, refused to back Yeltsin's effort. Chechnya, renamed Ichkeria, declared independence on November 1, 1991, and took advantage of the chaos prevailing in Moscow in the early 1990s to turn the declaration into reality.

Yeltsin ordered his army into Chechnya again in December 1994 with the goal of capturing its capital, Grozny. But the Chechen fighters ambushed Russian tanks and armored vehicles on the streets of Grozny, causing many casualties. The battle for the city lasted until March 1995, and the Russians succeeded in taking the Chechen capital only after destroying a good part of the city with aerial bombardment and artillery fire. The rebels retreated into the mountainous areas of the country, from which they continued their attacks on the occupying forces even after a Russian guided missile killed General Dudaev.

His successor, Aslan Maskhadov, managed to recapture Grozny in August 1996.

In the same month General Aleksandr Lebed, Yeltsin's head of the State Security Council, signed a ceasefire agreement with the Chechen leaders that resulted in the withdrawal of the Russian army. Chechnya was left largely to its own devices but, isolated and unrecognized not only by Russia but also by the international community, it was not doing well. Aslan Maskhadov, elected president in 1997, had little control of Chechen territory outside Grozny, which was held mostly by warlords. Kidnapping for ransom became one of the ways in which they filled their coffers. Radical factions among the rebels continued terrorist attacks on Russian territory.[36]

Many of the Chechen military leaders and their foot soldiers exchanged the national independence ideology of the late 1980s for the ideas and beliefs of radical Islam. Islamist circles in the Middle East were the only international actors prepared to recognize the self-proclaimed republic. The Chechen incursion into Dagestan in the summer of 1999 and their declaration of the Islamic State of Dagestan were fueled by new religious zeal and ideology. They were not approved by the top Chechen leadership, which had no interest in provoking Russia into a new offensive. But the crisis created by the Chechen fighters' venture into Dagestan brought war nevertheless, since it was highly advantageous from the viewpoint of Russian domestic politics. Too advantageous, some commentators have suggested, implying the involvement of the Russian security services in inciting the attack.[37]

Overseen by Putin, the Russian offensive began in late August 1999 with massive aerial bombardment of Chechnya, causing the exodus of up to 100,000 people and creating a refugee crisis in neighboring areas of Russia. In September, blasts rocked not only Chechen but Russian cities, including Moscow. Several apartment buildings were blown up with explosives strategically located in their basements, killing more than 300 civilians. The Federal Security Service (Russian acronym FSB), Putin's power base, blamed the blasts on Chechen fighters, but evidence pointed to the FSB itself. In Riazan, a city 200 kilometers (124 miles) southeast of Moscow with a population of half a million, the local police caught FSB agents planting bombs in an apartment building. The FSB declared that it was an anti-terrorist drill. Although the question of responsibility remains unresolved even now, terrorist acts caused indignation in Russia and provided Putin with a popular mandate to launch an all-out land invasion of Chechnya.[38]

Putin ordered the invasion in October 1999 after declaring the Chechen president, Aslan Maskhadov, illegitimate. The stated goal was to partition Chechnya, creating a northern buffer zone between rebel-held territories and the Russian Federation. Maskhadov's calls for peace talks were rejected. With the support of air power and artillery, Russian troops began moving deep into Chechen territory, causing hundreds of thousands of civilians to leave their homes. By December 1999 the Russian forces were once again at the walls of Chechnya's capital, Grozny. Whatever had not been destroyed by bombardment in 1995 was destroyed now. The city fell in February 2000 and was designated by the United Nations as the most devastated city in the world. By May 2000 Putin already had a puppet administration in place, ending the active phase of the Second Chechen War.[39]

By that time Putin had become president of Russia, moving officially into the presidential office on May 7, 2000. In his New Year's address on December 31, 1999, Yeltsin had surprised everyone by announcing his resignation. Putin, whose popularity with voters had crossed the 50 percent mark earlier that month, became acting president, assuming full control not only over the government and the army but also the state-run media and "administrative resources" needed to win the presidential elections Russia-style. Earlier in December a new law was adopted requiring candidates to collect at least one million signatures to qualify for the campaign. It also regulated election finances so as to privilege the candidate who enjoyed government support. Putin alone could count on it.

The elections that the opposition had expected in the summer of 2000 were now moved up to spring, leaving the opposition candidates, in particular the mayor of Moscow, Yurii Luzhkov, insufficient time

to prepare. Luzhkov withdrew his candidacy, as did Yevgenii Primakov, leaving the center of Russia's political spectrum free for Putin.
In March 2000 he easily won the presidential elections in the first
round, gaining 53 percent of the vote. The communist leader, Gennadii
Ziuganov, received 22 percent, while the liberal leader, Grigorii Yavlinsky, garnered 6 percent. The operation dubbed by the insiders "Successor" was complete. Putin's first decree in presidential office dealt with
guarantees for Boris Yeltsin, who was granted immunity from criminal
prosecution regardless of any accusations against him.[40]

The Yeltsin era in Russian politics was effectively over, and he left
behind an influential legacy. A former Communist Party official, Yeltsin wanted democracy so much that he was prepared to use authoritarian methods to achieve it. He had not only led the Russian Federation
out of the Soviet Union on the wave of democratic mobilization but
also established it as a superpresidential republic limiting the same
democracy that brought him to power. Yeltsin also inaugurated a succession system in which the new top official would be preselected by
the incumbent. After his election Putin took full advantage of the existing political system, advancing it from the superpresidential stage to
the autocratic one. That would have a tremendous impact not only on
Russian domestic politics but also on the country's foreign policy.

The Orange Revolution

In the fall of 1999, as Yeltsin was getting ready to step down and promote Putin as his successor, the president of Ukraine, Leonid Kuchma,
was preparing to run for a second term. During his first term he had
managed to stabilize the Ukrainian economy by launching large-scale
privatization and working closely with Western donors, especially the
International Monetary Fund.

Kuchma had also brought Ukrainian politics into temporary equi-
librium by adopting a new constitution that introduced a power-sharing
agreement between president and parliament. Yet the system was anything but stable, as the two political actors did not agree on the politi-

cal and economic direction of the country. The global financial crisis of 1997 and the Russian default of 1998 hurt the Ukrainian economy, enhancing the position of the communists as the most powerful parliamentary faction. In the parliamentary elections of 1998 they gained 25 percent of the popular vote. The national democrats, organized in Rukh and led by the former dissident Viacheslav Chornovil, came second with 10 percent of the vote, while the Kuchma-backed People's Democratic Party garnered a mere 5 percent.[41]

In 1999 Kuchma was pretty much in the same place as Yeltsin on the eve of his reelection in 1996. He decided to take a page from Yeltsin's electoral campaign, presenting himself as the only force capable of stopping a communist return to power. This stance appealed to the new industrial bosses in eastern Ukraine, who had managed to privatize former state-owned enterprises on Kuchma's watch and with his assistance. Electors in the western regions, who cherished Ukrainian independence, oriented themselves toward Europe and against a return to the USSR.

Using his control of state-run media and obtaining support from media controlled by the regional bosses and oligarchs who had emerged during his first term, Kuchma managed to carry both eastern and western Ukraine, losing only in the center, where the countryside was still controlled by holdovers of the collective farm system. He gained 58 percent of the popular vote versus 39 percent for his opponent, the Ukrainian communist leader Petro Symonenko. Like Yeltsin, Kuchma decided to use his victory over the communists to push market reforms forward. He was luckier than his Russian counterpart, as there was no Asian financial crisis to interfere with his plans.[42]

Upon his reelection, Kuchma initiated a new course toward integrating Ukraine into European political and economic structures. He appointed Viktor Yushchenko, the young head of Ukraine's national bank who was strongly supported by the International Monetary Fund (IMF), as the new prime minister. In slightly more than a year, Yushchenko and his ally Yulia Tymoshenko, who became deputy prime minister in the new government, managed to stop the economic decline, increase revenues by closing loopholes for big business and the newly emergent oligarchic clans, and repay unpaid wages, salaries, and pensions. The economy began a rapid recovery led by the metallurgical and mining industries, which doubled their exports. Economic growth would continue well into the first decade of the new millennium.[43]

Kuchma used his electoral victory to renegotiate the constitutional deal he had reached with parliament back in 1996. First, he forced the communists to accept the new parliamentary leadership formed by the pro-presidential parties, and then called a referendum on presidential powers. Eighty-one percent of the electorate took part in the referendum and, depending on the question, anywhere between 83 and 91 percent of voters supported a complete reshuffle of parliament as an institution, creating two chambers instead of one, reducing the number of deputies by one-third, allowing criminal prosecution of deputies, and permitting the president to dissolve parliament if it failed to create a stable majority within one month of beginning a session.[44]

Kuchma was now ready to rewrite the Ukrainian constitution in the spirit of Yeltsin's document but was checked by the opposition, whose parliamentary representatives would not recognize the outcome of the referendum. Kuchma, for his part, had too few votes to introduce the constitutional amendments approved by the referendum. The standoff exploded into a major political scandal in late November 2000, when Oleksandr Moroz, the leader of the Socialist Party and former speaker of parliament, made public secret tapes of conversations held in Kuchma's office. The tapes, allegedly made by one of Kuchma's bodyguards, caught the president discussing corrupt privatization schemes and prosecution of his political opponents.

Most damaging in the recordings were conversations in which Kuchma gave his interior minister an order to kidnap an oppositional journalist, Heorhii Gongadze. He had disappeared in September of that year, and his headless body was found in a forest near Kyiv in November. The political scandal rocked the foundations of Kuchma's regime. The president denied ever having given an order to kill the journalist, which was probably true, but the tapes had him demanding that his interior minister, Yurii Kravchenko, kidnap Gongadze and expel him from the country. It would later be proved that Kravchenko's secret death squad had murdered Gongadze, but it was never revealed who had given the order not just to kidnap but to kill the journalist. Kravchenko would eventually die under suspicious circumstances, having shot himself not once but twice in an apparent suicide attempt.[45]

In December 2000 the opposition, including socialists led by Moroz and populists led by Yulia Tymoshenko, marched in the streets of Kyiv, demanding the president's resignation and launching a massive campaign under the slogan, "Ukraine without Kuchma." The weakened president abandoned his reformist course. Yulia Tymoshenko was arrested, and the reform-oriented Viktor Yushchenko, who enjoyed Western support, was replaced as prime minister. With American and European leaders demanding an impartial investigation of the president's role in the kidnapping and murder of Gongadze, Kuchma abandoned his ambitions of European integration and turned for support to Russia and its new president, Vladimir Putin.[46]

While few doubted that Kuchma had indeed ordered the kidnapping and forcible deportation of Gongadze from Ukraine—the recording suggested that he had ordered his interior minister to send the journalist to Chechnya—it remained unclear who had ordered him to be killed, and why. The circumstances under which Kuchma was allegedly taped by one of his bodyguards, Mykola Melnychenko, remain murky to this day. What seems uncontested, however, is that Melnychenko worked on behalf of top officers in the Ukrainian security services and later collaborated with their Russian counterparts. It is quite clear that the main beneficiary of Kuchmagate was Vladimir Putin, who exploited the weakening of Kuchma's political authority and the worsening of his relations with the United States, caused by the scandal, to extract a number of concessions from him. Among those was Ukraine's accession to Russia-led Eurasian organizations and forums promoting the economic reintegration of the post-Soviet space. Kuchma also dropped the goal of joining NATO from Ukrainian military doctrine.[47]

The Ukrainian constitution did not allow the president to serve in office more than two terms, and after some hesitation Leonid Kuchma decided to abide by it, rejecting the idea of running for a third term on the grounds that his first election predated the adoption of the constitution and thus should not be counted. Once again Kuchma reached out for the Russian or, more specifically, Yeltsin's precedent, looking for a successor who would guarantee his personal safety and the integrity of his assets.

The choice fell on the leader of Ukraine's largest regional clan, the governor of Donetsk oblast, Viktor Yanukovych, who had led the largest grouping in the pro-presidential faction of parliament. Yanukovych had been appointed prime minister and approved by parliament in November 2002. The presidential campaign of 2004, which pitched Yanukovych, supported by Kuchma, against the former prime minister, Viktor Yushchenko, who led the largest faction in parliament, was the dirtiest in Ukrainian history. The Yanukovych camp used government media, administrative pressure, government handouts to the most vulnerable social groups, as well as the financial power of the Donetsk clan to prevail in the elections. It also resorted to an act of terrorism against Yushchenko.[48]

In September 2004, the fifty-year-old Yushchenko fell violently ill and was soon diagnosed with dioxin poisoning. The individuals suspected of arranging it had fled to Russia and were given safe haven there. Yushchenko miraculously survived the attack and managed to return to the electoral campaign defaced but alive. Instead of knocking Yushchenko out, the attack on the opposition candidate increased his popularity. When Ukrainians went to the polling stations on October 31, most of them voted for Yushchenko, not Yanukovych.[49]

That was the result of the exit polls conducted by numerous Ukrainian institutions on election day, but the Central Electoral Commission, controlled by Kuchma and Yanukovych, announced a different outcome. According to the commission's report, it was Yanukovych who had won the race with 49 percent of the vote over Yushchenko's 47 percent. Yushchenko's supporters, refusing to accept the forged result, flooded Kyiv's main square, the Maidan, and set up a tent city there. Kyivans were soon joined by supporters from the provinces. The Orange Revolution, which took its name from the colors of Yushchenko's electoral campaign, had begun.[50]

Numerous factors contributed to the outbreak of the Orange Revolution. Among them were the protracted and unresolved conflict between the presidential and legislative branches of government; the split within the political elite, including the oligarchs with their media resources, who supported opposite sides; and, last but not least, Kuchma's halfhearted support for Yanukovych, who was not his preferred choice for successor but was forced on him by circumstances. Ultimately it was Ukrainian regionalism, rooted in political and cultural differences, that came to the rescue of Ukrainian democracy. The supporters of the Orange Revolution, many of them residents of Ukraine's west and center, associated themselves with Ukrainian identity, language, and culture, as well as an orientation toward the liberal West.[51]

Faced with continuing mass protests and the split within the elite, Kuchma decided to put Yeltsin's precedent aside. Despite demands from Yanukovych, he refused to use the army against the protesters and open fire, as had been the case in Moscow in 1993. Instead, he opted for a compromise. The Yanukovych camp agreed to a new round of elections in exchange for Yushchenko's promise to amend the constitution to limit presidential prerogatives. On December 26, in the third round of the presidential elections, Yushchenko was elected with 52 percent of the vote against Yanukovych's 44 percent.[52]

The crisis that had begun in April 2000 with Kuchma's attempt to increase the power of the presidency by means of a referendum came to an end in December 2004 with the weakening of presidential powers. Some presidential prerogatives were transferred to the prime minister, whose appointment and political fortunes depended on the disposition of political forces in parliament. Ukraine was entering the new century as a presidential-parliamentary republic with divided governing power. It was anything but an ideal outcome, for under the new system neither the president nor the prime minister had sufficient power to implement policy independently. But it was the outcome that saved Ukrainian democracy.

During his last year in office, Kuchma had published his memoirs under the telling title, *Ukraine Is Not Russia*. After trying the Russian model more than once and inevitably failing to achieve the desired result, he knew exactly what he was talking about. The book was published in Moscow and launched there before its Ukrainian translation became available to readers in Kyiv. It sent a message that very few in Russia took seriously and no one in the Kremlin was prepared to accept.[53]

3

NUCLEAR IMPLOSION

Ukraine as an independent state was born nuclear, inheriting from the Soviet Union the third-largest nuclear arsenal in the world. The Soviet Union had deployed close to 1,900 nuclear warheads and about 2,500 tactical nuclear weapons on Ukrainian territory. Those weapons presented a major problem to the United States: as the USSR disintegrated, Washington was concerned that the Soviet collapse could set off a civil war among nuclear-armed republics, producing what was referred to at the time as "Yugoslavia with nukes." The possibility of war between Russia and Ukraine became more than theoretical when the Russian parliament declared that the Crimea had been illegitimately transferred to Ukraine and then claimed the city of Sevastopol for the Russian Federation.[1]

Russia wanted the Ukrainian nuclear weapons to be transferred to its territory as soon as possible, which would greatly strengthen its claim to an exclusive sphere of influence in the post-Soviet space. Ukraine was anything but eager to comply. It did not have operational control over the weapons—the codes required to launch the missiles were in Moscow—but had physical possession, and some officials in the Ukrainian parliament and government considered a transfer politically unacceptable. The reason was obvious—Russia's territorial claim to the Crimea and, potentially, other Ukrainian territories.

Ukraine's stance on nuclear weapons evolved over time. Kyiv began its career in the international arena with its declaration of sovereignty in 1990 as a strong proponent of denuclearization for two main reasons. The first was the legacy of the Chernobyl nuclear disaster in 1986, which contaminated a good part of Ukrainian territory and led the Ukrainian parliament to pass laws committing the country to a moratorium on the construction of new nuclear plants. Then there was the realization that a dispute with the Union center over control of nuclear weapons would be long and messy, possibly delaying Ukraine's progress toward full independence. It was considered expedient at the time to trade the weapons for recognition of Ukraine's independence and right to create its own armed forces. The declaration of Ukrainian sovereignty adopted by parliament in the summer of 1990 committed Ukraine to non-nuclear status.[2]

The first doubts regarding that commitment came in the fall of 1991, after the Ukrainian parliament's vote for independence, because of Russia's reaction. Boris Yeltsin's statement, issued by his press secretary, Pavel Voshchanov, indicated that Ukraine's borders could be guaranteed only in union with Russia. Many in Kyiv began to reconsider the nuclear issue. Volodymyr Filenko, an influential member of the Ukrainian parliament, told a British journalist in September 1991, "Most MPs think we cannot just give weapons to Russia. It would upset the balance of power between Russia and Ukraine." He then added: "We're afraid of Russia, if you like. We're fighting for independence from Russia. We cannot say there is a nuclear threat, but they did recently raise territorial claims."[3]

The Ukrainian political elite was faced with a dilemma: the fastest and perhaps only viable way of gaining international recognition of Ukrainian independence was to give up nuclear weapons, but the most effective and possibly the only plausible way of assuring the country's longevity was to keep them. In October 1991, to ensure American support for Ukrainian independence, parliament committed itself to non-nuclear status but also claimed the right to determine the disposition of the nuclear weapons in its possession. "Ukraine insists on its right to control the non-use of the nuclear weapons located on its territory," read the parliamentary resolution. In December 1991, parliament voted to ratify the documents creating the Commonwealth of Independent States on condition that Ukraine become a non-nuclear state by ensuring international control over the destruction of its nuclear weapons.[4]

The Crimean Knot

Territorial disputes are a hallmark of imperial disintegration, and the fall of the USSR was no exception. The Russian government had been challenging Ukraine's territorial integrity even before it became legally independent and left the Soviet Union. The first challenge to the Ukrainian borders came from the democratic government of Russia almost immediately after the Ukrainian parliament declared the country's independence on August 24, 1991. Two days later the Russian president's spokesman, Pavel Voshchanov, made a statement on behalf of his superior.

"In the most recent days, state sovereignty has been declared and withdrawal from the USSR announced in a series of Union republics," read the statement. "In that regard, I have been empowered by the President of the RSFSR to make the following declaration. The Russian Federation casts no doubt on the constitutional right of every state and people to self-determination. But there is the problem of borders, which may prove to be unregulated, a condition admissible only if provision is made for Union relations secured by an appropriate treaty. Should they be abrogated, the RSFSR reserves the right to pose the question of revision of borders."[5]

The statement was addressed to every Soviet republic that might declare its independence of the Soviet Union. But when Voshchanov was asked by journalists to be more specific, he singled out Ukraine and Kazakhstan. "If those republics enter into a union with Russia, then there is no problem," he explained. "But if they withdraw, then we must be concerned about the population living there and not forget that those lands were colonized by Russians. Russia will hardly agree to give them away so easily." Both Ukraine and Kazakhstan had large ethnic Russian minorities, and both republics, Ukraine in its entirety, and Kazakhstan in its northern lands, were eyed as parts of a future Russian state by no less a figure than Aleksandr Solzhenitsyn, whose article advocating the creation of such a state had been published by the major Soviet newspapers the previous year.[6]

Kyiv and Almaty protested, obliging Yeltsin to dissociate himself from Voshchanov's remarks. The spokesman was portrayed as someone who had got out of control and presented his personal views rather than the policy of Yeltsin's administration. But Voshchanov had in fact formulated the new policy of the Russian Federation for years to come. Treaties recognizing the borders of Union republics like the one signed between Russia and Ukraine in 1990 applied only if the republics, Ukraine in particular, remained in union with Russia. The understanding of what such union meant would change over time, from Gorbachev's Soviet Union to Yeltsin's Commonwealth of Independent States and, eventually, a number of Eurasian projects advanced by Putin. Models and rulers changed, but the basic principle remained the same: Russia's recognition of the territorial integrity and sovereignty of the post-Soviet states would be conditional on alliance with Moscow.[7]

Voshchanov later recalled that the Donbas and the Crimea were the Ukrainian territories that concerned the Russian leadership at the time. The Crimean peninsula was the most recent addition to Ukrainian territory, transferred from the Russian Federation to the Ukrainian SSR in 1954 for economic reasons, given that its economy was not functioning effectively without close coordination with the economy of the mainland, which happened to be Ukraine.[8]

The Crimea became the only region of Ukraine in which ethnic Russians constituted a majority, accounting for 1,635,000 people in 1989, compared with 625,0000 Ukrainians and 38,000 Crimean Tatars. On

December 1, 1991, 54 percent of the population of the peninsula supported Ukrainian independence. Similar numbers in Donetsk oblast of the Donbas were 77 percent and, in neighboring Luhansk oblast, 85 percent. Support for independence in the country as a whole exceeded 92 percent. The Crimea emerged as the most vulnerable region of Ukraine not only because of less popular support for independence but also because many in Russia, from democrats to communists and nationalists, believed that Russia had a historical right to the peninsula and should reclaim it.[9]

In January 1992 the Russian parliament questioned the legality of the transfer of the Crimea from Russia to Ukraine. It adopted a resolution to that effect in order to make Ukraine more tractable in the ongoing dispute about the future of the Soviet Black Sea Fleet. Kyiv argued that the fleet constituted its share of the USSR military infrastructure, with the rest of the Soviet Navy going to Russia. The Russian leadership, for its part, claimed the fleet as part of its strategic forces, which were to be placed under joint (de facto Russian) command. The Russian claim was tacitly made with regard not only to the navy but also to its base, the city of Sevastopol.

While Yeltsin and his government did not support the parliamentary resolution, Yeltsin agreed with some of his key allies, such as Anatolii Sobchak, the mayor of St. Petersburg and Putin's superior at the time, that the Black Sea Fleet should stay Russian no matter what position Ukraine and its leadership might take. Before the end of the month Yeltsin flew to the Russian port of Novorossiysk to meet with the commander of the Black Sea Fleet, Admiral Igor Kasatonov, on board the cruiser *Moskva*, which would be sunk by Ukrainian missiles thirty years later in the midst of the Russo-Ukrainian War. The purpose of the visit was to demonstrate Moscow's determination to keep the fleet under its jurisdiction.[10]

Yeltsin and his advisers followed a plan proposed by Vladimir Lukin, independent Russia's first ambassador to the United States. Before his departure for Washington in 1992, Lukin wrote a proposal that the issue of Crimean sovereignty be used to undermine Ukraine's position at negotiations on the future of the Black Sea Fleet. In April 1992, after President Leonid Kravchuk assumed control over former Soviet troops on Ukrainian territory, Yeltsin issued an order subordinating the Black Sea Fleet to himself. Yeltsin's vice president, Aleksandr Rutskoi, visited the Crimea and sided with the Russian parliament, claiming that the 1954 transfer of the Crimea to Ukraine had to be reversed. "Common sense dictates that the Crimea become part of Russia," declared Rutskoi. "Those who signed the decision of 1954 were evidently inebriated or suffering from sunstroke." He claimed that the Black Sea Fleet was and would remain Russian, while Yeltsin's adviser Sergei Stankevich questioned the legality of the 1954 transfer.[11]

That transfer had taken place alongside a propagandistic campaign marking the tercentenary of the "Reunification of Ukraine with Russia," the phrase used at the time for the acceptance of the Russian tsar's protectorate by the Ukrainian Cossack hetman Bohdan Khmelnytsky. He swore an oath of allegiance to Tsar Aleksei Romanov in the Ukrainian city of Pereiaslav in January 1654. The Soviet reunification paradigm was borrowed from imperial times, and in the Crimea it overshadowed another long-standing myth with strong imperial origins—that of Sevastopol as a city of Russian glory, born of its heroic defense in the Crimean War of 1853–56. The two mythologies complemented each other in the prevailing Russocentric narrative of the Soviet period but clashed after Ukraine left Russia's orbit.[12]

Tensions over the Crimea reached a danger point in May 1992, when the Crimean parliament—the Crimean oblast had become an autonomous republic within Ukraine and acquired its own parliament the previous year—proclaimed the republic a state in its own right. Declaring that the Crimea was to define its relations with Ukraine on the basis of a union treaty, parliament adopted a constitution and set a date for a referendum on Crimean independence. This initiative was supported by nationalist forces in Russia, and in the same month the Russian parliament raised the stakes, declaring that the transfer of the peninsula to Ukraine in 1954 had been illegal and proposing that Ukraine enter into negotiations on the status of the Crimea.

Kyiv fought back on two fronts, internal and external. The Ukrainian parliament refused to negotiate, denouncing Moscow's offer as interference in Ukraine's internal affairs. Meanwhile, the Ukrainian government convinced the Crimean authorities to amend their constitution and cancel the proposed referendum. The legal conflict was resolved without the use of force, which differed from the situation in neighboring Moldova. There, conflict between pro-Russian separatists in Transnistria had resulted in open warfare involving Russian troops and bringing about the de facto separation of the enclave from Moldova. But tensions in and around the Crimea did not abate. In Russia, they became part of the battle between parliament and the president.[13]

In July 1993 the Russian parliament adopted a resolution claiming the city of Sevastopol, the base of the Black Sea Fleet, as part of the territory and jurisdiction of the Russian Federation. "I am ashamed of parliament's decision," said Boris Yeltsin in response, adding: "We can't start a war with Ukraine, after all." In the following month Yeltsin met with Kravchuk at the Massandra resort in the Crimea, where the two presidents discussed the future of the Black Sea Fleet as well as Ukraine's growing debt to Russia for its supply of natural gas. The Ukrainians were threatened with a gas cutoff unless they "sold" their part of the fleet to Russia to pay off the debt. Kravchuk felt that he had no choice but to accept the "offer," but the Ukrainian parliament would refuse to ratify a deal made under coercion.[14]

The Massandra Accords helped Yeltsin take the initiative on the issues of the Black Sea Fleet and the Crimea away from parliament just a few weeks before he ordered his tanks to fire at the Russian parliament building. But the accords did little to promote a solution. The victory of communist and nationalist forces added to the new Duma in the autumn elections of 1993 emboldened the separatist movement in the Crimea. In 1994 the Crimea acquired a president of its own, Yurii Meshkov, who put the question of Crimean independence back on the political agenda, proposing a new referendum. Later that year the city council of Sevastopol, which remained the base of the Black Sea Fleet and depended on Moscow to pay its bills, voted to accept Russian jurisdiction over the city.

The Crimean crisis was resolved largely because Ukrainian democracy continued to function. The change of president in Kyiv as a result of the 1994 elections brought in a candidate strongly supported by Crimean voters. Leonid Kuchma received 90 percent of the vote in the Crimea as a whole and 92 percent in Sevastopol. Kuchma, a Russian speaker from Ukraine's industrial southeast, assured the peninsula's ethnic Russians that their linguistic and cultural rights would be protected by the central government. Ukrainian officials reached an informal power-sharing agreement with Crimean parliamentary leaders, who abolished the office of Crimean president and agreed to harmonize their constitution and laws with those of Ukraine.[15]

Tensions in the Crimea did not explode into civil war also because Russia refused to exploit its loyalists in the Black Sea Fleet to intervene on the side of the separatists, as it had done in Moldova. There were several reasons for Yeltsin's reluctance to fully embrace Crimean separatism. Secession of the Crimea would have been perceived as a concession to nationalists and communists in the Russian parliament, possibly emboldening Russia's own autonomies and offering them legal grounds to follow the Crimean example—this was particularly dangerous in the case of Tatarstan. Equally important, Russia's support for Crimean independence and de facto integration into the Russian Federation would have jeopardized the Yeltsin administration's attempts to strengthen its relations with the United States. This involved the joint efforts of Moscow and Washington to convince Ukraine to give up the nuclear arsenal that it had inherited from the Soviet Union.[16]

The Budapest Memorandum

Ever since the declaration of independence, Kyiv was prepared to accept a non-nuclear status of Ukraine but not to turn over its nuclear weapons to Russia without guarantees that they would be destroyed and not used against it. In March 1992, as tensions over control of the Black Sea Fleet began to increase, President Kravchuk ordered a stop to the transfer of tactical nuclear weapons to Russia, raising eyebrows and concerns not only in Moscow but also in Washington. The transfer was resumed only after the Ukrainians were allowed to observe the destruction of their weapons on Russian territory.[17]

In May 1992, under heavy American pressure, Leonid Kravchuk signed the Lisbon Protocol, which committed Ukraine to joining the Nuclear Nonproliferation Treaty as a non-nuclear state. The protocol also made Ukraine, along with Russia, Belarus, and Kazakhstan—the three other post-Soviet republics with nuclear weapons—a signatory to START-I, a 1991 Soviet-American treaty on the reduction of nuclear arsenals. But the signing of the protocol coincided with another rise in tensions between Russia and Ukraine over the Crimea, making the Ukrainian parliament anything but eager to ratify the Lisbon Protocol. The ratification of START-I encountered difficulty in July 1993, after the Russian Duma claimed Sevastopol as Russian territory. Yeltsin's attempts to force Ukraine to give up its nuclear weapons, as well as its claims to the Black Sea Fleet, in exchange for forgiveness of its natural gas debt to Moscow were rejected by the Ukrainian parliament. The more tensions increased over the Crimea, the stronger became Ukraine's grip on its weapons.[18]

In the United States, President George H. W. Bush spent the last year of his term, 1992, continuing the course he had adopted in the waning days of the USSR: Ukraine and other post-Soviet republics had to disarm and send their nuclear arsenals to Russia, whether they wanted to do so or not. But Bill Clinton's inauguration in January 1993 opened the door to reconsidering that policy, if only to try to understand the causes of Ukrainian resistance and eventually overcome it.

A few months into the Clinton presidency, the renowned political scientist and international relations expert John Mearsheimer published an article in *Foreign Affairs* arguing that Ukraine should be encouraged to keep its nuclear weapons, not pressured to give them up. In Mearsheimer's view that was the most effective way to prevent a Russo-Ukrainian war, which he characterized as a "disaster" that could lead to the reconquest of Ukraine and "injure prospects for peace throughout Europe." He argued: "Ukrainian nuclear weapons are the only reliable deterrent to Russian aggression. If the U.S. aim is to enhance stability in Europe, the case against a nuclear-armed Ukraine is unpersuasive."[19]

Clinton and his advisers were not prepared to take Mearsheimer's advice but became more considerate of Ukrainian concerns. Washington recognized Ukraine's ownership of the nuclear weapons on its territory and agreed to discuss financial compensation for their removal. When it came to security concerns, the administration was prepared to look into the possibility of offering Ukraine security assurances. More importantly, finally recognizing that Ukraine's main security concern was Russia, Washington replaced Moscow as the leading negotiator in the trilateral talks on Ukraine's nuclear disarmament. The new approach worked. Before the end of 1993, Washington and Kyiv reached agreement in principle on the conditions of Ukraine's denuclearization.

Under the new deal, the United States agreed to provide compensation for the Ukrainian weapons in the amount of one billion dollars. The United States and Russia jointly committed themselves to supply Ukraine's nuclear plants with fuel produced from the removed Ukrainian warheads. They also agreed to provide assurances of the sovereignty and territorial integrity of Ukraine. These became the foundations of the US-Russia-Ukraine treaty on the denuclearization of Ukraine, signed in January 1994. In February 1994, the Ukrainian parliament ratified the Lisbon Protocol, and in November of that year it voted for Ukraine's accession to the Treaty on the Nonproliferation of Nuclear Weapons (NPT) as a non-nuclear state.[20]

In December 1994, Clinton and Kuchma signed the Budapest Memorandum on the security assurances to be provided to Ukraine by the United States, Russia, and the United Kingdom. China and France later added their signatures to the document. Similar documents were signed by the leaders of Belarus and Kazakhstan, the two other post-Soviet republics to be denuclearized. The guarantors promised to "respect the independence and sovereignty and the existing borders of Ukraine" and "refrain from the threat or use of force against the territorial integrity or political independence of Ukraine, and that none of their weapons will ever be used against Ukraine."

The problem was the absence of commitments to protect Ukraine in case the promises were broken and Ukraine was attacked. If there should be a nuclear attack on Ukraine, the guarantors promised "to seek immediate United Nations Security Council action to provide assistance to Ukraine." They also promised consultations "in the event a situation arises that raises a question concerning these commitments." That was a poor substitute for the iron-clad guarantees requested by the Ukrainians, but it was the most they managed to obtain as a result of protracted negotiations.[21]

President Kuchma and his advisers hoped for the best but had few illusions. "If tomorrow Russia goes into the Crimea, no one will even raise an eyebrow," declared Kuchma, the former director of the largest missile factory in Europe and a proponent of the idea that Ukraine should divest itself of the nuclear weapons covered by START-I but leave the rest for its own security. Why did Kuchma, of all people, decide to accept the new deal offered by Washington? The reason was simple: he returned to the pre-independence position adopted by Ukrainian politicians. Once again, getting rid of the weapons became the surest way to secure Ukraine's independence and its recognition by the international community. Independence was under threat in 1993, not only because of Ukraine's continuing tensions with Russia and pressure from the United States but also because of the virtual collapse of the Ukrainian economy: in 1994, the year in which the Budapest Memorandum was signed, Ukraine lost almost a quarter of its GDP.[22]

The Budapest Memorandum filled the gap created in Ukraine's security by its forced nuclear disarmament with promises from the nuclear powers. The gap would grow wider and wider until, three decades later, Russian full-scale invasion of Ukraine exposed the ineffectiveness of the assurances offered by the Budapest Memorandum and accompanying treaties. But when the treaties were signed, they performed an important function for Ukraine, stabilizing its economy and statehood. American financial assistance began to be delivered to

Ukraine soon after Clinton, Yeltsin, and Kravchuk signed the Trilateral Agreement on nuclear disarmament in January 1994. The resolution of the nuclear issue also helped Kuchma stabilize the situation in the Crimea, as Yeltsin now had less incentive to support Russian separatism there and was in a stronger position to thwart such attempts on the part of the Russian parliament.[23]

In May 1997, Kuchma and Yeltsin signed a Friendship Treaty whereby Russia recognized the territorial integrity of Ukraine, now in its post-Soviet borders. The treaty was accompanied by a number of agreements resolving the long-standing dispute over the future of the Black Sea Fleet and its naval base in Sevastopol. Kyiv agreed to transfer to Russia most of the Soviet-era navy, retaining only 18 percent of the ships, and to lease the Sevastopol naval base to Russia for twenty years. In 2014, control of the Sevastopol base would allow Vladimir Putin to take over the entire peninsula in a few days, but at the time Kyiv managed nothing better in its negotiations with Russia. They were marred not only by Russian territorial claims but also by continuing Ukrainian dependence on Russian oil and gas. Ukraine was unable to pay the rising prices for those commodities in full and on time.[24]

The Budapest Memorandum of 1994 and the Treaty of Friendship of 1997 helped the Ukrainians get both Russia and the United States to commit on paper to the principles of Ukraine's sovereignty and territorial integrity. But it took two years for the Russian parliament to ratify the Friendship Treaty over strong opposition from nationalist and populist forces. Few in the Ukrainian government considered either treaty, or the two together, sufficient to guarantee Ukraine's security. With the last nuclear warhead leaving their territory in 1996, the Ukrainians began looking for a substitute to protect their sovereignty and integrity.[25]

The only substitute they could come up with was the North Atlantic Treaty Organization (NATO). A few months after Ukraine finally managed to sign the Friendship Treaty with Russia, two of Ukraine's western neighbors, Poland and the Czech Republic, were invited to join the alliance, solving their "Russia problem."[26]

Partnership for Peace

On the evening of April 21, 1993, President Clinton was late for his address at the reception for the opening of the US Holocaust Memorial Museum. He was not the only person who made the distinguished guests wait that evening. Late along with him were a number of leaders of East European states who had arrived for the occasion. "I spent a great deal of time talking to these world leaders about things that concern us all and that are very relevant to the occasion which has brought all of you here today," explained Clinton. The occasion was of course honoring the memory of Holocaust victims; the "things that concern us all" were requests of the East Europeans to open the doors of NATO to their countries.[27]

One of those leaders was Lech Wałęsa, the president of Poland and former leader of the Solidarity movement in that country. He pushed for his country's membership in the alliance. "After decades of Soviet domination, we are all afraid of Russia," Wałęsa told Clinton. "If Russia again adopts an aggressive foreign policy, this aggression will be directed against Ukraine and Poland. We need America to prevent this." Wałęsa was speaking not only about his own country but also about the three other members of the Visegrad Group, Hungary, Czerchia, and Slovakia, which had agreed to coordinate their efforts to join Western institutions. Another anti-communist dissident, then president of the Czech Republic, Vaclav Havel, told Clinton on a separate occasion that his country was "living in a vacuum" before adding: "that is why we want to join NATO."[28]

The East Europeans had been knocking on NATO's door since early 1990, when the issue of its eastward expansion was raised in the context of negotiations on the unification of Germany. In the course of those negotiations, the US secretary of state, James Baker, asked Gorbachev: "Would you prefer to see a unified Germany outside NATO, independent and with no US forces, or would you prefer a unified Germany tied to NATO, with assurances that NATO's jurisdiction would not shift one inch eastward from its present position?" Gorbachev objected to any expansion of the "zone of NATO." Ultimately, the agree-ment was limited to German unification alone. The final settlement, signed in September 1990, allowed the new, united Germany to join NATO without the movement of NATO infrastructure into the eastern part of the country.[29]

In March 1990 representatives of Czechoslovakia, Poland, and Hungary criticized the Kremlin for its opposition to eastward NATO expansion, and in May Gorbachev warned the Americans that he knew about their support for the aspirations of Moscow's former satellites to join the alliance. President Bush indeed refused to endorse the position taken by Baker during the negotiations, but neither would he make any concessions to the desires of the Soviet Union or of its former allies. Gorbachev later admitted that Baker's statement was made in the con-text of negotiations on Germany only. But that did not stop Russian leaders, including Putin, from using Baker's words as "proof" that NATO had agreed not to expand beyond eastern Germany.[30]

Concern about Soviet and then Russian objections to NATO mem-bership for East European countries was the key factor behind Presi-dent George H. W. Bush's refusal to contemplate NATO's expansion beyond Germany's eastern borders, although he insisted on keeping the organization in existence after the Cold War. It was also a major reason why many members of the Clinton administration rejected the pleas of East European leaders to join the alliance. By 1993 there was one more reason to question such expansion. That reason was Ukraine or, more specifically, its denuclearization. Clinton's secretary of state, Warren Christopher, formulated the Ukraine problem as follows: "[It is] hard to see how Ukraine can accept being the buffer between NATO, Europe and Russia. This will militate against our efforts to get rid of Ukraine's nuclear weapons."[31]

The direct link between nuclear weapons and the desirability of NATO membership for the East European countries was demonstrated in 1992, when some Polish officials suggested to their American coun-terparts that they would acquire nuclear weapons if not allowed to join NATO. The prospect of a nuclear-armed Poland facing a newly aggressive Russia frightened many in Washington, and some were prepared to offer NATO membership to the Ukrainians as a carrot to give up their nuclear arsenal. Frightened by the possibility of losing their weapons while getting stuck in the gray zone between NATO and Russia, Ukrainian diplomats tried to jump on the East European bandwagon to join the alliance. The deputy minister of foreign affairs, Borys Tarasiuk, stated that it would be "unacceptable for NATO to expand without Ukraine becoming a full member."[32]

In April 1993, when Clinton met with Wałęsa and Havel in Washington, and both leaders raised the issue of NATO membership, the US president began to rethink the more cautious policies of his predecessor. But there were two main obstacles on the East European road to the alliance. One was opposition from Russia; the other was concern about Ukraine, which still retained its nuclear weapons and was extremely apprehensive about finding itself in a no-man's-land between NATO and Russia.

Russian opposition to NATO expansion presented a problem, but the Clinton administration was also concerned that whatever position Yeltsin took, such expansion would embolden his domestic critics. "If NATO adopted an anti-Russian rationale for taking in new members, it could tip the balance of forces in Russian politics in exactly the direction that we ... most feared," wrote Clinton's point man on Russia and Eastern Europe, Strobe Talbott. The breakthrough on Russia came in August 1993, when Wałęsa reached an informal agreement with Yeltsin that ensured Poland's membership in NATO at the expense of Ukraine. The terms were that Russia would not oppose Poland's application to join the alliance, and in exchange Poland would not involve itself in Ukrainian affairs unless there were a military crisis in Ukraine. Although highly informal, the deal was upheld: Russia raised no objections to East Europeans joining the alliance, but the line was drawn at the Ukrainian border.[33]

With Russia seemingly at bay, the main issue for Washington became Ukraine itself. Talbott formulated Washington's task vis-à-vis Ukraine as follows: "[We] must be careful not to pull this off in a way that makes Ukraine feel it is being left out in the cold with its furry neighbor to the north." Washington's Ukraine problem was soon solved by the creation of the NATO Partnership for Peace Program, open to all East European countries, including Ukraine and Russia. This was Clinton's response to Yeltsin's letter of September 1993, written soon after Yeltsin made his deal with Wałęsa, in which he suggested to his American counterpart that Russia would agree to NATO enlargement if it could take part in the process. It was also a consolation prize for Ukraine, which Clinton offered President Kravchuk in Kyiv in January 1994 on his way to Moscow to sign the trilateral American-Russian-Ukrainian agreement on the transfer of Ukrainian nuclear weapons to Russia. The Partnership for Peace Program was announced in Brussels on the day before Clinton's stopover in Kyiv.[34]

The new program served as an anteroom for the East Europeans on their way to full membership in the alliance. It performed a different function for Russia and Ukraine, which were given no prospect of joining NATO. Membership in the program was meant to assure Moscow that Brussels was not conspiring against the Russian Federation. For Kyiv, it served as an assurance that Ukraine would not be left one-on-one with an unhappy and aggressive Russia. If the East Europeans and Russians took their time, the Ukrainians jumped at the opportunity. Ukraine became the first state to join the program, less than a month after it was announced. Partnership with NATO became its only hope of fending off Russia.[35]

The Partnership for Peace Program was short-lived. In July 1997 the heads of NATO member states, led by Bill Clinton, met in Madrid to invite Poland, the Czech Republic, and Hungary to join the alliance. At the same time they offered two separate agreements to Russia and Ukraine. The Russian document was called "The NATO-Russia Founding Act," while the Ukrainian one was titled "Charter on a Distinctive Partnership." The purpose of the draft agreements was the same as that of the Partnership for Peace Program—to assure Russia that NATO was not conspiring against it and Ukraine that NATO would keep Russia at bay.

Russia was also invited to join the G7 group of the largest demo-cratic economies, although its democratic credentials after the shelling of parliament in 1993 were questionable, while the size of its economy was unquestionably small. Bill Clinton later explained to President Kuchma that Russia was being granted a seat on the G7 (now G8) council with Ukraine in mind. "I took criticism on G8 and APEC for bringing Russia in," Clinton told Kuchma. "But I wanted them to see more benefits from cooperation with others, like Ukraine, than from dominating it." Yeltsin accepted G7 membership but tried to insert a clause in the NATO-Russia Founding Act giving Russia a veto over any future enlargement of the alliance. He was rebuffed but declared to his domestic audience that Russia had acquired that right.[36]

Russia's relations with NATO took a decisive turn for the worse in the spring of 1999, soon after the Czech Republic, Poland, and Hun-gary officially joined NATO. The immediate cause was unrelated to alli-ance expansion and resulted from NATO's decision to bomb Serbia, which, together with Montenegro, constituted the rump state of Yugo-slavia. The NATO countries began their bombing campaign to stop the atrocities being committed by the Yugoslav army against the popula-tion of Kosovo, a predominantly Muslim region within Serbia. Clinton and other Western leaders believed that they had to stop the genocide, but the UN Security Council refused to approve the airstrikes, because Russia and China were opposed. NATO therefore assumed responsi-bility for the military operation. Overnight, NATO had turned from a defensive into an offensive alliance—a development not lost on the Russians.[37]

Neither the Russian government, led after the Russian financial crisis of 1998 by the former head of the country's foreign intelligence service, Yevgenii Primakov, nor the communist and nationalist opposi-tion that backed Primakov's government were prepared to accept what was going on in Serbia. Although Yeltsin did not follow the course of the Serbian leader, Slobodan Milošević, and use his army to keep the Soviet Union together, turning it into a "Yugoslavia with nukes," Russia and Serbia developed friendly relations in the late 1990s. Completely forgotten were the years of hostility initiated by the Stalin-Tito breach of the late 1940s and the period of mistrust caused by Milošević's support for the coup of August 1991 in Moscow. The long relationship based on shared Slavic roots, Orthodox heritage, and the Russian Empire's assistance to the South Slavs in their nineteenth-century struggle against Ottoman rule was reinstated. Pan-Slavism, nationalism, and religion were becoming important elements of the new Russian policy, replacing the outdated Marxist ideology and faltering liberal democracy. As far as Russian nationalists were concerned, "fraternal" Serbia was enduring the same loss-of-empire shock as Russia itself.

Primakov was on his way to the United States by air when he learned on March 24, 1999, that NATO had begun its bombing of Serbia. He was so upset by what he considered an unfriendly American initiative that he ordered his pilot to reverse course over the Atlantic and head back to Moscow. Russia followed up by breaking relations with NATO to protest American intervention in what it regarded as its sphere of interest. Over time, this became a metaphor for a dramatic turn of Russian foreign policy away from cooperation with the United States. The bombing campaign, which lasted seventy-eight days, caused the wounding or death of thousands of Serbian military and civilians, as well as large-scale destruction of Yugoslav infrastructure. After the bombing stopped, Russian troops marched into Kosovo's capital of Priština, meeting a NATO force marching in from Macedonia and insisting on joint occupation of the area. In Priština, Russia and NATO were together and apart at the same time—pro forma allies and de facto rivals.[38]

4

THE NEW EASTERN EUROPE

The new millennium began with a promise of improved relations between Russia, the United States, and the West as a whole, which would presumably lead to a better Russia-NATO relationship. The promise came on September 9, 2001, with a telephone call from Vladimir Putin, who by then had been president of Russia for one year and a few months, to George W. Bush, at that time less than ten months into his first term as president of the United States. Putin warned Bush about a piece of intelligence that he had obtained from Afghanistan, where a key Moscow ally had been assassinated by the Taliban: something big "was about to happen, something long in preparation." The Al Qaeda attack of 9/11 took place two days later, changing Bush's presidency and the priorities, if not the direction, of American foreign policy for years to come.

Putin saw an opening and took advantage of it to offer Bush and his administration a partnership built on fighting the common threat from Afghanistan and radical Islam but extending beyond regional cooperation. "I am sure that today, when our 'destiny again meets history,' we

will not only be partners but may well be friends," declared Putin in
the course of his visit to Washington in November 2001. Putin's vision
included Russia's return to the status held by the USSR in world politics, an end to NATO expansion, and recognition of the territory of the
former USSR as a Russian sphere of influence. Putin was also there to
provide more intelligence about Afghanistan, the White House's main
concern at the time.[1]

Bush and his administration were grateful but not prepared to go as
far as Putin suggested. In exchange for the intelligence on Afghanistan
and other gestures of goodwill from Moscow, Washington was prepared
to share its own intelligence about the "war on terror," maintain public
silence about Russia's brutal pacification of Chechnya, designated by
Russia as a terrorist organization, and help Russia join the World Trade
Organization. The partnership worked for a while, but tensions were
apparent even in the area of common interest—the war on the Taliban.
The United States needed military bases in Central Asia, but Putin was
reluctant to admit the Americans into his exclusive sphere of influence.
Only after some hesitation did he agree to the opening of two American
bases in the region, one in Uzbekistan, the other in Kyrgyzstan.[2]

That was just the beginning. In June 2002 Bush withdrew from
the 1972 Anti-Ballistic Missile Treaty, citing the need to develop anti-
missile defenses in response to the threat posed by rogue states like
Iran. Putin felt that Bush's real target was Russia and withdrew from
the 1993 START II treaty signed by George H. W. Bush and Boris Yeltsin. Putin's attempt to influence NATO through the NATO-Russia
Council created in May 2002 also had scant success: in November of
that year NATO decided to accept new East European members, notably
the Baltic states (forcibly annexed to the USSR in 1940), encroaching
on what Putin wanted to be recognized as his sphere of influence. In
2003, Bush's decision to invade Iraq became another point of contention between Washington and Moscow.[3]

But it was Bush's "democracy crusade," or policies designed to promote and support democracy on a global scale in particular, that put
Washington and Moscow on a collision course. Putin's regime found

democracy promotion a threat to its stability at home and its political objectives abroad. The new Eastern Europe, the former western republics of the USSR, became the site where those competing interests collided to the same degree as they did in the "old" Eastern Europe during the Cold War. The focal point of the new competition became Ukraine, where in the fall of 2004 a democratic Orange Revolution had succeeded. A few months earlier, in March 2004, seven East European countries, including the three Baltic states—all of them democracies—had officially joined NATO. Could Ukraine be next?

The Democracy Crusade

As far as Russia was concerned, the victory of the 2004 Orange Revolution in Ukraine was a major blow to the Kremlin's interests at home and abroad. "It was our 9/11," declared the Russian political adviser Gleb Pavlovsky, who was close to the Kremlin. A native of Ukraine, he went to Kyiv to advise Prime Minister Yanukovych and his campaign. The Orange Revolution was also a personal defeat for Putin because it was supported by Boris Berezovsky, his onetime sponsor, later nemesis, and ultimately refugee from his regime. The Kremlin was concerned that under the Western-leaning President Yushchenko, Ukraine might leave the Russian orbit forever and join the Western camp.[4]

With the fall of communism, democratic rule became a prerequisite for post-communist and post-Soviet states aspiring to join Western institutions, both political, like the European Union, and military, NATO in particular. Ukraine, with its chaotic but viable democracy, could be a candidate for both, while Russia, failing one democracy test after another and eventually setting on the path of authoritarian rule, could not. The success and durability of Ukrainian democracy was a threat to the Putin regime, since it encouraged whatever remained of the pro-democratic forces in Russia and, in geopolitical terms, brought democratic institutions closer to Russia's borders. In Putin's eyes, this was not just undesirable but unacceptable.

By 2004, Putin was well on the way to laying the foundations for a future autocratic regime. He took control of the Russian Duma in the December 2003 elections, which saw his party, United Russia, obtain three times as many votes as the communists to become the largest party in parliament. He then exploited a hostage crisis produced by Chechen radicals who attacked a school in Beslan in September 2004. It was mishandled by the Russian security services, whose personnel stormed the school, contributing to the death of 314 hostages, including 186 schoolchildren. This gave Putin an opportunity to intervene and curtail whatever remained of Russian democracy: elections of regional governors were abolished, and new laws were introduced curtailing the activities of political parties and NGOs.[5]

Putin was eager to see a similar political system installed in Ukraine, openly campaigning for Yanukovych and secretly pushing Kuchma toward the use of force. He failed on both counts. In early 2005, mass protests also shook a number of other post-Soviet countries, including Uzbekistan and Kyrgyzstan, where the "Tulip Revolution" unseated the local ruler, Askar Akayev, who had been in power since the late Soviet period. A year before the Orange Revolution, the "Revolution of Roses" in Georgia had brought to power a young, charismatic, pro-Western reformer named Mikheil Saakashvili. In Russia, all these protest movements were labeled "Orange." Finding itself on the defensive, Moscow began to mimic the tactics used by the opposition during the Orange Revolution, creating and funding numerous pro-government youth organizations, the most notorious of which was "Nashi," or "Ours." "Ours" were there to defend the president against revolutionary upheaval, allegedly promoted by foreign powers. Ukraine was singled out in that regard, but behind Ukraine Moscow ideologues saw the threatening shadow of the West.[6]

Indeed, as expected in Moscow, the Orange Revolution produced a major geopolitical shift in Kyiv. President Yushchenko returned to the pro-European policies launched by Kuchma before the Melnychenko tapes scandal of 2001. Those included gradual integration into European structures, from the European Union to NATO. Yushchenko

wanted an invitation to join the alliance in the form of a Membership
Action Plan, or MAP. His requests did not fall on deaf ears in Brussels,
as NATO officials invited Ukraine to begin an Intensified Dialogue on
possible membership. The Czech Republic, Slovakia, Hungary, and
Poland, Ukraine's western neighbors who had not wanted their efforts
to join NATO to be compromised by association with Ukraine in the
1990s, now all supported Ukraine's aspirations to membership. They
were only too happy to yield their position on NATO's eastern flank,
vulnerable to possible Russian attack, to Ukraine.[7]

In February 2005, a few weeks after his inauguration, Yushchenko
attended a meeting of heads of state of NATO member nations in Brussels, where he publicly declared that he wanted his colleagues to regard
Ukraine as a future member of the alliance. He did so in the name of
the Orange Revolution that he had led and the people who had elected
him to the presidency. "I'm pretty much sure, dear friends," began
Yushchenko, "that the people who went onto Kyiv's squares and streets
were motivated because they wanted to see Ukraine in Europe, not as
a neighbor of Europe, because we are a country located in the center
of Europe. And we would like to see Ukraine integrated into the European Union and into the North Atlantic Alliance." Before leaving the
podium, Yushchenko went out of his way to reassure Russia that his
NATO aspirations and those of his country were not directed against
Russia. "Russia is our strategic partner," declared Yushchenko, "and
Ukraine's policy toward NATO will by no means be against the interests of other countries, including Russia."[8]

Ukraine was trying to solve its security dilemma as best it could.
Since NATO had established a strategic partnership with Russia, the
idea of Ukraine's acceding to NATO without antagonizing Russia was
theoretically feasible in the 1990s. But in the wake of the Orange Revolution, Kyiv faced a difficult choice: either to accommodate Moscow,
which had long-standing territorial claims on Ukraine and had inter-
vened directly in that country's presidential elections, or to seek protection in a military alliance that could guarantee its territorial integrity

and sovereignty. The threat from Russia was real and immediate, while membership in NATO was hypothetical and removed in time. After long vacillation, Kyiv opted decisively for NATO.[9]

Russia followed Yushchenko's foreign-policy moves closely but made no public statements with regard to Kyiv's NATO aspirations. Instead, Moscow used Ukraine's dependence on Russian gas and its role as a transit country for the export of that gas to Europe to interfere with Ukraine's drift toward the West. In March 2005, soon after Yushchenko's visit to Brussels with his request for a Membership Action Plan, Russia raised gas prices for Ukraine. This was part of its general policy of cutting subsidies to the former Soviet republics, but it was selective treatment at best, as Belarus, which was friendly to Russia, received better terms. This was followed by a number of gas crises in which Russia would cut its gas supply to Ukraine because of its inability to pay high prices (Ukraine's rates would eventually become higher than those paid by customers in central Europe).

These crises, also known as "gas wars," were timed to take place in winter, forcing Ukraine to take gas from the volume that Russia shipped to its central European customers. Moscow would accuse Kyiv of stealing European gas and threaten to cut supplies to Europe altogether. That was the situation in January 2006, when the supply of Russian gas to Hungary was cut by 40 percent, to France and Austria by 30 percent, and to Italy by 24 percent. This reflected badly on Ukraine and got the EU directly involved in the Russo-Ukrainian gas wars, but did little to dampen the Yushchenko administration's resolve to adopt pro-Western policies. Indeed, it only strengthened that resolve.[10]

The Bucharest Summit

Relations between Russia and the United States went into a crisis mode in February 2007, when Putin chose the platform of the Munich Security Forum to publicly challenge the United States as the world's political leader.

The Russian president was prepared to take full advantage of Washington's significantly diminished standing in the world owing to the Iraq War. He accused Washington of acting unilaterally and destroying the foundations of international order by its attack on Iraq. He also protested the expansion of NATO. "I think it is obvious that NATO expansion does not bear any relation to the modernization of the Alliance itself or to ensuring security in Europe," declared Putin. "On the contrary, it represents a serious provocation that reduces the level of mutual trust." He then referred to the promises allegedly made by the NATO leadership in 1990 not to expand NATO beyond Germany.[11]

Secretary General Jaap de Hoop Scheffer of NATO was anything but pleased, calling Putin's Munich speech "disappointing and not helpful." The American response to Putin was formulated by Senator John McCain, a leading voice in the Republican Party. It was expressed in the language of democracy rather than mutual trust or security. "Moscow must understand that it cannot enjoy a genuine partnership with the West so long as its actions at home and abroad conflict so fundamentally with the core values of Euro-Atlantic democracies," declared McCain.[12]

Democracy was Yushchenko's main theme when he and other leaders of Ukraine wrote to NATO headquarters in Brussels in January 2008 to request a Membership Action Plan for Ukraine. Yushchenko wrote: "Fully sharing European democratic values, our state identifies itself as part of the Euro-Atlantic security area and is willing, together with NATO and partners thereof, to counteract common threats to security under equal conditions." The letter asked NATO to consider giving Ukraine a MAP at its forthcoming Bucharest summit in April 2008.

Moscow was not pleased. Putin threatened Ukraine with a missile attack if it accepted NATO missiles. "It is horrible to say and terrifying to think that Russia could target its missile systems at Ukraine, in response to deployment of such installations on Ukrainian territory," he stated. "Imagine this for a moment. This is what worries me." Yushchenko engaged in his own acts of imagination, trying to calm nerves in Moscow. "Can one imagine that there will be a NATO base in Sevastopol? Of course not, and there never will be," he declared on one occasion. He still hoped that Russia could be convinced to drop its opposition to Ukraine's membership in the alliance.

But Moscow considered Ukrainian membership in NATO a breach of good relations with Russia. The Russian Foreign Ministry reacted to the news of Ukraine's request with a declaration that "apparently today's Ukrainian leadership considers closer ties with NATO as an alternative to good-neighborly relations with the Russian Federation." Russia's "Foreign Policy Concept," published in the same month, treated the extension of the alliance, the possible admission of Ukraine and Georgia, and the movement of "NATO military infrastructure" eastward as violations of "the principle of equal security," leading "to new dividing lines in Europe." "We will be forced to use appropriate measures," read the statement.[13]

Russia was determined to stop Ukraine and Georgia, another rebellious post-Soviet republic whose democratic credentials were rooted in its Revolution of Roses (2003), from joining the alliance. Considering its poor relations with NATO, Russia threatened to make them even worse. "Due to the fact that our relations with NATO are very challenging at present, I am not certain that the alliance will extend an invitation to Ukraine," declared the Russian representative to the UN, Dmitrii Rogozin.[14]

As NATO leaders arrived for the Bucharest summit on April 2, 2008, Russia's vocal protests against membership for Ukraine and Georgia were on their minds. Putin came to the Romanian capital in person to take part in the meeting of the Russia-NATO summit and warn the members of the alliance against extending invitations to the two post-Soviet republics. "The emergence of a powerful military bloc at our borders will be seen as a direct threat to Russian security," Putin told President Bush. Bush was not particularly impressed. Before going to Bucharest he made a stopover in Kyiv, where he told the Ukrainians: "Your nation has made a bold decision, and the United States strongly supports your request."[15]

But key European members of NATO, France and Germany in particular, blocked the decision advocated by the United States and supported by the new East European members of the alliance to grant Ukraine and Georgia a Membership Action Plan. "We agreed today that these countries will become members of NATO," read the declaration before making it clear that no accession would take place any time soon. The MAP was promised but not given on the basis that the two potential applicants still had to meet some specific criteria in order to qualify. "[W]e will now begin a period of intensive engagement with both at a high political level to address the questions still outstanding pertaining to their MAP applications."[16]

The matter was postponed and would not return to the NATO agenda at the next summit or the one after that. Everyone knew that the decision to deny MAP to the two post-Soviet republics was a concession to their former master, Russia. Otherwise it was impossible to explain why the Bucharest summit invited Croatia and Albania to join NATO. For the two countries now perceived as threats by Russia, NATO's nondecision on their membership was the worst possible outcome of the summit: their applications had been postponed indefinitely, leaving them with no protection from the alliance that they had publicly stated they wanted to join. While Russia would not dare to attack NATO, it could easily attack its aspirants, and it did so.

On August 8, 2008, a few months after the Bucharest summit, Russia launched a war on Georgia, ostensibly in defense of the Georgian enclave of South Ossetia, which had seceded from Georgia in the early 1990s. The Russian attack allegedly came as a response to the actions of the Georgian army, which had been ordered into South Ossetia, but there was no doubt that the war was directly linked to the outcome of the Bucharest summit. Russia had established official relations with South Ossetia and Abkhazia, the two Georgian provinces that it was now "defending," almost immediately after Putin's return from the Bucharest summit. The Georgians fought back under the leadership of President Mikheil Saakashvili, who had been educated in Ukraine and the United States, but the Russian army, larger and superior to Georgia's, moved deep into the country and threatened to occupy its capital, Tbilisi.

On August 12, Yushchenko, together with the leaders of Poland and the three Baltic states, flew to Tbilisi to show support for Saakashvili and his country. That day the Russian advance was stopped by means of a ceasefire negotiated by President Nicolas Sarkozy of France. Russian troops eventually left a good part of the occupied territory but stayed in Abkhazia and South Ossetia, ostensibly protecting the independence of the two provinces from Georgia and perpetuating its territorial division. That undermined Georgia's chances of ever joining NATO, as the alliance was reluctant to accept any state with unresolved territorial issues. The Russian war on Georgia became the first instance of its initiating a major war beyond its borders. It sent a clear signal to the West that Russia was prepared to use military force to stop any expansion of the alliance. It also demonstrated to other post-Soviet republics that NATO would not come to their rescue in case of Russian attack.[17]

The decision of the Bucharest NATO summit, coupled with the outcome of the Russo-Georgian War, dealt a devastating blow to Ukrainian aspirations to join the alliance. The changing of the guard in Washington and the inauguration of Barack Obama as president in January 2009 led to a thorough revision of all elements of US foreign policy and an attempted "reset" of US-Russia relations. In January 2010 Viktor Yushchenko, defeated in the first round of that year's presidential elections, left office to make way for Putin's old favorite, Viktor Yanukovych. The new president promptly dropped NATO membership from the Ukrainian foreign-policy agenda and signed a deal that was devastating for Ukrainian security because it extended the presence of the Russian Black Sea Fleet in Sevastopol until 2042.[18]

The Bucharest summit put Ukraine in the most vulnerable position that it had experienced since declaring independence. Without nuclear weapons and NATO membership, Ukraine found itself at the mercy of Russia, which saw the ambiguous offer of membership extended to Ukraine by the Bucharest summit as a threat to its own security.

Ukraine was a lone warrior on open ground pursued by hostile forces, running to take shelter in a secure fortress, only to find its gates closing because of disagreements among its defenders.

The Eurasian Union

Vladimir Putin thought about Russian security in the same way as the tsars and the commissars did: to make Russia safe they created and maintained a belt of buffer states. Putin wanted to bring most of the former Soviet republics under the leadership of Moscow, admittedly not in the form of a restored Soviet Union but of a political, military, and, most important, economic bloc to be known as the Eurasian Union. Ukraine, given its size and economic importance, was meant to be a cornerstone of the new union.

The reintegration of the post-Soviet space, renamed in Moscow and known throughout the world as Eurasia, was initiated by Boris Yeltsin in the 1990s with the signing of several agreements on the creation of a common market between Russia, Belarus, and a number of Central Asian states. Putin added momentum to the reintegration process by creating the Eurasian Economic Community—tacit recognition that the Commonwealth of Independent States created by Yeltsin was not uniting the post-Soviet space under Russian control, as Moscow had expected it to do in the early 1990s.

Putin's integrationist efforts met with success in 2003, when Ukraine, after having refused to join the Commonwealth that it had helped to create, signed an agreement on the creation of a common economic space with Russia, Belarus, and Kazakhstan. That was part of the turn away from Europe and toward Russia undertaken by President Kuchma after he was weakened by the Melnychenko tapes scandal. But the Orange Revolution of 2004 put an end to Ukrainian participation in Russia-led Eurasian integration projects. President Yushchenko was looking toward Ukraine's integration with Europe. Some form of Eurasian cooperation became much more likely in 2010, when Viktor Yanukovych became president of Ukraine.

In 2008, Putin switched roles with his former prime minister, Dmitrii Medvedev, to comply with the Russian constitutional ban on a president serving more than two consecutive terms in office. In October 2011 Putin, now prime minister, presented his vision of Eurasian integration in a highly publicized article. He announced plans for the formation of a common economic space encompassing Russia, Belarus, and Kazakhstan on January 1, 2012. This was conceived as just the beginning of a Eurasian Union under Russia's leadership. "We propose the model of a strong supranational union capable of becoming one of the poles of the contemporary world and, in that capacity, playing the role of an effective 'link' between Europe and the dynamic Asia-Pacific region," wrote Putin. He envisioned Russia leading a powerful bloc capable of competing with the European Union in the west and a rising China in the east.[19]

The article was addressed not only to the Russian public: Putin was also trying to recruit new members for his Eurasian Union. He faced competition in that regard, as a number of post-Soviet states were eyeing potential membership in the European Union. "Some of our neighbors explain their unwillingness to participate in advanced projects of integration in the post-Soviet space with the argument that this supposedly conflicts with their European choice," wrote Putin. He had a solution to that problem: "I consider that a false dichotomy. We are not about to hedge ourselves off from anyone or oppose anyone. The Eurasian Union will be built on universal integrationist principles as an inalienable part of Greater Europe, united by the shared values of freedom, democracy, and market principles."[20]

The article was part of Putin's pre-election program: by the time of its publication he had already announced his plans to return to the presidency. When he did so in May 2012, the reintegration of Eurasia became one of his key goals. In ideological terms, the Eurasian Union was very much a product of Eurasian and neo-Eurasian thinking, as it sought to reintegrate former Russian imperial and Soviet space on a transnational basis. In economic terms it was an attempt to secure markets for Russian industry, which was globally noncompetitive, in order to stave off future economic shocks and crises. To compete effectively with the European Union and a rising China, Russia needed new technology, which it could obtain only from the West. To that end Moscow conducted its own negotiations with the EU, not initially interfering with similar efforts on the part of Ukraine and other post-Soviet countries.[21]

But by mid-2013 it had become clear that while EU-Russia talks were unproductive, the association agreements that the EU was prepared to offer the post-Soviet states were incompatible with their prospective membership in the Eurasian Union. When Putin pressed post-Soviet states interested in association agreements with the European Union to drop their plans, Armenia, which depended on Russian support in its war with neighboring Azerbaijan, fell into line, but Georgia and Moldova did not. Ukraine found itself vacillating between Moscow and Brussels. For Putin, Ukraine was the key—without the second-largest post-Soviet republic, the Eurasian Union would not be able to perform its function as one of his "poles" of the contemporary world.

The new Ukrainian president, Viktor Yanukovych, jettisoned many of his predecessor's policies. He used his allies and clients in parliament to change the constitution and remove the limitations on presidential power adopted at the time of Yushchenko's election. These enhanced presidential powers allowed Yanukovych to embark on the formation of elements of authoritarian rule, followed by the establishment of a highly corrupt system of government that siphoned billions of dollars from the state budget into secret accounts held by the president, members of his family, and close advisers and associates. In the realm of foreign policy, Yanukovych publicly declared that his country was abandoning NATO aspirations and returning to non-bloc status. The Russian lease of the Sevastopol naval base, which Yanukovych extended by twenty-five years, was another sign of the new government's turn away from Brussels toward Moscow.[22]

One of the very few of Yushchenko's policies that remained on Yanukovych's agenda was the establishment of close economic and trade relations with the European Union, a huge market for Ukrainian metallurgy and other export-oriented branches of the economy, centered on

Yanukovych's native region of the Donbas. The oligarchs who backed him, fearing competition from their Russian counterparts, wanted to open European markets for their products. They also did not mind having the EU as an ally to check authoritarian tendencies in Kyiv— Yanukovych's growing power and appetite for capturing other people's assets presented a threat to their business interests.[23]

The EU was concerned about Yanukovych's assault on democracy and rule of law but prepared to offer Ukraine an association agreement in exchange for the release of political prisoners, in particular the former prime minister, Yulia Tymoshenko, whom Yanukovych had jailed, ironically enough, for signing an economically damaging gas deal with Russia. The EU's principal demand was the continuation of market reforms. That was the tricky part for Yanukovych, who wanted no reforms and was developing a kleptocratic system of rent collection. But he and his entourage hoped to imitate reforms, protect their business interests from Russia, and penetrate European markets. Polls suggested that in the presidential elections scheduled for 2015 Yanukovych would win if he delivered on his promise of bringing Ukraine into association with the EU. Pro-democratic and liberal voters would forgive him the rest.[24]

Yanukovych vacillated. While the EU was demanding the release of Tymoshenko and reforms, Moscow asked nothing of the sort. But it threatened Yanukovych with an economic blockade if he signed an association agreement with the EU. To show that he meant business, Putin embarked on a limited trade war with Ukraine, barring Ukrainian products from Russia and causing a 10 percent drop in Ukrainian exports. The cost of "tightening up" Russia's customs regulations was estimated at $1.4 billion. Moscow had not only a stick but also a carrot in its arsenal. Putin offered money if Ukraine did not sign the proposed agreement with the EU: the amount would later be specified as $15 billion, a lifeline for Yanukovych, whose kleptocratic rule had brought Ukraine to the verge of financial collapse. Yanukovych had finally made his choice.[25]

In November 2013 Yanukovych accepted an invitation to the EU summit in Vilnius, where he was expected to sign the association agreement but abruptly refused to do so. Speaking to his own entourage, he explained the about-face as the result of an exchange with Putin, who had allegedly told him that he would never allow the European Union or NATO to share a border with Russia. If Yanukovych signed the EU agreement, Putin threatened to occupy the Crimea and a good part of southeastern Ukraine, including the Donbas. Yanukovych, visibly shaken, decided to abandon the EU association agreement.[26]

Yanukovych did not tell his European counterparts about the money that he was getting from Russia. When he visited Putin in Moscow a few weeks later, the Russian president delivered on his promise. He offered his Ukrainian counterpart a discount price on Russian natural gas and a $15 billion loan. "Ukraine," declared Putin, "is undoubtedly our strategic partner and ally in the full sense of the word." The Eurasian integration project was alive and well, or so it seemed at the time.[27]

The Revolution of Dignity

By the time Yanukovych got his financial reward in Moscow, he was already in deep trouble in Kyiv. As soon as the Ukrainian government announced the results of the EU summit in Vilnius for Ukraine, young Kyivan urbanites gathered at the Maidan, Kyiv's Independence Square, to protest Yanukovych's refusal to sign the agreement. Like much of Ukrainian society, they associated their hopes for bringing European legal and business practices to Ukraine with the promised agreement. They were soon joined by students who camped on the Maidan. The Euromaidan protests were born, condemning Yanukovych's broken promises to bring his people closer to Europe.

The Euromaidan protests were transformed into what subsequently became known as the Revolution of Dignity early in the morning of November 30, when riot police attempted to dislodge students from the square by beating them up. On December 1, more than half a million Kyivans showed up in the city center to protest police brutality. The citizens had come to defend the students, but also to protect society in the face of crippling authoritarianism. On December 11, government police began to storm the Maidan encampment. Its defenders managed to withstand the pressure, and the police units withdrew. The government's assault on the protesters took place during the visit to Kyiv of the US assistant secretary of state, Victoria Nuland, who arrived in Kyiv together with an EU representative, Catherine Ashton, hoping to assist in resolving the crisis. They went to the Maidan to express support for the protesters.[28]

The timing of the police operation was anything but incidental. It was meant first and foremost to send a signal to Washington that its intervention was unwelcome. Putin would later refer to Nuland's visit to the Maidan as proof of the American role in instigating the protests. Less than a week later, Yanukovych flew to Moscow to accept Putin's bribe for not signing the association agreement with the EU. On January 8, 2014, the day after Orthodox Christmas, Yanukovych flew to Russia for another meeting with Putin. According to later reports, Russia was withholding the transfer of the next installment of the $15 billion loan until the protests were dispersed. In mid-January the Ukrainian parliament, in which Yanukovych's supporters had a majority, adopted the so-called dictatorial laws that banned the activities of Western-funded NGOs and outlawed certain forms of protest.[29]

But Ukraine was not Russia. Instead of intimidating the opposition and protesters into submission, the new laws mobilized popular resistance. In Kyiv, tens of thousands of protesters showed up on the streets, and the most radical of them broke with the tradition of peaceful protest to attack government buildings. In the western oblasts of Ukraine, where an absolute majority of the population supported the Revolution of Dignity, the protesters began to take control of government buildings. Yanukovych used police against protesters in Kyiv but could do little about developments in western Ukraine, where the local governments sided with the protesters.

By the end of the month, Yanukovych began a tactical retreat. Parliament reversed some of the "dictatorial laws," and Yanukovych dismissed his long-serving prime minister, the Russian-born and edu-

cated Mykola Azarov, who had drawn strong criticism for his inability
or unwillingness to learn Ukrainian. In mid-February the government
released more than 230 previously arrested protesters, and protesters
vacated some of the government buildings they had occupied. A compromise was in the works, with the immediate goal of forming a new
government and the medium-term goal of drafting a new constitution.

But the truce between the government and the protesters collapsed
on February 18, 2014, when thousands of protesters marched toward
the Ukrainian parliament building. They attacked and set fire to the
headquarters of Yanukovych's ruling Party of Regions. Riot police
responded with an all-out attack on the protesters, firing live ammunition, using tear gas, and pushing the crowd back to the Maidan. The
protesters' headquarters, the Trade Union Building, was set on fire by
agents of the Security Service, and the police managed to occupy part of
the square itself. At least eleven civilians and seven police officers were
killed or died in the fire. The government also employed bands of hired
thugs to terrorize the protesters.[30]

The violence of February 18 changed the course of the Revolution
of Dignity and the Ukrainian political process in general. The peaceful protests of the 1990s, the Orange Revolution of 2004, and the first
months of the Revolution of Dignity now belonged to the past. The next
few days brought significantly more violence as the protesters tried to
reclaim the Maidan but were met with gunfire opened by special police
forces and by snipers whose allegiance has yet to be identified. Among
those killed by gunfire were thirteen police offers, but they were greatly
outnumbered by the 108 protesters shot to death that day.[31]

On the night of February 20, in the presence of the foreign ministers of France, Germany, and Poland, who had flown to Kyiv to medi-
ate the crisis, Yanukovych reached an agreement with the opposition
leaders entailing the formation of a new government, early presidential elections, and a return to the constitution of 2004, with reduced
presidential powers. A representative of Russia, Vladimir Lukin, was
also present. A former ambassador to the United States, Lukin was
now his country's human-rights ombudsman. He refused to sign the

agreement reached in Kyiv, suggesting that Putin had not approved it. Earlier in the crisis, Russian representatives had called on Yanukovych to crush the protest or risk Russia's intervention under the pretext of defending Ukraine's sovereignty according to the terms of the Budapest Memorandum.[32]

As Yanukovych negotiated with the opposition, the Ukrainian parliament voted on a resolution prohibiting the use of police against the protesters. Once adopted, the resolution came into force on the morning of February 21. By midday, police units began to leave downtown Kyiv. Yanukovych followed suit, abandoning his lavish compound of Mezhyhiria near Kyiv late in the evening. He told one of his close allies "that his life was in danger; that there were many armed people in Kyiv, many bands had formed, so he had to leave Kyiv." Some protesters on the Maidan refused to accept the agreement reached by Yanukovych and the opposition leaders, and there were no more police officers to defend him if the protesters should decide to storm the presidential buildings or the Mezhyhiria compound.[33]

On February 22, the day after Yanukovych left Kyiv, parliament, now led by the opposition, voted to remove Yanukovych from office on the grounds that he had neglected his duties and abandoned his office. Oleksandr Turchynov, one of the leaders of the opposition and the Maidan protests, was elected interim president. Another opposition leader, Arsenii Yatseniuk, became the new prime minister. Parliament voted for the removal of Yanukovych by simple majority without invoking the impeachment procedure, which would have required a two-thirds majority, as the requisite quorum was lacking. Yanukovych refused either to resign or to return to Kyiv. A few days later, he left the country.

On the Maidan there was mourning of the dead and celebration of the victory: the revolution had won, a new government had been formed, and it had pledged to sign the EU association agreement, while the aspiring autocrat had gone into exile in Russia, the Eurasian autocracy that had supported him throughout. Unknown to people on the

Maidan, Viktor Yanukovych's flight from Kyiv on the night of February 21, 2014, initiated a sequence of events that led a few days later to the Russian annexation of the Crimea, which in turn served as a trigger for Russo-Ukrainian military conflict, the first stage of the all-out Russo-Ukrainian war.[34]

5

THE CRIMEAN GAMBIT

Where Russia begins and ends, and what territories the historical "gathering of the Russian lands" should encompass, are old questions that have preoccupied Russian thinkers and statesmen for generations. The disintegration of the Soviet Union put those questions back on the political agenda with unprecedented urgency. The new state borders of the former Soviet republics left approximately 30 million ethnic Russians and Russian-speaking members of other nationalities that associated themselves mainly with Russia beyond the borders of the Russian Federation. The leading Russian nationalist writer Aleksandr Solzhenitsyn, who returned to Russia from Cold War exile in the United States in 1992, decried the division of the "Russian people" by the post-Soviet borders, identifying it as the essence of the new Russian question. For the same reason, Putin called the Soviet collapse the greatest geopolitical tragedy of the twentieth century.[1]

Boris Yeltsin and his advisers faced a major challenge of transforming the post-Soviet Russia into a European nation-state according to the model established over the previous two centuries by the French Revolution and its successors. It was based on the definition of nationalism by the Czech-British philosopher Ernest Gellner as the "political principle which holds that political and national units should be congruent." Given the millions of non-Russians and non-Slavs within the borders of the Russian Federation and the tens of millions of "Russians" and Soviets of different stripes beyond those borders, the task of Russian nation-building was all but impossible without a major war, which had been the main instrument used to create the European system of nation-states. In the 1990s, the latest example was the Greater Serbia project of Slobodan Milošević.[2]

Yeltsin and his government could not afford such a war, nor did they want one. In fact, Moscow went to war with the non-Slavic and non-Christian Chechnya in defense of a different principle—the inviolability of the borders of the Russian Federation, challenged by Chechen separatism. The two ferocious Chechen wars brutalized Russian politics and society, strengthening the imperial model of Russian identity as transethnic and transcultural. They did so in part on the foundations but also at the expense of the Soviet identity developed in communist times. The new leaders in Moscow, who had come to power in opposition to communism and largely contributed to the collapse of the Soviet Union, now faced communist opposition to their rule. They rejected Soviet identity as an instrument of Russian nation-building or a means of maintaining Russian control over the post-Soviet space. They looked instead for an alternative, and Yeltsin even called for a new model of the Russia idea.[3]

In the course of the 1990s there emerged a number of political, cultural, and ideological concepts not based on the Soviet model. They competed with that model as possible means of uniting the political components of the Russian Federation and the post-Soviet republics no longer subject to Moscow's rule. One such concept was Eurasianism, which gave its name to a number of reintegrationist projects and institutions in the post-Soviet space. Rooted in the writings of Russian intellectuals including Prince Nikolay Trubetzkoy and Petr Savitsky, who found themselves in exile after the Bolshevik Revolution, Eurasianism sought to re-create the former Russian imperial and now post-Soviet space on the basis of Russia's imperial heritage, Russian culture, and Orthodox Christianity, which might integrate the non-Russian parts of the former empire into the present-day Russian Federation.

The old Eurasianism of the Russian émigrés captured the imagination of part of the intellectual elite that was dissatisfied with the liberal-democratic discourse embraced by Yeltsin's advisers, and some of its supporters and interpreters made their way into the Kremlin's orbit after Putin's rise to power. Aleksandr Dugin, a neo-Eurasianist who advocated the creation of a Eurasian empire and has been considered an ideologue of Russian fascism, became an adviser to Sergei Naryshkin. He served at that time as chief of the presidential staff, would go on to serve as the speaker of the Duma, and then the head of the foreign intelligence service, Putin's old institutional home.[4]

Putin adopted many elements of traditional and revived Eurasianism as parts of his world view. In his official pronouncements he spoke repeatedly of Russia as a unique multiethnic civilization not only different from the West but opposed to it in history, culture, and values. But he also embraced with equal if not greater enthusiasm the ideas of a different group of Russian thinkers who juxtaposed Russia to the West predominantly as a Eurasian Slavic or Russian civilization. That trend of thought, represented by such figures as Aleksei Khomiakov, Ivan Kirievsky, and Konstantin Aksakov, predated Eurasianism, going back to the first decades of the nineteenth century, which produced one of the most consequential schisms in Russian intellectual history, that between Westernizers and Slavophiles. The former insisted that Russia's destiny lay with the West, while the latter emphasized Russian uniqueness, rooted in history, language, culture, and nationality.

The nationality that the Slavophiles called Russian was in fact East Slavic. In imperial Russian terminology, it consisted of Great Russians, or Russians per se, Little Russians or Ukrainians, and White Russians or Belarusians. The model of a tripartite Russian nation, which the Rus-

sian historian Alexei Miller calls a "big Russian nation," was adopted
by the imperial elites in the second half of the nineteenth century and
became part of the ideological credo and personal belief, as well as identity, of many of the country's political, religious, and military leaders.
The Russian Revolution put an end to the dominance of the tripartite
nation in Russian political and ethnonational thought. In 1922, Lenin
resisted Joseph Stalin's attempts to incorporate non-Russian republics
into the Russian Federation and insisted on the creation of a Union
state in which those republics would be distinct polities with rights
equal to those of Russia.[5]

The idea of a big Russian nation went into the Russian emigra-
tion along with the White Guard generals defeated by the Bolshevik
Red Army and the intellectuals who supported their vision of Russia,
one and indivisible. Among the émigrés was General Anton Denikin,
whose memoirs would make a strong impression on Vladimir Putin,
and the philosopher Ivan Ilyin, an admirer of fascism, whose article,
"What the Dismemberment of Russia Promises the World," would
become a frequently quoted source in the speeches and pronouncements of Putin and other Russian officials. Ilyin argued that one day
Russia would gather its lands back under its tutelage.[6]

The key figure who linked the imperial thinking of the past with a
plan for dealing with post-Soviet Russian challenges and realities was
Aleksandr Solzhenitsyn. In his essay of 1990, *Rebuilding Russia: Reflec-
tions and Tentative Proposals*, Solzhenitsyn called for the separation of the
eastern Slavs from the non-Slavic republics of the Soviet Union and the
formation of a "Russian Union" consisting of Russia, Ukraine, Belarus,
and northern Kazakhstan. If one followed Ernest Gellner's definition
of nationalism as the establishment of congruence between political
and ethnonational borders, then Solzhenitsyn's "reconstructed" Russia
was to become quadripartite. But his plan never materialized, and several years later Solzhenitsyn went on to question the legitimacy of the
Ukrainian borders. In his essay *Russia in Collapse* (1998), Solzhenitsyn
argued for the annexation of eastern and southern Ukraine, denounc-

ing its "inordinate expansion onto territory that was never Ukraine until Lenin: the two Donets provinces, and the whole southern belt of New Russia (Melitopol–Kherson–Odesa) and the Crimea."[7]

Putin was an admirer of all these writers and shared many of their ideas. In May 2009, less than a year after the invasion of Georgia, he made a public show of his admiration for imperial Russian thinkers. Despite rainy weather, he showed up in the company of numerous reporters at the cemetery of the Donskoi Monastery in Moscow to lay flowers on the graves of General Denikin and his wife, along with the grave of Ivan Ilyin and that of Ivan Shmelev, another Russian émigré writer whose remains had been returned to Russia. Putin also laid flowers on the grave of Aleksandr Solzhenitsyn, who had died in Moscow the previous year.[8]

Referring to General Denikin, whose grave he honored first, Putin encouraged one of the reporters accompanying him at the ceremony to read Denikin's memoirs. "Denikin discusses Great and Little Russia, Ukraine," said Putin. "He writes that no one may meddle in relations between us; that has always been the business of Russia itself." Denikin was in fact following Aleksandr Pushkin, who had attacked the West for criticizing Russia's assault on Poland after it rebelled against the empire in 1830. If Pushkin referred to Russo-Polish relations, Denikin referred to those between Russia and Ukraine. In Putin's view, it was up to Russia to decide how to conduct its relations with a weaker neighbor. The Slavic roots of the two peoples became his excuse to condemn any Western support for Ukraine.[9]

Archimandrite Tikhon, who was rumored to be Putin's spiritual adviser at the time, confided to the assembled reporters that Putin had personally paid for the tombstones of the Denikins, Ilyin, and Shmelev. The archimandrite also told them of Putin's admiration for Solzhenitsyn, whom he called "an organic and committed statist."[10] Solzhenitsyn was not only a believer in a strong Russian state but also a promoter of Russia as an East Slavic state based on the Pan-Russian, imperial model of the Russian nation, including Russia, Ukraine, and Belarus. This was an awkward compromise between the Soviet and imperial visions of Russian national identity. In the Soviet tradition, Solzhenitsyn, who was half Ukrainian, referred to the Ukrainians as a separate nation, but, according to imperial tradition, he considered them one and the same people as the Russians.

Putin shared Solzhenitsyn's belief that parts of eastern and southern Ukraine were not its historical territories but, as he told President George Bush in 2008, were a gift from the Russian Bolsheviks. As for Solzhenitsyn's compromise view, that was not a major issue for Putin as long as the political project of Russo-Ukrainian unity and the imperial model of a tripartite Russian nation were realized. Like Solzhenitsyn, Putin accepted the Soviet division of the Russian nation into Russians, Ukrainians, and Belarusians, but continued to think of them as representatives of essentially one people. Solzhenitsyn's vision of Russia served as a bridge between imperial notions of Russian language, culture, and identity and views that began to become popular in Russian political circles with the arrival of Vladimir Putin in the Kremlin.

Russia was ready to move beyond the Soviet legacy when it came to its vision of itself and relations with its neighbors, but the movement was backward in history. Putin emerged as its leader. At his disposal he had the ideas of the Eurasianists, who offered justification for Russian control of the former imperial space; the proponents of a big Russian nation, who wanted a common East Slavic state; and, finally, the views of those who, in case other integrationist projects failed, were prepared to settle for a Greater Russia annexing historically or ethnically Russian enclaves.

The Race to the Crimea

Putin later claimed that he personally made the decision to annex the Crimea on the night of February 23 after conversing with a small group of advisers—the heads of the Ministry of Defense and the intelligence services. "I invited the heads of our intelligence services and the Ministry of Defense to the Kremlin," he recalled, adding that apart from him there were just four people present. The meeting lasted until 7:00

a.m. the following morning. In the end, according to Putin, "We were obliged to begin work on restoring the Crimea as a component of Russia." The decision was the autocrat's alone. There were no ministers, parliamentary deputies, or even members of the Security Council to advise him.[11]

The Crimea, the only part of Ukraine in which ethnic Russians constituted a majority of the population, and a bone of contention between Russia and Ukraine since the late Soviet years, had long been on the Kremlin's integrationist horizon. Back in 1994, Boris Yeltsin had decided not to intervene in Ukraine's internal affairs when Ukrainian voters elected the allegedly pro-Russian President Leonid Kuchma and Ukrainian politicians negotiated their relations with the Crimean elites. Now Putin, faced with the loss of his protégé in Kyiv, Ukraine's almost certain signing of an association agreement with the EU, and thus the fiasco of his plans to involve Ukraine in the Russia-led Customs Union and Eurasian Union, decided to take the peninsula by force.

There was no separatist movement in sight, as had been the case in 1994, but there were other factors that Putin sought to use to his advantage. They included the interregnum in Kyiv, the questionable legitimacy of parliament's removal of Yanukovych from power, the no less questionable credentials of his successor, and the inability of the new authorities to gain the trust of the Ukrainian security services, which they had fought with Molotov cocktails only a few days, if not hours, earlier. Soon the Ukrainian parliament gave Putin a political gift with its maladroit adoption of a new law supporting the use of the Ukrainian language, which pro-Russian politicians in Ukraine characterized as an attack on Russian minority rights. The Kremlin exploited the law to stoke the flames of Russian nationalism and separatism, thereby helping to justify the annexation.

Putin was in touch with Yanukovych throughout the most difficult parts of the Maidan protests, holding eleven telephone conversations with him between the start of shooting in Kyiv on February 18 and the bloodiest day of the confrontation, February 20. The Polish foreign minister, Radosław Sikorski, recalled that during the night of February 20, when he and other European representatives were negotiating a resolution of the crisis with Yanukovych, the Ukrainian president left the conference room to speak with Putin by telephone and agreed to early presidential elections only with Putin's approval.[12]

Putin later recalled that he had also spoken by telephone with President Barack Obama. "We discussed those questions. We spoke about how we would promote the fulfillment of those agreements. Russia took certain obligations upon itself. I heard that my American colleague was prepared to assume certain obligations." According to the Russian newspaper publisher Konstantin Remchukov, who had numerous meetings with Putin, "Obama was supposed to direct the protesters away from the Maidan, and Putin was to suggest to Yanukovych that he send armed law enforcement officers to the barracks. New elections of the president of Ukraine are to be held in the fall of 2014."

According to Ben Rhodes, Deputy National Security Adviser for Strategic Communications and Speechwriting in Obama's White House, the two presidents had indeed "agreed upon a formula that included a schedule for expedited elections in Ukraine. . . . But Yanukovych fled the country, and the protesters took control of Kiev." According to Remchukov, Putin blamed Obama, who allegedly "never called Putin back. He didn't even apologize, to say that everything had gone wrong, sorry, old man. He simply never called back, and that was the end of it." Rhodes recalled that the two presidents had numerous conversations about Ukraine in the following days and weeks. Putin blamed the United States for instigating the protests and called the events in Kyiv a coup.[13]

Putin never concealed his disapproval of Yanukovych's refusal to use massive force and possibly send in the army against the protesters. Putin remembered Yanukovych telling him that "I could not sign the order to use arms. My hand would not rise to do it." Putin commented: "Can he be blamed for that? I don't know. . . . Whether it's good or bad, the consequences of inaction are heavy." Putin apparently tried to convince Yanukovych not to leave Kyiv on the night of February 21, but Yanukovych insisted on doing so and called Putin once again to

inform him of his decision. "At least, do not dismiss the law enforcement agencies," Putin advised his client. "Oh, yes-yes, I understand
that perfectly," came the answer. In fact, riot police units were already
leaving Kyiv in response to the parliamentary vote. Yanukovych could
do nothing about that.[14]

On the next day, February 22, Yanukovych failed to show up at the
congress of deputies of the councils of eastern and southern Ukraine,
whose organizers hoped to declare the transfer of the Ukrainian capital
to Kharkiv and have Yanukovych attempt to rule the country from there.
Instead, Yanukovych asked Putin for a meeting, which Putin agreed to
hold in the city of Rostov-on-Don close to the Ukrainian border. But
Ukrainian border guards, following orders from Kyiv, prevented the
departure of Yanukovych's plane from his native Donetsk to Russia. In
the late afternoon of that day, as noted earlier, the Ukrainian parliament
voted to remove Yanukovych from office. Yanukovych called Putin once
again to ask for help: he was heading for the Crimea to see whether he
could establish a base there.[15]

The first instruction that Putin gave his security chiefs when they
met in the Kremlin to discuss the rapidly developing situation was to
exfiltrate Yanukovych to Russia. "I . . . gave them the task of saving the
life of the president of Ukraine; they [the Ukrainians] would simply
have done away with him," recalled Putin. "We made arrangements to
take him directly out of Donetsk, by land, sea, and air." Putin ordered
his security forces into the sovereign state of Ukraine, and they followed his orders. Helicopters were sent across the border, and the Russian military used its radio surveillance facilities to follow the advance
of Yanukovych's motorcade from Donetsk airport, where he had been
denied the opportunity to fly to the Crimea.[16]

Meanwhile, Putin had already decided to take the Crimea away
from Ukraine. The only question was how to provide such an act with
a veneer of legitimacy: the Russian constitution did not permit the
annexation of sovereign nations' territories. According to one Kremlin
insider, the majority favored a scenario tested after Russia's attack on
South Ossetia in 2008, when that enclave in Georgia declared indepen-

dence and was recognized by Russia as such. The same could be done in the Crimean case, followed by annexation. Putin allegedly dismissed any objections to such a scenario, saying that it was his aides' responsibility to work out the details of the operation.[17]

Putin told his advisers that the reason why they allegedly had no choice but to "return" the Crimea to Russia was the threat posed to its population by radical Ukrainian nationalists: "[We] cannot abandon that territory and the people living there to their fate, which would mean being steamrollered by the nationalists." No such threat existed, but Putin's larger purpose of annexing the Crimea to Russia would come to nothing if Yanukovych were to make the Crimea his base for attempting to return to Kyiv as a legitimate president. Yanukovych had to be prevented from barricading himself in the Crimea or, even better, stopped before he entered the peninsula. The Russian intelligence services, which were in touch with Yanukovych's security guards as the Ukrainian president made his way to the Crimea, told him that there was an ambush awaiting him. He was to stop short of the peninsula and wait to be picked up by Russian helicopters.

"Our radio tracking services began, in effect, to lead his motorcade," said Putin, recalling the events of that night. "We kept establishing his position as he proceeded on his route. But when they showed me the map, it became clear that he would soon encounter an ambush. Moreover, according to data in our possession, high-caliber machine guns had been installed there to make short work of him." No evidence has come to light to show that anyone besides the Russian government was trying to stop Yanukovych on his way to the Crimea. The Ukrainian security services were too disorganized at the time to attempt something of the sort, even if there was a plan to kill Yanukovych. But Yanukovych did as he was told by the callers from Moscow, stopped his motorcade, and was soon picked up by three Russian military helicopters. To his surprise, he was taken not to the Crimea, where he was heading, but to Russia—the pilots cited the need to refuel.[18]

There was no Putin waiting for him on Russian territory, and Yanukovych demanded that he be taken back to Ukraine, more specifically to the Crimea. According to one of Yanukovych's bodyguards, he was flown to the Russian town of Anapa on the Black Sea coast and from there to a Russian naval base in the Crimea. At one of the sanatoriums on the peninsula he met with the head of his presidential administration, Andrii Kliuiev, and other political allies. The situation was uncertain. The newly appointed head of the Ukrainian security service, Valentyn Nalyvaichenko, and the interior minister, Arsen Avakov, were already in the Crimea looking for Yanukovych. Since they had been leaders of protests on the Maidan, the two officials were unsure whether the Ukrainian security services and interior ministry officers would obey them if they gave orders to arrest Yanukovych, whose security detail remained loyal to him. But Yanukovych decided not to try his luck and leave the Crimea. "I decided to leave Ukraine when I saw that, given the situation, if I stayed in Ukraine, my life would be in danger," Yanukovych later told a reporter.[19]

Vladimir Putin had a different story to tell. "Because developments in Kyiv were very fast and furious, there was already no point in his returning to Kyiv under such conditions," argued Putin. Meanwhile the Crimeans, "seeing how events were developing, took to their weapons almost immediately and appealed to us to approve the measures that they were planning to take," claimed Putin. In other words, according to Putin, Yanukovych had no future in Kyiv and was now an obstacle to developments in the Crimea, which were allegedly instigated by the locals but led to the "return of the Crimea" to Russia ordered by Putin.[20]

Yanukovych left Ukraine on the evening of February 23, heading first for the Russian naval base of Sevastopol and proceeding from there by ship to Russia. His departure removed an important political obstacle to the Russian takeover of the peninsula. February 23 had been Red Army Day in the Soviet Union, and Putin, a former KGB officer, still celebrated it. On that day he basked in the glory of having organized the Winter Olympic Games. Russia was back on the world stage, proving its capacity to organize major international sports events, as the USSR had done back in 1980. The challenge now was to prove Russia's ability to avoid the trap that the USSR had fallen into a few months before the 1980 Olympics by entering Afghanistan.

The ouster of Yanukovych in Kyiv and the installation of a new Ukrainian government committed to an association agreement with the EU were major setbacks for Putin's plan to establish the Eurasian Union as one of the poles of the new world order. Perhaps even more endangered was his vision of Ukraine as part of a Slavic union with Russia. Having failed to keep all of Ukraine in his orbit, Putin opted for the annexation of part of its territory to develop his Greater Russia project, meant to integrate territories with ethnic Russian majorities into the Russian Federation. The hope was that the construction of Greater Russia would save Putin's Pan-Russian and Eurasian integration projects.

The Annexation

The Russian military operation to occupy the Crimea started early in the morning of February 27, when a band of heavily armed men in military fatigues, wearing no insignias, entered the Crimean parliament building in the peninsula's capital of Simferopol and seized control of it. It took Anatolii Mogilev, the prime minister of the Crimea appointed by Yanukovych, who had previously served as Ukraine's minister of interior, a few minutes to realize that these were professionals at work. The special forces acted strictly according to their manual, taking up positions around the building. Since this was a takeover, Mogilev called Kyiv but received no clear instructions. The new authorities had not yet established full control of the armed forces or the security apparatus.[21]

While one group of men in unmarked uniforms took over the buildings of the Crimean cabinet and parliament, another group crisscrossed the city to bring the parliamentary deputies to the seized building, where they were forced to vote on a prepared resolution approving the ouster of Mogilev and the appointment of Sergei Aksenov, a forty-two-year-old parliamentary deputy, as prime minister of the Crimea. Known in the criminal world as "Goblin," Aksenov was a key figure in the peninsula's underworld. He headed the Russian Unity Party, sponsored by the Russian security services. In the months leading up to the crisis, billboards along Crimean highways had featured nothing but portraits of Yanukovych and Aksenov. Yanukovych had no choice but to tolerate such competition. Aksenov's party had received a mere 4 percent of the vote in the Crimean parliamentary elections, but that no longer mattered: the men with Kalashnikovs were correcting the will of the electorate.[22]

The frightened members of the Crimean parliament complied with their instructions, making Aksenov the new Crimean prime minister. The deputies also voted for a referendum on a constitution establishing federal ties between Kyiv and Simferopol and providing broader autonomy for the Crimea within Ukraine. The Kremlin was not yet placing the issue of Crimean independence on the parliamentary agenda, as it wanted to gauge reaction to developments on the peninsula and beyond. In Simferopol, Crimean Tatars gathered at the walls of the parliament building, chanting "Glory to Ukraine!" Pro-Moscow demonstrators mobilized and funded by Russian agents chanted "Russia!"

Sergei Glazev, an aide to Putin, was caught by the Ukrainian security services complaining on the phone that Aksenov and other pro-Russian politicians long "fed" by Russia had failed to show up at the rally. The speaker of the Crimean parliament, Vladimir Konstantinov, referred to rumors that the parliament wanted to vote for independence as a "provocation." But the Russian intelligence services organized a push for independence from below. The rally organized by the Russian agents in Sevastopol demanded the return of Sevastopol to Russia. Another rally in the city of Kerch called for the federalization of Ukraine—a goal endorsed by parliament—and threatened secession if that demand was not met.[23]

On February 28 the acting president of Ukraine, Oleksandr Turchynov, called a meeting of the Security Council to discuss the territorial integrity of the country, telling the participants that the Russian authorities were considering the annexation of the peninsula. That day Russian special forces wearing unmarked military uniforms seized the

Simferopol and Sevastopol airports. Turchynov admitted that not all members of the new government were prepared at that point to work under extreme conditions but insisted that the people of Ukraine were demanding action.

The head of the Security Service, Valentyn Nalyvaichenko, reported the complete collapse of Ukrainian authority in the Crimea. Not only the new prime minister, Aksenov, but also the speaker of parliament, Vladimir Konstantinov, who had held that post before the Russian assault, were collaborating with Russian military and naval commanders. Police units, members of the riot police in particular, had joined the separatists upon returning from Kyiv after the victory of the Revolution of Dignity there. The military were demoralized. The situation was even worse in the Ukrainian navy, whose commander had submitted his resignation. Nalyvaichenko warned of provocations, possibly leading to shooting and civilian deaths, that might be used as pretext for a full-scale Russian military takeover of the peninsula.[24]

The acting minister of defense, Admiral Ihor Teniukh, reported to the leadership that the Russian army was preparing to invade Ukraine across its eastern border. Altogether up to 40,000 officers and men had been moved to the eastern borders of Ukraine under the pretext of maneuvers. "I will be frank," continued the admiral. "Today we have no army. It was methodically destroyed by Yanukovych and his circle on the instructions of the Russian security services." He reported that the Russians were moving their battle-ready units to the Crimea, with the number of troops reaching 20,000. Ukraine had 15,000 troops in the Crimea whose loyalty was uncertain, as most of them were recruits from the peninsula itself. Teniukh could count on no more than 5,000 officers and soldiers capable of following orders and carrying out military tasks. His only hope was an American frigate then deployed in the Black Sea. Teniukh wanted the ship to enter Ukrainian territorial waters as a demonstration of American support for Ukraine.

Turchynov had an idea: would NATO agree to admit Ukraine as an "associate" member of the alliance? That was an idea first proposed by the Ukrainians in the 1990s, but NATO had no such status. The former prime minister, Yulia Tymoshenko, just released from prison after having been incarcerated by the Yanukovych regime, was also opposed to the idea. "We should not talk about immediate membership in NATO, as that would provoke even stronger Russian aggression." The new prime minister, Arsenii Yatseniuk, explained that Russia had attacked Georgia in 2008 over the issue of a NATO Membership Action Plan for that country and was now doing the same in Ukraine. The West had refused to provide Ukraine with a MAP then, and now it was "absolutely unrealistic."

Nor did Yatseniuk expect much help from the signatories of the Budapest Memorandum—the United States, the United Kingdom, France, and China. "We will have to deal with that exclusively by reliance on ourselves," suggested Yatseniuk. He summarized the situation as follows: as the Russian government was well aware, Ukraine was not ready for a military confrontation, and an attempt to resolve the crisis through negotiations with the new Crimean leaders and concessions to them would be prevented by Russia. The only hope was to rally international support. Yatseniuk proposed to document Russia's violation of international agreements and convene the UN Security Council to stop its aggression.

In the middle of the meeting, Turchynov was summoned to a telephone in a separate room. On the line was the head of the Russian Duma, Putin's close ally, Sergei Naryshkin. He conveyed Putin's message—in fact, a naked threat: if even one Russian died in the Crimea, Russia would declare the new leaders of Ukraine war criminals and pursue them to any destination in the world. Naryshkin had one more warning: the persecution of Russians and Russian speakers would not be tolerated by Russia. Turchynov understood that as a threat to invade other parts of Ukraine in case Kyiv put up resistance in the Crimea. He shot back, stating that the Russian leaders had already made themselves war criminals by their aggression against Ukraine and would have to answer to an international court.

Putin's threat did not work. But without nuclear weapons, NATO membership, or an army to speak of, Ukraine had no way to stop the aggression. The head of the Security Service, Nalyvaichenko, reported that American and German officials were asking Ukraine not to resist Russia in the Crimea: according to their intelligence, Moscow would exploit such resistance as an excuse to launch a full-scale invasion of Ukraine. Appeals to the international community and condemnation of Russia in the UN became the only means to which the Ukrainian government could resort in its efforts to defend the country's territorial integrity.[25]

On March 1 the new Crimean prime minister, Aksenov, called on Vladimir Putin "to provide assistance in ensuring peace and tranquility." On the same day Putin asked the Federation Council, the upper house of parliament, for permission to deploy Russian armed forces on Ukrainian territory. When it was pointed out in the UN Security Council that the Crimean prime minister had no right to call on another country to intervene in Ukrainian affairs, Russia's permanent representative at the UN, Vitalii Churkin, produced a document signed by Viktor Yanukovych, by that time an exile in Russia. In his appeal to Putin, Yanukovych, now completely under Russian control, called on the Russian president to use his country's armed forces to restore order and protect the Ukrainian population from the threats created by the Maidan Revolution. Not only the Crimea but also southern and eastern Ukraine were allegedly under threat.[26]

The calls for intervention and permission to use Russia's armed forces in Ukraine were nothing but delayed attempts to provide a veneer of legitimacy for the military takeover of the Crimea, which was already under way. On March 4 Putin held a press conference in which he called the Revolution of Dignity a coup d'état and denied the role of the Russian military in the takeover of the Crimea, suggesting that it was being done by local self-defense units. He then spoke about the tactics that the Russian army was prepared to use if the Ukrainian armed forces should resist. "And let anyone from among the military servicemen try to fire at their own people, behind whom we will be standing," said Putin. He then repeated: "Not in front, but behind. Let them try shooting women and children." What he was saying amounted to nothing less than a war crime.[27]

Putin denied that he was planning to annex the Crimea, but two days later the Crimean parliament, now fully controlled by Russia, changed its earlier decision and revised the questions for the forthcoming referendum, scheduled for March 16. The main question now concerned the "reunification" of the Crimea with Russia. To avoid publicity risks, the Russian authorities prevented coverage of the referendum by journalists, with the exception of friendly representatives of Russia's right-wing allies from Serbia and some European countries. The turnout, according to independent estimates, was anywhere between 30 and 50 percent. According to the same estimates, between 50 and 80 percent of those taking part voted for "reunification." That was sufficient for Putin's purposes, but Moscow needed a decisive victory. When the official results of the referendum were announced, they reminded many of Soviet-era elections: 96.77 percent had allegedly voted in favor of reunification. The turnout was announced to have been 83 percent.[28]

On the following day, March 17, the "count" was complete, and the Crimean parliament asked the Russian authorities to accept the peninsula as part of their territory. In an article published on the eve of the referendum, the historian Andrei Zubov, a professor at the elite Moscow Institute of International Relations, compared the planned annexation of the peninsula to Hitler's Anschluss of Austria in 1938. He drew parallels between Hitler's vision of Greater Germany and Russia's reunification rhetoric, pointed out that both acts were justified to the public by the need to protect allegedly persecuted minorities, German (in Czechoslovakia) in the first case and Russian in the second, and mentioned the staged referendum as a sham to provide legal cover for the forcible annexation. Zubov was soon dismissed, losing his prestigious position at the country's top diplomatic school. But he did not lose the argument.[29]

Numerous parallels have been drawn between the Crimean "reunification" and the Austrian Anschluss, as well as the visions of Greater

Germany and Greater Russia that inspired them. There were also some similarities in public perception of those two acts. The Anschluss of 1938 aroused little concern in London and Moscow, as it was assumed that Hitler's appetite for expansion was limited to German ethnic territories. German reaction to Putin's annexation of the Crimea was similarly calm—up to 40 percent of the German public did not disapprove of his action. In both cases, there was hope that the aggressor would not go farther. It proved to be wishful thinking at its worst.[30]

6

THE RISE AND FALL
OF THE NEW RUSSIA

On March 18, 2014, Vladimir Putin delivered one of the most consequential speeches of his career. Addressing a joint session of the lower and upper houses of the Russian parliament—the deputies of the State Duma and the members of the Federation Council, joined by regional leaders and representatives of Kremlin-controlled civic organizations—Putin asked the deputies to approve a law annexing the Ukrainian Crimea and the city of Sevastopol to the Russian Federation. Two days after the referendum, Putin was ending the Crimea's short-lived independence by annexing the peninsula—the first annexation of a sovereign nation's territory in Europe by a foreign state since World War II.[1]

In his speech, Putin declared that the Crimean self-defense units had taken the initiative to bring about reunification, and the people of the Crimea had decided their fate, preventing Sevastopol from being turned into a NATO military base. He took advantage of the opportunity to remind NATO and the West of all the injustices allegedly committed against international law and Russia, from the bombing of

Serbia to the recognition of Kosovo's independence, as putative justification for Russia's actions in the Crimea, and denounced the "color
revolutions" as coups engineered by the West.

Putin made an unprecedented appeal to Russian nationalism. This
was a marked departure from his earlier statements and pronouncements, in which his main addressee and point of reference was the
multiethnic Russian political nation embodied by the citizens of the
Russian Federation, referred to as *rossiiane* rather than ethnic *russkie*.
Now he claimed that Russia and the Russians were the greatest divided
nation in the world. After the fall of the USSR, said Putin, when "Crimea
ended up as part of a different country . . . Russia realized that it was
not simply robbed, it was plundered." "All these years," he declared, "citizens and many public figures have come back to this issue, saying that
Crimea is historically Russian land and Sevastopol is a Russian city."

There were also elements of the speech that appealed to Russo-
Ukrainian unity, despite Putin's attack on Ukraine and annexation of
part of its territory. "Orthodoxy," claimed Putin, "predetermined the
overall basis of the culture, civilization, and human values that unite
the peoples of Russia, Ukraine, and Belarus." He even declared that
Russia was taking the Crimea on behalf of both Russians and Ukrainians to prevent its loss to a third party. "Crimea is our common historical legacy and a very important factor in regional stability," Putin went
on. "And this strategic territory should be part of a strong and stable
sovereignty, which today can only be Russian. Otherwise, dear friends
(I am addressing both Ukraine and Russia), you and we—Russians and
Ukrainians—could lose Crimea completely, and that could happen in
the near historical perspective."

Putin made a hybrid argument for the annexation: appealing to
Russian history, territory, and identity, he invoked the legacy of empire
to claim the Crimea under the banner of Russian ethnic nationalism, while also maintaining that Russians and Ukrainians were Slavic
brethren. The latter was meant to exploit the sense of Russo-Ukrainian
unity to which many citizens of Russia and Ukraine subscribed. Putin
assured Ukrainians that Crimea was a unique case—a part of Ukraine

historically, culturally, and ethnically belonging to Russia. The rest of Ukraine was safe. "Do not believe those who want you to fear Russia, shouting that other regions will follow Crimea," declared Putin. "We do not want to divide Ukraine; we do not need that." In fact, the division of Ukraine was exactly what Putin undertook in the weeks and months following his Crimean speech.[2]

In conclusion, Putin asked the Russian parliamentarians to ratify the treaty and create two new constituent entities within the Russian Federation, one for the Crimea, another for the city of Sevastopol. The parliament complied, and on March 21 Putin signed the law integrating the Crimea and the city of Sevastopol into the Russian Federation. The annexation of the Crimea was now a fait accompli, carried out in accordance with the Russian constitution but in blatant violation of international law and treaties signed by Russia, including the Budapest Memorandum of 1994 and the Russo-Ukrainian Friendship Agreement of 1997.[3]

The New Russia

The annexation of the Crimea made imperialism and nationalism key elements and driving forces of Russian foreign policy. The annexation suggested that Putin had given the Greater Russia project—annexation of the territories either settled by ethnic Russians or considered to be Russian on historical or cultural grounds—priority over the projects of Russo-Ukrainian unity and Eurasian integration. In fact, he was trying to pursue both, or even to exploit the annexation of the peninsula to keep the rest of Ukraine in Moscow's fold. How could that be accomplished?

The answer was given in a proposal that appeared on the website of the Russian Ministry of Foreign Affairs on March 17, 2014, the day after the Crimean referendum and one day before Putin's speech about the Crimea. It was claimed that the text had been made available to the United States and European powers one week earlier. The proposal called for the return of Yanukovych as president of Ukraine, the formation by Ukrainian parliamentary decree of a Constitutional Assembly representing "all Ukrainian regions," and the assembly's adoption of a new constitution turning Ukraine into a "federal" state that would declare its "political and military" neutrality. Russian would become Ukraine's second official language. The regions would manage their own economic, cultural, and educational affairs and establish "external transregional ties," breaking the center's monopoly on the formulation and execution of foreign policy.[4]

Although the proposal spoke of federalization, it would in fact have turned Ukraine into a confederation of semi-independent regions making policy on international affairs. Ukraine would have ceased to exist as a sovereign state, rendering the central government in Kyiv incapable of negotiating an association agreement with the European Union—the key demand of the Maidan protesters. The new Ukrainian government in Kyiv rejected the notions of adopting a new constitution or federalizing the country. It was prepared, however, to reform local government and amend the Ukrainian constitution accordingly—a concession made in April at talks with Russia, the United States, and the European Union in Geneva. Predictably, Russia was displeased, and it soon became clear that if Kyiv refused to make Ukraine a virtually ungovernable state open to Russian manipulation, Moscow had another solution for its "Ukraine problem"—partition.[5]

In the second half of March, soon after Russia's annexation of the Crimea, the governments of Poland, Romania, and Hungary received a proposal signed by Vladimir Zhirinovsky, the leader of the ultranationalist Liberal Democratic Party and head of its faction in the Russian parliament. Zhirinovsky invited the governments of those countries, which had controlled or occupied parts of Ukraine during the interwar period and World War II, to conduct referendums on the "return" of such territories to themselves. He offered to reestablish European borders existing prior to the signing of the Molotov-Ribbentrop Pact between Nazi Germany and the USSR in 1939. "It is never too late to correct historical errors," read the letter. It was not clear whether Zhirinovsky was writing on behalf of the Kremlin.[6]

A Polish Foreign Ministry spokesperson dismissed Zhirinovsky's letter as a "complete oddity," while his superior, Radosław Sikorski, revealed a few months later that he had heard the same proposal from Putin himself. The offer had been made during the visit of an official Polish delegation to Moscow in February 2008, just as Ukraine was applying for a NATO Membership Action Plan. Neither Poland nor any other central European country showed interest in the Russian proposal. But what would have happened if they had been prepared to consider it? At about the same time as Putin made his offer to the Polish delegation, "some not entirely academic quarters in Moscow"—to quote the source of that report, the Russian political scientist Dmitri Trenin—had discussed the idea of creating a buffer state to be called "New Russia" out of parts of southern Ukraine and Moldova. Its name was borrowed from that of the imperial province established by Catherine II in the northern Black Sea region in the last decades of the eighteenth century.[7]

During the Moscow discussions of 2008, it had been proposed that Transnistria, a separatist enclave of Moldova, become part of the new state, but by the spring of 2014 the geography of the imagined region had changed. In early April a British reporter heard anti-Kyiv protesters in the city of Donetsk, far away from Catherine II's historical province, chanting "New Russia." In mid-April Putin took it upon himself to define the geographic scope of the area that he called "New Russia." Answering questions during a televised marathon phone-in, Putin defined "New Russia" as the Ukrainian oblasts of Kharkiv, Luhansk, Donetsk, Kherson, Mykolaiv, and Odesa—the entire east and south of Ukraine. "These are all the territories that were transferred to Ukraine in the [19]20s by the Soviet government. Why they did it, God knows. All this happened after the corresponding victories of Potemkin and Catherine II in the well-known wars centered in Novorossiysk. Hence [the Russian name] Novorossiia ["New Russia"]. Then, for various reasons, these territories left [Soviet Russia], but the people remained there."[8]

Putin's geographic definition of "New Russia" was ahistorical, as the eighteenth-century province had been limited to the Pontic steppes north of the Black Sea and did not extend to Kharkiv, Luhansk, or Donetsk. But that definition corresponded to Solzhenitsyn's list of historically and linguistically Russian lands that had been included in Ukraine but did not properly belong to it. Solzhenitsyn's historical excursus was as misguided as Putin's: after the Bolshevik Revolution, Russians constituted only 17 percent of the population of the lands that Catherine II had designated as a province and that Putin was now claiming, allegedly for historical reasons, as the "New Russia" province of the Russian Federation. The Ukrainian majority in those regions was the reason why they had been allotted to the Ukrainian SSR in the 1920s. Putin, for his part, was now referring to imperial Russia's annexation of the Crimea and southern Ukraine in the late eighteenth century to make not only a historical but also an ethnonational claim to a much larger region.[9]

By the time Putin described the geographic scope of "New Russia," that region had already become the scene of rallies and riots inspired, orchestrated, and funded by the Russian Federation. On April 7, crowds organized by Russian nationalists who had moved to mainland Ukraine from the Crimea after the end of the military operation there proclaimed the formation of the Donetsk People's Republic, centered on the city of Donetsk. Before the end of the month, the Luhansk People's Republic was declared in another center of the Donbas, the city of Luhansk. The same happened in Kharkiv, where rioters took over government buildings. Ukrainian forces pushed back, securing the Kharkiv government center. On May 2, clashes between pro-Kyiv and pro-Russia activists took place in Odesa—the heart of historical New Russia. The confrontation ended in a tragedy: forty-two anti-Kyiv activists died in a fire in a building to which they had retreated after a confrontation with pro-Ukrainian forces.[10]

In early May the Kyiv government, backed by local activists and business leaders, managed to crush the Russia-inspired and -financed revolts in Kharkiv, Odesa, Zaporizhia, Dnipropetrovsk, and other centers of southeastern Ukraine—the region described by Putin in mid-April as "New Russia." But Kyiv lost control of most of the industrial

Donbas—the Donetsk and Luhansk regions. The relative ease with which Russian mercenaries, supported by local separatist forces, were able to capture and hold hostage the inhabitants of the Ukrainian Donbas, most of whom wanted to stay in Ukraine, has a number of explanations.

One of them is the weakness of the interim government in Kyiv and its inability to command the loyalty of the security forces: police units that associated themselves with the anti-Maidan political camp during the Revolution of Dignity had no trust in the new government. The Donbas was also the home base of the ousted President Viktor Yanukovych, and both the local elites and the population at large considered themselves losers in the Euromaidan revolution that succeeded in Kyiv. The managers of machine-building factories were especially concerned about the future of their enterprises under the new agreement with the European Union and counted on Russian markets for their products. The Donbas, whose origins as the industrial hub of Ukraine and the Soviet Union as a whole went back to the metallurgical and mining boom of the late nineteenth century, never reinvented itself as a center of the post-industrial economy and degenerated into a classic rust belt, devoid of economic opportunities for its inhabitants.

The standard of living in Donetsk and Luhansk oblasts was one of the lowest in the country, and the local population had been mobilized for years by politicians who stoked resentment against Ukrainian-speaking western Ukraine among their Russian-speaking electors in order to win votes. The ethnic composition of the region—Russians constituted 48 percent of the population of Donetsk, the region's largest city—helped to make such propaganda work. In April 2014, 30 percent of those polled in the Donbas oblasts of Ukraine favored union with Russia—not a majority by any means, but enough to garner support for groups of Russian mercenaries and nationalists moving into the area.[11]

The "New Russia" of Putin and Russian nationalists now found its new geographic boundaries in the Ukrainian Donbas. Russian and separatist propaganda exploited the Odesa tragedy of early May to mobilize votes for the independence of the Donetsk and Luhansk oblasts. The referendums that took place in the same month were organized even more hastily than the one in the Crimea, and the organizers predictably declared victory for the pro-independence side. Those who showed up for the referendums voted for the independence not of Putin's "New Russia" but of the two separate "people's republics" of Donetsk and Luhansk. The idea of such republics harked back not to imperial but to early Soviet times, in particular to the short-lived Donets-Kryvyi Rih Bolshevik-controlled polity during the Russian Revolution. Soviet mythology resonated with the locals much more strongly than distant memories of empire.

"New Russia" soon became a badge of identity and a battle cry for the numerous groups of Russian Eurasianists, Russian nationalists, Orthodox monarchists, and neo-Nazis who flocked to the area in hopes of building the polity of their dreams. One of the major supporters of "New Russia," the leader of neo-Eurasianism, Aleksandr Dugin, even adjusted his theories to allow for the existence of a "Big Russia" as part of Eurasia, producing a curious mélange of Eurasian and Russian nationalist ideas. Backed by Russian money and instructed and directed by the Russian intelligence services, the Russian nationalists and Eurasianists soon took control of the newly proclaimed republics.[12]

The Russian political consultant Aleksandr Borodai made the most spectacular career of all the new arrivals in the region, becoming prime minister of the newly proclaimed Donetsk People's Republic. But the most famous of the Muscovites now running the Ukrainian Donbas was Igor Girkin, nom de guerre Strelkov, a former officer of the Russian security services who assumed the post of the republic's defense minister. Both were Russian nationalists, Girkin a devoted monarchist, with a record of participation in regional conflicts across the post-Soviet space, from Moldova to Chechnya. Girkin had also taken part in the Yugoslav wars. The importance of Russian agents in destabilizing the Donbas and turning it into a separatist enclave is hard to overestimate. Girkin, for example, led a group of Russian mercenaries in seizing the key transportation center of Sloviansk in the Donetsk oblast. He also began a shooting war in the Donbas by opening fire on Ukrainian security officers and killing one of them.[13]

The Minsk Agreements

Russia's annexation of the Crimea and de facto takeover of the Donbas occurred during an "interregnum" in Ukraine—the period between the ouster of Yanukovych in late February and the election of a new president, Petro Poroshenko, in late May 2014. Historically speaking, interregnums are the most dangerous periods in the life of states, provoking predatory actions of neighboring states that would use the opportunity offered by the lack of universally recognized rules to seize a rival's territory. That is a story familiar to historians of the Middle Ages and early modern times, but it was revived by Moscow's actions in the Donbas in the spring of 2014.

But interregnums end, as this one did in Ukraine on May 25, when Petro Poroshenko, a politician and businessman who had been a victim of the trade war unleashed by Putin against Ukraine in the summer of 2013 to stop the signing of the EU association agreement, was elected president. The interim president, Oleksandr Turchynov, stepped down to head the National Security and Defense Council under the new president. During his campaign, Poroshenko had declared more than once that his goal as president would be to restore Kyiv's control over the two Donbas oblasts.

By early June, when Poroshenko took office, the shock from Russia's annexation of the Crimea and the de facto loss of the Donbas had given way in Kyiv to a determination to fight. The first volunteer battalions, consisting of activists of the Revolution of Dignity, were formed by the Ministry of the Interior and funded by Ukrainian oligarchs. Notable in that regard was the oligarch Igor Kolomoisky, who also became governor of the Dnipropetrovsk oblast, bordering on the Donbas. The volunteer battalions showed that the Russian mercenaries and their supporters could be pushed back: in May, they took control of some rural areas of the Donbas. The army, demoralized by years of neglect—

some units did not know how to react to protests staged by separatist forces and surrendered their weapons in April 2014—was finally prepared to do battle. Ukrainian business helped to feed and supply not only the volunteer battalions but the army itself, and tens of thousands of volunteers were eager to deliver all they could to the front lines.[14]

Since mid-April, the Kyiv government had fought the separatist insurrection under the banner of the Anti-Terrorist Operation—ironically, the same set of laws used by Yanukovych during the Maidan protests to combat activists of the Revolution of Dignity. But now the operation was switching from defense to offense. The first victory of the government forces came immediately after Poroshenko's election on May 26, when Ukrainian National Guard units, assisted by the air force, attacked separatist militias occupying the Donetsk airport and reclaimed that important transportation hub. The separatists suffered major losses, with dozens killed; most of the dead turned out to be mercenaries from Russia. Much greater success came in mid-June, when the Azov volunteer battalion, together with interior ministry forces, fought a six-hour battle to retake the city of Mariupol, a major industrial center and port on the Sea of Azov.[15]

A major development in the Ukrainian counteroffensive in the Donbas came on July 5, when Igor Girkin, the self-proclaimed defense minister of the Donetsk People's Republic, abandoned his stronghold of Sloviansk and, under attack by Ukrainian forces, fled with his troops to Donetsk. Propaganda sites associated with the Kremlin heaped criticism on Girkin for abandoning Sloviansk. But Moscow also realized that the light weapons and shoulder-launched missiles with which it had supplied the separatist units were insufficient to stop the Ukrainian offensive. In order to survive, the breakaway republics needed heavy artillery, self-propelled rocket launchers, surface-to-air missiles, and possibly Russian boots on the ground. Russia was prepared to supply all that but needed a pretext. On July 13, the Russian media claimed that a Ukrainian shell had hit a city on the Russian side of the border. The response, on the same day, was a massive attack by Russian Tornado multiple rocket launchers on Ukrainian positions.[16]

The war then entered a new stage. On July 14, a Ukrainian plane was shot down by a surface-to-air missile. Four days later, on July 17, Ukrainian radio surveillance intercepted a conversation between two separatist commanders about shooting down another Ukrainian plane. It turned out to be Malaysian Airlines Flight MH 17, en route from Amsterdam to Kuala Lumpur, flying at an altitude of 10,000 meters, or approximately 33,000 feet. A Russian Buk TELAR self-propelled surface-to-air missile launcher fired a rocket that brought down the plane, killing 283 passengers and 15 crew members. It was later proved that the launcher and its crew had come from Russia and belonged to the 53rd Anti-Aircraft Missile Brigade stationed in the Russian city of Kursk, close to the Ukrainian border. The tragedy of those killed on the Malaysian Airlines flight awakened the world to the ongoing war in Ukraine, which had long moved from the Crimea to the mainland. The United States, the European Union, and Western allies responded with sanctions. They were not strong enough to influence Russia's behavior in the long run and, by definition, could do little to affect short-run behavior.[17]

Moscow denied any involvement in the attack on the Malaysian airplane, blaming Ukraine. It tried to avert a repetition of such attacks on civilians and avoid direct responsibility for subsequent conduct of the war by recalling Aleksandr Borodai from his post of prime minister of the self-proclaimed republic and Igor Girkin from the post of minister of defense, replacing them with locals. Once the most obvious signs of Russian involvement in the Donbas puppet states had been removed, Putin sent Russian military units into the region, attempting to save the separatist enclaves from crushing blows delivered by the Ukrainian army. By early August the Ukrainians had split the separatist-held territories in half, reaching the Russian border, where they were shelled by Russian artillery.[18]

Russia's direct invasion of eastern Ukraine began on August 24, 2014, Ukrainian Independence Day, less than ten days after the removal of Girkin as self-proclaimed minister of defense. Hundreds of Russian tanks, armored vehicles, artillery pieces, trucks, and thousands of regular troops crossed the Ukrainian border in multiple locations. By August 26, Ukrainians already had proof that regular Russian forces were being deployed in the offensive: ten Russian paratroopers were taken prisoners and paraded in front of television cameras. The Russian side stated that the soldiers, captured 20 kilometers (12 miles) from the Russian border, had simply lost their way. The offensive continued. Advancing Russian troops surrounded Ukrainian units near the key railway hub of Ilovaisk. As one of the Ukrainian units admitted defeat and negotiated the right of safe passage, the Russians opened fire, massacring the column. The Ukrainian forces suffered unprecedented losses: 366 killed in action, 429 wounded, and 128 taken prisoner. The defeat showed the strength of the Russian army and the inability of the Ukrainian forces to stop the new invasion.[19]

President Poroshenko's military campaign to retake the Donbas was now over. He was forced to negotiate in the most unfavorable conditions possible. On September 5, 2014, Poroshenko agreed to the conditions of the Minsk Protocol, signed that day in the capital of Belarus by representatives of Ukraine, Russia, the Organization for Security and Cooperation in Europe, and the leaders of the two Donbas "republics." The protocol called for an end to hostilities, the withdrawal of illegal armed units and mercenaries from Ukrainian territory, and the establishment of an OSCE mission to monitor movement across the Russo-Ukrainian border—a measure that was supposed to prevent the influx of new Russian troops. Superficially, those conditions favored Ukraine, but the protocol also recognized the existence of new entities on Ukrainian territory not controlled by Kyiv. The Ukrainian government undertook to adopt a law on the special status of the regions captured by the separatists. That was part of Russia's original plan to "federalize" Ukraine. The Ukrainian government, which had earlier agreed to reform local administration, now had no choice but to accept the conditions dictated by Russia and its proxies.[20]

The Minsk agreements were broken by Russia almost immediately after they were signed, as the OSCE was either unable to monitor the border or the missions reporting on the continuing influx of Russian troops were ignored. In January 2015, Russia resumed a large-scale military campaign as it tried to improve the position of its puppets on the front lines and to enforce the conditions imposed on Ukraine by the Minsk Protocol. That month separatist troops managed to capture the ruins of the Donetsk airport, which were held by the Ukrainians. (The heroic months-long defense of the airport by Ukrainian soldiers, who had become popularly known as "Cyborgs," provided Ukraine with an important narrative of martial mythology.) In the same month, 8,000 Russian troops, most of them professional contract soldiers supported by local separatist forces organized by Russian officers, launched a major operation against the Ukrainian-held city of Debaltseve—an important transport junction located between the territories held by the separatist Luhansk and Donetsk republics. The Russian troops proved unable to repeat the encirclement that they had managed at Ilovaisk, and Ukrainian troops retreated from the area.[21]

In mid-February 2015, as the battle for Debaltseve continued on the snow-covered fields of eastern Ukraine, Vladimir Putin met with his Ukrainian counterpart, Petro Poroshenko, the chancellor of Germany, Angela Merkel, and the president of France, François Hollande, to negotiate a new deal. The meeting took place in Minsk, and the new agreements subsequently became known as Minsk II. The Ukrainians kept fighting long after the end of the negotiations, and Putin no longer had the leverage over Poroshenko that the Ilovaisk debacle had given him the previous September, but he was still on the offensive and managed to improve his position. Ukraine undertook not only to adopt a law on the status of the breakaway republics, but also to amend its constitution to accommodate that law.

The new protocol explicitly referred to Ukraine's reestablishment of control over its border with Russia, but prescribed that Kyiv conduct local elections in the breakaway parts of the Donbas first, and only then gain control of the border. That provision suggested that the elections would be held under Russian control, leaving Ukraine to deal with Russian-appointed authorities in regions that would have enough power under the revised Ukrainian constitution to stall the country's movement toward the European Union. The question of which should come first, Ukrainian control over the border (and thus its sovereignty) or the elections, would become an obstacle to the implementation of the Minsk agreements. But for the moment they brought Ukraine the long-awaited promise of peace. There would be desultory fighting and shelling across the border in the years to come, raising the overall number of war casualties in the Donbas to some 14,000 by the beginning of 2022. Those numbers would be dwarfed by the casualties incurred after the war resumed in February of that year.[22]

By the time the Minsk agreements were signed, "New Russia" had disappeared from Moscow's official lexicon—the last time Putin referred to it was in late August 2014, when the battle of Ilovaisk was going on. The Russian president put the New Russia project on hold, replacing it with that of the partial "federalization" of Ukraine. According to the new plan, the two Donbas puppet states were to remain separate, later to be reintegrated into Ukraine by means of the implementation of the Minsk agreements in their Russian interpretation. The Ukrainians were concerned that once the Donetsk and Luhansk statelets became part of Ukraine, they would use their special status to block Ukraine's political and economic integration into the European structures and put an end to Kyiv's aspiration to join the EU.

The annexation of the Crimea and the launch of Russia's war in the Donbas demonstrated Putin's opportunism and flexibility in geopolitical and ideological thinking. Unable to seize all of Ukraine for his Eurasian Union, he decided to occupy part of it, postponing the rest of the takeover project. Putin's nationalist allies, who lost influence over developments in the Donbas with the dismissal of Borodai and Girkin in the summer of 2014, felt betrayed. Nevertheless, they clung to their imagined but never-materialized nationalist vision of New Russia. Girkin would travel around on the FSB-issued passport in the name of Sergey Runov. He would also make YouTube videos on developments in Ukraine under the banner of the nonexistent state of New Russia well into the new Russian war, which was launched in February 2022.[23]

The New Ukraine

The eight years of hybrid warfare that Russia had waged against Ukraine in the Donbas, divided by the Minsk agreements, turned Ukraine into a different country and society from those of 2014. A country divided by issues of history, culture, and identity when the Crimea was annexed was now united by the desire to defend its sovereignty, democratic order, and way of life at almost any price.

The war had changed the electoral map of Ukraine. The first wartime presidential elections, held in May 2014, yielded unprecedented results: Petro Poroshenko won in the first round with 55 percent of the vote—the first time this had happened since 1991. Even more important, Poroshenko carried 187 precincts out of 188 remaining under Ukrainian control. The dividing line of the previous presidential elections, which had split Ukraine in half between pro-European and pro-Russian candidates, was now gone. The war had produced a much more homogenous country.[24]

Russia's annexation of the Crimea and takeover of significant portions of Ukraine's Donbas removed the traditionally most pro-Russian areas, with the greatest number of ethnic Russians and Russian speakers in Ukraine, from Ukrainian political and cultural space. Those areas had also served as bases for Russia-friendly political parties. Russia did its utmost to support former allies of the ousted president, Viktor Yanukovych, but they were divided and weak after losing a significant part of their electoral base. The forces led by the Ukrainian businessman and politician Viktor Medvedchuk, who was close to Putin, also remained weak despite the support of television channels and newspapers funded with Russian assistance.[25]

The growth of Ukrainian political identity began with the rejection of symbols of the Soviet past. The Maidan protests of 2014 unleashed a wave of demolition of monuments to Vladimir Lenin, the main symbol of communist and, in the eyes of many, Russian domination of Ukraine. More than 500 such monuments were toppled by anti-communist activists in the first half of 2014, mostly in the center of the country. The rest, more than 1,500 that remained in the regions of southeastern Ukraine controlled by Kyiv, were removed in the course of the next few years by decision of parliament, which adopted the so-called "decommunization laws" prohibiting the public display of communist symbols.[26]

Ukrainians survived the Russian onslaught during the first stage of the war, in 2014–15, by uniting across ethnic, linguistic, religious, and cultural lines. The war itself also promoted popular identification with the Ukrainian language and culture. Since Putin's official rationale for invading Ukraine was the defense of Russian speakers, many Ukrainians and Russians who knew Ukrainian but used Russian as their language of preference began to switch to Ukrainian as an act of defiance. The number of those self-reporting their use of Ukrainian at home and at work spiked in 2014–15. That number returned to the previous norm once the immediate danger of all-out invasion passed, but readiness to adopt Ukrainian as the dominant language of government and education remained. In 2019, parliament adopted a new law making the Ukrainian language mandatory for government officials and public-sector employees. The Russian Foreign Ministry protested, claiming that the law would deepen divisions in Ukrainian society. That did not prove to be the case.[27]

City and village bookstores were flooded with Ukrainian-language books, reducing Russian-language publications to secondary status. Works on Ukrainian history and culture began to top bestseller lists. Before the war, the government had spent little or no money on the promotion of Ukrainian culture abroad; now it created a special Ukrainian Institute under the auspices of the Ministry of Foreign Affairs. Its task was to emulate Germany's Goethe Institute and similar agencies in other countries, familiarizing foreign countries with the Ukrainian language and culture. At home, the Ukrainian Cultural Fund and the Ukrainian Book Institute were charged with supporting cultural events and promoting Ukrainian publications.[28]

In 2018 the government provided strong support for the unification of the two branches of the Ukrainian Orthodox Church that were independent of the Moscow Patriarchate, which still dominated

Orthodoxy in Ukraine, while striving to restrain competition between them. President Poroshenko attended the unification council of the two churches, which were placed under the jurisdiction of the Patriarch of Constantinople—a major blow to the prospect of continuing Russian Orthodox hegemony. Moscow protested and severed ties with the Patriarch of Constantinople but could do little more to maintain its position. The newly united Orthodox Church of Ukraine (OCU) had mass popular support, and, given the ongoing if undeclared war with Russia, many Orthodox Ukrainians preferred a church independent of Moscow. The transfer of parishes from the Moscow Patriarchate to the OCU began in the first months of 2019.[29]

Active government involvement in matters of language, memory politics, and religion met with substantial criticism not only from traditionally pro-Russian political forces but also from part of the country's liberal establishment. Nevertheless, it was either supported or accepted by the population at large. After Russia's aggressive weaponization of issues of culture and history in 2014–15, much of the population agreed that the new laws and policies were necessary elements of nation-building, designed to prevent further Russian aggression.[30]

The new Ukrainian government fulfilled the promise of the Revolution of Dignity by moving closer to the European Union and Euro-Atlantic institutions, including NATO. The association agreement that had triggered the Maidan protests in 2013 was signed in June 2014. In March 2017 the European Union Council granted Ukrainians visa-free travel to the EU. The EU member nations provided badly needed financial assistance, altogether up to $14 billion, to help Ukraine deal with its losses of territory, population, and economic assets. An additional $2.2 billion came from the United States. Washington became the main sponsor of reform in the Ukrainian security sector, providing $1.6 billion for that purpose alone. Ukraine was rapidly acquiring a new professional army, and the government placed NATO membership back on its agenda by including it in the Ukrainian constitution. The Kremlin did not like what they saw.[31]

7

PUTIN'S WAR

In the fall of 2008, Vladimir Putin, then the prime minister of Russia, who had just left the office of the president, asked Aleksei Venediktov, the editor in chief of the radio station Echo of Moscow, which was liberal but still tolerated by the authorities, what aspects of his two presidential terms would make it into school history textbooks.

Venediktov, who had begun his career as a history teacher, responded that it would be Putin's initiative leading to the reunification of the Moscow Patriarchate with the Russian Orthodox Church abroad—an émigré institution that had remained anti-Bolshevik and loyal to the Romanov dynasty after the Revolution of 1917. Surprised, Putin asked, "And is that all?" In 2015, seven years after their original conversation and one year after the annexation of the Crimea, Putin asked Venediktov the same question. "Putin knows perfectly well," remarked Venediktov in an interview, "that history books for both Russian and Ukrainian schools will say that 'Khrushchev gave away the Crimea, and Putin took it back.'"[1]

Putin compared himself not only to the Soviet leaders like Khrushchev but also to the Russian emperors Peter I, Catherine II, and Alexander II. Their busts and portraits made their way into Putin's antechamber in the Kremlin, and his press secretary, Dmitrii Peskov, attested to his superior's interest in history. "Putin reads all the time," confided Peskov on one occasion, "mostly about the history of Russia. He reads memoirs, the memoirs of Russian historical state figures." Putin's reading of history clearly intensified during the COVID lockdown of 2020–21. This time around he was not just reading but also writing.[2]

In July 2021, Putin had surprised Russia watchers throughout the world by releasing a long historical essay, which to all appearances he had written himself, with some assistance. The essay, titled "On the Historical Unity of Russians and Ukrainians," reflected his already well-known views, elaborated with a long excursus into history. After the failure of his Eurasian integration project in Kyiv and the implementation of his Greater Russia scenario by the annexation of the Crimea, Putin was returning to the imperial vision of a big Russian nation, a Pan-Russian project endorsed by Aleksandr Solzhenitsyn, among others. "I said that Russians and Ukrainians were one people— a single whole," wrote Putin in the opening statement of the lengthy essay. "These words were not driven by some short-term considerations or prompted by the current political context. It is what I have said on numerous occasions and what I firmly believe."[3]

What followed was an extended discussion of the history of Russia and Ukraine whose basic premises followed the line established in the nineteenth century by Count Sergei Uvarov and his favorite historian, whom he had commissioned to write school textbooks on Russian history, Nikolai Ustrialov. Like Ustrialov, Putin dwelled on what he regarded as the original unity of the big Russian nation, established in medieval times, when the Russian people were not only ruled by the same princes and belonged to the same Orthodox Church but also allegedly spoke the same language. Kyivan Rus' had in fact been a multiethnic polity whose territory spanned thousands of miles. But Putin, like

Ustrialov and many others who followed the historian's lead, attributed the loss of presumed Russian unity to bad rulers and foreign enemies.[4]

"The wall that has emerged in recent years between Russia and Ukraine, between the parts of what is essentially the same historical and spiritual space, to my mind is our great common misfortune and tragedy," wrote Putin. "These are, first and foremost, the consequences of our own mistakes made at different periods of time. But these are also the result of deliberate efforts by those forces that have always sought to undermine our unity." When it came to "our own mistakes," Putin pointed first and foremost to those allegedly committed by the Bolsheviks, Vladimir Lenin in particular. The list of Russia's historical enemies was long, from the thirteenth-century Mongols to the Poles of the fifteenth and sixteenth centuries, then the Austro-Hungarians and again the Poles in the nineteenth century, as well as the Germans in the twentieth century.

The Poles played a special role as the nation responsible for the breakup of the united Russian people in all imperial Russian narratives, and Putin's version did not depart from that long-established tradition. "The idea of the Ukrainian people as a nation separate from the Russians started to form and gain ground among the Polish elite and part of the Malorussian [imperial term for Ukrainian] intelligentsia," wrote Putin, all but following the argument put forward by the imperial authorities in 1863 as grounds for prohibiting Ukrainian-language publications. He then tried to explain the Russian Empire's prosecution of leaders of the Ukrainian movement, and especially its prohibitions on Ukrainian-language publications, by blaming the Poles once again. "These decisions were taken against the backdrop of dramatic events in Poland and the desire of the leaders of the Polish national movement to exploit the 'Ukrainian issue' to their own advantage," wrote Putin.[5]

Putin's contribution to his predecessors' historical schemas was the notion of Ukraine as an anti-Russia or, as he described it, "a barrier between Europe and Russia, a springboard against Russia." It was allegedly a concoction of evil Western forces. "Inevitably, there came a time when the concept of 'Ukraine is not Russia' was no longer an option," wrote Putin. "There was a need for an 'anti-Russia' concept, which we will never accept. The owners of this project took as a basis the old groundwork of the Polish-Austrian ideologists to create an 'anti-Moscow Russia.'" Putin pledged action: "[W]e will never allow our historical territories and people close to us living there to be used against Russia."

Putin was clearly upset with the Ukrainian democracy that kept generating political leaders dedicated to the idea of the independence of Ukraine. He complained that "presidents, members of parliament, and ministers would change, but the attitude of separation from and enmity toward Russia would remain." That was allegedly the result of the political system established by the "Western authors of the anti-Russia project." Without naming the new Ukrainian president Volodymyr Zelensky, Putin accused him of lying to his electorate. "Reaching peace was the main election slogan of the incumbent president," wrote Putin. "He came to power with this. The promises turned out to be lies. Nothing has changed. And in some ways the situation in Ukraine and around Donbas has even degenerated."[6]

The Servant of the People

Volodymyr Zelensky, a forty-one-year-old comedian, entrepreneur, and television personality, won the Ukrainian presidency in the spring of 2019. A few years earlier he had played the role of an honest and decisive president in a television series titled Servant of the People. Many liked the TV persona created by Zelensky and supported his presidential bid. Others, especially the younger voters, were tired of the old politics and politicians and wanted change.

The incumbent, President Petro Poroshenko, campaigned as a pro-European and anti-Russian candidate, hoping that Zelensky would be regarded by the electorate as occupying the pro-Russian niche previously held by candidates such as Yanukovych. But attempts to divide the electorate into pro-Russian and pro-Ukrainian factions were no longer effective. Ukraine was now fairly united, and Zelensky, who ran on an anti-corruption platform, won handily over a candidate widely perceived as a representative of the economic oligarchy. Zelensky won more than 73 percent of the vote in the second round of elections, carrying every region of Ukraine but one.[7]

Ukrainian society had rallied around the government to embrace its new linguistic and cultural identity and the creation of a professional army, but most Ukrainian citizens were not prepared to tolerate continuing governmental corruption. Curbed to some extent under President Poroshenko, it nevertheless remained a major concern both at home and abroad. Poroshenko himself exemplified the failure of the system to free itself from oligarchic influence. A billionaire as of 2012, he lost that status as the war began but regained it in office. More importantly, anti-corruption activists in Ukraine considered Poroshenko complacent about ongoing corruption schemes and soft on embezzling government officials.[8]

The concerns of Poroshenko's supporters that Zelensky would sell out Ukraine to Russia or prove incapable of standing up to Putin did not materialize. Under Zelensky's leadership there would be no change of Ukraine's commitment to join NATO, and the nation-building initiatives and cultural policies introduced by Poroshenko were maintained. Zelensky, adept at reading the popular mood, understood that the war had changed Ukrainian society. He soon fully mastered not only the Ukrainian language but also the art of politics. A Russian-speaking Jew from eastern Ukraine, he won a solid electoral majority of the largely ethnic Ukrainian and often Ukrainian-speaking electorate, and remained popular longer than any of his predecessors in office.[9]

Zelensky had won the presidency with the promise of bringing lasting peace to Ukraine. "We will continue in the direction of the Minsk [peace] talks and head toward concluding a ceasefire," he declared upon election. Zelensky based his hopes for peace on a personal meeting with Putin. They did indeed meet in Paris in December 2019, accompanied by Chancellor Angela Merkel of Germany and the host of the talks, President Emmanuel Macron of France. They agreed on a new ceasefire in order to break out of the existing stalemate: shelling across the demarcation line in the Donbas had been proceeding in desultory fashion for years, as had prisoner exchanges. But there was no progress on the fundamental question of the Minsk agreements—whether local elections in the Donbas or Russian withdrawal should come first. "It is necessary to synchronize the process of achieving a ceasefire with the implementation of political reforms in Ukraine, envisaged by the Minsk Agreements," commented Putin on the results of the negotiations. Some Russian émigrés with good contacts in Moscow would argue later that Putin felt betrayed by his aides, especially Vladislav Surkov, who had promised him that Zelensky would accept the Russian conditions. It was allegedly after the Paris meeting that Putin not only fired Surkov but also started to think about going to war with Ukraine.[10]

Zelensky repeated again and again that he would not trade Ukrainian territory for peace. But he vacillated on the issue of the implementation of the constitutional reforms envisioned by Putin. The reforms would have given the Donbas special status and turned it into a Russian enclave if the Russians had been allowed to take charge of the elections. Poroshenko had tried to pass laws to that effect in the Ukrainian parliament, only to provoke mass protests instead. Zelensky faced similar difficulties when in October 2019 he agreed to the formula endorsed by Russia, Germany, and France for the reintegration of Donbas. Almost immediately, mass protests erupted all over Ukraine under the slogan, "No to the capitulation." Looking for a way out of a difficult situation, Zelensky said "no" to Putin in Paris. Now he had nowhere to go but west and no door to knock on but that of NATO.[11]

In December 2019, the month in which Zelensky met with Putin in Paris, the Ukrainian parliament dominated by Zelensky's Servant of the People party adopted a resolution reaffirming Ukraine's course toward NATO membership. Zelensky stood by the constitutional pledge to make Ukraine a member of the North Atlantic alliance and implemented a number of measures, including the adoption of a new National Security Strategy, to move closer to the Alliance. In December 2020, with the conflict in the Donbas showing no signs of subsiding, the Ukrainian defense minister, Andrii Taran, raised the issue of a NATO Membership Action Plan (MAP) in his address to the ambassadors and military attachés of the NATO countries in Kyiv. "Please inform your capitals that we count on your full political and military support for such a decision [granting Ukraine a MAP] at the next NATO summit in 2021. This will be a practical step and a demonstration of commitment to the decisions of the 2008 Bucharest Summit," requested the minister.[12]

Annoyed by Russia's continuing interference in Ukrainian affairs through Moscow-backed television channels, Zelensky soon opened another front against Russia, clamping down the Russian-funded channels and their de facto owner, Viktor Medvedchuk. A Ukrainian politician and businessman close to Putin, Medvedchuk had also served as a back-channel intermediary for President Poroshenko in his dealings with the Kremlin. In February 2021, Zelensky used the powers of the National Security and Defense Council to shut down a number of television channels controlled by Medvedchuk. "Ukraine strongly supports freedom of speech," Zelensky tweeted his followers. "Not propaganda financed by the aggressor country that undermines Ukraine on its way to EU and Euro-Atlantic integration. The fight for independence is a fight in the information war for truth and European values."[13]

The United States supported Zelensky's move, but Putin was displeased: Russia was losing its presence in Ukrainian public space, limiting its ability to influence the Ukrainian public and intimidate the Ukrainian political elite. As always, Putin saw Western influence behind Kyiv's move. "Look, in Ukraine they've taken three leading channels and just shut them down! With one stroke of the pen. And everyone is keeping quiet! And some are even slapping them on the back with approval. What can one say about that? Nothing, except that they use those instruments for one's own geopolitical purposes," declared the Russian president in February 2021, a few weeks after the action taken by Zelensky and his National Security and Defense Council.[14]

A few weeks later, in April 2021, Russia moved an unprecedented number of troops to the Ukrainian border—the largest such deployment of men and arms since the hot war of 2014–15. The alarms sounded in the Western capitals, while Zelensky called on NATO to review Ukraine's request to join the alliance. Russia gave no reasons for the sudden escalation, nor were they immediately obvious. A Ukrainian analyst suggested that the deployment had been provoked by inquiries from the Zelensky administration about a MAP for Ukraine and that it was meant as a warning to the newly elected American president, Joe Biden, to whom those inquiries were ultimately addressed.

Concerned about the sudden buildup, Zelensky once again called on NATO to expedite his country's admission to the alliance. Biden telephoned to assure him of American support for Ukrainian sovereignty, and the United States discussed the situation with its NATO allies. The crisis of April 2021 dissipated as Moscow moved most of its troops away from the Ukrainian borders in May, but elements of their infrastructure and some equipment were left in the area—a clear sign that they might well return.[15]

The International Crisis

The American and British intelligence services, working together, began to notice preparations for a possible invasion of Ukraine in the spring of 2021, when satellite images showed a concentration of Russian troops on the Ukrainian borders. President Biden met with Vladimir Putin in Geneva in June 2021 and made some progress on matters of cybersecurity—a major irritant in US-Russia relations owing to ransomware attacks on American business that the United States attributed to Russia, as well as a cyberattack on US government institutions. Ukraine was on the agenda, but no progress was made to resolve the ongoing crisis in the Donbas.[16]

About the time of the Biden-Putin meeting, the American and British intelligence services received the first reports that Russian military strategists had started planning an all-out invasion of Ukraine. By October, the US intelligence services were suggesting that Putin was determined to invade and occupy most of Ukraine. "We assess that they plan to conduct a significant strategic attack on Ukraine from multiple directions simultaneously," General Mark A. Milley, chairman of the Joint Chiefs of Staff, told President Biden, adding: "Their version of 'shock and awe.'" The attack, planned for winter, included the "removal" of President Zelensky.[17]

The White House decided that it could not just sit on the increasing data pointing to such an invasion. In an unprecedented move, possibly risking the disclosure of sources and methods of intelligence gathering, the two governments began to share information with allies to build a coalition that could stop Putin. In early November the CIA director, William Burns, flew to Moscow to tell his counterparts that their plans were no longer secret. Putin did not question the American intelligence. Instead, he complained about NATO expansion. In early December, reporting about plans for an invasion involving 175,000 Russian troops appeared in the *Washington Post*.[18]

On December 17, 2021, as the world began its last weekend before the Christmas break, the Russian authorities presented their Western counterparts with an unexpected ultimatum. The list of demands was rather long and included a commitment in writing from NATO to halt any further expansion of the alliance, remove multinational NATO troops from Poland and the Baltic states, and even withdraw American nuclear weapons from Europe. The most important demand was a formal NATO commitment that Ukraine never be allowed to join the alliance. The context in which these demands were made, especially the concentration of almost 200,000 Russian troops within striking distance of the Ukrainian borders, suggested that if the West did not comply, then Russia would launch a major military offensive against Ukraine, reigniting the war that had begun in 2014.[19]

The key task that Biden and his advisers were trying to solve was summarized by General Milley in the following way: "How do you underwrite and enforce the rules-based international order" against a country with extraordinary nuclear capability, "without going to World War III?" His response entrusted to the note cards read as follows: "No. 1: 'Don't have a kinetic conflict between the U.S. military and NATO with Russia.' No. 2: 'Contain war inside the geographical boundaries of Ukraine.' No. 3: 'Strengthen and maintain NATO unity.' No. 4: 'Empower Ukraine and give them the means to fight.'"[20]

In the months and weeks leading up to the invasion, President Biden adopted a two-track policy with regard to a possible Russian assault. On the one hand, the president and his administration kept warning the world about Putin's aggressive intentions and plans, sharing intelligence with anyone prepared to listen about the number of Russian troops approaching the Ukrainian borders. That intelligence included possible dates of an invasion. On the other hand, the Americans never tired of repeating that neither they nor their NATO partners would fight in Ukraine, thereby taking the military option off the table and reassuring Putin that no matter what he might do in Ukraine, there would be no military response.

The United States would not send its troops to Ukraine even to rescue American citizens, declared Biden. Many believed that it was a mistake to remove the threat of military intervention, since it gave Putin carte blanche to invade without fear of encountering superior forces. But Biden apparently wanted to reassure both his own people and the Western public at large that American opposition to Russia's possible new war against Ukraine would not lead to a global and potentially nuclear conflict. The disincentive for Putin to invade was a threat that the united West would impose personal and sectoral sanctions on the Russian economy. A Western media campaign began in order to deny Putin the benefit of surprise, perhaps even to shame him into canceling or postponing his invasion.[21]

If all that were to fail, the United States threatened Putin with support of a potential Ukrainian insurgency against Russian occupying forces, as no one in Washington, London, or other Western capitals expected the Ukrainian armed forces to last more than a few days. Thus, the United States was not planning to send weapons to Ukraine in significant numbers if the war dragged on. The concern was that they would end up in Russian hands sooner or later. The weapons sent by the United States and its allies in limited numbers included Javelins and Stingers, powerful anti-tank and anti-aircraft missiles that could be managed by small partisan forces to inflict casualties on an occupying army, as the Afghan resistance had done with Stingers toward the end of the Cold War.[22]

As Russia presented its ultimatum to NATO in December 2021, demanding that the alliance's borders be moved back to their 1997 positions, Biden and Putin held a videoconference call on December 30. There was no progress of any kind, although they agreed to continue talking. The Russians were interested in the appearance of negotiations, but not in substantive progress. Subsequent talks involving the United States, Russia, NATO representatives, and Ukraine as a member of the Organization for Security and Cooperation in Europe also produced no results. The Russian demands were considered nonstarters in Washington and found unacceptable by all members of NATO—a rare instance of unanimity in an alliance often strained by disagreements about Russia. All member nations agreed that no external power could dictate which countries could join the alliance.[23]

The failure of the negotiations served as a prelude to a hacker attack on official Ukrainian websites, which the Ukrainian government blamed on Russia. The US Congress began to consider bills imposing major sanctions on the Russian financial sector and top officials, including President Putin himself. As the Russians threatened the United States and NATO with an "asymmetrical response," rumors began to swirl around Washington suggesting that nuclear-armed missiles might be installed close to American shores. After Russian officials suggested sending their troops to Cuba and Venezuela, concern grew that such missiles might not only be carried on submarines but also based on land. Putin's threats of the previous few months concerning a repetition of the Cuban missile crisis of 1962 suddenly acquired new meaning and urgency.[24]

Now it was the West's turn to hit the history books and draw lessons, if not inspiration, from the past. Parallels were drawn between the rising tensions over Ukraine and the Western democracies' dealings with Hitler's Germany over Czechoslovakia in 1938. The question

on everyone's mind was whether there would be another Munich—
Western appeasement of an aggressive power. In January, the German/
British drama *Munich—The Edge of War*, released by Netflix, attracted
attention throughout the world. The *New York Times* characterized the
film as a feature-length attempt to glorify Neville Chamberlain, the
British prime minister who had engaged in the much-debated diplomatic strategy of appeasement in the run-up to World War II.[25]

Whatever might be said about France and Germany, there was no
appeasement on the part of the United States. Secretary of State Antony
Blinken first informed President Zelensky of US intelligence about
the coming war in early November. A few weeks later, a senior State
Department official told the visiting Ukrainian foreign minister, Dmytro Kuleba, "dig trenches." CIA Director William Burns, who visited
Kyiv on January 12, 2022, informed President Zelensky about the Russian plan to seize Kyiv by landing at Hostomel airport near the Ukrainian capital. He also told the president to take his personal security and
that of his family seriously. More warnings came from Antony Blinken
when he visited Kyiv a few days later and learned from Zelensky that he
was not going to leave the capital.[26]

Zelensky did not appear to be impressed by the American warnings. He would later explain his attitude at the time as follows: "You can
say a million times, 'Listen, there may be an invasion.' Okay, there may
be an invasion—will you give us planes? Will you give us air defenses?
'Well, you're not a member of NATO.' Oh, okay, then what are we talking about?'" When President Biden called Zelensky in late January to
let him know that the Russian attack was almost certainly coming next
month, Zelensky asked his American counterpart to "calm down the
messaging." He later told reporters that the constant signals of "war
tomorrow" were causing "panic in the markets and in the financial sector." He estimated Ukraine's losses from public statements about the
coming war at US $15.5 billion.[27]

Given the successive American warnings, the economic losses,
and no hint of possible Western involvement in the approaching military conflict, the Ukrainians intensified their negotiations with Russia.

The head of Zelensky's presidential administration, Andrii Yermak, met with Putin's trusted ally Dmitrii Kozak, a native of Ukraine and deputy head of Putin's presidential administration, to negotiate a solution to the Donbas conflict. The media reported on their failed talks, but informal consultations continued, resulting in a draft agreement whereby Ukraine was to deter possible Russian aggression by assuring the Kremlin that it would not join NATO.[28]

Meanwhile, the Ukrainians kept up a brave face, seemingly in complete denial of the ever more serious situation. In late January, with the American and other Western embassies leaving Kyiv and incessant warnings from Washington and London about an imminent Russian attack, the Ukrainian defense minister, Oleksii Reznikov, reassured the Ukrainian parliament and public, saying: "As of today, there are no grounds to believe [that Russia will invade]," and "Don't worry, sleep well. No need to have your bags packed." But behind the scenes, the Ukrainian administration was asking its friends for weapons. The secretary of the National Security and Defense Council, Oleksii Danilov, had a message for the Western allies: "Don't scream about this so much. Do you see a threat? Give us ten planes a day. Not one, but ten, and the threat will disappear."[29]

That was the position taken by Zelensky on February 19, three days before the invasion, when he surprised everyone by leaving Kyiv to attend the Munich Security Conference. "Whatever happens, we will defend our wonderful land, whether there are 50,000, 150,000, or a million soldiers of any army on our borders," declared Zelensky. "To really help Ukraine, there's no need to say how many of them there are—soldiers and equipment. What needs to be said is how many of us there are. To really help Ukraine, there's no need to keep talking about dates of probable invasion. We will defend our land whether it's February 16, March 1, or December 31. What we need much more are different dates. And everyone understands perfectly well which ones." He was referring to weapons delivery.[30]

Zelensky also reminded the conference participants about the responsibility that great powers had assumed in signing the 1994

Budapest Memorandum and removing nuclear weapons from Ukraine. "Ukraine has received security guarantees for abandoning the world's third nuclear capability," stated Zelensky. "We don't have that weapon. We also have no security. We also do not have part of the territory of our state that is larger in area than Switzerland, the Netherlands, or Belgium. And most importantly—we don't have millions of our citizens. We don't have all this. Therefore, we have something. The right to demand a shift from a policy of appeasement to ensuring security and peace guarantees."[31]

According to one member of the Ukrainian delegation at the Munich conference, some Western leaders advised Zelensky not to return to Ukraine in light of an imminent invasion and to form a government in exile instead. London or Warsaw, the capitals of Ukraine's two staunchest allies in Europe, were suggested. Zelensky allegedly refused. "I had breakfast in Ukraine this morning, and I will have dinner in Ukraine," responded the Ukrainian president. Few had expected such an answer from a former comedian who, with no prior political experience, had assumed the presidency of a troubled country and promised to end the ongoing conflict with Russia as soon as possible.[32]

The Declaration of War

In late 2021, as rumors about Putin's failing health started to circulate with new intensity in Russia and abroad, observers began to notice changes in his appearance, including his puffy face—possibly an effect of medication. And it was impossible to ignore Putin's desire to protect himself from COVID-19 or other infections by seating foreign dignitaries who came to see him at the opposite end of a ridiculously long table. This led Russian political commentators to concern themselves with the question of Putin's legacy, in which the Crimea and Ukraine featured prominently. The political consultant and expert on Ukraine Sergei Markov, who was close to the Kremlin, suggested that "Putin cannot step down leaving Ukraine occupied, given that Russians there are being turned into anti-Russians by means of terror." He then explained his thought in terms of the Pan-Russian project: "Because Ukraine is in fact part of Rus'."[33]

Putin first publicly subscribed to the imperial idea of a big Russian nation and declared that Russians and Ukrainians were one and the same people in the course of his visit to Kyiv in the summer of 2013. He was there with Patriarch Kirill of the Russian Orthodox Church to mark the supposed 1,025th anniversary of the baptism of Kyivan Rus'. "We understand today's realities," declared Putin, speaking to the friendly audience of conference participants in an address appropriately entitled "Orthodox Slavic Values: The Basis of Ukraine's Civilizational Choice." "We have the Ukrainian people and the Belarusian people and other peoples, and we are respectful of that whole legacy, but at the foundation there lie, unquestionably, our common spiritual values, which make us one people."[34]

Putin would repeat his mantra about the Russians and Ukrainians being one and the same people again and again, but now Markov argued that the time had come for Putin to turn his words into actions. But there were also those in the Russian nationalist camp who did not believe that the war between the Russians and Ukrainians was a good idea. The head of the All-Russian Officer Assembly, Colonel General Leonid Ivashov, published an open letter to Putin opposing the war on the grounds of Russian national interest and Slavic unity. "The use of military force against Ukraine will, in the first place, put into question the existence of Russia itself as a state," wrote Ivashov. "Secondly, it will make Russians and Ukrainians mortal enemies forever. Thirdly, thousands (tens of thousands) of healthy young men will perish on both sides, and that will unquestionably affect the future demographic situation in our countries, which are dying out."[35]

Vladimir Putin spent the weeks, months, and days leading up to the war publicly denying his intention to start it. He went on record on February 12, less than two weeks before the invasion, denying any plans of launching it, despite ongoing American reports that Russian troops were continuing to mass on the Ukrainian borders, reaching totals of 100,000 and then 150,000 men. Altogether, according to US estimates, by the time of the invasion the Kremlin had mobilized 120 battalions of tactical groups with an overall strength of 150,000 to 190,000 men. "The facts are that the Americans are artificially whipping up hysteria around an alleged Russian plan for invasion, even providing the dates of such an invasion," declared the Russian president.[36]

Putin made the formal decision to go to war at the February 21 meeting of the Russian Security Council, which approved the de facto denunciation of the Minsk Agreements and supported the proposal to recognize the "independence" of the two puppet statelets in the Ukrainian Donbas. As Putin suggested in front of cameras, he had not discussed his decision to denounce the agreements and recognize the independence of the Donbas "republics" with the members of the council beforehand. What he wanted was to hear their opinion. Heavily edited television footage of the meeting left little doubt that few had any opinions of their own. The majority did their best to provide arguments in favor of a decision that had already been made, and the head of foreign intelligence, Sergei Naryshkin, even incurred reprimands from Putin, first for vacillating about recognition of the two "people's republics" and then for overshooting the target by proposing to annex them to Russia.[37]

The footage strongly suggested that the decision to go to war was Putin's own. The rest were there merely to voice support. Among those present was the Russian foreign minister Sergei Lavrov, whom Putin, according to the investigative journalist Christo Grozev, allegedly never consulted on the issue of going to war with Ukraine. According to the anecdote shared by the Western Russia watchers, when asked who Putin's advisers were, Lavrov allegedly answered: Peter the Great, Catherine the Great, and Alexander II—Russian emperors of the eighteenth and nineteenth centuries.[38]

After Russian television showed the footage of the Security Council meeting, it broadcast a lengthy speech by Putin explaining his decision to denounce the Minsk Agreements of 2015. The speech indicated that Putin was not about to limit himself to the Donbas, whether the statelets were to be declared formally independent or annexed outright, as Naryshkin had suggested. Putin was after Ukraine as a whole. He returned to the main themes of his historical essays of July 2021 in an attempt to delegitimize the existence of Ukraine as both state and nation.

"Modern Ukraine was entirely created by Russia or, to be more precise, by Bolshevik, Communist Russia," declared the Russian president. "This process started practically right after the 1917 revolution, and Lenin and his associates did it in a way that was extremely harsh on Russia—by separating, severing what is historically Russian land." That theme was deeply rooted in the writings of Russian White Guard émigrés such as General Anton Denikin and was a prominent thread in Solzhenitsyn's thinking and writing. Putin decided to add weight to his argument by pointing out that he had studied the topic on the basis of archival documents.[39]

In Ukrainian social media, the reaction to Putin's statement was ridicule. Within a few hours, Facebook was flooded with images of Vladimir Lenin surprised to learn that he had created Ukraine. Another montage inserted Lenin into the monument to the legendary founders of Kyiv, the brothers Kyi, Shchek, and Khoryv and their sister, Lybid. Lenin replaced Lybid at the prow of the boat carrying the founders of the Ukrainian capital. The monument expresses popular Ukrainian belief that their country's roots go back to the Middle Ages. Putin had scant interest in the Ukrainian reaction—his decision had already been made.[40]

On February 21, the day of the Security Council meeting, Putin recorded another address, this one to be released on the morning of the Russian attack. In it he justified the coming aggression as a response to what he called "genocide" committed by "the forces that staged the coup in Ukraine in 2014: against the millions of inhabitants of the Donbas." He argued that the actions of the Kyiv authorities left Russia no choice but to act. "In these circumstances," declared Putin, "we have to take bold and immediate action. The people's republics of the Donbas have asked Russia for help." The reference was to a request made by the leaders of the puppet states in the Russian-occupied part of the Donbas, recently recognized by Moscow as independent. Their request gave Putin a formal casus belli, set the minimum goal of Russian aggression—the takeover of the entire Donbas—and misled the Ukrainian side into thinking that the war might be limited to the Donbas alone.

Other parts of the address suggested that the Donbas was a mere pretext. Although Putin called his aggression a "special military operation," he characterized it as a global struggle, in the tradition of Stalin's Great Patriotic War, against the hostile West and the Ukrainian fascism that it supported. "Focused on their own goals, the leading NATO countries are supporting the far-right nationalists and neo-Nazis in Ukraine, those who will never forgive the people of the Crimea and Sevastopol for freely making a choice to reunite with Russia," claimed Putin. "They will undoubtedly try to bring war to the Crimea just as they have done in the Donbas, to kill innocent people just as members of the punitive units of Ukrainian nationalists and Hitler's accomplices did during the Great Patriotic War. They have also openly laid claim to several other Russian regions."[41]

Putin formulated the goal of his "special military operation" as follows: "demilitarize and denazify Ukraine, as well as bring to trial those who perpetrated numerous bloody crimes against civilians, including against citizens of the Russian Federation." The meaning of demilitarization was quite clear: Ukraine was to be left defenseless, at the mercy of Moscow. But what did "denazification" mean? Putin's propaganda had spent years portraying some of the Ukrainian volunteer military formations of 2014 as Nazi. But more was at stake than those battalions. A few days earlier, the United States had warned the United Nations that Russian intelligence services were compiling lists of people "to be killed or sent to camps." They included "Russian and Belarusian dissidents in exile in Ukraine, journalists and anti-corruption activists, and vulnerable populations such as religious and ethnic minorities and LGBTQI+ persons." There was also little doubt that anyone resisting the invasion would be killed or put on trial. Putin called on the Ukrainian military "immediately to lay down arms and go home."[42]

The Invasion

Putin's address was aired on Russian television in the early hours of February 24, on the eighth anniversary of Putin's decision to start the Crimean annexation in 2014. He expected the results to be as quick, decisive, and positive as they had been then.

Putin concluded the speech with an appeal to Russian citizens: "I believe in your support and the invincible force rooted in love for our Fatherland." The key motifs of his address, including the denazification of Ukraine, would be picked up and popularized by the Russian media in the days and weeks to come, although it was difficult to change the propaganda line right away. Leonid Slutsky, the head of the Russian State Duma Committee on Foreign Affairs, denied the invasion even on the very day it began. "We do not intend to unleash any war. We are not going to invade Ukraine as we are being accused of in Ukraine itself, and not only there," he told journalists. As he spoke those words, Russian columns were moving toward the Ukrainian capital.[43]

The Russian assault on Ukraine began shortly before 4:00 a.m. Kyiv time on February 24, 2022, on multiple fronts. The citizens of Kyiv, Kharkiv, Odesa, Zaporizhia, Zhytomyr, Mykolaiv, and Kherson, to list only the main regional centers, woke up to the sound of explosions—Russian aviation and missiles were attacking airfields and military installations all over the country. Radio and television covered the news on the basis of posts in social media from around Ukraine. There were also reports of Russian amphibious landings in Odesa on the Black Sea and Mariupol on the Sea of Azov. Those later turned out to be false.[44]

The Russian armed forces bombarded Ukrainian command and control centers, air defenses, and critical infrastructure with more than 100 short-range ballistic missiles launched from the air and from the sea. Columns of Russian tanks and personnel carriers began to cross the Ukrainian borders from Belarus toward Kyiv, from Russia toward Kharkiv, and from the occupied Crimea toward Kherson and Nova Kakhovka in the south. Tens of thousands of troops were suddenly on the move. Ukraine, where neither the government nor the general population believed in the possibility of large-scale Russian aggression, was in for a rude awakening.[45]

The entire military operation, underpinned by Putin's belief in the nonexistence of the Ukrainian nation and the desire of Ukrainians to live under Russian rule, was modeled on the Russian takeover of the Crimea. In the first echelon of ground troops advancing on Kyiv immediately after the paratroopers were units of riot police, and in burned-out tanks and vehicles Ukrainians would find parade uniforms of Russian soldiers prepared for a victory march down Kyiv's main avenue, Khreshchatyk. The soldiers had rations for only two or three days, as they were promised that the operation in Ukraine would take no longer. Since the invasion was billed as a mission of liberation, the officers and soldiers were ordered not to show any hostility whatever to the local population. They were told that the military operation was ordered to prevent the installation of NATO bases in Ukraine.[46]

"Orders have been given to the Russian army not to assault cities or their inhabitants. The leadership of the Russian Defense Ministry emphasizes that the population of a fraternal country has nothing to fear from the Russian army," confided the political consultant Sergei Markov to a reporter on the second day of the invasion, February 25, 2022. Regarding the further plan of the action, Markov suggested: "All groupings of the Ukrainian Armed Forces will be surrounded (mainly from the air) and given an ultimatum. They will have to surrender their arms. If everything proceeds normally, a process of disarmament will begin. Wherever normality does not prevail, those groupings will be destroyed. I think that most subunits of the Ukrainian Armed Forces will surrender their weapons. Part of them will continue to offer resistance. Those are the neo-Nazi military subunits."[47]

That was not just Markov's plan but Putin's as well. In his address at the start of the war, Putin had appealed to the Ukrainian military to lay down their arms. But the Ukrainian army continued to fight. Not a single unit would surrender, to say nothing of switching sides. Putin and his propagandists like Markov were in for a rude awakening.

8

THE GATES OF KYIV

Among those most surprised by the Russian all-out invasion was the Ukrainian president, Volodymyr Zelensky. For weeks before the invasion he had tried to reassure himself and the Ukrainian people that it would not take place. "It wasn't fear on his face," said the speaker of the Ukrainian parliament, Ruslan Stefanchuk, who remembered meeting Zelensky that morning. "It was a question: How could this be?" The shock was shared by Stefanchuk and other top leaders of the country. "We sensed the world order collapsing," recalled Stefanchuk a few weeks later.

The president's wife, Olena, woke up early that morning to realize that her husband was gone. She found him in the next room, already dressed. "It has begun," Zelensky told her. There was no need to explain what had begun—the unthinkable had happened. Volodymyr and Olena awakened their seventeen-year-old daughter and nine-year-old son. Soon explosions became audible from the president's quarters. Two days previously, Zelensky had been warned by his intelligence service that the Russians had plans to assassinate him. He had responded with irony. Now the situation was different: the family had to go, while the president stayed.[1]

"Well, then? We'll fight!" said Zelensky by way of welcoming Oleksii Danilov, the secretary of the National Security and Defense Council, when he showed up in the president's office. "It was immediately clear that the president was not about to go anywhere and would stay in Ukraine despite the risk of being killed," recalled Danilov. Danilov reported the latest news to Zelensky. According to the first reports, which had begun to arrive in Danilov's office after 3:40 a.m., the Russians had begun the invasion by attacking the town of Mylove on the border between the Russian- and Ukrainian-held parts of the Donbas. Now it was about 5:00 a.m. At 5:30 a.m., the members of the National Security and Defense Council voted to declare martial law.[2]

At some point that morning, Zelensky must have realized that his hopes of appeasing the Kremlin by promising not to join NATO were futile. The previous day, when meeting Ukraine's leading businessmen, he had assured them that he was doing everything possible to avoid war. One of them, Vadim Novinsky, who had close ties with the Moscow patriarch, assured the president that he was fully on board. Until the last moment, there was hope that the negotiations between Zelensky's chief of staff, Andrii Yermak, and Putin's aide Dmitrii Kozak would help to avoid war. But Kozak failed to convince Putin to accept Ukraine's assurances not to join NATO and called Yermak that morning to demand a surrender. Yermak swore and hung up. The negotiations were over.[3]

After the meeting of the Security Council, Zelensky recorded a brief video address to the nation, calling for calm and assuring Ukrainians that he, the government, and the armed forces were doing their job. He concluded with a promise to stay in touch with video reports. Zelensky's next video, released at 7:48 a.m., referred to the invasion as Putin's war against Ukraine, launched with the goal of destroying the Ukrainian state. He called on the Ukrainian people to do everything in their power to assist their armed forces and on Ukrainians abroad to help form an international anti-Putin coalition to save Ukraine and democracy at large. Zelensky reported that he had already spoken by phone with President Joe Biden of the United States, Prime Minister Boris Johnson of the United Kingdom, President Andrzej Duda of Poland, and other leaders. From them, he wanted support and the "closure of the Ukrainian skies."[4]

Russian air superiority was the primary concern of Zelensky and his military, and it would remain so for weeks and months to come. But maintaining unbroken communication with his people and assuring them that the president was in Kyiv, holding the fort no matter what, were the top priorities that he established that day. They would literally change the course of the war. There were two big surprises the first day. The first of them, which shocked Kyiv, was Russia's all-out attack on Ukraine and the bombing of its capital. The second stunned Moscow. Unlike Yanukovych, Zelensky refused to flee, and Ukrainians throughout the country, unlike those in the Crimea and many of those in the Donbas, refused to stay housebound. They fought back.

The Battle for Kyiv

The all-out invasion came as a shock not only to the politicians and ordinary citizens but to the military as well. "We still thought and, you could say, hoped that the opponent would begin his active military measures from the occupied territory of parts of Luhansk and Donetsk oblasts," recalled the commander in chief of Ukraine's Northern Command, General Dmytro Krasylnykov. "Again, using subunits of illegal military formations of the 'Luhansk and Donetsk People's Republics' to mask the basic formation of seconded troops, volunteers, and mercenaries, somewhat diluted with regular troops, perhaps supported by long-distance multiple rocket launchers and aviation. Perhaps. To the end, we believed that our enemy would not intrude with large-scale aggression on every front across all lines."[5]

The Ukrainian military had been preparing for the last war or, rather, the war they had been fighting in the Donbas since 2014. Despite the ever more tense situation on the borders, the Ukrainian military units were not yet manned according to wartime standards. Western intelligence services turned out to be right when they warned repeatedly that the attack would not be limited to the Donbas. In fact, one of the main thrusts of the Russian offensive was directed against Kyiv, on the northeastern segment of the front. On the second day of the invasion Sergei Markov, a political adviser close to the Kremlin, told reporters that "Kyiv had to be taken because there should have been no orders coming from there to kill Russian soldiers. Such orders are being issued now. We need a man in Kyiv issuing different orders. That is why Kyiv had to be taken."[6]

The officer issuing Ukrainian military orders was the commander in chief of the Ukrainian Armed Forces, Lieutenant General Valerii Zaluzhny. Round-faced, his appearance suggesting that of a teddy bear, the forty-eight-year-old general had not served a day in the Soviet Army. He represented a new generation of Ukrainian officers, trained according to NATO standards, who were proving themselves in battles with Russia and its satellites in the east of the country. Together with the commander of ground forces, Colonel General Oleksandr Syrsky, who took over the defense of Kyiv, Zaluzhny moved the command posts from their usual locations closer to the border with Russia. He also moved jets and helicopters to secondary airports, making it hard to detect and destroy them in a surprise strike. Syrsky would create two defensive circles around Kyiv and divide the city itself into defense sectors headed by the commanders of Kyiv military schools. These actions would help to save not only the army but the city as well.[7]

The most direct way for the Russian troops to reach Kyiv was via the Chernobyl exclusion zone, the site of the world's worst nuclear disaster. Close to 30,000 Russian troops had been deployed as part of the "Union Resolve 2022" military maneuvers before the invasion. On February 24, some of those troops took control of the Chernobyl nuclear power plant and the adjacent exclusion zone with its Arch, a €1.5 billion containment structure over the damaged reactor no. 4 and the spent-fuel storage facility. The lightly armed Ukrainian guardsmen surrendered without a fight as they were not prepared to resist an over-whelming enemy force on the territory of a nuclear site.

Anton Herashchenko, an adviser to the Ukrainian minister of the interior, posted an announcement on his Facebook page that Ukrainian guardsmen had been attacked in the zone. He issued a general warning that shelling could damage the storage facilities, producing a radioactive plume that would cover a good part of Ukraine, Belarus, and the European Union. That did not happen, as the Ukrainian guardsmen surrendered without a fight in the face of overwhelming force, but Russian tanks and heavy machinery advancing from the Belarusian border through the Chernobyl exclusion zone stirred up radioactive dust remaining from the explosion of 1986.[8]

By 8:30 p.m., Ukraine's State Inspectorate for Nuclear Regulation had lost control over all facilities in the Chernobyl zone. Ukrainian guardsmen had been taken prisoner by a much larger and better-equipped invading force, and the operators of the Arch and other Chernobyl-zone facilities had been taken hostage. Kyiv informed the Vienna-based International Atomic Energy Agency (IAEA) about the assault on the station by a foreign military force. In a tweet, Zelensky called the attack on Chernobyl "a declaration of war against the whole of Europe," but the agency, which belongs to a UN family of international organizations, could do nothing to stop the seizure of the nuclear site by the military forces of a permanent member of the UN Security Council. IAEA officials could not even bring themselves to mention Russia in their initial statements on the crisis. The aggressor got away without so much as a slap on the wrist. It was left to the Ukrainians to deal with the brewing nuclear crisis on their front line.[9]

The first major battle of the new war took place at the Antonov International Airport in the town of Hostomel, 35 kilometers (22 miles) northwest of central Kyiv. Home to the Antonov 225, the world's largest cargo plane, the airport was not only close to the city but also capable of receiving all types of airplanes in the employ of the Russian Air Force. The Russian military command planned to seize the airport with the help of a relatively small detachment of airborne troops and special forces. That would allow a much larger paratroop force to land in the vicinity of Kyiv, capture the city's bridges across the Dnieper River, and limit the ability of the Ukrainian armed forces to maneuver and move units through the Kyiv transportation hub. The rumored operation to capture or kill President Zelensky was also to be conducted from there. Chechen fighters loyal to the Russia-backed strongman Ramzan Kadyrov would later be dispatched to Hostomel by land, allegedly to carry out that task.[10]

The armada of Russian KA52 attack helicopters, known as Alligators, and MI8 transport helicopters with paratroopers on board, accompanied by airplanes, approached the Hostomel Airport around 10:30 a.m. on February 24. By that time Russian strikes had managed to destroy the Ukrainian air defenses around the airport. Despite a warning from CIA director William Burns to President Zelensky that the Russians were going to land at Hostomel, there were no Ukrainian Army units at the strategic airport, only a lightly armed detachment of a rapid-response brigade of National Guards. Although most of the brigade's personnel had been dispatched to the Donbas, those who stayed at the airport—about 300 men, including draftees—managed to offer stiff resistance. They shot down three of the approximately thirty-five Russian helicopters and hit another three. The remaining MI8 helicopters managed to land their troops but left them without air support under enemy fire.

For the Russians, things did not go according to plan. They managed to hold the airport, but Ukrainian artillery fire aimed at the airstrip made it impossible for heavy transport airplanes to land there. Ukrainian paratroopers of the 95th Brigade moved in with their own helicopters, and soldiers of the 72nd Motorized Brigade, the main military unit defending the capital, would contest Russian control over Hostomel for days to come. Their efforts saved the Ukrainian capital from a surprise attack and Zelensky and his government from possible captivity, if not death. The offensive against Kyiv was stalled as Ukrainian armed forces destroyed the dam on the Irpin River, cutting off the Russian troops in Hostomel from Kyiv. Hostomel and its airport became the site of the first and longest battle to be fought during the initial stage of the war, which would last into April.[11]

The Russian attempt, a few days later, to capture another strategic airport in Vasylkiv, approximately 40 kilometers (25 miles) south of central Kyiv, also failed thanks to the effective work of Ukrainian air defense units. A small Russian detachment that managed to land on the airfield was destroyed by Ukrainian ground forces. With Hostomel Airport contested and attempts to capture Vasylkiv defeated, the Russian assault on Kyiv came to a halt in mid-March near the village of Moshchun northeast of Kyiv.[12]

Russian troops moved toward Kyiv not only from Belarus via the Chernobyl zone but also from Russian territory through the Sumy and Chernihiv regions, east of the Ukrainian capital. Ukrainian infantry and tank brigades located in that region left their locations before the Russian attack, survived air strikes and, reinforced by reservists, began fighting Russian columns advancing on Kyiv. "The first strike, directed against the withdrawal zone, proved unsuccessful for the opponent, and we retained our basic battle strength," recalled the commander of Ukraine's northern flank, General Krasylnykov. "And in the course of further operations that allowed us to inflict serious losses." The Ukrainians turned the city of Chernihiv, with a population of more than a quarter million, located less than 150 kilometers (93 miles) northeast of Kyiv, and Sumy, a regional center with a similar population located more than 350 kilometers (127 miles) east of Kyiv, into their strongholds.[13]

The Russian commanders achieved a 12 to 1 force ratio on the northern approaches to Kyiv but failed to turn that advantage into a victory because they lacked tactical competence. The Russian columns had to make their way around cities; on narrow forest roads their personnel, vehicles, arms, and equipment became easy targets for Ukrainian mobile groups. Using Javelins and their Ukrainian and Soviet-era analogues, and assisted by the local population, they destroyed Russian tanks and armed personnel carriers, stalling the approach to Kyiv from the east. Videos shot in the area showed columns of Russian tanks burned by artillery fire, drones, and lightly armed Ukrainian mobile groups. Russian officers and men abandoned their vehicles and equipment, much of it malfunctioning or simply running out of fuel. The invaders had fuel and food for only a few days.[14]

The Russian troops advancing on Kyiv had only limited air support. The complete Russian air dominance predicted by Western experts never materialized. The Russians were rushing things: instead of the lengthy air bombardment that had characterized US operations in Iraq, they combined air bombardment with their ground offensive into a single stage. "Russia's inability to suppress or destroy Ukrainian strategic anti-aircraft systems in the first days of the conflict limited its ability to assist ground maneuvers with tactical air support, contributing to the failure of the advance on Kyiv," wrote British intelligence experts assessing the causes of the stalled Russian offensive in northern Ukraine.[15]

Defiance

On February 25, the second day of the invasion, the Kremlin press service released Putin's new appeal to the Ukrainian military: "I address myself once again to the servicemen of the armed forces of Ukraine. Do not allow the neo-Nazis and Banderites to make use of your children, your wives, and seniors as a living shield. Take power into your own hands. It will probably be easier for us to reach agreement with you than with the band of drug addicts and neo-Nazis that has ensconced itself in Kyiv and taken the whole Ukrainian people hostage." The appeal followed personal messages of the same nature sent by the Russian military commanders to their Ukrainian counterparts and anonymous letters addressed to almost every colonel in the Ukrainian armed forces. According to later reports, the Russian intelligence services had been working on a military coup against the Ukrainian government, but its participants allegedly refused to act once the Russian attempt at a quick takeover of Hostomel failed.[16]

Putin's repeated appeals to the military to rebel went unanswered. The Ukrainian troops were motivated and fought bravely. "We assess

Moscow underestimated the strength of Ukraine's resistance and the degree of internal military challenges we are observing, which include an ill-constructed plan, morale issues and considerable logistical issues," the director of national intelligence, Avril Haines, informed the US Congress at the beginning of March, less than two weeks after the start of the invasion. The assessment was right on the mark. Putin and his "special military operation" fell victim to the Russian president's distorted view of history and complete lack of understanding of Ukrainian society and its democratic foundations.

Russian spies, especially the special directorate of the Federal Security Service (FSB), which was charged with clandestine operations in Ukraine, were feeding Putin descriptions of the attitude of the Ukrainian population toward its own government and Russia that conformed to his historical fantasies. The FSB reported that Ukrainians would greet their Russian liberators. A vast network of agents was recruited in Ukraine not only to spy on the Ukrainian government, military, and people, but also to organize mass demonstrations in support of liberating Russian troops and take over key government installations as they approached, replicating the takeover of the Ukrainian Crimea and Donbas in the spring of 2014.[17]

Putin expected Ukrainians to welcome with flowers the Russian forces sent to liberate them from Nazism and nationalism. Instead, they met the Russians with Javelins, Stingers, and Ukraine's own Skif (Scythian) or Stuhna anti-tank guided missiles. Faced with stiff resistance, the "liberation army" was frightened, confused, and disoriented. If Putin was the victim of his own delusions, historical and otherwise, his troops became victims of his propaganda efforts. By claiming that Russians and Ukrainians were one and the same people, Putin left his soldiers unprepared for a war in which the entire population would oppose the invading army and support its own armed forces.

To the surprise of Putin and his entourage, the government and people of Ukraine were united, as they had not been in 2014, when the ouster of Yanukovych incapacitated the government and divided society. Zelensky refused to flee. When the Americans offered to exfiltrate him from Kyiv, Zelensky reportedly answered: "The fight is here; I need ammunition, not a ride." In a video address to the Ukrainian people filmed on the street in front of a Kyiv building, he told his compatriots: "I am here. We are not putting down our arms. We will be defending our country, because our weapon is truth, and our truth is that this is our land, our country, our children, and we will defend all this."[18]

Zelensky's decision to stay in Kyiv—some claimed that it was partly motivated by the decision of his archrival Petro Poroshenko not to leave the capital—had a major impact on government personnel, many of whom, according to Secretary Danilov of the National Security and Defense Council, were getting ready to leave the city after the first hours of the attack. No less important were Zelensky's videos rallying citizens to resist the aggression. Data released in Ukraine on the day before the invasion, February 23, rated Zelensky as the country's most popular politician, with 42 percent support. Now he used that trust to the fullest and showed that it was not misplaced.

Many who had been disappointed by Zelensky's earlier statements downplaying the threat of Russian aggression now began to think of him as their leader. The former actor had a talent that many professional politicians could only dream of. He had good rapport with his audience and knew what people wanted at a particular moment. He was there to amplify their voice in both peace and war. The absolute majority of Ukrainians did not believe that war was coming, and Zelensky was there to articulate that disbelief. But when the invasion came, Ukrainians were ready to fight after absorbing the initial shock, and Zelensky amplified and communicated that message to domestic and international audiences alike.[19]

A telephone poll conducted on February 26–27, the third and the fourth days of the war, showed 79 percent of Ukrainians believing in victory, 90 percent of men expressing readiness to defend their country with arms in hand, and 70 percent of women responding in the same way. In the east, endangered by the Russian advance, 60 percent were prepared to join the army; in the south, the figure was 80 percent. Nationwide, 86 percent of Ukrainians wanted to join the EU, and 76 percent supported plans to join NATO. In early March, with the Russian "blitzkrieg" faltering but no Ukrainian victories in sight, the number of believers in victory jumped to 88 percent. Ninety-eight percent supported the Ukrainian armed forces, and 44 percent were prepared to endure the hardships of war as long as it might take to ensure peace on Ukrainian conditions.[20]

Zelensky's popularity soared to an unprecedented 93 percent. Support for heads of local administration was next, at 84 percent. This was unprecedented in Ukrainian history. The need to unite around the state authorities was part of the explanation. Even more important was the behavior of government officials in the face of the Russian invasion—not only Zelensky but, with very few exceptions, heads of local administration did not flee and stood with their people. Ukraine had been undergoing a reform of local government devolving greater rights and resources from the center to the localities. Ironically, that reform was the Ukrainian response to Russian demands for the "federalization" of the country. It strengthened the population's trust in Ukrainian state institutions, which was fully demonstrated in the cities, towns, and villages overrun by Russian forces in the first days and weeks of the war. People marched, carrying Ukrainian flags, in defense of mayors kidnapped by the occupiers.[21]

In the city of Kyiv, nights were full of the sounds of gunfire coming not only from the vicinity of Hostomel, where the fight for the airport was still going on, but also from within the city, where Russian commando units were trying to reach the government compound and centers of military and critical infrastructure but were stopped by defenders. People began to leave the city en masse, but the longest lines were those of men in front of military commissariats enlisting in territorial defense units. Those without military experience were often turned back, but still there were more volunteers than the commissariats could accept and provide with weapons.[22]

Putin's continuing public responses to Biden's accusations that the Russian president had promised not to start a war with Ukraine left many officers and soldiers bewildered. Last-minute propaganda efforts to make soldiers believe that the war was being waged to liberate fraternal Russians and Russian speakers were also problematic. Between 35,000 and 40,000 Russian officers and men took part in the Russian army's unsuccessful attempt to take Kyiv. By the end of March, Moscow had declared unrecoverable losses of more than 1,300 individuals in Ukraine. NATO estimates were closer to 10,000, while the Ukrainians claimed to have killed as many as 20,000 Russians. "Russia has failed in its objective of capturing Kyiv. It has failed in its objective of subjugating Ukraine," declared the US National Security Council spokesperson, John Kirby, at the time.[23]

Faced with the failure of his plan, Putin blamed others, especially spies, who had been reporting what he wanted to hear. The FSB directorate, headed by General Sergei Beseda, spent millions of dollars recruiting agents and running clandestine networks in preparation for the special operation, but their work came to nothing when the invasion, which the spies themselves probably did not expect to materialize, actually took place. Information on the current status of Ukraine and prospects of its immediate collapse was supplied by highly biased former aides of Viktor Yanukovych, who had fled the country with their boss back in 2014.

In March, rumors circulated in Moscow that Putin had ordered the arrest of generals and officers, who apparently had not only misled him but also embezzled millions of dollars, allegedly to support nonexistent agents and networks but actually spent on apartments, mansions, cars, and vacations. The rumors, if anything, reflected a growing internal struggle at the center of Russian power which pitched the chiefs of the security services against one another.[24]

Occupation

Despite Putin's illusions about his mission of "liberation" in Ukraine and the propaganda used to portray the Ukrainian government as a Nazi band, many Ukrainians saw the Russian invaders as the true Nazis. The Russian occupation of Ukrainian cities and villages was reminiscent of scenes of the Nazi occupation of Ukraine in World War II. Those memories never faded away in Ukraine, as they were passed from one generation to the next. "They called the people together and demanded that they elect headmen (*starosty*). Headmen! Village dwellers exchanged meaningful glances, immediately recalling that word from the days of the German occupation," said the prominent Ukrainian lawyer Svitlana Musiienko, recalling her experience under the Russian occupation in the small village of Obukhovychi next to the Chernobyl zone.

An address to locals by a Russian political officer also reminded them of World War II in Ukraine. The officer, named Yevgenii, told them: "Generally speaking, we are peacekeepers. But if even a hair falls from the head of a Russian soldier, you'll all be fucked. Otherwise, live as you please. We don't bother you, so don't bother us. Just don't go beyond the bounds of the village, wear white armbands when moving about, don't cross from one garden to another, and hang a list of residents on the gate of every building—we'll check them." And so, like ghetto Jews forced to wear the Star of David in wartime, local residents had to wear white armbands and hang lists of dwellers on their front gates. Svitlana Musiienko, who was partly of Jewish descent, saved a photo of herself wearing a white armband next to the list of residents of the house where she spent the occupation.[25]

In Ukrainian villages occupied by the Russian army, local leaders were targeted and urged to cooperate with the military authorities. Those who refused were liable to be kidnapped or even killed. Yurii Prylypko, the mayor of Hostomel, where the first major battle of the war had been fought, was gunned down by automatic fire as he drove his car to deliver food and supplies to city dwellers. His corpse was then booby-trapped, targeting those who might try to help him or bury his body. A Russian soldier removed the booby trap when he saw an Orthodox priest approaching to bury the dead mayor. In the village of Motyzhyn, 45 kilometers (28 miles) west of Kyiv, Russian troops arrested mayor Olha Sukhenko with her husband and son. All three were executed by the occupiers and buried in a shallow grave.[26]

Anatolii Fedoruk, the mayor of the nearby town of Bucha, which would become known to the world at large because of the massacre of civilians there, was spared only because his name was misspelled on a list of local officials and activists compiled by the occupiers. Bucha, the home of more than 35,000 citizens located immediately south of Hostomel, became the site of a major battle on February 27. On that day Ukrainian artillery destroyed a column of Russian tanks and armored troop carriers proceeding along a street in Bucha from Hostomel toward Kyiv. Fedoruk was there soon after the battle and recorded a video address to his citizens against the background of burned-out Russian armored vehicles, promising that everything destroyed as a result of the battle would be rebuilt.

Four days later, on March 3, the Russians reoccupied the town. As Fedoruk was on his way out of Bucha, he returned home to pick up some personal items, only to find a Russian officer with a machine gun in one hand and a list of Bucha officials in the other. The Russians were looking for him. Fedoruk pretended to be a neighbor keeping an eye on the mayor's house after he had allegedly left the city. When the officer asked for a passport, Fedoruk told him that he had left it at home. As the two walked toward Fedoruk's alleged home, the officer received a radio message and let Fedoruk go: he was supposed to return with the passport but never did.[27]

Lena Chychenina, an art critic who spent the first days of the occupation in Bucha, documented the change of the occupiers' attitude toward the local population. At first they behaved in friendly fashion, apparently believing that the people of Ukraine, oppressed by nationalists, were waiting to be liberated by the Russian army. When an old man in the house where Chychenina was staying approached a Russian soldier, he advised the civilians to go into the cellar and stay there for a few days, as he expected that the town would soon become a major battleground. When asked what the Russians were going to do in the town, he responded: "I have no idea. In general, we don't understand what's going on here."

In a few days, two Russian soldiers checked on the house and asked for passports and cell phones. Chychenina accompanied one of the soldiers to the cellar—he was apparently looking for men of fighting age. There were none. "Along the way he became shockingly frank," recalled Chychenina. "He complained about Putin and the commanders: 'They promised we'd be here three days, but a week and a half has gone by.' There's no food—one ration kit for six men. And its 'best before' date has passed. No place to sleep." On the first day of Russian presence in the town, Chychenina saw hungry soldiers breaking into a local food store. "They were taking chips and bread crusts of some kind out of there and starting to eat as they walked," she recalled. "It was obvious that they were hungry." The soldiers were also confused about their mission. "What's going on here in general and what their task is, they also don't know," said Chychenina, summarizing her conversation with the soldiers who checked her cellar.[28]

But the soldiers' friendly attitude toward the locals soon began changing to anger and violence. On March 4, the second day of the occupation of Bucha, Svitlana Kizilova, who was staying in Kyiv, learned that the Russians had killed her father-in-law, Valerii, in Bucha. He and his wife had just completed the renovation of their house in Bucha, where they were planning to spend their retirement. They refused to evacuate, saying: "This is our building and our land; we should protect what belongs to us." Valerii was ill, recovering from COVID. He was in the yard when Russian soldiers shot him in the head, apparently without warning. They then stormed into the house, where they found an old hunting rifle and claimed that the seventy-year-old Valerii had been a military man. They put his wife in the cellar and moved into the house, which they turned into their command post. From there they could clearly see the bridge from Bucha to Irpin—the last town on the way to Kyiv.[29]

Valerii was killed in the house with a view on the corner of Yablunska Street, where a satellite captured images of dead civilians. One man was killed while riding a bicycle, others executed in cold blood, their arms tied behind their backs. The first satellite images of corpses on the street are dated March 11. The bodies would remain where they lay until the Russians left the town on March 31. No one was allowed to remove them. The mayor of the city, Anatolii Fedoruk, who stayed incognito with his friends near Bucha, recalled: "Practically every evening at that time, there would be shooting of automatic weapons and machine guns." He did not know why the attitude of the Russians had changed but he had a plausible hypothesis. "My own conclusion is that it began when they understood that they would not be able to take Kyiv." Chychenina had a different explanation: "The longer they sat in Bucha, the angrier they became. With their own rulers and with us. And given that they could do nothing about their superiors, nothing remained but to start solving the 'Ukrainian question.' They grasped very quickly that no one was about to present them with flowers. Obviously, that was the collapse of their speculation."[30]

Vladyslav Verstiuk, a seventy-two-year-old historian, Ukraine's top expert on the history of the 1917 Revolution, spent a good part of March in a house on Yablunska Street in the town of Vorzel. A long street, it ran through both Vorzel and Bucha, and it was there that the bodies of the Ukrainian citizens killed in cold blood were found after the liberation of Bucha. The war caught Verstiuk, his wife, Iryna, and Iryna's elderly father, whom everyone addressed by his patronymic, Danylovych, in Hostomel, by surprise. In a few days they managed to escape to what seemed at the time a safer place, the house of Verstiuk's son, Bohdan, in Vorzel. But soon the war came to Vorzel as well.

On March 10, one day before satellite cameras caught images of dead bodies on Yablunska Street, Verstiuk saw a Russian armored vehicle stopping in front of his son's house. "The soldiers spread out across the meadow and started looking through the yards. Ours included. They fired into the air," wrote Verstiuk, recording the encounter with the occupiers in his diary. "Bohdan had a nervous conversation with them," continued Verstiuk. "They were evidently on edge. They said that they had no food or gas. They were from the Altai region." Miraculously, the encounter ended without violence. "They drove off. It was quiet again," continued Verstiuk. "But how will the next incident end (there is no doubt that there will be one sooner or later)?" Verstiuk and his family were able to leave their house on Yablunska Street on March 14 and made their way back to Kyiv.[31]

The Russians left Bucha in late March because of a successful Ukrainian counteroffensive that began on March 22. As the occupiers left the Kyiv suburbs and areas around Chernihiv and Sumy, they also abandoned the Chernobyl exclusion zone. On March 31 they forced representatives of the Ukrainian site administration to sign a document claiming that they had no complaints about the actions of the Russian troops, who had allegedly been protecting the site. The officials, feeling they had little choice, signed the document. In reality, the Russian occupation of the zone almost ended in nuclear disaster when electricity needed to cool spent fuel at the Chernobyl site was cut off because military action in the area damaged the transmission line.

The damage done to the power line incapacitated the pumps that supplied water to the cooling pond with fuel assemblies from reactor no. 3 at Chernobyl, which had been shut down in 2000. The fuel assemblies, which were still very hot and needed a constant supply of water to prevent overheating, could burst and release radiation into the environment. Only the use of the diesel generators and the supply of electricity from Belarus saved Chernobyl and the world from another nuclear accident. What the Ukrainians found at the site after the Russians left suggested that the story of Chernobyl contamination was far from over. After occupying the station, the Russian soldiers had dug trenches in the immediate proximity of the still radioactive Red Forest. Radiation thus unleashed may prove damaging to their health years from now.[32]

On April 10, Ukrainian forces moved into Bucha and other suburbs of Kyiv. The following day the mayor of Bucha, Anatolii Fedoruk, announced that the Russian occupiers had killed as many as 300 of his fellow citizens. Images of the civilian corpses were shared on social media throughout the world, producing outrage at the barbarity of the Russian troops, who had committed war crimes that President Biden described as genocidal. By April 4, the estimated number of civilians killed in Bucha was increased to 340. In the Kyiv region, one month after the liberation, the number of the dead was raised to 1,000, with more than 650 having been shot point-blank by Russian soldiers; the rest were victims of shelling from both sides. The Kyiv regional police announced in July that their officers had managed to locate and identify 1,346 civilians killed by the aggressors. Approximately 300 individuals were unaccounted for.[33]

On April 18, a few days after Biden had accused Russian troops of committing genocide, Vladimir Putin signed a decree awarding one of the units stationed in Bucha at the time of the massacres with the honorary title of "Guards Brigade." The same month, Lt. Col. Artyom Gorodilov, the commander of the 234th Air Assault Regiment, whose soldiers used the cell phones of the Ukrainian victims they killed to call home, was promoted to the rank of colonel.[34]

The news from Bucha put an end to the Russo-Ukrainian negotiations, the latest round of which had ended in Istanbul on March 29. Ukraine asked for a ceasefire, but Moscow was not interested. Disheartened, Kyiv was prepared to make a deal abandoning its plans to join NATO and accepting neutrality in return for the security guarantees provided by a number of countries, including the United States and Turkey. The final document was supposed to be negotiated by Putin and Zelensky. But a few days later, Zelensky visited Bucha to declare that the crimes committed by the Russian forces were making it harder to negotiate with Moscow. As the Russian offensive stalled and the Ukrainians reclaimed areas around Kyiv and Chernihiv, the negotiations had stalled as well. Kyiv recognized that Ukraine's best chance to stay independent and regain its territorial integrity was at the battlefield, not at the negotiation table.[35]

Exodus

The Russian invasion of Ukraine produced the largest refugee crisis in Europe since the end of World War II. Most of the displaced Ukrainians stayed in their country, moving from the east, north, and south to its central and western lands. The number of internally displaced persons was estimated at more than 8 million in mid-May. As of late August

2022, over 7 million citizens of Ukraine found temporary refuge abroad. Almost 3.5 million were received, housed, and fed in Poland, more than 9,000 in Romania, 700,000 in Germany, 620,000 in Hungary, and 466,000 in Moldova—the highest percentage per capita for any country that accepted Ukrainian refuges. The figure in Slovakia was 430,000, with 350,000 in the Czech Republic.

With men staying to fight, or not being allowed to leave the country if they were younger than sixty, the gender and age profile of Ukrainian war refugees in Europe was dramatically different from every other since the end of World War II. They were mostly women and children, the latter constituting 40 percent of the overall number. And they behaved differently from previous waves of refugees. European Union countries helped to place children in schools and allowed their parents to stay and work. Many jumped at that opportunity, but most wanted to return home at the first news that their town or village had been liberated, the front line had moved away from their hometown, or the danger had subsided. By mid-May 1.8 million Ukrainians had returned, with approximately 30,000 people per day crossing the Ukrainian border eastward rather than westward at that time. By the end of August 2022, only 1.36 million out of 3.5 million stayed in Poland—the rest had returned to Ukraine once the Russian advance was halted by the Ukrainian army.[36]

Every refugee had a story that was both unique and typical. They had all fled the destruction brought by the Russian invasion, abandoning all their possessions and trying to save their lives. They were driven out by the fear of death, not by the hardships of war, and often risked their lives in the process. "They destroyed everything . . . every building was damaged, there were fires. . . . I was scared that we would be killed trying to leave the city; we saw a car with two dead civilians," testified a refugee from Ukraine called Oleksandr on March 24, speaking at a press conference in Brussels. With his family, which included two small children, he had fled the town of Bucha, which at the time of the press conference was just another unfamiliar name on the map of Ukraine. Less than a week later, with photos from Bucha exploding on the Internet, everyone knew exactly what Oleksandr feared and was fleeing from.

"We felt our skin shaking from the shelling and the bombs. The first night in the bomb shelter was the coldest one in my life. I couldn't sleep, I couldn't close my eyes . . . the bombs just continued dropping," testified Diana, a student from Kharkiv, at the same press conference. "My colleague was inside the building," recalled Maria, a refugee from Mariupol, referring to the experiences of her male friend during the Russian bombing of the drama theater in that city. The theater was hit despite a huge sign saying "Children" painted on the plaza in front of the building. Six hundred people, including children, died in the bombing. "He told me of the screams of the children buried under the rubble," recalled Maria. "Emergency services could not get to them because the bombing didn't stop." Maria escaped from encircled Mariupol by bribing her way through Russian checkpoints with bottles of vodka and packs of cigarettes.[37]

What lay ahead for those who escaped Russian occupation or shelling were excruciatingly long lines on Ukraine's western borders with Poland, Slovakia, Hungary, Romania, and Moldova. "We are staying here for a long time, maybe six or seven hours already," Tamara Kulman, a refugee from the large city of Zhytomyr west of Kyiv, told a Western reporter when she was interviewed on the Polish border on the second day of the war. "I don't know how to leave my native country," continued Tamara, in all likelihood reflecting the sentiments of everyone in the seemingly endless line. "Actually, I don't want to leave my native country, but because of the invaders, I must leave it as fast as possible."[38]

In the coming days and weeks the lines would grow, with the time spent by refugees at the border crossings increasing from twenty-four hours to multiple days and nights. The only thing that compensated them for that long wait was the welcome that they received on the other side from Polish, Romanian, and other volunteers. Eastern Europe, which had turned into "Fortress Europe" a few years earlier with regard to Syrian refugees, was now becoming "Hotel Europe," a Europe without borders. If the physical borders were still there, cultural and emotional ones were gone. Eastern Europeans had seen Russian tanks before and knew better than anyone else what the Ukrainians were going through. They wanted the Ukrainian men to fight and were prepared to take care of their women and children. Now they were all in the same boat—a flotilla of ships endangered by the storm of Russian aggression.

In May 2022, the UN announced that the Ukrainian refugees had increased the number of displaced persons throughout the world to more than a billion. "It's a record that should never have been set," declared the UN High Commissioner for Refugees, Filippo Grandi. The *New York Times* editorial board appealed to world public opinion in an article entitled "Putin Knows What He's Doing with Ukraine's Refugees. This Is the World's Big Test." The article called for global solidarity in support of the countries that had taken refugees. The editors had been concerned mainly about the lack of unity among Western nations as they opposed Russian aggression and supported Ukraine's fight for independence. They also worried about Syrian and other refugees, seeing signs of global instability ahead. "As the world enters a period of greater instability," went the appeal, "its leaders can no longer ignore the need for a coordinated and humane response to all of those fleeing war and other desperate circumstances."[39]

9

EASTERN FRONT

With Russian troops unable to capture Kyiv, Moscow redirected the main thrust of its attack toward the east, preparing for a major battle to take the highly urbanized Donbas region of Ukraine. The takeover of the territories of the Donetsk and Luhansk regions was not only the declared goal of the "special military operation," but also the likely reason why Moscow rejected Kyiv's calls for the ceasefire at the Istanbul talks in late March. That was the chance to end the war on favorable-for-Moscow terms that Kremlin would never acquire again.

The first months of the war demonstrated several features of the coming new stage of Russia's war on Ukraine. One of them was that the Russians had limited air resources for bombing military targets and relied on missiles, many of which were anything but accurate and often hit civilian targets. Contrary to the expectations of some and the concerns of others, the Russian Air Force was never able to establish air superiority in Ukraine. Warned by intelligence data, quite possibly provided by Ukraine's Western allies, the Ukrainians managed to remove most of their planes immediately before Russian missile attacks on Ukrainian airfields in the early hours of February 24. No matter how few and outdated the available Ukrainian airplanes, they were saved from destruction and could contest the Russians in the skies.

Ukrainian anti-aircraft defense also turned out to be resilient. Stingers—American-made portable air defense systems provided by Western partners in the weeks leading up to the invasion—increased Ukrainian anti-aircraft resources. As the Russians lost planes and helicopters in growing numbers, they relied on missiles, some of them launched from ships in the Caspian Sea. The missiles would often fail to hit their targets, striking civilian objects instead of military ones. The Ukrainians shot down Russian cruise missiles as best they could in an effort to protect their cities.[1]

The Russian army also had different reasons for targeting Ukrainian cities so indiscriminately. They used artillery to destroy city infrastructure and deny the Ukrainian army defensive positions—a strategy they would use to the fullest in their attack on Mariupol and several Ukrainian cities in the Donbas. They also used artillery and missiles as weapons of terror, trying to break Ukrainians' will to resist. The main victims of terror bombing were Ukraine's eastern cities—the main battlefield of the war, where most of the population spoke Russian and the percentage of ethnic Russians was the highest in the country. It was Russians and Russian speakers, whom the Russian army had allegedly come to liberate, who would be the main victims of this war of attrition.

The First Capital

Among the first Ukrainian cities that found themselves under direct attack by the advancing Russian forces was Kharkiv, Ukraine's second-largest metropolis and first capital during the Soviet era. A major administrative and cultural center with a population of 1.5 million, it is located only 50 kilometers (30 miles) from the Russian border. Kharkiv was first assaulted by ground forces and then subjected to unrelenting bombardment.

Kharkiv had been the center of Cossack settlements in the region called Sloboda Ukraine since its founding in the mid-seventeenth century. At the turn of the nineteenth century, while the Romanov dynasty remained in power, the first university in Russian-ruled Ukraine was founded in Kharkiv. In the 1830s the city became the center of Ukrainian literary Romanticism, whose adherents formulated the cultural foundations of the modern Ukrainian project. In the 1920s Kharkiv became the capital of Soviet Ukraine and witnessed a Ukrainian cultural renaissance, passing on to subsequent generations the constructivist architectural masterpiece of the government center and the works of modernist writers. The cultural revival was short-lived, becoming known as the "executed renaissance"—quite a few Kharkiv authors either committed suicide or were killed by Stalin's terror machine in the 1930s. After the declaration of Ukrainian independence in 1991, Kharkiv became the publishing capital of Ukraine and home to some of the country's leading cultural figures, such as the poet, novelist, and performer Serhii Zhadan.[2]

The Russians badly wanted to take control of Kharkiv, bypassing other major urban centers of eastern Ukraine for several reasons. First, Kharkiv was a major transportation hub needed for the military campaign. Second, it was an almost exclusively Russian-speaking city, home to scores not only of Ukrainian but also Russian writers, poets, and actors. This heightened hopes in Moscow that Russian troops would be welcomed there, as required by the ideological slogan of the war—the protection of Russian speakers allegedly oppressed by Kyiv. Recent history also came into play. In 2014 the city had been on the verge of falling into the hands of Russian-backed separatists, like other cities and settlements of the Donbas. Third, Kharkiv was close to the Russian border; Russian troops could reach it without overextending their supply lines—the bane of their attack on Kyiv.

For all those reasons, war planners in Moscow must have considered Kharkiv not only a desirable but also an easy target. But here, as in many other cases, the campaign did not go according to plan. Unlike defenders of Ukrainian territory north of Kyiv along the basically open

Belarusian border, Ukrainian troops near Kharkiv were better prepared for the coming assault and resisted the Russian advance from the start. Russian ground forces began their offensive on the morning of February 24, crossing the border and attacking Ukrainian defensive positions close to the city with artillery fire. They also hit the city itself, with Russian shells claiming their first victims among civilians, including children.

On February 25, Russian advance units reached the outskirts of Kharkiv. The Ukrainians fought back, but in the following days the Russians broke into the city itself, and the Russian Defense Ministry announced it was accepting the surrender of Ukrainian troops in the city center. The announcement was premature at best: by the end of the day, the Ukrainians had expelled the Russian attackers. Kharkiv stayed Ukrainian.[3]

On February 27, the fourth day of warfare, with resistance continuing, the Russian military began to bombard the city they had failed to conquer. Dozens of civilians were killed and injured. That was just the beginning. More deadly strikes, often on residential areas, followed the next day, killing more people. The Russian army was using cluster bombs, which open in mid-air, split into hundreds of submunitions, and scatter indiscriminately over a huge area, killing anyone within a radius equal to several football fields. The use of such bombs was prohibited by the 2008 Convention on Cluster Munitions, signed by more than 100 countries. Russia was not a signatory, and now its troops were using cluster bombs against a city of 1.5 million inhabitants.[4]

A CNN journalistic investigation counted 11 cluster munition strikes on Kharkiv in the course of February 27 and 28. All of them were fired by Smerch (Tornado) multiple rocket launchers of the 79th Missile-Artillery Brigade of the Russian armed forces. Given the proximity of Kharkiv to the Russian border, the strikes were launched from Russian territory. The investigators concluded that the order to fire could have been given only by the commander of the Russian Western Military District, Colonel General Aleksandr Zhuravlev, a veteran of the brutal campaign in Syria, where he had twice served as commander of the Russian task force. On February 28 Zhuravlev's rockets killed scores of civilians in the city, including three children.[5]

"Klochkivska Street. Kharkiv. Bodies already recovered, bodies of Kharkiv civilians," wrote Kateryna Novak, a Kharkiv resident and book editor, in a Facebook post on February 28. She had led the revival of publications of Ukrainian historical nonfiction after the start of the 2014 war. Kateryna added a link to the video recorded on the spot: blood, fragments of human bodies, and the shell of the cluster bomb missile sticking up from the asphalt near the entrance to the apartment building. She added: "What remains is blood and THIS," referring to the human remains.

Kateryna's husband joined the city's territorial defense unit. She stayed at home with her aged mother and daughter, unable to leave them and go to a bomb shelter or seek safety outside Kharkiv, as some of her coworkers and neighbors had done. Kateryna stayed in the apartment, fearing a missile strike on her building every time she heard the siren, which sounded often. Before February 28, Kateryna had largely reposted other people's photos, videos, and posts; now she began a Facebook diary describing life under siege.[6]

"The occupiers have been terrorizing my Kharkiv for two days in succession with particular cruelty: aerial bombardment and rockets cease for a few hours at most," wrote Kateryna on March 1. "I'm writing now, and the sirens are wailing. Bombs have been pounding residential sections of the city for a second day. The suburbs are burning, and it's terrible to watch. There are blasts in the city center. Explosions near me: Paul's Field, Klochkivska Street . . . The remains of a shell whose name I don't know is sticking up from a linden tree in front of the meat store, whose windows have all been blown out. The 'liberators' are killing children, destroying civilian buildings, targeting facilities vital to the life of my city. . . . They are pounding, and pounding, and pounding, and pounding us! The occupiers couldn't take the city, so now they're bent on destroying us, 'liberating' us from our lives, rubbing us out! I'm at home. My family is with me. My husband is fighting. Glory to Ukraine!"

Kateryna started counting the days of the war. On March 2, she wrote: "Day 7. Now I know the sound that a plane makes when, flying very low, it maneuvers before making an airstrike. It seems to be flying straight for your head, not even into your head but right through it. I also know how the building shakes from that airstrike. And I also know what it's like to write to your colleagues on Messenger when they're hiding in the subway: Don't come out! There'll be another one right away! Yesterday there were powerful airstrikes, terrible and cruel. Then we went to sleep to the sounds of shooting on Culture Street. Our forces were driving out enemy sabotage and reconnaissance groups. In the morning they [the Russians] hit the National Police building and Karazin University ... Terrible blasts and smoke. They're terrorizing us! But my husband called this morning and said that he's all right. Glory to Ukraine!"

March 3, the eighth day of the war. Kateryna continued her diary: "Kharkiv is holding on. The terror continues. The suburbs are devastated. They are killing civilians. They are ruining the city. Colleagues have spent several days in the subway. Grad rockets again. Plane overhead again. I think of the sky as an enemy, as a potential threat. I'm beginning to hate it! This is abnormal. Close the sky. In any way whatever. I'm addressing the countries that support us. Up-to-date air defense forces of some kind, planes ... Anything. But right away!" Kateryna wrote her posts in German as well as Ukrainian in order to reach out to her friends in Europe. One of the comments on her original post was very brief but clear: "We need a second Front." There was no second front, and Ukraine's Western partners refused to provide planes or antiaircraft systems. They would come, but much later.

Kateryna kept writing about her own life and the deaths of others. "Looking at ruins is terrible, but knowing that children are constantly dying beneath those ruins tears at the heartstrings!" She then listed recent attacks on Kharkiv and environs: "Effects of an airstrike on the village of Yakovlivka in Kharkiv oblast." There, on the night of March 3, bombardment destroyed all forty-five buildings of the village, twenty-one of them completely. Two people were killed, two were missing, and

eleven wounded. "Effects of an attack on Kharkiv city center," continued Kateryna before adding: "Palace of Labor." On March 2, a Russian cruise missile hit the city council building. An airplane dropped a
bomb and destroyed half of a Kharkiv landmark, a building erected in
1916 and known since Soviet times as the "Palace of Labor."[7]

The bombardment of Kharkiv and environs continued throughout
March and April, and well into May, with Russian artillery located close
enough to the city to target all parts of it. By the end of April, close to
2,000 buildings had been either damaged or completely destroyed, and
hundreds of citizens killed. But the city and its defenders withstood the
assault. By mid-May Western observers declared the Ukrainian armed
forces victorious in the battle for Kharkiv. British intelligence reported
the sacking of one of the key Russian commanders in the area, Sergei Kisel of the First Guards Tank Army, allegedly for his failure to
take Kharkiv.[8]

The mayor of Kharkiv, Ihor Terekhov, went on record saying that
the citizens' attitude toward Russia had become radically negative, even
more so than in western Ukraine, which Putin considered the hotbed
of Ukrainian nationalism. The bombing of Kharkiv was the first case
of the mass killing of Russian speakers in the name of their liberation.[9]

The Steel of Azov

With a population of more than 430,000, two major metallurgical enterprises, and the largest port on the Sea of Azov, Mariupol, or the city of
Maria, was among the primary targets of the Russian invasion. Back in
May 2014, the city that accounted for 7 percent of the Ukrainian GDP
had been captured by Russian-backed separatist militias. But in June
of that year the Ukrainians managed to reclaim the city, thanks largely
to two volunteer battalions formed by the Ukrainian interior ministry.
One of the battalions, Dnipro-1, was recruited by the regional administration of nearby Dnipropetrovsk oblast. The other, Azov, included
former activists of the Revolution of Dignity, among them a group of

radical nationalists led by Andrii Biletsky, who became the battalion's first commander.[10]

In February 2015 Azov, now part of the National Guard of Ukraine, recaptured five settlements east of Mariupol from the pro-Russian rebels, moving the front line farther away from the city that had become its home base. By that time Biletsky had left the service, as had some of his nationalistically minded lieutenants. Over the next few years, the composition of the regiment changed dramatically. It cut its ties with far-right parties and ideologies but remained a prime target of Russian propagandistic attacks, which characterized the Revolution of Dignity and the Ukrainian government resulting from it as "fascists" and referred to the fighters of Azov as Nazis.[11]

On the morning of February 24, the officers and soldiers of the Azov regiment joined Ukrainian military formations in the battle for Mariupol. The city was subjected to heavy bombardment on the first day of the war, the demarcation line established by the Azov regiment in 2015 being only 40 kilometers (25 miles) to the east. The ground assault on the city began on the morning of February 24, only to be repelled by defenders, and was followed by a Russian amphibious landing west of the city. The goal was to take Mariupol and cut it off from Ukrainian armed forces in the area. The fall of Berdiansk to Russian forces breaking out of the Crimea on February 27, followed by the Ukrainian army's loss of its important defensive position at Volnovakha, north of Mariupol, all but sealed the fate of Mariupol itself.[12]

By March 2, the encirclement of Mariupol was complete: the Russians, advancing westward from the parts of the Donbas that they held, and from the recently captured Berdiansk in the west, covered all exits from the city. Within Mariupol, the Russians had both regular troops and units recruited in the Donbas "republics," reinforced with Chechen detachments loyal to the Russian-appointed governor of Chechnya, Ramzan Kadyrov. All these forces were under the command of General Mikhail Mizintsev, who had made a name for himself in the destruction of Aleppo in Syria and was now intent on doing the same in Mariupol.[13]

The defenders of the city inflicted heavy losses on the advancing Russian troops, and in mid-March they killed the commander of the Russian 151st Motorized Rifle Division, Oleg Mitiaev. But the opposing forces were highly unequal. The Azov regiment, led by the thirty-year-old Lieutenant Colonel Denys Prokopenko, the grandson of a Finnish soldier who had fought the Russians in the Winter War of 1939–40, found itself encircled along with the 36th Independent Marine Brigade under the command of Colonel Volodymyr Baraniuk and the 12th Operational Brigade of the National Guard of Ukraine under Colonel Denys Shleha. They were joined by border guards and local police detachments.

Unable to dislodge the defenders of Mariupol from their positions, the Russian forces intensified the shelling of the city that had begun on the first day of the war. Aerial, artillery, and missile attacks on the city had been methodically destroying one block after another, making no distinction between military and civilians, who found themselves under constant bombardment. The civilians suffered from a shortage of food, but most severely from the cold weather, as heat and electricity had been lost a few days after the start of the siege.

A ceasefire established on March 5 to start the evacuation of civilians was violated by the Russians as they continued shelling the city. That would become a pattern. The so-called "green corridors" for the evacuation of civilians would open, only to be closed either before or during the evacuation, making it difficult for inhabitants to leave the city for Ukrainian-controlled territory. Meanwhile, the Russian occupying forces encouraged—in the opinion of the Ukrainian side, forced—the evacuation of between 20,000 and 30,000 citizens of Mariupol to Russian-controlled areas.[14]

Russian aircraft used unguided bombs in their raids on the city, while artillery and missile fire was anything but precise, even if directed against military targets. On March 9 the Russians bombed a maternity hospital in Mariupol, killing dozens. Photos of pregnant women fleeing the half-destroyed building sent shock waves around the world. Seven days later, on March 16, even more gruesome images hit the world media services: an air attack on the city destroyed the Mariupol Drama

Theater, which served as a shelter for civilians. The authorities, running out of time and resources, began to bury the dead in mass graves.

By early April, the bodies were simply left lying on the streets—the city government had no people or resources to collect the dead, and it was too dangerous to do so, as the battle had long moved into the city itself. In the parts of the city captured by the Russian army, mobile crematoriums were used to burn the corpses. Vitalii Liubomirsky, who managed to get out of the city on April 7, told an American reporter: "You might know the smell of rotten meat, but this was deeper. The smell of rotting human bodies and of bodies being burned in crematoriums was everywhere." Mayor Vadym Boichenko estimated the death toll at greater than 21,000.[15]

In March the Ukrainian military made an attempt to de-blockade the city, but the armored group at their disposal was too weak to achieve the goal and had to retreat. During the last week of March, Ukrainian military intelligence started to organize helicopter raids from territory under its control to the besieged Ukrainian forces in Mariupol. Between late March and the end of April, sixteen MI-8 helicopters took part in seven missions that helped to bring out seventy-two volunteers of the Azov regiment, supply armaments and medication, and evacuate the wounded. That daring operation ended after the loss of three helicopters. During the first week of April, with the Ukrainian armed forces unable to provide air or artillery support, and the defenders running low on ammunition, medication, and food, Russian troops managed to take the city center and drive the Ukrainian forces back to the port area and the Azov Steel (*Azovstal'*) iron and steel works.[16]

On the night of April 11, Colonel Baraniuk led his marines in a desperate attempt to break through the Russian lines, but the sortie failed, with the troops suffering major losses and the survivors, including Baraniuk himself, forced to surrender. The remaining marines left their positions at the Ilyich metallurgical complex, the second of the city's major steelworks, and joined Prokopenko's Azov regiment at Azov Steel. They were also reinforced there by national guardsmen, remaining members of police units, and border guards retreating from the port area, making the Azov Steel complex the last part of the city under Ukrainian control. In the underground facilities of the complex, the Ukrainian military were joined by their families and other civilians fleeing the bombardment of the city.[17]

During the last week of April, Secretary-General Antonio Guterres of the United Nations, meeting with Vladimir Putin in the Kremlin and conducting negotiations across an extremely long table meant to protect the Russian leader from the visitor's germs, managed to get Putin's agreement to establish a humanitarian corridor in order to evacuate civilians from the Azov Steel complex. The first group of twenty left the city on April 30. The evacuation continued throughout the following week in breaks between heavy bombardment and attacks on the plant. It was over by May 7, with close to 500 people managing to leave the hellish underground chambers of the complex.[18]

With the civilians fleeing, the remaining Ukrainian troops continued fighting, although it was clear that their days were numbered. President Zelensky publicly declared more than once that he was doing all he could to save them. President Recep Tayyip Erdogan of Turkey apparently offered to evacuate the Ukrainian defenders to his country and keep them interned until the end of the war. A similar offer came from Switzerland. On May 11 the twenty-seven-year-old Kateryna Prokopenko, the wife of the Azov regiment's commander, Denys Prokopenko, and the wife of another defender of Azov Steel met with Pope Francis to ask him to intervene directly with Putin on behalf of their husbands. Kateryna was adamant that "Russian captivity is not an option." What they had in mind was the sort of "extraction" discussed by Volodymyr Zelensky and other European leaders.

Vladimir Putin turned down all the offers made by intermediaries. The Ukrainian government was left with no alternative but to negotiate an agreement with Russia according to which the defenders of Azov Steel would surrender to Russian troops on condition of their later exchange for Russian prisoners of war in Ukrainian custody. Zelensky announced that he was engaged in negotiations with France, Turkey, Israel, Switzerland, and the United Nations in an attempt to broker the deal. He also disclosed that he had begun those negotiations after his appeal to Western partners to provide arms for a Ukrainian break-through to Mariupol went unanswered.[19]

On May 16, the first fifty-three wounded defenders of Azov Steel surrendered and were taken to Russian-held territory. The surrender was authorized by the Ukrainian General Staff, which issued a state-ment praising the heroism of the officers and soldiers who were about to become prisoners of war. "The defenders of Mariupol are heroes of our time. They will live forever in history," read the statement. They were credited with tying up Russian forces and preventing "the imple-mentation of the [Russian] plan for the rapid capture of Zaporizhia."[20]

On May 20, the Russian military authorities declared the surrender of the last group of Ukrainian defenders of Azov Steel, the overall num-ber of prisoners of war being given as 2,439 officers. The statement, which observers at the time considered to have inflated the number of captured Ukrainian soldiers, called the officers and men of the Azov battalion "Nazis," raising the question of whether Russia would keep its part of the bargain and allow the exchange of Lieutenant Colonel Pro-kopenko and his comrades for Russian prisoners of war. The speaker of the Russian parliament made an announcement that its deputies would consider passing a law prohibiting the exchange of members of the Azov regiment.[21]

On the last day of the defense of Azov Steel, May 20, the press offi-cer of the Azov regiment, Dmytro Kozatsky, who had left his studies at the Ostrih Academy, Ukraine's oldest institution of higher learning, to join the army, wrote a final post on his Twitter account. "So this is all," read the post. "I give thanks for the shelter of Azov Steel, the place of my death and my life." The post was accompanied by photos taken by Dmytro on the spot. Many of them, including a photo captioned "Light will prevail," portraying a soldier standing in a beam of light coming from the roof, damaged by bombs, high above him, had already gone viral on Ukrainian social networks. But there were new images as well. Commenting on the photos, Kozatsky continued tweeting: "By the way, while I'm in captivity, I'll leave you some premium-quality photos; submit them to be considered for all journalistic prizes and photo contests; if I win something, that will be a great pleasure once I get out. My thanks to all for your support. Until we meet again."[22]

Kozatsky would return home in September to the news that his photos had won gold and silver at an international exhibition in Paris. He also received the Polish Grand Press Photo award. Kozatsky was released under the terms of a prisoner exchange in which the Ukrainians swapped the leader of the Russian lobby in Ukraine, Viktor Medvedchuk, allegedly Putin's personal friend, and fifty-four Russian military captured on the battlefield in Ukraine, for 215 Ukrainian prisoners of war, including 108 Azov fighters. Although Lieutenant Colonel Prokopenko, the commander of the Azov regiment, was released, most Azov fighters remained in Russian captivity. More than forty of them had been killed in late July by a staged explosion at the prisoner barracks in the prisoner-of-war camp at Olenivka in the occupied Donbas.[23]

For Putin, the fall of Azov Steel was the kind of victory for which he had hoped in the first days of the war: the capture of a Ukrainian stronghold in the Donbas and the surrender of "Nazis" from the Azov regiment. But the victory was pyrrhic at best, coming almost three months after the start of the offensive. It was won only by turning a major urban center into rubble: 90 percent of the buildings in Mariupol had been damaged and 40 percent of its housing completely destroyed. The Russian onslaught killed tens of thousands of civilians, forcing hundreds of thousands more to become refugees. This was done to a city in which, before the war, ethnic Russians had constituted 44 percent of the population, and Russian had been the dominant language in all aspects of life.[24]

The Battle for the Donbas

The fall of Mariupol allowed the Russian military command to focus on what Moscow had considered the main goal of the war's new stage—the takeover of the rest of the Donbas. That task had been formulated by Russian defense minister, Sergei Shoigu, back in late March, when he

had called off the troops from northern Ukraine and insisted on focusing "basic attention and basic efforts on attaining the principal goal—
the liberation of the Donbas." A few weeks later Shoigu's colleague,
minister of foreign affairs Sergei Lavrov, explained that with reference
to the Donbas, the Russian government and military had in mind the
entire territory of the Luhansk and Donetsk oblasts of Ukraine, not
only the parts controlled by their puppet regimes. "The point is that
when the referendum took place in 2014, the question concerned the
entire territory of those former oblasts," explained Lavrov, referring to
the referendums in the Donbas, which had not been recognized by the
international community.[25]

The Russian offensive began in earnest during the last week of
April, proceeding on a broad front along the existing demarcation
line of 2014. After withdrawing their troops from Kyiv and northern
Ukraine and freeing large military formations by pushing the defenders of Mariupol into the catacombs of Azov Steel, the Russian command had amassed as many as 60,000 troops—sixty-seven Battalion
Tactical Groups (BTGs)—for its broad new offensive. The Ukrainian
General Staff said at the time that there had been eighty-seven Russian BTGs in Ukraine as a whole, so three-quarters of all the Russian
troops were now committed to advancing in one direction. According to
President Zelensky, the Ukrainian armed forces, which were fighting
in brigade formations, had close to 44,000 men in the Donbas, while
Western assessments ranged from 40,000 to 50,000. It was generally
expected that the battle for the Donbas, or the second stage of the war,
would decide the outcome of the conflict as a whole.[26]

The Ukrainian forces in the Donbas were holding the 2014 line near
the city of Donetsk and east of Luhansk, which they had had eight years
to fortify. Indeed, it turned out to be very difficult for Russian troops
to break through that line. Their initial success occurred in the second
week of May, when they took the towns of Popasna and Rubizhne in the
center of the Ukrainian defensive lines east of Luhansk. Popasna was
reduced to rubble by Russian artillery fire, which surpassed in intensity anything that the Ukrainians could offer in return. The explana-

tion given by Ukrainian officials for the retreat of their forces was both simple and horrifying—there was no longer anything to defend, as the defensive positions had been razed to the ground.[27]

The Ukrainians expected the Russians to conduct pincer-type operations and create pockets by surrounding Ukrainian troops, as had often been done in fighting on the Eastern Front during World War II. Although the Russians tried to do so, their pincer movements from Izium in the north and from the northern shore of the Sea of Azov in the south, intended to create a large pocket, proved futile because of a successful Ukrainian counterattack near Izium, which halted the Russian advance. Further Russian attempts to conduct a pincer-type operation and create a smaller pocket also failed after their unsuccessful attempts to cross the Siverskyi Donets River. On May 11, Ukrainian artillery wiped out an entire battalion of the 74th Motorized Rifle Brigade near the village of Bilohorivka. Out of 550 officers and men who tried to ford the river, 485 were either killed or wounded, and eighty vehicles and pieces of equipment were destroyed.[28]

Having failed to create encirclements or pockets for almost a month after their offensive, the Russians had to engage in urban warfare of the type they had experienced in Mariupol. In late May, Russian troops fought their way through the Ukrainian defenses to the city of Siverodonetsk in eastern Luhansk oblast. House-to-house fighting ensued, with the Russians once again using aviation and artillery fire to destroy Ukrainian defensive positions. It was a slow and bloody but tried and true way of winning the war, with the attackers incurring enormous casualties; the Russians succeeded once again. Ukrainian troops left Siverodonetsk on June 24 and took up positions in the nearby city of Lysychansk.[29]

Lysychansk was the twin city of Siverodonetsk, located on the high bank of a river, which made it easy to defend and hard to capture. But this time the Russians confronted the Ukrainians with a real threat of encirclement in Lysychansk. They broke through Ukrainian lines and surrounded Ukrainian units near the villages of Hirske and Zolote, forcing them to withdraw along back roads. Once Russian troops all but encircled Lysychansk, the Ukrainians had no recourse but to abandon the city. Lysychansk, the last major urban center of Luhansk oblast still under Ukrainian control, fell to Russian troops and units formally belonging to the Luhansk People's Republic on July 2, less than ten days after Ukrainian forces abandoned Siverodonetsk.[30]

According to later estimates, during the fighting in the Donbas the Ukrainians were outgunned ten to one in artillery fire. Ukrainian munition depots had been among the prime targets of Russian missile attacks during the first days of the invasion, and now the Ukrainians had very few munitions left, leaving them barely capable of participating in artillery duels with the Russians. Their casualties mounted, reaching anywhere between 100 to 200 soldiers killed and as many as 800 wounded every single day of warfare. It was now Ukrainian infantry fighting Russian artillery. President Zelensky and Ukrainian officials sounded the alarm for weeks, but Ukraine's Western allies among the former Soviet-bloc countries had little Soviet-type ammunition to share, while NATO-type artillery pieces and artillery rocket systems were still on their way to the Ukrainian front lines.[31]

In Moscow, defense minister Shoigu reported to Putin that the "liberation" of the Luhansk People's Republic was complete. Putin, seemingly pleased, awarded the commander of Army Group Center and one of his subordinates with the Order of Hero of the Russian Federation. He told the troops to take a rest. It was the first such high-profile award and the first break for Russian troops since the start of the Donbas operation in late April. While the capture of Siverodonetsk and Lysychansk was lauded as a major victory, few independent observers doubted that the goals of the offensive had not been achieved. Only Luhansk oblast, where the Russians had been in control of most of the territory before February 2022, turned out to have been "liberated." There was no significant progress to report in the neighboring "Donetsk People's Republic," to say nothing of control of southern Ukraine and a bridge to Transnistria.[32]

The battle for the Donbas did not become the turning point in the war, as many had hoped or feared. In the second half of July, the head of Britain's MI6, Richard Moore, called the Russian advances "tiny" and suggested that the Russian army was about to "run out of steam." "Our assessment," continued Moore, "is that the Russians will increasingly find it difficult to find manpower and materiel over the next few weeks. . . . They will have to pause in some way, and that will give the Ukrainians the opportunity to strike back." Indeed, by mid-July the situation on the Donbas front line had stabilized. The previous few weeks had seen the arrival in Ukraine of Western artillery pieces, including the M777, 155-mm pieces of howitzer class, and ammunition for them.[33]

A major supplement to those artillery pieces were American High Mobility Rocket Systems (HIMARS), precision-targeted heavy artillery weapons that surpassed their Russian equivalents in accuracy and effective range. Ukrainians supplied with HIMARS ammunition could now hit targets within a 50-mile radius, finally giving them an advantage over the Russians. Although the number of HIMARS systems supplied at first was insignificant, within a few weeks a dozen of them destroyed as many as 100 so-called value targets, striking ammunition depots and command centers deep behind the Russian lines. "The introduction of HIMARS and M270 firing GMLRS into the UAF therefore can be seen as the point where the Russian offensive on Donbas ended and the war entered a new phase," wrote experts of the UK Royal United Services Institute for Defence Studies.[34]

The damage done by the HIMARS systems to Russian defensive and offensive capabilities became so significant that on July 18 the Russian media reported on Minister Shoigu's order to the Russian forces to find a way of destroying them. Four days later, Shoigu's ministry announced the destruction of four HIMARS, but on the same day General Mark Milley, the chairman of the US Joint Chiefs of Staff, speaking at a press conference in the Pentagon, stated that the claim was false. "To date, those systems have not been eliminated by the Russians," Milley told the journalists in attendance. A few days earlier he had told them that HIMARS strikes were "steadily degrading the Russian ability to supply their troops, command and control their forces, and carry out their illegal war of aggression." Milley promised that four more HIMARS systems would be shipped to Ukraine.[35]

The Death of the Russian Utopia

The Russian invasion destroyed the last vestiges of the belief that Ukrainians and Russians were fraternal peoples, to say nothing about their being one and the same people. That was true even of those features of common heritage to which Putin had sought to appeal in his articles and speeches, including historical roots, religious tradition, and joint resistance to the Nazi occupation.

In the city of Pereiaslav in the Kyiv region, where Hetman Bohdan Khmelnytsky had sworn allegiance to the Russian tsar in 1654, the city authorities removed the monument to the "reunification of Russia and Ukraine," the centerpiece of propaganda about Russo-Ukrainian unity. The Kyiv monument to the "Motherland" defending the city against Nazi aggression, a sword raised in one hand and a shield in the other, built by the Soviets in the 1980s and known as a symbol of Kyiv, remained intact but changed its meaning. It was now considered a symbol of resistance to the Russian invasion. There was also a new attitude toward the lyrics of one of the most popular Soviet songs, which began with lines known to every schoolchild in the USSR: "On June the twenty-second / Precisely at four in the morning / Kyiv was bombed / And we were told that the war had begun." The lines referred to the German bombardment of Kyiv in June 1941, but now the invaders bombing the city were Russians.[36]

In mid-July UNESCO identified 163 cultural sites destroyed or damaged by the Russian war on Ukraine. It was a sad irony that Russian bombardment was killing Russian speakers and destroying landmarks and locations claimed by Russian imperial and then Soviet culture. Andrei Krasniashchikh, a professor at Kharkiv University and an author who had been writing and publishing in Russian, decried the demolition of Kharkiv by Russian bombardment as destruction of pre-Soviet and Soviet Russian culture in Ukraine by those who had allegedly come to protect it.[37]

"Bernes," wrote Krasniashchikh, referring to the famous Soviet actor and singer Mark Bernes. "His house is in Kharkiv. I don't know whether it has survived. It's not far from Seminary Street, which was struck by a bomb." Bernes, an ethnic Jew and a native of Nizhyn in Chernihiv oblast, was one of the most recognized names in Soviet Russian culture, a performer of World War II–era hits, as well as the coauthor and performer of the 1961 Soviet antiwar song, "Do the Russians Want War?" According to the song, having sacrificed so much in World War II, the Russians did not want war. "Ask the soldiers / Who lie beneath the birches," went the lyric. "And their sons will answer you / Whether the Russians want war!" In early March 2022 the song was performed on the satirical show *ZDF Magazine Royale* in protest against Russia's attack on Ukraine.[38]

"I don't know what has become of the homes of Shulzhenko, Bunin, and Khlebnikov," continued Krasniashchikh, listing the names of other famous residents of Kharkiv, the Soviet singer Klavdiia Shulzhenko and the Russian writers Ivan Bunin and Velimir Khlebnikov. "His house," wrote Krasniashchikh about Khlebnikov's old place, "is next to the oblast police department, which was bombed on March 2, and a bomb fell on the art museum with works by Aivazovsky, Repin, and Levitan." All three painters mentioned by Krasniashchikh were considered the pride of Russian culture. "The home of [Isaak] Dunaevsky," he continued, referring to the famous Soviet composer and conductor, "on Yaroslav the Wise Street, there was bombing there as well. They are bombing everywhere. 2,055 buildings. The fine university campus has shattered windows. Our department is on the sixth floor opposite." Krasniashchikh then reported on the news from Bucha: "In the rucksack of a Russian soldier killed in Ukraine they found a book by Bulgakov, a little gold cross, a child's earrings with ladybird ornaments, and gold teeth." He titled his article "How Russian Culture Is Burning under Bombardment."[39]

In the first week of May a Russian missile destroyed the museum of Hryhorii Skovoroda, a famous eighteenth-century philosopher who has been considered the founder not only of Ukrainian but also of Russian religious philosophy—a major influence on Vladimir Soloviev and Nikolai Berdiaev. The museum was located fifty kilometers (30 miles)

northeast of Kharkiv in the village of Ivanivka, renamed Skovorodynivka after the philosopher, who died there. The Ukrainian minister
of culture, Oleksandr Tkachenko, believed that the destruction of the
museum had been deliberate. "Skovorodynivka is distant from other
villages and infrastructure; in fact, there are only fields in the vicinity,"
said the minister. "I have no doubt that they were aiming at Skovoroda
in particular. I think that he himself once said, 'Don't fraternize with
those hiding evil intentions.'"[40]

Also under attack were monuments of Kyiv's princely era—a heritage that Putin and Russian nationalists of all stripes considered their
own. That was the case in the city of Chernihiv, one of the princely
capitals of Kyivan Rus' claimed by Russian writers, thinkers, and politicians of every persuasion as the cradle of their civilization. First mentioned in the Kyivan Chronicle under the year 907, Chernihiv was
the site of a number of architectural monuments of the medieval era,
including the eleventh-century Holy Savior Cathedral and the Dormition Cathedral, the Yelets Monastery, and the Church of St. Elijah, all
dating from the twelfth century. There were also buildings of the early
modern era, built in what has been known in Ukraine as the Cossack
baroque style.[41]

With a population approaching 300,000, located less than 90
kilometers (56 miles) from the Russian border and 155 kilometers (96
miles) northeast of Kyiv, Chernihiv was in the path of Russian troops
advancing toward Kyiv on the left bank of the Dnieper. They reached the
city on the first day of the war but were repelled by Ukrainian defenders, who even took some Russians prisoner. The Russian commanders
decided to bypass the city, moving on toward Kyiv. Instead of storming
Chernihiv, they bombarded it, beginning on February 25, the second
day of the war. Two days later, explosions could already be heard in the
historic center of Chernihiv.[42]

On March 6, the bombardment was particularly intense. Forty-
seven people were killed, and bombs hit the building of the literary and
art museums. The twelfth-century Yelets Monastery was damaged on
the following day. The bombardment of the surrounded city contin-

ued through the rest of March, claiming hundreds of additional civilian victims and destroying more of the city's museums, libraries, and university buildings. The siege came to an end on March 31, when the Ukrainian army recaptured the strategic highway connecting Kyiv and Chernihiv. The city, partly ruined, with half its population turned into refugees, began to return to some semblance of normality and count its losses—human, physical, and emotional.[43]

The sixty-one-year-old professor of history Serhii Lepiavko, author of numerous books on the history of Chernihiv and its environs, who had joined the city's territorial defense unit together with his two sons, gave an interview to the local media. "It was important for me, as a Chernihivite, to remain on the streets of my city and defend it," said Lepiavko, explaining his decision to stand and fight. He then betrayed his greatest fear, which was not that of dying but of losing the city's architectural jewels: "I personally feared that it would come to fighting in the ruins of the Church of St. Catherine or the Holy Savior Cathedral. But I knew for certain that I would never leave. It would have been the last act of my life."[44]

Russian bombs cracked open not only church buildings but also the edifice of the Moscow Patriarchate. The Ukrainian Orthodox Church under the jurisdiction of Moscow rebelled against Patriarch Kirill, who had issued a statement at the beginning of the war calling on "all parties to the conflict to do everything possible to avoid civilian casualties" and invoked the tenth-century baptism of Kyivan Rus', the state from which both Ukrainians and Russians trace their origins, as part of a tradition that should help to overcome "the divisions and contradictions that have arisen and have led to the current conflict."[45]

Kirill's formal subordinate and ally in Ukraine, Metropolitan Onuphry, the head of the Ukrainian Orthodox Church subject to the Moscow Patriarchate, had little tolerance for his superior's refusal to name and condemn the aggressor. "Russia has launched military actions against Ukraine, and at this fateful time I urge you not to panic, to be courageous, and to show love for your homeland and for one another," stated the metropolitan, who had been considered a staunch supporter of Ukraine's ties with Moscow, in an address to his flock. He then appealed to the Russian president, all but accusing him of the "sin of Cain" by offering a very different interpretation of the common baptism of Rus' in 988 by Prince Volodymyr of Kyiv, to which Patriarch Kirill had alluded.

"Defending the sovereignty and integrity of Ukraine," continued Onuphry, "we appeal to the President of Russia and ask him immediately to stop the fratricidal war. The Ukrainian and Russian peoples came out of the Dnieper baptismal font, and the war between these peoples is a repetition of the sin of Cain, who killed his own brother out of envy. Such a war has no justification either from God or from people." Metropolitan Onuphry's statement was one of many similar pronouncements, public and private, issued in Kyiv and other cities of Ukraine after the Russian attack. In June Bishop Lonhyn, who was close to Onuphry, challenged Kirill by "thanking" him during a church service for the bloodshed that he had *endorsed*. "Your Holiness, we thank you for your blessing. For the fact that people are dying, and blood is being shed. For having bombed our monasteries, our churches. For continuing to kill our monks, our priests. We thank you, Your Holiness, for your great blessing of bloodshed."[46]

The council of the Ukrainian Orthodox Church subordinate to the Moscow Patriarchate, convened in late May 2022, registered its "disagreement" with Patriarch Kirill and made a step toward independence from Moscow, allowing his flock not to pray for the patriarch and its churches to use consecrated oil supplied by Kyiv rather than Moscow— a major step toward full autocephaly according to Orthodox practice. The Moscow Patriarchate responded when one of its eparchies in the "Donetsk People's Republic" refused to pray for Metropolitan Onuphry. Despite the war, Kyiv still maintained formal control over parts of its former eparchies on the territory of the Donetsk and Luhansk "republics." But now, with those statelets recognized by Moscow as independent, and Kyivan bishops rebelling against Patriarch Kirill's endorsement of the war, all bets were off. The parishes of the Moscow Patriarchate in Ukraine were splitting as well. In December, President Zelensky initiated a law prohibiting activities of the religious organizations affiliated with the "centers of influence" of the Russian Federation.[47]

The stubborn resistance of the Ukrainian government and public to Western warnings about the coming invasion was at least partly based on the belief that Russia, historically and culturally close to Ukraine, might launch a new round of hybrid warfare but would not dare to wage a large-scale war against Ukraine. And surely Russia would never attack Kyiv, which Putin himself, like many predecessors, had called the "mother of Russian cities." That definition came from the medieval Kyivan Chronicle. But far from inspiring gratitude for ostensible "fraternal assistance," the war helped to destroy a number of Russian imperial and Soviet myths. Instead of arresting the development of the Ukrainian nation and destroying its commitment to sovereignty, the Russian invasion in general and the assault on Kyiv in particular strengthened the Ukrainian people's sense of identity and unity, endowing it with a new raison d'être, new narratives, and new heroes and martyrs.[48]

10

—

THE BLACK SEA

On April 15, 2022, reporters in downtown Kyiv photographed a scene unusual for a city under threat of missile bombardment: dozens of people formed a long line beginning on Khreshchatyk Boulevard, turning left toward Maidan Square, and disappearing into the doorway of the city's main post office.

Someone suggested that this lineup was longer than those for the latest iPhone. Indeed, given that sirens could go off any minute announcing another missile attack on the Ukrainian capital, those standing in line were not risking their lives to get another iPhone. Nor were they waiting to pick up packages or send money transfers. Instead, they were there to buy a stamp costing 23 hryvnias (approximately 8 cents). It had been released three days earlier but was unavailable online. At one of the local online marketplaces, 5,000 sets of the stamp were sold in three minutes, with 2,500 customers buying it every second. To get the stamp, one had to stand in line.[1]

The stamp had a somewhat unusual design. It depicted a soldier standing with his back to the viewer, holding an automatic rifle in his left hand and raising his right hand. The soldier stood on a yellow beach with the blue sea in front of him, replicating the colors of the Ukrainian national flag. The Ukrainian coat of arms was displayed in the upper right corner of the stamp. But it was not the colors or the coat of arms that attracted the viewer's attention. If one looked closely enough at the soldier's raised hand, it became apparent that he was giving the finger to the heavily armed cruiser depicted in the blue waters of the sea. Those in the lineup knew that the cruiser was Russian. They also knew what the soldier on the stamp had replied to the captain of the cruiser when ordered to surrender along with his fellow Ukrainian soldiers. "Russian naval ship, go fuck yourself!" were the words immortalized on the newly released stamp.

It was the "based on a true story" stamp that everyone in Ukraine wanted to have. The episode it depicted had taken place on the first day of the war, February 24, when the flagship *Moskva* of the Russian Black Sea Fleet approached Snake Island, a tiny piece of rock 0.4 miles long and less than 0.3 miles wide, approximately 35 kilometers (22 miles) off the Ukrainian Black Sea coast. The island had been known to the ancient Greeks as the Island of Achilles. The Greeks referred to the Black Sea itself as Euxinos Pontos, and the Romans simply as Pontus, after the name of the Greek god of the sea. The strategically important Snake Island was defended by thirteen Ukrainian guardsmen. The Russian approach to the island became the first act of the Pontic War of the new era, which was fought both on the Black Sea and in the Pontic steppes north of it.[2]

The captain of the *Moskva* introduced himself by radio with the words: "This a Russian military ship" and demanded surrender. A Ukrainian border guard named Roman Hrybov used the words that would go viral after a Ukrainian radio surveillance unit on shore intercepted the exchange, which quickly became known to the media. The Ukrainian radio operators soon lost contact with the border guards. It was assumed that they had been attacked and killed. The first reports on the matter turned out to be false: the guards had been captured by the Russian navy and were later exchanged for Russian POWs. Hrybov returned home from Russian captivity a hero.[3]

For Ukrainians, the episode, the words spoken, and now the stamp served as symbols of their defiance in the face of overwhelming odds. The Ukrainians simply did not have a navy to repel the Russian onslaught on the Black and Azov Seas. The shore of the Sea of Azov was almost entirely lost to Russia within the first few days of the war. The Russian takeover of Snake Island was part of their preparations for amphibious landings on the Ukrainian mainland to capture or assist ground troops in capturing the city of Odesa, Ukraine's third-largest urban center, with a population of more than one million.

The Fall of Taurida

President Zelensky's headquarters in Kyiv and the city itself were the prime targets of the Russian attack on Ukraine when it began on February 24. But the Russian assault also proceeded along the old front line of 2014 in the Donbas. The Russians and their proxies, the military forces of the two puppet statelets, found the Ukrainian defenses hard to penetrate. The Ukrainians had been fortifying their positions for almost eight years, placing their best-trained and -equipped troops there. The Russians were much more successful in the south, where their most effective troops broke out of the Crimea and advanced deep into the Ukrainian mainland region between the Dnieper and Molochna Rivers historically known as Taurida (called Tauris by the ancient Greeks) because of its proximity to the Crimea.[4]

On the first day of the war, Ukraine suffered a major defeat not at the walls of the Chernobyl power plant in the north but at the Kakhovka Dam across the Dnieper River in the south of the country. The dam was captured late in the morning of February 24 by Russian troops that advanced toward it along the main highways in tanks, armored personnel carriers, and trucks with the letter "Z" painted in white on their fronts, backs, and sides to help distinguish Russian forces from the Ukrainian units. They drove from the Crimea with apparent ease, meeting no Ukrainian resistance to speak of. The Ukrainian troops were elsewhere, and the city's territorial defense unit, consisting of some eighty men, had no arms. The Russians arrived around 11:00 a.m. and raised their banner over the city. "There are tanks without insignia at the hydroelectric station," reported the Ministry of Energy in Kyiv that day.[5]

Tavriysk, a satellite city of Nova Kakhovka, housed the headquarters of the North Crimean Canal, which had been built to bring water from Dnieper to the Crimea. The mayor of Tavriysk, Mykola Rizak, could not get into the headquarters of the canal administration because a tank was pointing its gun at his car. He called the regional authorities in Kherson, but they did not believe him. "I tell them about this, and they don't believe it. But I have a question: how could Russian tanks, Grad missiles, and armored personnel carriers make it to Tavriysk from Armiansk [in the Crimea] in four hours? Where are our first and second defensive echelons?" Rizak asked a Ukrainian reporter. Those were the questions on the minds of many citizens of Tavriysk and Nova Kakhovka, but there were no immediate answers either from Kherson or from Kyiv.[6]

After the Russian annexation of the Crimea, Ukraine blocked the North Crimean Canal, which had brought Dnieper water to the peninsula. The Crimean economy, the agricultural sector in particular, was immediately affected. The occupying authorities tried unsuccessfully to find other sources of water, but the problem worsened with every passing year. Russian politicians spoke openly about establishing a corridor from the Russian-held areas of the Donbas to the Crimea along the northern shore of the Sea of Azov, and the new Russian-installed leaders of the Crimea made no secret of their desire to control the flow of Dnieper water to the peninsula.[7]

The Ukrainian authorities were cognizant of the danger posed to the Kakhovka Dam and the Tavriysk channel by possible Russian military action. But like the Russians in their attempt to capture Kyiv, they were preparing for the last war, not the coming one. The Russians expected the Ukrainians to put up scant military resistance and counted on the population to greet them as liberators—the scenario engineered by Russian intelligence in the Crimea. The Ukrainians, for their part, were getting ready for a repetition of the Crimean scenario in southern Ukraine—an attempt to create chaos in that region, followed by a limited Russian military operation. Russian forces would be "invited" into the region by their agents, proclaimed as "people's mayors" of cities and villages.

In mid-February, as the world media were bursting with articles predicting a possible Russian attack on Ukraine, President Zelensky, accompanied by a large group of Ukrainian and foreign reporters, visited Ukrainian villages north of the Crimean isthmus to observe exercises conducted by 1,300 police officers, border guards, and emergency workers. The scenario to which they were preparing to react was described as follows: "An infopsychological operation is being conducted by electronic and social media broadcasting on occupied territories and regions of mainland Ukraine. Information is being circulated among the population of border towns according to which there is a serious problem in the energy sector. This produces mass disorder and attempts to blow up dams on the North Crimean Canal in order to restore water supply to the Autonomous Republic of the Crimea and seize administrative buildings."[8]

The Ukrainians were preparing for a police action, not a military operation. What they got on the morning of February 24, less than two weeks after the exercise, was an all-out military assault on the Ukrainian mainland. It began at 4:00 a.m. with heavy bombardment of three Ukrainian checkpoints on the Crimean isthmus—Chonhar, Kalanchak, and Chaplynka. The approaches to the peninsula and the roads had been mined by the Ukrainian side long before the invasion. But none of the bridges crossed by Russian tanks, armaments, equipment, and soldiers had been blown up. The mines did not work. Ukrainian experts would later suggest a number of possible reasons for that: the officers who were supposed to activate the explosives were killed in the assault; Russian commandos had disarmed the system before the attack; or someone on the Ukrainian side had betrayed the location of the mines or did not follow the order to activate the system in case of attack.[9]

The Russian troops passing through the Ukrainian checkpoints toward Nova Kakhovka and other cities and towns on the Ukrainian mainland belonged to the 49th and 58th armies, whose units were either stationed in the Crimea or moved there before the invasion. They broke out of the peninsula facing little Ukrainian resistance—the Ukrainian General Staff would later claim that their forces in the region were outnumbered 15 to 1—and used the existing road and railway network to proceed quickly to Nova Kakhovka, northwest of the Crimea, and to the city of Melitopol, northeast of the peninsula. Russian paratroopers would be flown by helicopters to seize bridges ahead of troops advancing by land. They often wore unmarked uniforms or even put civilian clothing atop their uniforms to confuse the Ukrainian military.[10]

There were numerous bridges in the area crossing the North Crimean Canal, but the most important one was the bridge across the Dnieper itself. The Antonivka Bridge connects the left bank of the river, from which the Russian invasion of mainland Ukraine had been proceeding, with its right bank and the city of Kherson, the regional capital, with a population of 300,000. To reach Kherson, proceed to the city of Mykolaiv, and go on to Odesa, the invaders needed to capture and control the Antonivka Bridge. That became the task of units of the 49th army, commanded by a veteran of the Russian war in Syria, the forty-eight-year-old Lieutenant General Yakov Rezantsev.

The Ukrainian armed forces expected battle north of the Crimea, but with the Russian troops proceeding quickly along the main roads and threatening the Ukrainians from the rear, the order to the troops was to retreat and avoid encirclement. The twenty-three-year-old commander of the tank company of the 59th Ukrainian brigade, Yevhen Palchenko, was awakened about 4:30 a.m. in the brigade's camp north of the Crimea by sounds of bombardment. A youngster who looked at least five years younger than his actual age, Palchenko was already a veteran of the anti-terrorist operation in the Donbas, as the Ukrainian government called its war there. Following his battalion commander's order, Palchenko first led his company north toward Nova Kakhovka to block a possible attack by Russian troops that had already captured an area on the flank of his brigade, which was retreating toward the Dnieper.[11]

He was then ordered to proceed to the Antonivka Bridge and secure it for the movement of Ukrainian units toward Kherson. His tanks arrived there close to 8:00 p.m., only to discover that the bridge was already in the hands of Russian paratroopers. Palchenko's tanks opened fire at the Russian amphibious vehicles, destroying two of them and securing the bridge. For the next hour he watched as retreating Ukrainian troops crossed the bridge and regrouped on the right bank of the Dnieper. Toward midnight, the Russians returned with an air attack on Palchenko's company and the rest of the tank battalion that had joined him later. Russian infantry followed. It was the start of a three-day battle for control of the bridge, defended by two Ukrainian brigades. For his role in the battle, Palchenko would be awarded the Star of Hero of Ukraine by President Zelensky.[12]

The heroism of Palchenko and men like him notwithstanding, the Ukrainian armed forces eventually lost control of the Antonivka Bridge. Russian troops had crossed the Dnieper across the Kakhovka Dam north of the bridge and now threatened the Ukrainian units from the rear. The Ukrainians also failed to blow up the bridge when retreating, and their attempt to do so from the air failed. The strategic bridge ended up under Russian control. The city of Kherson, along with its key airport near the village of Chornobaivka, was taken by Russian troops on March 3 after having been fully encircled. This was a major victory for the Russians. Palchenko's unit and the other Ukrainian troops retreated from Kherson to accept battle on the approaches to Mykolaiv.[13]

The Russian soldiers, angry, cold, and hungry, marched into Kherson and immediately began to help themselves to whatever they could lay their hands on. "We reached the seaport of Kherson," wrote the thirty-three-year-old Russian paratrooper Pavel Filatiev, recalling his entrance into the city. "Everyone began to scout buildings in search of food, water, a shower, and a place to sleep. Some started to bring in computers and anything else of value that they could find. I was no exception: I found a hat in a wrecked wagon in the area and took it. The offices had dining rooms with kitchens and refrigerators. Like savages, we consumed all that was there. Overnight we turned everything upside down." The Russian occupation of Kherson had begun.[14]

On the first day of March, Russian troops approached Enerhodar, a city approximately 200 kilometers (124 miles) north of the Crimean isthmus. It is home to the Zaporizhia nuclear power plant, the largest in Europe, which includes six of Ukraine's fifteen nuclear reactors. The citizens of Enerhodar refused to let the aggressors in, putting up roadblocks at the entrance to the city and staging a mass demonstration with Ukrainian flags. The Russian military originally backed off, not daring to storm a nuclear installation. Instead, they asked the mayor, Dmytro Orlov, to let them in just to take a selfie against the backdrop of the power plant and report to Moscow that they had taken control of the facility. The mayor refused.[15]

The Russians soon returned in full force. In the early hours of March 4, under cover of darkness, they attacked the nuclear power plant. It was protected by a small detachment of the Ukrainian national guard that fought back. The operators began the lengthy process of shutting down the reactors by reducing their power levels. The public address system transmitted a message to the attackers: "Stop shooting at a dangerous nuclear facility. Stop shooting immediately! You are threatening the security of the whole world!" It had no effect. The shelling continued, setting one of the buildings of the nuclear complex on fire. Thanks only to the heroism of the firefighters, the blaze was extinguished. But the Russian military captured the plant, took its personnel hostage, and placed it under the command of a Russian military officer.[16]

President Zelensky declared the military takeover an act of nuclear terrorism. Rafael Mariano Grossi, the head of the International Atomic Energy Agency, issued a statement of his own: "Firing shells in the area of a nuclear power plant violates the fundamental principle that the physical integrity of nuclear facilities must be maintained and kept safe at all times." He once again avoided direct reference to Russia. But the American representative to the United Nations, Ambassador Linda Thomas-Greenfield, was much more straightforward. "Russia's attack last night put Europe's largest nuclear power plant at grave risk. It was incredibly reckless and dangerous," she declared at an emergency meeting of the UN Security Council. She added: "The world demands that Russia abide by international humanitarian law, which prohibits intentionally targeting civilians and civilian infrastructure."[17]

Loyalty and Betrayal

How could the Russians break out of the Crimea and march toward Nova Kakhovka and the Antonivka Bridge almost unopposed? That question was on the minds of many Ukrainians who ended up under the Russian occupation, as well as those living and fighting in other parts of Ukraine. Rumors began to circulate that the minefields blocking the exit from the Crimea had been deactivated prior to the invasion. The Ukrainian General Staff called the rumors groundless, appealing to the public to await a full investigation at the end of hostilities and suggesting that the Ukrainian armed forces had simply been outnumbered by the Russians.[18]

The Security Service of Ukraine (SBU) was already at work. Surprisingly, they soon arrested one of their own, the commander of the Kherson anti-terrorist center, Lieutenant Colonel Ihor Sadokhin, on charges of high treason. He had apparently supplied the Russians with maps of the minefields and then coordinated Russian air attacks once the SBU team under his command abandoned Kherson. Zelensky demoted Sadokhin's superior, General Serhii Kryvoruchko, the head of the Kherson branch of the SBU, stripping him of his rank. Kryvoruchko and his men had apparently left Kherson on the first day of the war. It appeared that the SBU was sharing Ukraine's secrets with the enemy.

The head of the SBU, Zelensky's childhood friend Ivan Bakanov, lost the president's confidence. The problems were not limited to Kherson. A few hours before the Russian invasion, General Andrii Naumov, the deputy of the head of the SBU in charge of internal security, fled the country. He would be arrested a few months later by Serbian authorities on charges of money laundering. The customs officers found €600,000 (about US $575,000) and an undisclosed number of diamonds in his car. In July Zelensky fired Bakanov, citing numerous cases of high treason by SBU officers. A few days earlier, there had been media reports about the arrest of Oleh Kulinich, the former head of the SBU department in charge of Crimean intelligence networks. He was charged with high treason.

Problems with loyalty of the leaders of Ukraine's main intelligence service were not new. Charged with fighting corruption, some departments of the service became involved in corruption schemes themselves, and their officers were easy targets for recruitment by their Russian counterparts. As politicians valued personal loyalty over professional qualifications and tried to use the SBU to undermine their opponents and protect themselves, unqualified candidates were appointed to senior positions. Bakanov's deputy, Andrii Naumov, had previously directed the center managing the Chernobyl exclusion zone, while Bakanov himself, a lawyer by training, had no experience working in the intelligence services, or indeed government services of any kind, before becoming head of the SBU. Zelensky was learning the hard way that personal loyalty was no substitute for competence and loyalty to the country.[19]

The real heroes of Ukraine's time of troubles in the south were the local mayors. With their cities and towns surrounded by Russian forces, they were faced with the dilemma of staying in office or leaving their cities and electors. Instructions from Kyiv were at first nonexistent and then confusing. Many mayors decided to stay and keep running their cities but refused to cooperate with the occupiers, even moving their offices to different places if the Russian military took over city halls and mayor's offices. That tactic could work for a while, but not indefinitely—a lesson learned the hard way by the popular mayor of Melitopol, Ivan Fedorov. He was arrested by the occupiers and, luckily for him, later exchanged for nine Russian prisoners of war.[20]

In Kherson, mayor Ihor Kolykhaev refused to remove Ukrainian flags from city buildings, stayed in touch with Kyiv, and gave interviews to the Ukrainian media weeks after the occupation. The Russian military command did not target him right away, apparently concerned about the reaction of hundreds of thousands of citizens in the large southern cities. The Russians simply lacked the resources to deal with so many people during the first days and weeks of the war. Besides, Kolykhaev had the full support of the city council, which rejected a proposal to proclaim the "Kherson People's Republic," an analogue of the puppet states created by the Russians in the Donbas in 2014.

Sunday, March 13, ten days after the occupation of Kherson, was the 76th anniversary of the city's liberation from the Nazis in 1944. Thousands of citizens marched with Ukrainian blue-and-yellow flags to protest the occupation. They chanted: "Go home," "Go home while you're still alive," "Ukraine above all," "Glory to the nation, death to enemies," "Fuck off, Russian soldier," "Kherson is Ukraine," "Russian soldiers are fascist occupiers."[21] The Russian military opened fire, aiming at the ground in front of the protesters and injuring one of them. When protests resumed the following Sunday, the Russian military used tear gas grenades against the demonstrators. The newly created Russian military administration went after the organizers of the demonstrations, threatening and kidnapping them. Kolykhaev was removed from office by the Russian military command in late April and abducted in late June.[22]

In March, demonstrations against the occupation were broken up not only in Kherson but also in other occupied southern cities, including Nova Kakhovka, the major transport center of Melitopol, and Berdiansk on the Sea of Azov. By April, public resistance had been crushed by units of the Russian Guards, trained to disperse mass protests and serve as an occupying force. They blocked the broadcasts of Ukrainian television channels and either cut mobile communications or brought them under control. The Russian ruble was introduced as the new currency. The occupiers established new civilian administrations, recruiting local politicians predominantly from pro-Russian parties. Eventually they would send local officials from Russia to take over the government of the occupied territories and recruit teachers from Russia to introduce the new school curriculum.[23]

The main ideological message of the occupiers was unambiguous: southern Ukraine was part of historical Russia, and its citizens were in fact Russians. In early April, the leading Russian news agency, RIA Novosti, published an article by a prominent Russian political consultant, Timofei Sergeitsev, which explained that denazification should mean de-Ukrainization. "Denazification will inevitably be de-Ukrainization as well—rejection of the artificial inflation of the ethnic component of personal identification of inhabitants of the historical territories of Little Russia and New Russia," wrote Sergeitsev. "Ukrainism is an artificial anti-Russian construction devoid of civilizational content, a subordinate element of foreign and alien civilization."[24]

Putin's thesis, "Russians and Ukrainians are one and the same people," was now directly linked to the official goal of the war—the denazification of Ukraine. In May the ruling Russian party, United Russia, sponsored the installation of billboards in Kherson with the headline: "Kherson is a city with Russian history." They featured portraits of Grigorii Potemkin, a courtier of Catherine II who was credited with founding the city, the imperial Russian general Aleksandr Suvorov, and the founder of modern Russian poetry, Aleksandr Pushkin, noting their links with Kherson and presenting the city's past as part of Russian history. This was done in a city whose population was 75 percent ethnic Ukrainian, with more than half the citizens claiming Ukrainian as their mother tongue. In the Kherson region, the share of Ukrainians is 82 percent, and the share of those who claim Ukrainian as their mother tongue exceeds 73 percent.[25]

The Road to Odesa

While the Russians succeeded in taking Kherson, their offensive toward Zaporizhia, a major industrial center north of Melitopol, was stopped in its tracks by mid-March. They also failed in their attempt to take

Mykolaiv, a ship-building capital of Ukraine and a city of half a million people, located 70 kilometers (43 miles) northwest of Kherson. Without Mykolaiv they could not advance toward Odesa, Ukraine's largest seaport, handling 65 percent of all Ukraine's sea cargo, which in turn accounted for 70 percent of all the country's imports.[26]

The Russians attempted to take Mykolaiv on February 26, but Ukrainian troops commanded by General Dmytro Marchenko, one of the legendary "cyborgs" who had defended the Donetsk airport in 2014–15, destroyed the attackers with artillery fire and the support of the local population, which informed the Ukrainian military about the movement of the Russian forces. The Russians resumed the attack, bringing in more troops and breaking into the city, but their units were defeated, splintering into small groups that lost contact with their commanders.

On March 5, after days of fighting, Vitaly Kim, a youngish-looking entrepreneur and politician of Korean descent, serving as governor of Mykolaiv, released a video announcing the complete defeat of the Russian attackers. He also mocked the Russian soldiers, who he said were running around Ukrainian villages asking for food, by offering them a deal: exchange their armaments for food and a ticket back to Russia. Kim's videos, full of resilience and belief in victory, made him an instant celebrity in Ukraine. In Mykolaiv they helped to mobilize resistance that stopped the Russian attack.[27]

Unable to capture Mykolaiv, Russian troops bypassed it from the north and approached Voznesensk, a major transportation hub and another gateway to Odesa. North of Voznesensk they tried to reach the city of Pivdennoukrainsk, with its southern Ukrainian nuclear power plant, but were stopped. The Ukrainian army had learned a lesson from the loss of Kherson, where they had failed to blow up the Antonivka Bridge in time and lost the city. Now they were destroying bridges across the Southern Buh and smaller rivers—a tactic that had been used successfully in the defense of Kyiv. It worked in southern Ukraine as well: General Marchenko and his men foiled the Russian attack on Voznesensk and Pivdennoukrainsk, compelling their forces to retreat. The road to Odesa remained closed.[28]

The Russian commanders returned to their original plan of capturing Mykolaiv or at least bypassing it, taking control of the highway leading from the city toward Odesa. The key Russian logistical center for the offensive against Mykolaiv became the airport in the village of Chornobaivka, 10 kilometers (6 miles) west of Kherson. The Russians captured the airfield in late February, even before they occupied Kherson, and now used it to concentrate the helicopters, tanks, trucks, and heavy equipment needed for the assault on Mykolaiv. But the Ukrainians were never far away, bombarding Chornobaivka from their artillery positions near Mykolaiv and turning the airfield into a mass grave of Russian personnel and equipment.

Ukrainian artillery first opened fire on Chornobaivka on the night of March 7. The bombardment was very successful, destroying dozens of Russian helicopters, pieces of artillery, and heavy equipment. The devastating attacks on Chornobaivka continued with significant success, and the name of the village became a meme and a term that the Ukrainian media applied to every major Russian target destroyed by Ukrainian forces in the region. As the Ukrainians grew extremely skillful in targeting top Russian commanders, with numerous generals killed by Ukrainian fire, Chornobaivka was identified as the real or imagined place where some of them had met their death, including the commander of the 49th Russian Army, General Yakov Rezantsev.[29]

The Russians lost not only two top generals in their attempt to take Mykolaiv and break through to Odesa but also thousands of officers and men, to say nothing of tanks, armored vehicles, and equipment. The Ukrainians counterattacked in early April, reaching the outskirts of Kherson. The Russians responded with the continued bombing of Mykolaiv. On March 30, Russian missiles deliberately targeted and destroyed the building of the regional administration, the headquarters of always optimistic Vitalii Kim. He survived the attack. More often than not, those killed by artillery were civilians.[30]

The Russian advance on Odesa was stalled by mid-April, and the only remaining hope of the Russian command was an amphibious landing at the key Ukrainian port. The Russian navy in the Black Sea was ordered to shell the city. It had been shelled before, but on March 21 the bombardment was done in the most public way possible: two Russian warships showed up at the approaches to the port and opened fire on the city before being driven away by Ukrainian artillery. Missile attacks from the Black Sea followed in the next several days.[31]

The Ukrainians could do little to protect Odesa from the sea short of laying sea mines, which they had already done. Their land-based missiles could not reach the Russian ships because of the anti-aircraft systems on the flagship *Moskva*, which had taken part in the capture of Snake Island and made it onto the Ukrainian stamp. The *Moskva* was a late Soviet-era guided-missile cruiser built, ironically enough, at the Mykolaiv shipyard. It served as the flagship of the Black Sea Fleet, being the headquarters of the fleet's commander, its brain, command center, and location of radar and anti-aircraft missiles that held an "umbrella" above the entire fleet. With its anti-ship and surface-to-air missiles, guns, anti-submarine mortars, and torpedoes, the *Moskva* had formidable firepower.[32]

Because the *Moskva* would be a key component of any future landing to capture Odesa, the Ukrainians were determined to take it out. They succeeded beyond all expectation or belief on the night of April 13, when two Ukrainian-made ground-based Neptune missiles outsmarted the *Moskva*'s air defense systems with the help of a drone, hitting the cruiser. Both missiles struck the ammunition hold, detonating the missiles and torpedoes on board. The entire cruiser eventually sank, with the Russian command too embarrassed ever to admit that it had been hit by Ukrainian missiles, and that the flagship had been lost in battle with a country that had no navy. Instead, it was officially announced that the cruiser had sunk because of a combination of factors: an explosion of unknown nature on board and a storm at sea.[33]

The sinking of the *Moskva* changed the course of the war at sea. Without its air defenses, the entire Russian Black Sea Fleet became vulnerable to Ukrainian Neptune anti-ship missiles and ran for cover to Sevastopol harbor under the protection of shore-based air defenses. British intelligence reported that the commander of the Black Sea Fleet was dismissed. The Ukrainian postal service reacted by issuing a new stamp—the old image augmented with that of a rubber stamp featuring the English word "Done" and the date of the sinking, April 14, 2022. In May, the post office issued five million two-stamp sets with the soldier giving the finger, one showing the cruiser, the other just the sea. Kyiv declared the cruiser's wreckage an item of the country's underwater cultural heritage. In the heritage records it was given the number 2064.[34]

But the story of the *Moskva*'s dealings with Snake Island was not yet over. With the loss of the cruiser, the small island acquired special strategic importance for the Russian navy. They could install missile launchers there to hit Odesa and the Ukrainian coast. Radar and anti-aircraft defense systems could also be installed to replace the logistical support previously provided by the sunken ship. The first Ukrainian attack on the Russian positions on Snake Island was launched in late April, destroying the Strela (Arrow) anti-aircraft missile complex. Further attacks on Russian targets, including missile complexes and small ships, picked up in May. The Ukrainians made effective use of their air force, artillery, and, apparently, new Western-supplied missile complexes to prevent the Russian navy from turning the island into a sea fortress at the approaches to Odesa. The Russians were forced to withdraw from the island in late June. The Ukrainians lost no time in sending commandos there to hoist their national flag.[35]

The Annexation Playbook

In June 2022, Russia celebrated the 350th anniversary of Peter I, better known as Peter the Great—the first Russian tsar also to be called an emperor. The anniversary was marked with academic conferences and meetings as well as public events, not only in Moscow and St. Petersburg but also in regional centers. In Moscow, on the premises of the VDNKh—the Russian Exhibition of Achievements of the National Economy—the authorities organized a multimedia exhibition dedicated to Peter and his legacy. Titled *Peter I. The Birth of the Empire*, the exhibition covered his role in state-building, diplomacy, and the creation of a "civic society," as well as reforms of education and development of culture.[36]

On June 9, Peter's official birthday, Vladimir Putin arrived at the VDNKh to open the exhibition in person. He also met with young Russian entrepreneurs, engineers, and scientists. Peter did a great deal for the development of Russian entrepreneurship and science, founding the Russian Academy of Sciences, and a meeting of that kind in conjunction with the exhibition seemed appropriate. But when Putin addressed the young entrepreneurs and scholars, his emphasis was not so much on Peter's contribution to Russian science and technology—Putin mentioned in passing his "borrowing" of Western knowledge when the tsar traveled to Europe—but rather on Peter's wars and territorial acquisitions, a subject much closer to Putin's heart at that moment.

"Peter the Great waged the Great Northern War for 21 years," said Putin, apparently suggesting that his own "special military operation," though dragging on much longer than expected, was still a reasonable undertaking. He then proceeded to the question of Peter's territorial acquisitions. "On the face of it, he was at war with Sweden, taking something away from it," suggested Putin. But he then proposed a very different interpretation of Peter's conquests: "He was not taking anything away; he was returning." Putin then addressed the issue of the legitimacy of such actions. "When he founded the new capital, none of the European countries recognized this territory as part of Russia," stated Putin. "Everyone recognized it as part of Sweden."

In Putin's mind, the conquest was justified because "from time immemorial, the Slavs had lived there along with the Finno-Ugric peoples, and this territory was under Russia's control." That was a stretch at best when it came to describing the population, and the claims of the medieval Novgorodian republic to that territory belonged to the distant past by the time Peter's forces moved into the area. But Putin continued in the same vein: "He was returning and reinforcing; that is what he was doing." He then added, with a smirk: "Clearly, it fell to our lot to return and reinforce as well." Putin's remarks stood in clear contrast to his "declaration of war" speech of February 24, when he proclaimed that Russia did not "plan to occupy Ukrainian territory."[37]

The Ukrainian response to Putin's remarks was swift. Mykhailo Podoliak, a senior adviser to President Zelensky, saw the Russian president's comments as evidence that imperialism was the true motive behind Russia's aggression against Ukraine. "Putin's confession of land seizures and comparing himself with Peter the Great proved there was no 'conflict,' only the country's bloody seizure under contrived pretexts of people's genocide," tweeted Podoliak. Reports from independent Russian journalists supported Podoliak's interpretation. A few days earlier *Meduza*, a website run by opposition journalists who had left Russia and found safe haven in Latvia, reported that "the Kremlin was planning to combine all the lands into a new federal district that could be annexed by Russia as soon as this autumn."[38]

"This is a different war to the one Putin began on 24 February 2022," wrote Lawrence Freedman, emeritus professor of war studies at King's College, London, soon after Putin made his remarks about Peter's legacy. "He has now presented himself as a reincarnation of Peter the Great and admitted that this is a war of conquest rather than liberation. It is territory now that he is after, having largely given up on the people of the Donbas, whose supposed vulnerability to a Ukrainian attack provided the pretext for the war. The separatist armies from Donetsk and Luhansk have been used as cannon-fodder, sent into battle unprepared and ill-equipped, to spare regular units."[39]

Putin's remarks left little doubt that he was on the path of territorial aggrandizement, but they also suggested that the Kremlin had scaled down its war aims. The capture of Kyiv and control of the rest of Ukraine by a puppet government, an apparent goal in February, was unachievable and had to be abandoned by the end of March. But Putin kept a good part of southern Ukraine, which he had seized in the first weeks of the war, and hoped to expand his possessions in the eastern part of the country. The war initially meant to gain complete control of Ukraine was redesigned to extend Russia's borders. Once again, as in the annexation of the Crimea in 2014, the "Greater Russia" project filled the gap between Russia's aspirations and its capacity to satisfy Putin's imperial ambitions.

As the Russian offensive stalled in the Donbas without achieving either its primary or secondary goals, the Ukrainian defense minister, Oleksii Reznikov, made public President Zelensky's order to his troops to recapture the south of the country. Western weapons were to help achieve that goal. Indeed, HIMARS rockets were soon used to bombard the Antonivka Bridge across the Dnieper near Kherson, the main link between Russian troops in the city and its outskirts and the principal Russian forces on the right bank of the Dnieper and in the Crimea. Many saw that as a sign of a coming Ukrainian counteroffensive in the south.[40]

But as news of the expected Ukrainian counteroffensive reached the front pages of the world media, more information started to come out of Russia and occupied parts of Ukraine about Moscow's plans to annex those territories. Apart from the territories of the Donbas puppet states, they included the port city of Berdiansk and the city of Melitopol, both within the boundaries of Zaporizhia oblast, as well as the entire Kherson oblast, with the cities of Kherson and Nova Kakhovka. Russian troops doubled their efforts, reinforcing their positions along the front line between Kherson and Mykolaiv. "They are mining the fields on the approaches from Mykolaiv," a local Ukrainian journalist told a *Guardian* reporter in the second half of July. "They are mining everything, and their soldiers are digging trenches."[41]

In May the official Russian news agency, Novosti, had published a statement by a Russian-appointed administrator of the occupied parts of Kherson oblast, suggesting that the region should become part of Russia. "Russian lands from time immemorial should return to their historical course of culture and values," declared the official. Journalists asked Putin's spokesperson, Dmitrii Peskov, about the Kremlin's plans of annexation. Peskov did not deny such plans but suggested, "Nothing can be done without the expression of the will of the inhabitants of these regions, without them deciding how to go on and with whom they want to live."[42]

Given Moscow's experience of organizing pseudo-referendums in the Crimea and the Donbas, that did not sound reassuring. In early June, soon after Sergei Kirienko, the former prime minister of Russia and now deputy chief of Putin's presidential administration, visited the occupied part of Zaporizhia oblast, a local occupation official there spoke about preparations for a referendum on the future of the region. In mid-July the media reported an astonishing piece of news: Russian occupation forces were no longer relying on locals to administer occupied territory, as had been the case in the Crimea and the Donbas. Instead, the former deputy governor of the Vologda region of Russia had been installed as head of government of the occupied parts of Zaporizhia oblast.[43]

In Washington, John Kirby, the coordinator for strategic communications at the National Security Council, referred to intelligence and open-source information as he claimed that Russia was preparing for the annexation of Kherson, Zaporizhia, and all of Donetsk and Luhansk oblasts. Moscow, according to Kirby, was following its 2014 "annexation playbook," installing its own illegitimate officials in the occupied regions to organize sham referendums about joining Russia, which would be used as a basis for annexation. "Ukraine and its Western partners," Kirby told the journalists, "may have a narrowing window of opportunity to support a Ukrainian counteroffensive into occupied Ukrainian territory before the Kremlin annexes that territory." With Russian intentions no longer enigmatic, the big question was who would be first, the Ukrainian armed forces retaking parts of southern Ukraine or Russian officials formally annexing them. It turned out the two processes were following their separate paths.[44]

11

THE COUNTEROFFENSIVE

The first publication to break the news about the coming counteroffensive of the Ukrainian armed forces in the Pontic steppes was *The (Sunday) Times*. On July 10, 2022, the newspaper quoted the Ukrainian defense minister, Oleksii Reznikov, as saying: "The president has given the order to the supreme military chief to draw up plans." It was supposed to be the mother of all counteroffensives. "Ukraine is massing a million-strong fighting force equipped with western weapons to recover its southern territory from Russia," wrote the newspaper with reference to Reznikov. But where would Ukraine attack? Reznikov pointed to southern Ukraine—the Pontic steppe occupied by Russia in the first weeks of its aggression.[1]

A clear sign that a counteroffensive in the south was indeed in preparation came one day before the publication of Reznikov's interview. On July 9, Iryna Vereshchuk, Ukraine's deputy prime minister in charge of temporarily occupied territories, called on the residents of southern Ukrainian territories occupied by Russian forces to leave the Kherson and Zaporizhia provinces as soon as possible. She suggested that if they could not reach Ukrainian-held territories directly, they should try to do so via the Russian-occupied Crimea. "Our artillery must do its work, since deoccupation includes the use of armed force, as we are of course aware," declared Vereshchuk. Therefore people must leave and take their family members with them by all means available."[2]

President Zelensky did not deny the existence of an order to launch a counteroffensive but was not prepared to announce the thrust of the attack. On the day after the publication of Reznikov's interview, Zelensky spoke to journalists in the presence of the visiting prime minister of the Netherlands, Mark Rutte: "I can say that it is the task of all our armed forces to deoccupy all our territory. I think that this is the task of every citizen of our state. I will not share the details of any particular plan." Although neither Zelensky nor his civil or military officials would disclose details of the coming counteroffensive, some in Ukraine expressed concern about Vereshchuk's message to residents of southern Ukraine, which had ostensibly indicated the direction of Ukraine's impending attack.[3]

A leading Ukrainian newspaper, *S'ohodni* (Today), turned to its military experts to figure out whether the announcement was an indication of actual plans or an attempt to misinform the enemy. The expert opinions were divided. Some assumed that the announcement was intended to mislead the Russians and prevent a possible new attack on Kyiv, but others believed that Reznikov had been referring to actual plans. Everyone agreed that the liberation of Kherson was not only very important but also the most promising target for a Ukrainian counteroffensive.[4]

The Russian troops posted on the right bank of the Dnieper River around Kherson and further north, near the city of Beryslav, located on the opposite bank of the river from Nova Kakhovka and its dam, continued to present a threat to the cities of Mykolaiv and Kryvyi Rih, the hometown of President Zelensky. The road to Odesa and Moldova, by now declared targets of Russian aggression, led through Mykolaiv. But the Russian units near Kherson and Beryslav were cut off from their forces on the left bank of the Dnieper and might become relatively easy prey for the advancing Ukrainian troops.

The Game of Bridges

"It's a rare bird that can reach the middle of the Dnieper," wrote Nikolai Gogol in his description of Ukraine's largest river, referring metaphorically to its width. The Dnieper was in fact very broad near Kherson, presenting the Russians with an obstacle of 700 meters, or approximately 2,300 feet, that they had had to cross back in February. If they wanted to hold Kherson and Beryslav on the right bank, they would have to maintain full control over the river crossings.[5]

The Russian supply lines across the Dnieper depended on three bridges: the Antonivka railway and highway bridges north of Kherson and a bridge connecting Nova Kakhovka with the Beryslav area in the vicinity of the Kakhovka Dam.[6] The Antonivka highway bridge, 25 meters (82 feet) wide and 1,366 meters (4,482 feet) long, is the main artery linking Kherson with the left bank of the Dnieper. The Ukrainians paid a high price for having failed to destroy that bridge because the Russians took control of it, gaining a direct route toward Mykolaiv and the southern Ukrainian nuclear power plant in the city of Novoukrainsk. If the Ukrainians were serious about their counteroffensive, they would have to demolish the bridges to isolate the Russian troops on the right bank, cutting off their supply lines.[7]

Whatever the rationale for releasing information about the coming Ukrainian offensive in the south, the Russian commanders in Kherson clearly took it seriously. On July 12, two days after the publication of Reznikov's interview, the citizens of Melitopol, a key transportation center on the left bank of the Dnieper, saw columns of Russian vehicles heading toward the river in the direction of Kherson. On the following day, Russian troops began to fortify the approaches to the Antonivka highway bridge. They also increased the number of patrols in Kherson. On July 20, the Russian foreign minister, Sergei Lavrov, declared that Russian territorial ambitions were no longer limited to the Donetsk and Luhansk oblasts but now extended to Zaporizhia and Kherson.[8]

These timely measures to repel the coming Ukrainian offensive availed the Russians little when the Ukrainians began to shape the battlefield to suit their purposes. They hit Russian ammunition depots and command centers with HIMARS (high mobility) rockets before using them against the bridges. On July 3 the Ukrainians used the HIMARS system to strike a Russian ammunition depot in Melitopol, the key transportation hub linking the Crimea with Russian-occupied southern Ukraine. The ammunition depot in Kherson was destroyed on July 6, and the one in Nova Kakhovka two days later.[9]

On July 19, nine days after the publication of Reznikov's interview, the Ukrainian armed forces dealt their first major blow to the Antonivka highway bridge, hitting the bridge itself and the fortifications next to it. On the same day, the English-language *Kyiv Independent* published a long article suggesting that the destruction of the two Antonivka bridges, for the highway and the railway, and the Kakhovka Dam Bridge were prerequisites for a successful counteroffensive. The newspaper quoted the deputy head of the Kherson regional administration, Yurii Sobolevsky, stating that "orcs [Russian military] and those who sympathize with them in Kherson may soon find themselves without supplies and ways of organized retreat."[10]

The July 19 HIMARS attack was just the beginning. More missile strikes against the Antonivka highway and railroad bridges followed in the next days and weeks. They began on the next day, July 20, causing enough damage to the highway bridge to close it temporarily. The third strike came on the evening of July 26, making the bridge unusable for heavy machinery. Satellite images showed at least sixteen holes in the southern part of the bridge. The Russian military got busy repairing the bridge once again, only to witness new attacks on August 14 and 30, forcing the Russian commanders to abandon repairs and focus instead on the construction of pontoon bridges and ferry crossings to traverse the Dnieper.[11]

The Antonivka highway bridge was not the only target of the Ukrainian-operated HIMARS systems. Routine strikes were made on the nearby Antonivka railroad bridge and the bridge at the Kakhovka dam, which was severely damaged on September 3, causing approximately 20 meters (65 feet) of one of its sections to collapse into the water.

Also attacked on numerous occasions was the Darivka bridge across the Inhulets River, a tributary of the Dnieper. It was the only bridge connecting the Russian troops in and around Kherson with army units in the Beryslav area. The Ukrainians also routinely attacked the pontoon bridges that the Russians were building to replace the damaged highway and railroad bridges. "Ukrainian generals clearly aim to starve the 49th Combined Arms Army and block reinforcements in order to weaken Russian defenses north of Kherson—and tilt the battlefield in favor of Ukrainian brigades that, since May, slowly have been fighting their way south toward Kherson," wrote David Axe, a reporter for *Forbes* magazine, in late July.[12]

To "tilt the battlefield," the Ukrainians not only used long-distance missile strikes but also sent commando and sabotage units across the demarcation line to collect intelligence, destroy ammunition depots and command centers, and spread terror among Russian troops in the rear. In late July, the Ukrainian media reported on the return to Mykolaiv of General Dmytro Marchenko, the hero of the city's defense in March and April. This time his task was to organize and coordinate the activities of Ukrainian commandos and partisan groups behind enemy lines. In mid-August the Ukrainian media reported on the detonation by "Ukrainian partisans" of a railway bridge near the key transportation hub of Melitopol. Similar reports came from Kherson and environs.[13]

Among Marchenko's targets were not only logistical hubs, ammunition depots, and barracks of Russian troops but also Ukrainian citizens who had joined the occupation administration. The Ukrainian media would refer to them as "gauleiters," the term used in Hitler's Germany to denote regional party leaders, closely associated in Ukrainian public opinion with Nazi rule in Ukraine during World War II.

On August 6 the deputy head of the occupation administration of Nova Kakhovka, Vitalii Hul, was gunned down by persons unknown. On August 28, the media reported the assassination of a former Ukrainian parliamentary deputy from Zelensky's party, Servant of the People, Oleksii Kovaliov, who had overseen the export of Ukrainian grain from the occupied Kherson region to the Crimea. That was the second attempt on his life. Four days later the media reported the death of Ivan Sushko, the head of the occupation administration in the village of Mykhailivka in the Zaporizhia region. He was blown up in his car. Members of commissions created by the Russian authorities to administer a referendum on Russian annexation of the occupied territories also found themselves under attack. Ukrainians were doing their best to prevent the Russian authorities from conducting a fake referendum before their armed forces were driven out of southern Ukraine.[14]

Judgment Day

"If anything of that kind takes place, Judgment Day will dawn for all of them in a single moment. Very swift and severe. Shelter will be very hard to find," declared Dmitrii Medvedev, the former president of Russia, now Putin's deputy in the Security Council, on July 17. He warned the Ukrainians against possible strikes on the Crimea, the main supply base for Russian troops around Kherson, threatening them with nothing less than nuclear attack.[15]

Unlike Luhansk and Donetsk, the Crimea had been officially incorporated as part of Russian territory, and throughout the first months of all-out warfare it enjoyed immunity from Ukrainian retaliatory attacks to the same degree as the parts of the Russian Federation and Belarus from which Russian troops attacked and shelled Ukrainian targets. But as the Ukrainians stepped up their missile attacks on Russian supply lines, television commentators began to question whether the attacks on the Antonivka bridge would be followed by similar attacks on the Crimean bridge. It was a 19-kilometer (11.8-mile) structure across the Kerch Strait linking the Russian Federation with the occupied Crimea and providing a lifeline for Russian troops in southern Ukraine.[16]

Volodymyr Zelensky brushed off Medvedev's threats, saying, "Yet another not particularly sober declaration was heard from Russia today about a supposed 'Judgment Day' for Ukraine. Of course, no one is going to take such intimidation seriously." Zelensky was referring to rumors about Medvedev's drunkenness then circulating in Moscow.

Some argued that Medvedev, completely sidelined by Putin, had unsuccessfully attempted suicide. But the problem was by no means limited to a key Kremlin official: many top Russian functionaries were hitting the bottle as they tried to cope with stress caused by the worsening situation at the front, which led to infighting among various groups of Putin's lieutenants. Putin himself apparently became worried by crumbling discipline among his aides and began to talk about the problem of alcoholism both privately and publicly.[17]

While Zelensky dismissed Medvedev's threats as the rambling of an alcoholic, the Ukrainian armed forces opened a new front in the Crimea. In late July, a drone missed by Russian anti-aircraft batteries hit the headquarters of the Russian Black Sea Fleet in Sevastopol. No casualties were reported, but the attack spoiled the mood in the city: celebrations of Russian Navy Day were canceled. August 9 brought a true shock to the Russian military as Ukrainian missiles hit the Russian airfield near the city of Saki, which had hosted President Roosevelt and Prime Minister Churchill when they arrived for the Yalta Conference in February 1945. The strike detonated a munitions depot on the airfield, contributing to the destruction of ten Russian airplanes—the core of the Russian Black Sea Fleet's air force. The explosions were seen and heard far from the airbase, causing a massive exodus of Russian tourists from the Crimea across the Kerch Bridge.

Russian officials blamed the explosions on violations of safety procedures by Russian personnel, as admitting a successful Ukrainian attack would have suggested a failure of Russian anti-aircraft defenses to protect what Moscow considered Russian territory. But Ukrainian attacks on the peninsula continued, making it impossible for the Kremlin to blame explosions at various Crimean locations on lax safety procedures. Russian officials admitted that the Crimea was under Ukrainian attack after the detonation of an arms depot near the city of Dzhankoi, a key railway station on the line connecting the Crimea with the southern Ukrainian mainland. The Ukrainians remained silent at first but claimed responsibility for the attacks in September. The Crimea ceased to be a secure arms depot for Russians fighting in southern Ukraine and became a legitimate target for the Ukrainian armed forces. They had not yet hit the Kerch Bridge, but it was now clear that they would do so once they had the means.[18]

While Russia initially reacted to Ukrainian attacks on the Crimea with silence and denial rather than the use of nuclear weapons, as Medvedev had suggested, the Kremlin had reached for the nuclear card about the time the Ukrainians began their attacks on the Crimea. The name of the Kremlin's nuclear card was the Zaporizhia nuclear power plant, captured by Russian forces in early March after the shelling that set one of the plant's buildings on fire. The Russian army used the plant as a safe haven for its troops as well as for armaments, heavy equipment, and ammunition, assuming that the Ukrainians would not dare to fire on a working nuclear power plant. They also used the plant as cover for shelling Ukrainian positions on the right bank of the Dnieper (the plant and company town, called Enerhodar, was located on the left bank), especially the city of Nikopol, a population of more than 100,000.

The Ukrainians used social media to ask the citizens of Enerhodar to inform them of instances when Russian artillery left the plant to execute strikes so that they could hit the Russians outside the plant. They also used drones to attack Russian forces outside the nuclear facility. A Ukrainian drone attack on Russian positions near the power plant took place on July 22. Two weeks later, on August 5, there was another attack on the plant, but this time it was artillery shelling of the plant itself. The Ukrainians denied any involvement in the attack, and President Zelensky accused the Russians of "nuclear blackmail." The Ukrainian official Oleksii Arestovych, an adviser to the presidential office, argued that by shelling the plant Putin was trying to force Ukraine to halt its counteroffensive in the south and conclude a ceasefire. This involved pressure not only on Kyiv but also on its Western allies, for an accident at Europe's largest nuclear power plant could affect eastern and central Europe, as well as Turkey and the Middle East.[19]

On September 1, after long negotiations, a team of experts from the International Atomic Energy Agency led by the IAEA director, Rafael

Grossi, made its way to the Zaporizhia nuclear power plant to assess the situation on site. By that time the shelling of the plant had injured one of the operators and caused a fire near the plant's nitrogen-oxygen station. The inspectors either could not or refused to identify who was shelling the plant but confirmed earlier Ukrainian reports that the Russians had indeed placed their vehicles and equipment in its turbine halls. The IAEA team produced a report calling for the establishment of a no-fight zone around the plant—in fact, its demilitarization. "What is urgently needed now, today, is that we agree on establishing a protection (if you want), a shield, a bubble around the perimeter of the facility," Grossi told the CNN anchor Christiane Amanpour a few days after returning from the station. The Ukrainians praised the report, while the Russians called for "clarifications."[20]

On September 15, the Board of Governors of the IAEA called on the Russians to leave the plant. The resolution was supported by thirty-three of the thirty-five board members, with the representatives of Russia and China opposed. Moscow's nuclear blackmail of Ukraine and the world continued as the reactors were switched off but not cooled, and so still dangerous. Shelling continued in the vicinity of the plant, forcing the operators on September 11 to shut down the last operating reactor providing electricity for the pumps that supplied water to cool the active zone of the reactor and keep the plant's safety systems operational. The safety of the reactor would now depend on outside power lines supplying electricity to the pumps. They had been damaged before and could be damaged again, triggering a Fukushima-type disaster. Judgment Day had been postponed but not cancelled.[21]

Going on the Offensive

By mid-August it appeared that the counteroffensive announced by Ukrainian officials the previous month was still as far from realization as it had been back then. The Ukrainian advance pretty much stopped after a handful of villages were brought under control. The destruction of ammunition depots, along with artillery and missile strikes on bridges and Russian communication lines, had only limited impact on the Russian army group near Kherson and Nova Kakhovka, whose numbers had greatly increased.

To the surprise of many, the Ukrainians either could not destroy the bridges across the Dnieper completely or make them unusable within the first few weeks after announcing their counteroffensive, or they had decided not to do so. These intended or unintended delays in cutting the key transportation arteries across the Dnieper allowed the Russian commanders to reinforce their forces on the right bank of the river. By mid-August Western intelligence had recorded mass redeployment of Russian troops from the Donbas, the takeover of which had been the declared goal of the new stage of Russia's war on Ukraine, as well as from the Crimea, from where eight tactical battalion groups, altogether close to 8,000 men, were moved to the region. According to Oleksii Arestovych, Russia had accumulated up to thirty battalion tactical groups on the right bank of the river.[22]

In late July, as Ukrainian forces struck the Antonivka bridge and their commanders announced first modest successes of the counteroffensive—the liberation of two villages in the region previously captured by the Russian army—the secretary of the Ukrainian Defense Council, Oleksii Danilov, admitted that there had been a massive redeployment of the Russian military to the south, toward Kherson in particular, and suggested possible delays in the counteroffensive. "I know for certain that our forces will do everything in their power to manage within the timelines put forward by the president," stated Danilov. He then added: "But victory will be ours in any event. A week early or late is a matter for the army."[23]

By mid-August the question was not how quickly the Ukrainian offensive would advance but whether the Russian battalions, many of them consisting of elite paratrooper detachments, would launch a counteroffensive of their own. Indeed, on August 20, Russian troops went onto the offensive, trying to make inroads toward Mykolaiv in the west and Kryvyi Rih in the north. The Russian tactical battalion formations that had moved into the area after the announcement of the

Ukrainian plans for a counteroffensive advanced up to 35 kilometers (22 miles) deep into Ukrainian-held territory, capturing the town of Blahodatne, a mere 45 kilometers (30 miles) east of Mykolaiv.[24]

As more and more Ukrainians expressed concerns about the wisdom of announcing the counteroffensive, thereby seeming to provoke a Russian advance toward the right bank of the Dnieper, news broke on August 29 about the start of the long-promised Ukrainian offensive. The Kakhovka Operational Group of the Ukrainian armed forces made a statement about its troops breaking through the lines of the Russian 109th regiment, which formally belonged to the armed forces of the "Donetsk People's Republic." "Ukraine has a brilliant chance to regain the territories with the help of HIMARS," read the statement of the operational command. It was a most unusual announcement, coming as it did from a military command as yet unknown to the general public. It had been an unwritten rule of Ukrainian wartime information strategy for major announcements to be issued by the president, his administration, or the General Staff, and only days after the actual developments. It was not clear why the Kakhovka Operational Group had shown such haste, but few people asked that question at the time. The main thing was that the long-awaited offensive had not only begun but also gained immediate success.[25]

Ukrainian troops had indeed broken through the first line of Russian defenses manned by conscripts from the Donetsk People's Republic, most of whom had been mobilized against their will, and whose morale was generally known to be low. But the Ukrainian offensive had soon stalled. The Russians brought in reinforcements and stabilized their front at the second line of defenses. On September 2 the Russian defense minister, Sergei Shoigu, announced the earlier Russian capture of the village of Blahodatne and questioned the Ukrainian forces' ability to conduct successful offensives. "Let me emphasize," stated Shoigu, referring to the start of the Ukrainian counteroffensive in the south, "that this action was planned by Zelensky's office with one single goal—to give their Western sponsors the illusion of the Ukrainian Armed Forces' capacity to manage an assault."[26]

But the Russian advance toward Mykolaiv was now effectively over, while the Ukrainians kept pushing. They claimed their first major success on September 4, when Zelensky's office released a video of troops raising the Ukrainian flag over the recently retaken village of Vysokopillia in the northern section of the right-bank enclave controlled by the Russian army. Ukrainian forces had taken the village after the withdrawal not of forcibly mobilized citizens of the Donbas "republic" but of elite Russian units avoiding encirclement. "That elite ran, abandoning everything it had, both weapons and equipment; they ran shamefully," commented Oleksandr Samoilenko, the head of the Kherson regional council. President Zelensky noted the recapture of Vyskopillia, stating that "Ukrainian flags are returning to places where they should be by right."[27]

Despite the celebratory mood in Kyiv, Vysokopillia was hardly a major administrative center or transportation hub. Established by German farmers in southern Ukraine in the nineteenth century and originally named Kronau, the village was one of the region's northernmost settlements, located 146 kilometers (91 miles) north of Kherson. According to Oleksii Arestovych, the Russians had been in tactical encirclement since late July, suggesting that the victory was long in the making. Its capture became a bigger public relations success than a military one. The Ukrainian public needed good news, and there had been none for a while, only promises of the coming offensive. Zelensky finally had something to show for all the buildup, both to his people and abroad.[28]

The good news from the southern front was especially welcome because the eastern one did not look promising. The Russians continued their offensive there, announcing the takeover of two villages on the border with the Donbas on September 6. On the following day, the Russian General Staff announced the capture of the village of Kodema, suggesting a continuing Russian offensive toward the Ukrainian positions near Bakhmut. That was the main Russian thrust, aiming at the occupation of Ukraine's entire Donetsk region. On the same day the Russian Ministry of Defense reported that because of major casualties, the Ukrainian armed forces had halted their attacks near Kherson and Beryslav on the right bank of the Dnieper.[29]

Ironically, that turned out to be the last victorious report of the Russian military. By the time they made it public, the Russian forces were already on the defensive. Unexpectedly for Moscow, a major new Ukrainian offensive had begun where the Russian commanders were least prepared for it—north of the Donbas, in the Kharkiv region. Unlike the southern counteroffensive publicized by Zelensky and his team, this one was prepared in complete secrecy and immediately began to produce results. A prominent Ukrainian political commentator, Taras Berezovets, even suggested to *Guardian* reporters that the previously announced counteroffensive in the south had been "designed to trick Russia."[30]

A Cossack Raid

The Ukrainian counteroffensive south of Kharkiv began on September 6, the day on which the IAEA released its report documenting the presence of Russian military equipment in the turbine halls of the Zaporizhia nuclear power plant. The news came not from the Ukrainian side, as with the southern advance, but from Russian military bloggers who decried the success of the Ukrainian surprise attack toward the city of Balakliia, located close to the Russo-Ukrainian front line southeast of Kharkiv. Satellite images confirmed the presence of Ukrainian forces on the outskirts of Balakliia. They also confirmed earlier reports that Russian troops were withdrawing and blowing up bridges in the wake of their retreat to stop or slow down the Ukrainian advance.[31]

The Ukrainian offensive took not only Russian troops but also Western military experts by surprise. The latter were also baffled by the Russian inability to predict or stop it. Phillips O'Brien, professor of strategic studies at the University of St. Andrews in the United Kingdom, commented on Twitter on the morning of September 6: "If the Ukrainians have achieved operational surprise around Kharkiv, [it] will demonstrate just how the Russian military is in disarray. I assumed through all the different monitoring devices (from satellites to UAVs to cyber and more) that such operational surprise would be." Later in the day, experts of the Washington-based Institute for the Study of War provided a possible explanation of the Ukrainian success. "The September 6 Ukrainian counterattack in Kharkiv was likely an opportunistic effort enabled by the redeployment of Russian forces away from the area to reinforce Russian positions against the Ukrainian counteroffensive in Kherson Oblast," read the institute's daily bulletin.[32]

The Ukrainian troops were led by Colonel General Oleksandr Syrsky, who had saved Kyiv in February and made Russian troops retreat from the Ukrainian capital in March. President Zelensky thanked the officers and soldiers of those units on September 8, the second day of the offensive. He listed altogether five brigades: one airborne, one mechanized, one assault, one artillery, and one infantry. He started with the 25th Airborne Brigade, which had received the honorific name of Sicheslav Brigade, referring to the glorious past of the Zaporozhian Host, a few months before the start of the all-out war. There was also a reference to the Cossack past in the name of another brigade that took part in the operation. The 92nd Mechanized Brigade was named after Ivan Sirko, a seventeenth-century Zaporizhian Cossack leader known for his daring raids.[33]

Ukrainian military formations named after Cossacks, along with Ukrainian troops in general, were now employing pretty much Cossack tactics, attacking the enemy where he did not expect them, penetrating enemy lines in multiple places, and attacking the Russians from the rear to create the impression that they were already encircled, thereby sowing panic. Taking on a Russian military grouping consisting of up to twelve battalion tactical groups, the Ukrainians lacked numerical superiority but showed the ability to coordinate artillery, infantry, and aviation, producing what the experts called a "cascade collapse" of the Russian front. The Cossack heritage and NATO training emphasizing the initiative of mid-level field commanders, as opposed to the highly centralized command and control system employed by the Soviet and now Russian army, were bearing fruit.[34]

In their offensive, the Ukrainians struck an area with little more than a first line of defense, as troops that could have manned second and third lines had been moved to the south. The least motivated troops Moscow could find, forcibly mobilized from the puppet "republic" of Luhansk, were left to hold the fort. In Verbivka, the first village captured by Ukrainian troops at the start of the offensive, there were roughly 100 such soldiers. They lived in houses abandoned by the locals, confiscated their cars and, according to the citizens of Verbivka, took from them whatever they wanted. If local men tried to protest, Russian soldiers would hit them in the chest with rifle butts. The Russians told the villagers that they were fighting for money, making no effort to convert them to any ideological cause, since they had none. When Ukrainian troops shelled Russian positions in the village, the soldiers, according to the local welder Vitalii Bychok, "ran into the houses and changed into whatever clothes they could find. They ran where they could, in small groups."[35]

The Ukrainian army passed through Verbivka toward the city of Balakliia, which counted 30,000 residents before the war and now had a Russian garrison manned by a detachment of rapid-response forces belonging to the Russian Guard who had been dispatched from Samara and Ufa, the capital of Bashkiria. The Ukrainians bypassed the city, moving deeper into Russian-held territory farther east. The Russian guardsmen were now encircled and giving in to panic. The first to flee Balakliia were the officers, leaving their soldiers behind. "You left us behind, you got out," residents of Balakliia heard Russian soldiers telling their commanders on the radio. Soon the soldiers followed their commanders, leaving clothes, supplies, ammunition, and heavy weapons behind. "Trucks drove through the city honking, and they climbed on and left," recalled the local resident Ihor Levchenko. He told a reporter: "They didn't have a fighting spirit. They were afraid."[36]

Ukrainian troops entered Balakliia on September 8, the third day of the offensive. By that time they had liberated twenty settlements and advanced up to 50 kilometers (31 miles) into enemy-held territory. The troops proceeded eastward to what appeared to be their main objective, the town of Kupiansk, which had served as temporary capital of the Russian-occupied part of the Kharkiv region. A major transportation hub roughly the size of Balakliia, it had a prewar population of about 27,000. The railroad connected Kupiansk with Russia in the east and two Russian strongholds in the occupied parts of Ukraine, the town of Vovchansk to the north and the city of Izium to the south. Located on the Oskil River, Kupiansk was strategically important to any battle that might take place in the region. Capturing the town also meant cutting the key supply line for Russian troops in Vovchansk and Izium, where a major grouping of Russian forces had been located.[37]

The Russian commanders realized the importance of Kupiansk for their position in the region but could do nothing to stop the Ukrainian offensive. Their front simply collapsed, their troops fled in panic, and reinforcements were unavailable, since the most battle-ready and motivated units were fully engaged on the right bank of the Dnieper around Kherson and Beryslav. The Russian command dispatched to Kupiansk whatever troops they could gather from Russia at the time. Russian television showed transport planes working around the clock to deliver heavy arms to the region and columns of vehicles crossing the Russo-Ukrainian border on their way to the front. Television announcers referred to the hastily gathered troops as "the Courageous." Many of them were killed by Ukrainian artillery fire before they reached their destination, partly because of information that the Ukrainians gathered from Russian television reporting. On September 9, Ukrainian troops were already on the outskirts of Kupiansk. By the following day they had reached the city center, posting a photo on social media showing soldiers of the 92nd Ivan Sirko Mechanized Brigade in front of the Kupiansk city council building. They scuffed the Russian tricolor with their boots in a photo that went viral on Ukrainian social networks.[38]

The most consequential part of the Kupiansk operation was the disruption of railway connections going through the city. Russian supply lines to Vovchansk in the north and Izium in the south were severed. The Russian military command finally decided that a planned retreat was better than uncontrolled flight. It publicly announced the withdrawal of units located east of the Oskil River, allegedly to reinforce units in the Donbas—the declared primary goal of Russian military activity on the eastern front. Experts at the Institute for the Study of War predicted the fall of Izium, the center of Russia's largest military grouping in the area, within 48 hours, adding, with reference to the Ukrainian troops, "if they have not already done that."[39]

Indeed, the Ukrainian 25th Sicheslav Brigade had entered the city on September 10, the same day the Ivan Sirko Brigade entered Kupiansk. The Ukrainians found an abundance of armaments, ammunition depots, and equipment left by the hastily retreating Russian troops. In the north, a few days later, Ukrainian troops entered the key town of Vovchansk, taking positions north of Kharkiv and along the Russo-Ukrainian border. It was a major development that prevented further Russian shelling of the long-suffering city. On September 14, the ninth day of the operation, the Ukrainian Ministry of Defense announced the liberation of 8,500 square kilometers (3,300 square miles) of Ukrainian territory, encompassing 388 towns, villages, and settlements with a combined population of close to 150,000.[40]

The same day Volodymyr Zelensky paid a surprise visit to the liberated city of Izium in the company of Colonel General Oleksandr Syrsky, the commander of the offensive. Zelensky greeted his troops, who were eager to take selfies with the president, and helped to raise the Ukrainian flag over the city. "Earlier, when we looked upward, we always sought blue sky and sunshine," said Zelensky. "But now we, and especially people in the temporarily occupied territories, looking up, seek only one thing—the flag of our state. It means that the heroes are here. It means that the enemy is gone; he has fled." What the enemy left behind were graves with more than 440 bodies and accounts of summary arrests, rape, and executions that reminded one of the Russian occupation of Bucha. "Russia is leaving death behind it everywhere and must be held responsible," stated Zelensky after his return from Izium.[41]

Zelensky's visit to Izium was an act of personal courage, as the front line was only a couple of dozen miles away. After a long and disorderly retreat, the Russians finally managed to stabilize their defensive lines. From Kupiansk in the north almost all the way to Izium in the south, they used the Oskil River and its reservoir as a defensive position. South of the Oskil River reservoir, the Ukrainian armed forces took the town of Sviatohirsk, known for its Orthodox monastery, but the Russians established effective defenses around the city of Lyman, farther east of Sviatohirsk. The Ukrainians slowed down their advance in the area but continued the counteroffensive. By the end of the month they had encircled the Russian troops near Lyman, delivering another major blow to their morale and to Russian defenses in the area.[42]

The Liberation of Kherson

The Kharkiv offensive ended the stalemate that developed at the front after the Ukrainians lost Siverodonetsk and Lysychansk in the Donbas. "Ukraine has the initiative and Ukraine gets to decide what the focus will now be," commented the Polish defense analyst Konrad Muzyka in an interview with the *Financial Times*. It was the beginning of the third stage of the war: the first had been characterized by Russian advances and, despite a setback in the battle for Kyiv, had lasted until early July. The second, in which the front lines stopped moving, had continued for more than two months. In the third stage, as the *The Economist* noted, Ukraine had seized the initiative. In full agreement with Western observers, Putin's nationalist critic Igor Girkin now claimed that "the opponent has already won the struggle for the initiative."[43]

The surprising and fast-paced offensive in the Kharkiv region showed that the Ukrainians could advance on more than one front. Their slow-moving offensive on the right bank of the Dnieper near Kharkiv and Beryslav continued, with Ukrainian troops recapturing eastern parts of the country. Despite the suggestions of some observers, Ukrainian actions in the south never amounted to mere distraction: it was a well-planned and -executed theater offensive in its own right. The planning of the counteroffensive had begun in midsummer as a response to President Zelensky's request to his commanders to prepare

THE COUNTEROFFENSIVE   237

an advance that would allow Ukraine to reclaim the south and cut off Mariupol from the rest of Russian-held territory.

According to *New York Times* reporting, the Ukrainians had done as their president requested, but their American advisers doubted that such a large-scale operation could succeed without significant Ukrainian casualties. Moreover, a war game conducted by the American and Ukrainian military projected failure, suggesting that the Ukrainians had to reduce their ambitions. Once American intelligence confirmed that the Russians were moving their troops southward and exposing their northern flank, the Ukrainians proposed two operations instead of one—a slowly developing one in the Kherson region and a quick one near Kharkiv. The Americans and the British reviewed the plans and gave their blessings. The rest was up to the Ukrainians, who executed their plans brilliantly.[44]

A signal outcome of the Ukrainian advance was the realization in world capitals from Moscow to Washington that the Ukrainian armed forces could not only defend their positions but also launch major offensives. Western supporters of Ukraine could now argue convincingly that the best way to end the war was to provide the Ukrainians with the means to defeat the Russians. "You won't really hear anyone talking against more weapons now, just a chorus of supporters and one or two staying silent," a senior European diplomat told the *Financial Times*, commenting on a meeting of Western defense ministers discussing future arms deliveries to Ukraine. "It is 100 per cent true that more weapons mean more Ukrainian territory. And less blood, less tears," said another official.[45]

The Ukrainian counteroffensive in the northeast was a major blow to Putin, shaking his grip on Russian society. It had begun on September 6, when Putin visited the Russian Far East to observe war games with his defense minister, Sergei Shoigu, and chief of staff, General Valerii Gerasimov. Putin never commented publicly on the defeat at Kharkiv. On September 10, as the Ukrainians took Kupiansk and entered Izium, he took part in the ceremonial opening of a Ferris wheel in Moscow. Ironically, it broke down a few hours after Putin left. On September 30, 2022, as Putin declared the Russian Federation's annexation of Ukraine's Donetsk, Luhansk, Zaporizhia, and Kherson oblasts, the Ukrainian counteroffensive continued, giving the lie to the ceremonial announcement in Moscow.

Inside Russia there were signs of growing opposition to the regime on the part of both liberals and nationalists. Dozens of members of local councils, predominantly from St. Petersburg and Moscow, called for the dictator's resignation, citing his war on Ukraine. "We, the municipal deputies of Russia, believe that the actions of its president, Vladimir Putin, are detrimental to Russia's and its citizens' future," read one of the petitions. "We demand Vladimir Putin's resignation from the post of President of the Russian Federation." Igor Girkin, the mouthpiece of the ultranationalist and pro-war lobby, suggested the possibility of "betrayal" within Putin's circle. He did not dare to accuse Putin himself, but Girkin's viewers understood that their guru held Putin and his defense minister personally responsible for the failure of the "special military operation" and reluctance to order a national mobilization.[46]

Putin was caught between two fires—growing dissatisfaction with the war in Russia's major cities, which made the mobilization of badly needed troops problematic and dangerous for the regime, and nationalist demands to proceed with such mobilization. To deflect criticism from the Kremlin, Putin instructed his regional officials, including Ramzan Kadyrov of Chechnya, to initiate mobilization drives within their administrative units. He also followed in Stalin's footsteps, turning to the penal system to solve his recruitment problem. Stalin had exploited inmates of the Gulag not only to build his industrial base but also to augment the ranks of the Red Army during World War II. Putin was now resorting to the same tactic to save the situation on his Ukrainian front, but the effort was proving insufficient.[47]

Soon after the Russian defeat near Kharkiv, a video went viral. It showed so-called Putin's chef, Yevgenii Prigozhin, a businessman and former convict close to the Kremlin, visiting a penal colony to recruit criminals into private Kremlin military companies, including Wagner and Liga, that he was helping to finance. Prigozhin promised the inmates money and presidential pardons if they joined his formations. That was Putin's original response to Girkin and others who were demanding mobilization. Then, on September 21, after some apparent vacillation, Putin made his choice, declaring the mobilization of reservists. He had seemingly concluded that discontent in Russia was a lesser threat to his regime than the possibility of losing the war in Ukraine. The protests in Chechnya, Dagestan, and other ethnic enclaves of Russia soon forced him to admit the "excesses" of the mobilization, but it went ahead nevertheless.[48]

As military commissions drafted Russian men into the army and sent them to the front lines of Ukraine with no training whatever, Putin's sham referenda were conducted in four partly occupied oblasts of Ukraine. They involved armed soldiers visiting the apartments of Ukrainian citizens and forcing them to vote in favor of Russian annexation of their regions. On September 30, 2022, Putin cited the "will of millions" as he signed decrees formally annexing four oblasts of Ukraine, some of them under Ukrainian control, as was the case with the city of Zaporizhia and its population of some 750,000.[49]

In his "annexation" speech, Putin quoted his favorite Russian émigré philosopher Ivan Ilyin and repeated many themes of his earlier pronouncements. He recalled the imperial history of New Russia—the term he now used to denote the Kherson and Zaporizhia oblasts; decried the destruction of that "great country," the USSR; and spoke about the allegedly free choice of "millions of people who, by their culture, religion, traditions, and language, consider themselves part of Russia." But the overriding subject of the address was Putin's hatred of "the West," which he mentioned thirty-three times. The West, insisted Putin, was guilty of "the plunder of India and Africa" and "the wars of England and France against China." He blamed the West for the economic hardships of the post-Soviet era, accusing its leaders of neocolonialism—a bizarre claim coming from the leader of a former empire now waging a colonial war against its former subject. Putin claimed that the West "continues looking for another chance to strike a blow at us, to weaken and break up Russia, which they have always dreamed about, to divide our state and set our peoples against each other, and to condemn them to poverty and extinction."[50]

Ironically, as Putin delivered his speech, Ukrainian forces were concluding the encirclement of the city of Lyman in the newly "annexed" Donetsk oblast of Ukraine. It would fall into the Ukrainians' hands the next day, becoming the first town of those formally annexed by Russia to be liberated from its armed forces. In the course of the next week, over sixty settlements were recaptured by the Ukrainians in the Kherson region, where the Russian front had collapsed. To add insult to injury, on October 8, one day after Putin celebrated his seventieth birthday with the government-organized rally in his native city of St. Petersburg, the Ukrainian dream of blowing up the Kerch bridge in the Crimea finally came true: a huge explosion demolished two flights of the highway bridge and damaged the railway one. Putin responded with massive missile strikes on Kyiv and other cities of Ukraine, aiming at civilian targets and destroying the country's energy infrastructure. That became his new target in the war, the goal being the destruction of the Ukrainian economy and the will of Ukrainians to resist.[51]

But the Ukrainians kept fighting. The successful attack on the Crimean bridge added to the enormous logistical problems that Russia already had experienced supplying its military formations on the right bank of the Dnieper River, in and around the city of Kherson. As the Ukrainian armed forces continued their HIMARS attacks on the Russian pontoon bridges across the Dnieper, pressure increased on the Russian military to cut their losses and withdraw from the right bank of the river. On October 18, ten days after the Ukrainian attack on the Crimean bridge, General Sergei Surovikin, the newly appointed commander of Russian operations in Ukraine, announced imminent "difficult decisions" with regard to the Russian troops in and around Kherson. In the following days, the Russians moved their military and civilian administrations to the left bank of the Dnieper River, and began the removal of armaments, military equipment, and cultural artifacts, including paintings from local museums, rare-book-library collections, and even the remains of Grigorii Potemkin, the favorite of Catherine II, and first Russian governor general of the region, who had been buried in Kherson. They also announced the evacuation of civilians and used the civilian population as cover against Ukrainian artillery attacks as they moved their troops and equipment across the Dnieper crossings.

Then, on November 9 in a televised meeting with the Russian defense minister Sergei Shoigu, Surovikin proposed the withdrawal of the Russian troops to the left bank of the river. The general cited the lack of prospects for any future success of the Russian army on the right bank. Shoigu, who claimed that the most important task he and Surovikin faced was saving the lives of Russian soldiers, gave his consent and ordered the withdrawal. He thereby assumed political responsibility for the withdrawal, humiliating for Putin, from the capital of a region that had just been declared part of the Russian Federation.[52]

The Ukrainians were surprised by the speed with which the Russians crossed the Dnieper. On November 10, the day after Surovikin's televised statement, Oleksii Reznikov, the Ukrainian minister of defense, estimated that it would take the Russian troops up to one week to leave their positions in and around Kherson. But as Reznikov spoke, the Russians were already leaving the region, looting the area and blowing up smaller and larger bridges behind their retreating columns. They began the retreat on the night of November 8, even before Surovikin's public announcement, and abandoned the city of Kherson on November 11.

Even before the Ukrainian army moved in, the citizens of Kherson raised the Ukrainian banner over the city administration building. Ukrainian special forces, the first to move in, were welcomed by cheering crowds in the city center. They wasted no time in removing the Russian propaganda images with the words "Russia is here forever" from the city's billboards. The internet exploded with photoshopped images of the billboards now stating, "Russia is here till November 11."[53]

The Ukrainian siege of Russian troops on the right bank of the Dnieper had finally produced the results Oleksii Reznikov hoped for when announcing the coming counteroffensive back in July. The

Ukrainians succeeded in liberating the only regional center that the Russians had managed to capture and did so without a frontal attack on the city. The difference between Mariupol, captured by the Russians after its almost complete destruction, and Kherson, reclaimed by the Ukrainians without a street fight, could not have been more striking: the city stayed pretty much intact. That was not the case with the rest of the region. As the Russians retreated, they destroyed every bridge they had ever crossed, a clear indication that they were not preparing to return any time soon. Russia was losing the war that it had started in a desperate attempt to regain its superpower status. Some US observers believed that Putin's loss of Kherson constituted a turning point in the war, placing the Ukrainians in a position to reclaim the rest of the south, including the Crimea annexed in 2014. In the course of his surprise visit to Kherson on November 12, President Zelensky declared that for him, peace meant the liberation of Ukraine's entire territory.[54]

The Ukrainian successes at Kherson were celebrated not just by the Ukrainians but also by their allies in the West. "Kherson is a step towards victory and demonstrates what can be achieved if there is a steady supply of western military technical assistance," wrote Jack Watling of the Royal United Services Institute soon after the Russian retreat from the right bank of the Dnieper. By that time the United Kingdom had committed £2.3 billion, or over $2.7 billion, in military assistance for Ukraine, making the second largest contribution to the cause of stopping Russia after the United States with its $19.3 billion contribution. The Ukrainian counteroffensives in the east and south would have been all but impossible without that massive military assistance. But Western assistance did not come at once, and not without hesitancy and debate, especially among Ukraine's European allies.[55]

12

THE RETURN OF THE WEST

The darkness of a spring evening had already fallen on the Royal Castle in downtown Warsaw when President Biden arrived to deliver what White House officials told journalists would be a landmark speech of his presidency.

The time was 6:15 p.m. on March 26, 2022, the thirtieth day of the war. A few hours earlier, the Russians had launched a missile attack on Lviv, a major Ukrainian city close to the Polish border, sending a clear message to President Biden that he was not welcome in what Moscow considered its backyard. Biden was on the third day of his diplomatic tour of Europe, which had begun in Brussels with summit meetings of the European Union and NATO discussing Russian aggression against Ukraine. The next stop was Warsaw, where the president met with Polish officials and members of the Ukrainian government, including the ministers of defense and foreign affairs, Oleksii Reznikov and Dmytro Kuleba. Biden also visited a location close to the Polish-Ukrainian border, where he spoke with Ukrainian refugees. By that point 3.5 million people had left their homeland and found shelter in Poland and other eastern and central European countries.[1]

Now some of those refugees joined Polish and Ukrainian dignitaries at the Warsaw Royal Castle to await the American president's address. When Biden showed up in front of the crowd, he was met with applause and American and Polish flags as well as cell phones flashing in an attempt to capture the historic moment. Biden struck a chord with the audience right away as he quoted Poland's favorite son, Pope John Paul II: "Do not be afraid!" John Paul had pronounced those words during his first papal visit to his homeland in the summer of 1979. They had sounded then as a call not to succumb to fear of the tyrannical communist state. "In the face of a cruel and brutal system of government, it was a message that helped end Soviet repression in Central and Eastern Europe 30 years ago," said the president, going on to make a direct connection between Poland in 1979 and Ukraine in 2022. "It was a message that will overcome the cruelty and brutality of this unjust war."[2]

With his reference to the pope, Biden established not only a bond with his audience but also a sense of continuity between the new war and the Cold War battles of the past. "We emerged anew in the great battle for freedom: a battle between democracy and autocracy, between liberty and repression, between a rules-based order and one governed by brute force," declared Biden. He went on to warn that the new crisis would not pass in a few days or weeks but would take years, if not decades, to overcome. "This battle will not be won in days or months either," declared Biden. "We need to steel ourselves for the long fight ahead." He defined the new struggle in the language of the Cold War.[3]

But there was also a different ring to his speech. Unlike such certified Cold Warriors as Winston Churchill and Ronald Reagan, who had avoided direct attacks on their opponents—Reagan's challenge to Gorbachev to "tear down this wall" in Berlin was an exception—Biden went directly after his nemesis, Vladimir Putin. "Putin has the gall to say he's 'de-Nazifying' Ukraine. It's a lie. It's just cynical. He knows that. And it's also obscene," Biden told the crowd before referring to

Ukraine's president, Volodymyr Zelensky, his democratic election, and the fact that most of his Jewish ancestors had been murdered in the Holocaust. "And Putin has the audacity, like all autocrats before him, to believe that might will make right," continued Biden. He concluded with an unscripted emotional outburst: "For God's sake, this man cannot remain in power."[4]

The White House tried to walk back the remark, issuing a statement to the effect that Biden's words did not imply regime change as an American goal in relations with Russia. The remark was not included in the official White House transcript. Nevertheless, it was clearly in the spirit of Biden's earlier comments about Putin. In March 2021 he had already agreed in public with an interviewer's suggestion that Putin was a killer and then found it necessary to explain himself to the Russian president. There was no indication that an explanation or tepid excuse would be forthcoming this time. When meeting with Ukrainian refugees at the Warsaw sports arena, Biden had called Putin a "butcher."[5]

This denunciation harked back to Winston Churchill's verbal attack on no less odious a figure than Adolf Hitler in a speech given on June 22, 1941. "Hitler is a monster of wickedness, insatiable in his lust for blood and plunder," Churchill declared in a radio broadcast. "Not content with having all Europe under his heel or else terrorized into various forms of abject submission, he must now carry his work of butchery and desolation among the vast multitudes of Russia and of Asia." Ironically, the speech was delivered on the very day of Hitler's invasion of the Soviet Union and was intended to express some form of solidarity with Stalin.[6]

Although the Biden administration was at pains to make clear that it had no intention of involving the United States in the Russo-Ukrainian war, the president's rhetoric was redolent of the Cold War. In that tradition, his speech was billed as remarks "on the United Efforts of the Free World to Support the People of Ukraine." There were four references to "the West" or "the Western World," and twenty uses of the words "free" and freedom."[7]

For anyone listening to Biden's speech on that March evening in Warsaw or watching it on television around the world, there was no doubt that the United States was back in Europe to lead its allies in the battle for freedom against an old enemy, and that the West as a whole was involved in the struggle. The joint actions of Americans and Europeans—provision of military and economic assistance to Ukraine, sheltering of refugees and, most controversially, the imposition of joint sanctions on Russia—indicated a revival of the Cold War era alliance.

The Sanctions Coalition

Joseph Biden had begun to build a transatlantic front against Russian aggression long before February 2022. The focus then was on sanctions against individuals responsible for Russia's aggression in 2014 and the Russian economy as a whole. The first sanctions were imposed by the United States and the European Union after Russia's annexation of the Crimea and the beginning of its hybrid warfare in the Donbas. Diplomats and economists in Washington and the European capitals were soon busily preparing new sanctions in case Putin should actually declare war. Public discussion of possible new sanctions was intended to dissuade him from doing so.

In late January the White House announced that the United States and its European partners were prepared to implement "massive consequences that were not considered in 2014." One week before the start of the war, Vice President Kamala Harris declared a similar but more specific threat at the security conference in Munich: "We have prepared, together, economic measures that will be swift, severe, and united. We will impose far-reaching financial sanctions and export controls. We will target Russia's financial institutions and key industries. And we will target those who are complicit and those who aid and abet this unprovoked invasion." Whatever the reaction in Moscow, this time the West was not bluffing: Biden had indeed put together a powerful sanctions coalition.[8]

As soon as Putin declared on February 21 that he was abandoning the Minsk Agreements and recognizing the "independence" of his puppet states in Donbas, the sanctions began to roll out. The United States immediately banned all economic relations with the puppet states, and the European Union imposed a travel ban on five prominent Russians in addition to a freeze of their assets. That was just the beginning: more sanctions were declared on the following day. The United States adopted measures denying Russian entities the ability to borrow money on international markets and blocked financial transactions of two Russian banks and three oligarchic groups. Europe was not far behind, as the German government stopped the licensing of the $11 billion Nord Stream II natural gas pipeline, the centerpiece of Berlin-Moscow economic cooperation in the previous few years.[9]

All this took place before Russian tanks and troops crossed the Ukrainian border. The message was: this time we are serious and united. Putin ignored it. The start of the war triggered a new wave of sanctions. The United States and Europe were joined by their Asian allies, including South Korea and Taiwan. Before the end of February 2022, Russian assets amounting to $1 trillion had been frozen throughout the world, the largest portion consisting of the Russian Central Bank's $630 billion in foreign-exchange reserves. "The West declares economic war on Russia," ran a headline in the influential American online publication *Politico*.[10]

In the course of ten months of warfare, between February 23 and December 16, 2022, the United States and the European Union agreed on nine packages of sanctions against Russia. Sanctioned for the first time were Vladimir Putin himself, the Russian foreign minister, Sergei Lavrov, and hundreds of members of the Russian political and business elite, including hosts of television programs engaged in war propaganda and the spread of misinformation at home and abroad. Sanctions against individuals included travel bans and freezing assets. The European Union also suspended the broadcasting activity of state-owned Russian media outlets on its territory, most notably the Kremlin's prime mouthpieces, Sputnik and Russia Today.

Sanctions in the financial sector led to a freeze on more than half of Russia's reserves and a prohibition on the use of Euro-dominated banknotes in EU transactions in or with Russia. Russian banks were cut off from the SWIFT messaging service, making it impossible to conduct international financial transactions involving foreign currency. New technologies, especially those that were or could be used in Russian weapons production (new Russian weapons were all built with the use of Western technology and microchips provided from abroad), were placed out of Moscow's reach.

It became illegal for countries participating in the sanctions to purchase, import, or transfer Russian-produced gold. Bans and embargoes were placed on Russian petroleum products, oil in particular. The European Union agreed to end the import of Russian oil by sea within six to eight months, reducing the amount it consumed by 90 percent. Those measures fit the EU green agenda of reducing carbon gas emissions but were introduced largely to limit the Russian government's revenues and ability to fund the war. Moscow's income from those sales alone amounted to $1 billion per day. In December, the EU countries agreed to introduce a cap on the price of Russian oil sold outside of the EU. The imposition of the embargo and introduction of the cap were estimated to cost the Russian budget $120 million per day in revenue.[11]

Arming Ukraine

"The birds are flying in, as if returning from a vortex!" wrote the Ukrainian defense minister, Oleksii Reznikov, on his Facebook page on February 11, 2022. He then explained what he had in mind: "another 90 tons of ammunition arrived from the United States for Ukraine's Armed Forces." He estimated the overall weight of the donated military assistance at 1,300 tons. Such posts, along with footage of weapons being unloaded from foreign airplanes, boosted Ukrainian morale and helped repel the Russian attack on Kyiv during the first days of the invasion.[12]

The weapons came from a number of Ukraine's European allies, with Britain leading the effort to supply arms, but most of them would come from the United States. On February 26, President Biden approved a $350 million military aid package. In Washington, law firms and lobbyists worked around the clock, sometimes pro bono, to help the government come up with that package. It was a major change of course. In the spring of 2021, Washington had prepared a $100 million package of military assistance to Ukraine but put it on hold, expecting a possible breakthrough at the Geneva summit with Putin in June. A $60 million package was announced in August, but the weapons and munitions would not be delivered to Ukraine in full until November. In December 2021, as the Ukrainian crisis led to growing international tensions, the Biden White House had to be nudged by members of Congress to provide Stinger and Javelin missiles requested by the Ukrainians. The administration was reluctant to do so at the time, but the outbreak of war changed that attitude.[13]

Weapons began to arrive en masse when it became clear that the Ukrainians were resisting successfully and that whatever assistance they received would increase their fighting power instead of falling into enemy hands, as had been the case with US supplies to the Afghan army a few months earlier. Seventy percent of the weapons in the package approved by Biden on February 26 were delivered to Ukraine within the next five days. Much of that delivery came from American bases in Germany and moved across the Polish and Romanian borders before the Russian army, shocked by the Ukrainian resistance, could take any countermeasures. The Ukrainians made good use of what they received. "All of us have been tremendously impressed by how effectively the Ukrainian armed forces have been using the equipment that we've provided them," the Pentagon's senior Russia hand, Laura Cooper, told the *New York Times*.[14]

There would be much more assistance to come. On March 16, Biden announced an additional $800 million in military aid to Ukraine, bringing the total amount that he had approved in the course of the previous week to $1 billion. Another billion would follow. The new package included 800 Stinger anti-aircraft systems, increasing the number of those missiles supplied by the United States to 1,400, as well as 2,000

Javelin anti-tank missiles, bringing their overall number to 4,600. New to the assistance program were 100 Tactical Unmanned Aerial Systems, or drones. On April 21 there was a further announcement from the White House and an additional $800 million in military assistance. This time the package included Switchblade or kamikaze drones and howitzers, or long-range artillery pieces. "We're in a critical window now of time where they're going to set the stage for the next phase of this war," declared Biden in connection with the new assistance.[15]

The Russian withdrawal from Kyiv and northern Ukraine did indeed mark a new stage of the war. It began with a jolt—terrible news and heartbreaking images of crimes committed by the retreating Russian troops in Bucha and other Ukrainian towns and villages. The world reacted with horror and resolve that the war criminals had to be defeated and destroyed. The Ukrainians had proved capable of doing so as long as they received plenty of military assistance: disrupting Russian supply lines with Javelin and drone attacks was not enough. The Russians, who had much shorter and well-protected supply lines in southern and eastern Ukraine, could only be dislodged with tanks and airplanes. East European NATO members who had inherited Soviet weapons with which the Ukrainians were familiar were already transferring what they could to Ukraine. It was up to the United States and its West European partners to provide more.

Biden was prepared to increase American support for Ukraine. A new program of American military assistance was announced on May 9, Victory Day in Russia, when Vladimir Putin held a parade on Red Square in Moscow. There was doleful irony in the coincidence of Russia's "Victory Day" with the Lend-Lease program for Ukraine that Biden had requested and obtained from Congress. The United States had not initiated a Lend-Lease program for an ally since World War II, and the allies at that time had been the United Kingdom and the Soviet Union. The United States had provided more than $50 billion ($690 billion in today's currency), with more than half that amount going to the United Kingdom and roughly one-fifth to the Soviet Union. The new Lend-Lease Act allowed the president to authorize up to $33 billion in military aid to Ukraine in addition to the $3.8 billion already spent for that purpose since the beginning of the war. The House of Representatives overwhelmingly supported the bill with a majority of 417 to 10. "The cost of the fight is not cheap, but caving to aggression is even more costly," declared Biden on signing the act into law.[16]

The United States was again involved in the kind of war in which it had not participated since the mid-twentieth century. As in March 1941, when President Franklin D. Roosevelt signed the original Lend-Lease Act, the United States was not joining the war directly. The goal now, as it had been then, was to help victims of aggression. The Biden administration was determined to remove Russia as a threat to peace not only in Ukraine but globally, to ensure its defeat in the current war and degrade its ability to wage new wars. That was the leitmotif of the pronouncements made on April 26 by Secretary of Defense Lloyd Austin, who, together with Secretary of State Antony Blinken, had paid a surprise visit to Kyiv one day earlier. "We want to see Russia weakened to the degree that it can't do the kinds of things that it has done in invading Ukraine," declared Austin upon his arrival in Poland from Kyiv. He added: "We believe that we can win," and then corrected himself: "they can win if they have the right equipment, the right support."

Later that day, Austin joined the chairman of the Joint Chiefs of Staff, General Mark A. Milley, the Ukrainian defense minister, Oleksii Reznikov, and military and civil officials from more than forty countries at the US air base Ramstein, Germany. Representatives of the United States, Ukraine, and Germany were seated at the head table. The participants included not just delegates of NATO member states but also those of Israel, Morocco, and Qatar, among others. The Japanese defense minister joined the meeting online. They had all gathered to discuss the coordination and acceleration of military aid to Ukraine. "We are going to keep moving heaven and earth," Austin told the assembled journalists to emphasize his determination and that of his colleagues to assist Ukraine in defending its independence. The participants agreed on immediate steps, created a coordinating center to manage assistance, and decided to hold regular monthly meetings.[17]

It was the first gathering of the "Ukraine Defense Consultative Group"—in fact, a new war coalition. The United States was in the driver's seat with regard to initiative, political clout, and quantity and quality of current and future arms supplies, but the help of the other participants was essential as well. In Ramstein, the free world of which President Biden had spoken in Warsaw the previous month had come together. Further developments in the war and in the world at large depended on the ability of that group to remain united. It achieved that goal and increased its membership to over fifty countries by the fall of 2022. The military supplies provided by the members of the group allowed Ukraine to regain initiative at the battlefield in September of that year.[18]

The British Charge

In June 2022 the Ukrainian edition of *Forbes* published a list of twenty friends of Ukraine—the countries that had contributed most to its defense. The United States was the unchallenged leader, with its commitment of $46 billion (0.22 percent of its GDP) for that purpose. But the list also took note of visits of national leaders to Kyiv and other forms of support, including participation in sanctions against Russia, which put Poland one line above the United States and made it the unrivaled champion, scoring 97 of 100 possible points. In terms of share of GDP dedicated to assistance to Ukraine, the leader was Estonia, with 0.81 percent of its GDP, followed by Latvia with 0.72 percent and Poland with 0.26 percent. The United Kingdom stood at 0.18 percent, while France contributed 0.08 percent, Germany 0.06 percent, and Italy 0.03 percent of its GDP.[19]

European assistance to Ukraine measured in percentage of GDP was quite revealing of the divisions in the Western bloc with regard to the war in Ukraine, despite unprecedented solidarity among European capitals in condemning Putin's unprovoked aggression against a sovereign country. The Baltic states, formerly Soviet republics that had joined the EU and NATO but still felt threatened by Russia, were concerned that if Putin won in Ukraine, they would be next. Accordingly, they formed the most pro-Ukrainian group in Europe. Their position was best expressed by Prime Minister Kaja Kallas of Estonia, who declared in her speech in Berlin that gas might be expensive, but freedom is priceless. "It's up to every government to decide how much of the burden its people are ready to carry. But it is equally necessary we get the message through to our people—what is our neighbor's problem today will be our problem tomorrow. We are in danger when our neighbor's house is on fire."[20]

Equally eager to support Ukraine was a group of former East European satellites of the USSR, which was led by Poland and included Slovakia and the Czech Republic. Although members of the EU and NATO, they were concerned about the possibility of Russian troops showing up on their borders. They not only marshaled their diplomatic, economic, and military resources to help Ukraine defend itself but also took in most of the Ukrainian refugees—more than 3.5 million were welcomed, housed, and fed in Poland alone. The only exception to that group had been Hungary, led by its strongman, Viktor Orban, who modeled his illiberal populist regime on the one built by Vladimir Putin, perhaps his closest political ally. Besides Orban's political sympathies for Moscow, hard-nosed calculation was involved: dependent on Russia for the lion's share of Hungary's energy supply, Orban gave only limited support to the anti-Russian coalition, arguing against supplying weapons to Kyiv and against the sanctions regime imposed by the collective West.[21]

The countries of "Old Europe," not immediately threatened by invasion, split into two groups. In a class by itself was the United Kingdom, which had left the European Union but was now very decisively reinserting itself into European politics. London emerged as the leader of the pro-Ukrainian European front, committing more money to the Ukrainian cause than any other country except the United States—more than $5 billion as of June 2022. Germany, France, and Italy were lower down on that list. Their leaders were reluctant to introduce sanctions against Russia and not eager to provide much military assistance.

Before the war and during its first stage, they tried to position themselves as possible mediators in future peace talks rather than participants in a political, economic, and military conflict threatening not only Ukraine but Europe as a whole.[22]

The British prime minister, Boris Johnson, emerged early as the champion of Ukraine and its interests on the European scene. On April 10 he became the first Western leader to visit Volodymyr Zelensky, walking with him in central Kyiv soon after the Russian withdrawal from the Kyiv suburbs. A camera caught a middle-aged Kyivan thanking Johnson for what he had been doing for Ukraine and saying that he would be grateful for the rest of his life. By then Johnson had become a household name in Ukraine, a symbol of Western support for the embattled country. According to well-informed Ukrainian journalists, Johnson's visit to Kyiv and the discovery of Russian war crimes in the Kyiv suburb of Bucha ten days earlier convinced Zelensky and his team that negotiations with Russia at that stage of the war were impossible and pointless. Johnson's visit also opened the door to subsequent visits to Kyiv of other Western leaders, including the American secretaries of defense and state, Lloyd Austin and Antony Blinken, later that month.[23]

Many, especially in Britain, accused Johnson of using his self-appointed role as principal cheerleader for Ukraine to distract attention from the parliamentary inquiry into his hosting of parties at a time when government-imposed COVID restrictions had prohibited such gatherings. If the critics were right, then Johnson clearly knew what he was doing. The sympathy of the British public for Ukraine during the first month after the Russian invasion was overwhelming, as was its condemnation of Russia's actions and desire to free Britain from the influence of numerous Russian oligarchs who had made London their second or even first home and, in the eyes of many citizens, corrupted British politics and culture with their money. A book by the journalist Oliver Bullough on that subject, titled *Butler to the World* and published in March 2022, became an instant bestseller.

In early June 2022, on the hundredth day of all-out war, Johnson's close ally, Foreign Secretary Liz Truss, issued a statement listing various forms of British assistance to Ukraine. She began with UK-imposed sanctions on 1,000 Russian individuals and 100 entities, including oligarchs with a total net worth of more than £117 billion. Johnson had been heavily criticized by his opponents and the public at large for appointing one of those oligarchs, Yevgenii Lebedev, the son of a former KGB agent, to the House of Lords without proper security clearance. There were also accusations that the prime minister's Conservative Party had taken money from donors with links to Russian oligarchs. But Johnson and Truss were now cleaning up relations with the oligarchs. They could also demonstrate substantial aid for Ukraine. While it was still very difficult for Ukrainian refugees to come to Britain and for British families to support their applications, the United Kingdom supplied Ukraine with 1,000 missiles and trained 22,000 of its troops.[24]

Although domestic politics undoubtedly played a role in Boris Johnson's support of Ukraine, the prime minister had not only a domestic but also an international agenda in mind. The author of a best-selling book about Winston Churchill who tried to model himself on his hero, Johnson was intent on maintaining Britain in its traditional role as a key European and indeed global political actor despite the enormous damage to its international reputation delivered by Brexit. "Oh the irony!" wrote the *Guardian*, always critical of the prime minister, in mid-May 2022. "Boris Johnson, the Brexit ringleader who turned his back on the EU, now boldly leads the defense of Europe in the face of Russian aggression. An exaggeration? Yes, but behind the hype lies an intriguing story. . . . Johnson is using the Ukraine crisis to mend fences with some old European allies. His aim: to re-establish the UK as a continental power."[25]

The Russo-Ukrainian war indeed provided London with an opportunity to rebuild old alliances with the East European and Nordic countries, traditionally skeptical about the power of Brussels and, in the case of Poland and the Baltic states, also displeased with the lukewarm attitude of the countries of Old Europe toward Russian aggression. Johnson had embraced and heartily supported the decision of the Finnish and

Swedish governments to become members of NATO in 2022. In 2017 both countries had joined the UK-led Expeditionary Force, a NATO-allied grouping of north European countries that also included Norway, Denmark, Iceland, the Netherlands, and the Baltic states. The Expeditionary Force became a European army in the making—the armed force that France had talked about but Britain was actively creating. In March, Johnson invited the leaders of the Expeditionary Force countries to London, where President Zelensky addressed them by video link, asking for military assistance.

Johnson also engaged the East European countries, trying to create a pan-European structure that would include Ukraine under London's auspices. In February, less than a week before the invasion, London, Warsaw, and Kyiv announced the creation of a British-Polish-Ukrainian military initiative that the Ukrainian foreign minister, Dmytro Kuleba, called a "tripartite format of cooperation." According to reports in the Italian media, during his April visit to Kyiv Johnson proposed to Zelensky the creation of a potential rival to the European Union—a UK-led European Commonwealth including Poland, the Baltic states, and Ukraine. Clearly, for Johnson, Brexit did not mean abandoning European politics. He was planning a power center alternative to Brussels and challenging the legitimacy of a policy toward Russia made in Paris and Berlin, which favored the economic concerns of the old Europe over the security concerns of the new one.[26]

German Fears

Russia's invasion of Ukraine was a major blow to the policy, advocated by the long-serving and recently retired chancellor Angela Merkel of Germany, of encouraging economic cooperation with Russia not just to solve Germany's and Europe's energy problems but also to turn Russia into a reliable economic and political ally. Merkel's policies toward Russia were rarely criticized in Germany during her long tenure, which lasted from November 2005 until December 2021. She helped to negotiate the Minsk II agreements that ended the active phase of the Russo-

Ukrainian war in the Donbas in February 2015 and played an important role in imposing and maintaining German and thus European sanctions on Russia after Putin's annexation of the Crimea.

Merkel was also instrumental in providing political backing for the construction of Nord Stream II, the gas pipeline from Russia to Germany, more specifically to the settlement called Lubmin in her Bundestag constituency. This project, undertaken after the imposition of sanctions, was criticized abroad but perceived largely positively at home. When Merkel left office in December 2021 to general accolades celebrating her numerous political achievements, there was little reason to believe that Nord Stream II would not become operational. Even American opposition had ceased after Biden replaced Trump in the White House. Germany was about to further increase its dependence on Russian gas, and it was believed that Russia's need for Western revenue would make Putin more friendly toward collective Europe.[27]

Although there were dark clouds on the horizon, with the United States and the United Kingdom warning the world about imminent Russian aggression against Ukraine, many in Germany believed that the problem could be solved with concessions to Russia. In January, a German naval officer, Vice Admiral Kay-Achim Schönbach, was caught on tape suggesting that the Crimea would stay Russian anyway, and that Putin only wanted some show of respect. "It is easy to give him the respect he really demands—and probably also deserves," stated Schönbach, after exclaiming: "And, my God, giving someone respect is low cost, even no cost." The tapes became public and went viral, forcing Schönbach's resignation. But his words reflected the thinking of the good part of the German political, military, and business elite at the time.[28]

The sixty-three-year-old Social Democrat Olaf Scholz, who replaced Angela Merkel as chancellor in December 2021, was immediately faced with the international crisis caused by Putin's demand that NATO's borders be shifted westward and his concentration of Russian troops on Ukraine's borders. What only a few months earlier had seemed a wise policy toward Russia conducted by Merkel was now increasingly perceived as the appeasement of an aggressor. The international climate changed, and Nord Stream II suddenly found itself in hot water: Germany's allies, the United States in particular, wanted the German government to stop the certification of the controversial pipeline.

In February, Scholz visited Washington and apparently agreed with Biden to cancel Nord Stream II certification if Putin went to war. "If there is military aggression against Ukraine, tough, mutually agreed and far-reaching sanctions will be imposed. It will be extremely costly for Russia to take such a step," declared Scholz at a joint press conference with his American counterpart. He then flew to Moscow to convince Putin not to go to war, assuring Putin that Ukraine had no chance of being admitted to NATO for the next thirty years. Rebuffed there, Scholz made a stop in Kyiv on his way back to Germany. Zelensky was quick to remind him that Nord Stream II was a Russian geopolitical weapon, and his visit produced little public enthusiasm in the Ukrainian capital. While the United States, the United Kingdom, and the East Europeans were already helping Ukraine with weapons, Germany offered 5,000 helmets. The mayor of Kyiv, Vitalii Klychko, a former professional boxer and multiple heavyweight champion, who had lived in Germany and still had celebrity status there, quipped that Germany's next delivery to Ukraine would consist of pillows.[29]

The start of all-out warfare on February 24 took Scholz and the German political elite completely by surprise. "We have woken up in a different world," stated Scholz's foreign minister, Annalena Baerbock. On February 27, in an unprecedented Sunday session of the Bundestag, Scholz declared a major shift in German foreign policy: on the previous day the government had approved a shipment of 1,000 anti-tank and 500 surface-to-air missiles to Ukraine. The requests of Estonia and the Netherlands to transfer some of the German weaponry in their possession to Ukraine, previously declined, were now granted. But most striking was the decision to allocate €100 billion toward Germany's defense and raise the country's military expenditure to more than 2 percent of GDP, a NATO requirement that Germany had heretofore ignored.

Scholz defined the change in his government's policy on two levels. The first was moral and ethical. Ukraine, he argued, had fallen victim to unprovoked aggression, and Germany would stand by it. The second level was geopolitical. "In attacking Ukraine, Putin doesn't just want to eradicate a country from the world map; he is destroying the European security structure we have had in place since Helsinki," said the chancellor. He was referring to the Final Act or Helsinki Accords of 1975, which recognized the post–World War II international borders, including those of the two German states, the Federal Republic of Germany (West Germany) and the German Democratic Republic (East Germany). Ukraine had joined the accords, along with other post-Soviet countries, in 1992. Thus, according to Scholz, the violation of Ukraine's territorial integrity was an attack on the integrity and security of all European states, including the present-day Federal Republic of Germany, reunified in 1990.

Putin, argued Scholz, wanted to "create a new order in Europe, and he has no qualms about using military capabilities to achieve it." The chancellor blamed the war on an individual rather than a country or a nation. "It was Putin who chose this war, not the Russian people, so we must see clearly that this is Putin's war," Scholz told the Bundestag. While Germans of his generation would never question their nation's responsibility for "Hitler's war," Scholz was not about to apply the same standard to the Russians—accusing Russians as a people of aggression had been a taboo in post–World War II Germany—even though polling data would soon demonstrate the Russian population's strong support for their government's "special military operation" in Ukraine. Scholz also warned the public about the need to avoid another world war. The German government was joining the transatlantic wartime alliance but doing so late, reluctantly, and with multiple qualifications.[30]

Despite proclaiming this paradigm shift in foreign policy, Scholz and his government failed to recapture the initiative on the European scene, where the agenda was now being set by the United States, Britain, and the East European countries, all insisting on greater support for Ukraine. Some members of Scholz's government as well as key figures in the Bundestag were of the same persuasion, but Scholz was reluctant to take their advice. In May 2022, a German political scientist summarized his strategy as one that "for the most part, rather hesitantly carries out what allies have already done (such as embargoes and arms deliveries)."[31]

In mid-March, when Volodymyr Zelensky was invited to address the Bundestag by video link from Kyiv, he did not pull his punches but addressed his critique to the previous German government. Zelensky accused Scholz's predecessors of blocking Ukraine's accession to NATO and the EU, funding Russian aggression by means of gas deals with Moscow, and delaying sanctions against the aggressor. The German government had built a new Berlin Wall in Europe, said Zelensky, leaving his country on the wrong side of it. He then appealed to the new leader: "Chancellor Scholz! Tear down this wall. Give Germany the leadership you deserve. And what your descendants will be proud of. Support us. Support peace. Support every Ukrainian. Stop the war. Help us stop it." The address began and ended with a standing ovation by the German parliamentarians, but Scholz's change of rhetoric produced little change in policy: the German government promised military assistance without delivering it.[32]

Zelensky kept up the pressure on Berlin. In early April, after the corpses of civilians murdered by Russian soldiers were discovered in Bucha, Zelensky made a point of publicly inviting Angela Merkel and the former French president, Nicolas Sarkozy, "to visit Bucha and see what the policy of concessions to Russia has led to over the past 14 years. See with your own eyes the tortured and slain Ukrainians." He then reminded the audience about the anniversary of the NATO Bucharest summit of 2008, where the two European leaders, now out of office, had blocked Ukraine's accession to the alliance, perpetuating what the Ukrainian president called "the gray zone, where Moscow thinks it's allowed to do anything. Even the most terrible war crimes."[33]

Soon after Boris Johnson's visit to Kyiv, Zelensky turned down an offer from President Frank-Walter Steinmeier of Germany to visit the Ukrainian capital. Ukrainian officials cited the image of Steinmeier as a supporter of Russia, prevalent in Ukraine, as the reason. Earlier in his career, Steinmeier had served as chief of staff to Chancellor

Gerhard Schröder, who, after ending his political career, became the chief lobbyist of Russian natural gas projects in Germany. But more important to Ukrainians was the role Steinmeier had played as foreign minister in Angela Merkel's government, proposing the "Steinmeier formula" for the implementation of the 2015 Minsk agreements, negotiated with Merkel's help, that were generally believed in Ukraine to have favored Russia.[34]

Zelensky's naming and shaming of Germany seemed to go nowhere as Scholz resisted pressure from abroad and from his own public. Half the nation believed in late May that Germany was not doing enough to support Ukraine, and many ministers in Scholz's own governing coalition were frustrated by German promises made but not kept to supply Ukraine with heavy weapons. Johann Wadephul of the opposition Christian Democratic Union accused the chancellor of "trying to substitute actual deliveries with announcements." The Ukrainian foreign minister, Dmytro Kuleba, expressed his government's frustration with Scholz when he stated: "There are countries from which we are awaiting deliveries, and other countries for which we have grown tired of waiting. Germany belongs to the second group."[35]

Scholz never explained the reason for his delaying tactics. He was probably playing for time, hoping that the war would somehow end without Germany being obliged to deliver the heavy weapons he had promised. There were at least two reasons for his maneuvering, both having to do with Russia. The first was historical and psychological: since World War II, the Germans had felt guilty about their war crimes against *die Russen*, even though Hitler's war in the east had been waged overwhelmingly against Ukrainians and Belarusians on their territory, and wanted to avoid repeating anything that might be construed as aggression against "Russia," broadly defined. The second reason was economic: 55 percent of the natural gas consumed in Germany was purchased from Russia.[36]

Accordingly, Olaf Scholz presented himself first and foremost as a peacemaker, a potential mediator in future peace talks rather than an uncompromising supporter of Ukraine—the role assumed by Washington and London and championed by the leaders of the Baltic and East European states.

The Peacemakers

No other European leader worked as long and as hard to claim the laurels of peacemaker in the newest iteration of the Russo-Ukrainian war as the French president, Emmanuel Macron. Back in December 2019 he had served as host of the first and only meeting between Putin and Zelensky, which ended on a positive note but brought few positive results. In February 2022 Macron was one of the last high-profile Western visitors to Moscow and Kyiv, trying to broker a deal that would prevent the war.[37]

Macron had never given up on the idea, long championed in Paris, of integrating Russia into Europe as a counterbalance to the United States and Germany. It had all but materialized on François Mitterrand's watch in the Gorbachev era, only to slip away with the collapse of the USSR. Macron now hoped to create a new security structure in Europe that would include Russia and diminish the American role in guaranteeing European security. "Macron's goal is to initiate a dialogue on NATO's role in Europe and Ukraine, and potentially a new treaty on arms control, some sort of Helsinki Accords 2.0," argued Carole Grimaud Potter of the Center for Russia and Eastern Europe Research in Geneva a few days before Putin's invasion. "He knows it will take time, and that NATO and the EU will have to give in to some of Russia's demands, [since Russia] wants to guarantee its security and restore the might it lost when the USSR disappeared."[38]

In late May, Macron joined Scholz in trying to convince Putin to end the war. In a three-way telephone conversation they asked Putin for a ceasefire, withdrawal of Russian troops, and opening of direct negotiations with Zelensky. Nothing came of that initiative, as Putin complained about Western arms supplies to Ukraine. But Putin promised Macron and Scholz to resolve the massive food shortage he had created by blocking the Ukrainian Black Sea ports and occupying those on the

Sea of Azov. Ukraine could no longer export its grain and, without it, Africa was poised to succumb to hunger and send hundreds of thousands if not millions of refugees across international borders. Putin had publicly blamed the emerging food crisis on the West and proposed that the Ukrainians either ship their grain through ports occupied by Russia, thereby recognizing their de facto occupation, or demine the Odesa ports, making the city vulnerable to Russian seaborne attack.[39]

A few days after the three-way telephone call with Putin and Scholz, Macron gave an interview in which he referred to France's role as a mediating power and suggested that the West avoid humiliating Russia, "so that the day the fighting stops we can pave a way out through diplomatic means." The "humiliation" remark did not go down well in Kyiv. Foreign minister Dmytro Kuleba tweeted the following day: "Calls to avoid humiliation of Russia can only humiliate France and every other country that would call for it. Because it is Russia that humiliates itself. We all better focus on how to put Russia in its place. This will bring peace and save lives." Macron had warned publicly before about avoiding humiliation of Russia, but this was the first time that the Ukrainians had responded in such a manner.[40]

Zelensky, for whom Macron had been a guide to international politics after the young and inexperienced former comedian became president of a country at war, clearly respected his French mentor but had also had enough of Macron's peace initiatives, which, in Kyiv's eyes, benefited only Russia. Zelensky publicly rejected the idea of trading Ukrainian territories for peace, which Macron had allegedly suggested to him. Kyivan diplomats did not like the French president's public observation that it would take decades for Ukraine to join the European Union. Macron suggested that Ukraine should join a "parallel European community"—a European security arrangement open to non-EU members. The idea was rejected in Kyiv. Zelensky wanted candidate status for Ukraine in the existing European Union, not vague promises of some future parallel accommodation.[41]

Scholz and Macron, Germany and France were not the only members of the Old Europe pushing for a speedy end of the war at the cost of Ukrainian concessions. They were joined wholeheartedly by Italy's Mario Draghi. While most Italians sympathized with Ukraine, the traditional pro-Russian sympathies of the Italian left, fascination with Putin among some elements of the right, and resentment of perceived American hegemony in Europe on the part of both left and right made the Italian media and the public at large more than skeptical when it came to military support for Ukraine and economic punishment of Russia. Fifty-six percent of Italians believed that the American position on the war was "bullish," and 62 percent agreed that the West should find a way to end the military conflict "at all costs."

In May, when the poll was conducted, Draghi visited Joe Biden in Washington to deliver a simple message: while the United States was prepared to support the Ukrainians until the Russian capacity for aggression was fully eliminated or significantly degraded, Europe, meaning Old Europe, wanted the war to end as soon as possible. On what conditions? Foreign minister Luigi Di Maio presented a four-point plan to the secretary-general of the UN and his counterparts in the G7 countries. Kyiv also received a copy, as did Moscow. The plan called for a ceasefire and demilitarization of the front line under UN supervision, the opening of negotiations on the neutral status of Ukraine, and negotiations between Moscow and Kyiv on the status of the Crimea and the Donbas. The Russo-Ukrainian talks were to lead to a multilateral agreement on peace and security in Europe, the last item clearly reminiscent of Macron's ideas. The withdrawal of Russian troops from Ukraine was to lead to the lifting of Western sanctions against Russia.[42]

Washington welcomed the plan as an effort to achieve peace, while Kyiv remained silent, and Moscow rejected it as "not serious." The authors of the plan were rebuffed by the Russian foreign minister, Sergei Lavrov, who suggested that they did not know the history of the crisis. He left it unclear what part of the history he had in mind. The attempts of the leaders of Old Europe to serve as mediators had now been rejected not only by the Ukrainian foreign minister's snide Twitter post about Macron's call not to humiliate Russia but also by the Russian foreign minister's remark on the Italians' poor knowledge of history.[43]

Common Front

The European leaders' peace crusade had effectively run its course by early June. Their efforts were either rejected entirely or met with scant success, appearing to smack increasingly of appeasement. The initiative if not the leadership in European affairs seemed to be passing into the hands of outsiders. They had to change course.

On the night of June 16 Macron, Scholz, and Draghi made their riskiest move since the start of the war. The risk was not only political but also physical. They flew to Poland, where they boarded a train across the Ukrainian border to Kyiv, pursued by the sound of air raid sirens as they approached the Ukrainian capital. They were no longer coming to suggest to Zelensky what peace with Moscow should look like but to express support for whatever position Kyiv would decide to take and catch up in the court of public opinion with those leaders who had visited Kyiv before them—Boris Johnson, Andrzej Duda of Poland, and the Americans. While Biden had not visited Kyiv in person, his secretaries of state and defense had done so, and his wife, Jill Biden, had visited Ukraine's westernmost regional center, Uzhhorod, in early May.[44]

Many in Kyiv were concerned about the message that the trio was bringing to Zelensky. Macron, speaking to reporters at the Kyiv railway station, tried to reassure the Ukrainians by characterizing the visit as "a message of European unity toward the Ukrainians, and of support about the present and future." The three leaders met with Zelensky in Kyiv and then toured the suburb of Irpin and the neighboring town of Bucha, where they observed the destruction caused by Russian troops. Macron walked back his earlier remarks about not humiliating Russia. "Today, Russia is waging war against Ukraine. How on earth could I explain to any Ukrainian the idea that 'You must not humiliate Russia, the Russian people, nor its leaders'?" Macron told reporters. "Today, they must win this war. France clearly supports Ukraine so that it wins."

Macron and his companions were ready to let Zelensky determine the terms of victory. Zelensky, for his part, commented that he and

Macron had turned the page in their relations, setting aside the "not humiliating Russia" remarks. "Zelensky must define what would be a military victory for him," commented a member of Macron's delegation. "We are in favor of a complete victory with the reestablishment of [Ukrainian] territorial integrity over all the territories that have been conquered by the Russians, including Crimea." Macron promised to increase French arms supplies to Ukraine. Old Europe was now fully backing Ukraine not only rhetorically but also diplomatically and institutionally, prepared to embrace it as a potential member of the European Union.[45]

One day after Macron, Scholz, and Draghi visited Kyiv, the European Commission recommended that the heads of the EU states grant Ukraine membership candidate status. Following on the commission's recommendation, the European Parliament indicated strong support with 529 votes in favor, 45 against, and 14 abstentions. The European heads of state approved the decision. Ukraine had applied for candidate status immediately after the start of the invasion and was now accepted, together with the neighboring republic of Moldova, whose Transnistria region had been declared a target by the Russian military—their next stop after Odesa. Candidate status was a de facto invitation to join the European Union: even though accession was not guaranteed and could take years, if not decades, the decision gave Ukraine access to a number of EU programs, sending a clear signal to Russia that the European community was prepared to stand by Ukraine.[46]

Transatlantic unity against Russian aggression was once again on display on June 29, three days after the European Council's decision on candidate status for Ukraine and Moldova. At the NATO summit meeting in Madrid, Finland and Sweden, which had applied for membership in the wake of the Russian invasion of Ukraine, were formally invited to join. Turkey's objections against the invitation on the grounds that both countries were harboring Turkish refugees branded as terrorists by Istanbul had been overcome on the eve of the summit. The decision was historic in more ways than one. Finland, which has a border of 1,340 kilometers (832 miles) with Russia and had stayed out of NATO during the Cold War, was now joining the alliance, while Sweden was abandoning more than 200 years of political neutrality.[47]

There was yet another historic moment at the Madrid summit. The communique issued by the summit's press office designated Russia as the "most significant and direct threat to the allies' security," the first such designation since the end of the Cold War. The members of NATO pledged further support for Ukraine's war effort. "We will continue and further step up political and practical support to our close partner Ukraine as it continues to defend its sovereignty and territorial integrity against Russian aggression. Jointly with Ukraine, we have decided on a strengthened package of support," read the communique. The participants also agreed to deploy more forces on the eastern borders of the alliance, pledging to increase the size of their eight battlegroups from battalion to brigade level when and where required.[48]

Putin was displeased. He had warned Finland that its membership in the alliance would impair relations between Moscow and Helsinki but now had to accept the new reality. He would downplay the importance of Sweden's and Finland's membership in NATO on the grounds that Russia had no territorial disputes with them, as it did with Ukraine. The dispute he had in mind was the one concerning the Crimea. It was in order to avoid such disputes that Finland, which had been under imperial Russian rule from 1809 to 1917 and had part of its territory annexed by Stalin in 1940, was now joining the alliance.[49]

The West was back in full strength. Despite the different and sometimes conflicting concerns and agendas of the United States and Europe, and varying degrees of readiness to participate in sanctions or arm Ukraine, Washington and its European allies managed to develop a common platform, drawn together by Russia's aggression and the threat it posed to Europe and international order. This was not the response that Putin had imagined when he decided to attack Ukraine. His aggression of 2014 had been linked to his attempt to stop Kyiv from signing an association agreement with the European Union. Ukraine had now become a candidate member of the EU. Putin's pretext for invasion in 2022 was NATO's eastward expansion and Russia's desire to keep Western armies away from its borders. Now, not only had Ukraine become a "close partner" of NATO, but the borders of the alliance itself, with Finland's membership, would advance to a distance of less than 200 kilometers (124 miles) from St. Petersburg, the birthplace and hometown of Putin and his closest associates.[50]

13

THE PIVOT TO ASIA

The USS *Ronald Reagan*, a nuclear-powered aircraft carrier, and its strike group left Singapore on July 25, 2022, and headed north toward the South China Sea and Taiwan. A few days later the carrier was spotted cruising at a distance of 115 miles from Fiery Cross Reef, a Chinese-occupied and militarized island also claimed by Taiwan, Vietnam, and the Philippines. Two Chinese military vessels, a destroyer and a frigate, were seen nearby. Soon more American and Chinese ships would enter the area, causing widespread concern about a possible accident and ensuing military confrontation between the two powers.[1]

Tensions had begun to build up weeks earlier, when rumors began about a possible visit by Nancy Pelosi, the speaker of the House of Representatives and third-highest-ranking US government official, to Taiwan, the island that Beijing considers a breakaway province of China, and President Biden had recently pledged to protect against any military aggression. As the news spread and protests from Beijing became more insistent, the US Seventh Fleet moved the *Ronald Reagan* and its striking group closer to Taiwan. China treated Pelosi's possible visit as a violation of its "one China" policy, which defines Taiwan as part of China and had been recognized by the US government in the late 1970s. A Chinese journalist called on the Chinese military to shoot down Pelosi's plane if she flew to Taiwan. The Chinese foreign ministry threatened the United States with "forceful measures." The White House reaffirmed its commitment to the "one China" policy.[2]

On July 28, when the *Ronald Reagan* was spotted cruising near Fiery Cross Reef and the Chinese made their statement, Biden and the Chinese leader, Xi Jinping, held a phone conversation lasting two hours and seventeen minutes. Taiwan was on the agenda, and, according to the Chinese readout of the conversation, Xi warned Biden against "playing with fire." Biden had earlier suggested that Pelosi's visit to Taiwan was "not a good idea right now," according to the US military's assessment of the situation. China, the world's first- or second-largest economy, was also in possession of the world's largest navy.[3]

But despite fiery rhetoric from Beijing and cautious discouragement from the White House, Pelosi visited Taiwan on August 2, 2022, as part of her Pacific tour. She declared her visit a symbol of "America's unwavering commitment to supporting Taiwan's vibrant democracy" and was greeted at the airport by Taiwanese citizens wearing blue-and-yellow masks (the colors of the Ukrainian flag) and carrying signs with the words "Freedom and Friendship" and "Taiwan =/ China." The Chinese media reported that People's Liberation Army military jets were flying over the Taiwan Strait. Indeed, twenty Chinese jets, including Russian-made Sukhoi SU-30 fighters, had entered the Taiwanese air-defense zone. Both the Chinese and the Russian foreign ministries protested and condemned the visit, and the Chinese army announced the start of live-fire military drills around the island later in the week.[4]

Pelosi's Taiwan visit created the worst crisis in US-Chinese relations since the end of the Cold War. The visit had bipartisan support in Congress, where the Democrats wanted their country to take a tougher stand vis-à-vis Beijing with regard to human rights and democracy, and the Republicans wanted a more aggressive economic and trade policy.

But the crisis was by no means welcome in the White House, where Biden and his advisers were doing their best to avoid simultaneous diplomatic and economic confrontation with Russia and China and were desperate to keep China from developing even closer relations with its northern neighbor.[5]

The key principles of the Biden administration's policy toward China had been formulated by Secretary of State Antony Blinken in a speech given in late May at George Washington University. The speech spelled out the administration's policy agenda vis-à-vis China, but Blinken began by speaking about Russia. "Russian President Vladimir Putin poses a clear and present threat," Blinken told his audience. "In attacking Ukraine three months ago, he also attacked the principles of sovereignty and territorial integrity, enshrined in the UN Charter, to protect all countries from being conquered or coerced." But Blinken did not believe that Russia would succeed. "So many countries have united to oppose this aggression because they see it as a direct assault on the foundation of their own peace and security," he continued. Referring to Putin, he said: "Instead of asserting Russia's strength, he's undermined it. And instead of weakening the international order, he has brought countries together to defend it."[6]

It was a different story with China, whose policies Blinken presented as the "most serious long-term challenge to the international order." "China is the only country with both the intent to reshape the international order and, increasingly, the economic, diplomatic, military, and technological power to do it," stated Blinken before continuing: "Beijing's vision would move us away from the universal values that have sustained so much of the world's progress over the past 75 years." His reference was to the post–World War II era. Blinken reassured the audience that "We are not looking for conflict or a new Cold War. To the contrary, we're determined to avoid both."

The catchwords "invest, align, compete" were the formula with which Blinken proposed to stop China and avoid future conflict. "We will invest in the foundations of our strength here at home—our competitiveness, our innovation, our democracy," Blinken told the audience. "We will align our efforts with our network of allies and partners, acting with common purpose and in common cause. And harnessing these two key assets, we'll compete with China to defend our interests and build our vision for the future."[7]

It sounded like the Soviet policy of "peaceful coexistence" and economic competition with the capitalist West that had caused the Sino-Soviet split in the 1950s. At that time Beijing had wanted a more confrontational approach toward the West, military as well as economic. The new Beijing wanted no restraints on its economic development. Wang Wenbin, a Chinese foreign ministry spokesman, suggested that America's goal was to "contain and suppress China's development and uphold US hegemony." He objected to the formation of alliances against China and dismissed international rules as impositions by the United States and its allies. "As to the rules-based international order that the U.S. advocates, all people with insight can see that they are nothing but rules formulated by the U.S. and a few other countries with the aim of upholding the U.S.-dominant international order," stated Wang Wenbin.[8]

The world's two largest economies, the United States and China, were on a collision course, and although neither was willing to engage in direct confrontation, the Russian war in Ukraine was increasing great-power tensions and accelerating the restructuring of the world order created at the end of the Cold War. The American-dominated unipolar world that had replaced the bipolar world when the Cold War ended in the early 1990s was facing the greatest threat since its creation.[9]

Washington's Dilemma

The first big blow to the unipolar American world was delivered by President George W. Bush, the man most determined to defend and preserve it.

Bush launched the Afghan war as a direct response to the 9/11 Al Qaeda attack on the US mainland and sent American troops into Iraq a year and a half later to complete the war against Saddam Hussein's regime, begun by the president's father, George H. W. Bush, in 1991 but never completed. Reflecting America's new vision of its role in the world, the wars were based on two key paradigms associated with the neoconservative turn in the American foreign policy establishment. The first suggested that preventive war was permissible, even desirable, as a means of maintaining American supremacy in the unipolar world that had emerged after the Cold War. The second was ideological, urging the transformation of the world into a community of democratic states. The wars envisioned in these paradigms were meant to be limited military engagements, but in practice they turned into prolonged colonial-type conflicts that exposed American political, economic, and military weaknesses, demonstrating the dangers of overextension.[10]

President Barack Obama wanted to end the wars in Iraq and Afghanistan, get out of the Middle East, and focus on the Pacific. This "pivot to Asia" could be traced to Obama's background—he had grown up in Hawaii and spent part of his childhood in Indonesia—but, more than anything else, it was informed by the realization that the long-term challenge to American economic, political, and potentially even military power was coming from China, a rapidly rising competitor that overtook Japan in 2010 as the world's second-largest economy. With annual growth of 10 percent, China was poised to overtake the US economy as well, and indeed it became the world's largest economy in 2014 if its GDP were measured on the basis of PPP (purchasing power parity). Obama hoped to pull American troops out of the Middle East in order to develop trade and enhance political alliances in the Pacific to rival China's growing economic and political power there.[11]

As for Russia, the Obama White House wanted a fresh start, blaming the growing tensions between Moscow and Washington on its predecessors, George W. Bush and his team. The Obama-Biden administration hoped to improve relations with Russia, significantly damaged the previous year by Washington's desire to invite Ukraine and Georgia to join NATO and by Russia's invasion of Georgia. Not only was the Georgian "accident" completely forgiven and plans for Ukraine and Georgia to become members of NATO abandoned, but the White

House also scrapped plans made by the Bush team to place missile defense systems in Eastern Europe. Putin, then switching roles from president to prime minister, praised the decision.

In March 2009 the new US secretary of state, Hillary Clinton, made headlines when she gave her Russian counterpart, Sergei Lavrov, a small souvenir—a red "reset" button. "I would like to present you with a little gift that represents what President Obama and Vice President Biden and I have been saying, and that is: 'We want to reset our relationship, and so we will do it together.'" As the two smiled and traded jokes, a bright future seemed to beckon for the Cold War–era rivals. But there were also lingering questions about Russia's intentions and the new administration's understanding of them. The button that Clinton gave Lavrov was labeled with a mistranslation of the word "reset." In Russian, it read *peregruzka* (overload) instead of *perezagruzka* (reset). "We worked hard to get the right Russian word. Do you think we got it?" asked Clinton. "You got it wrong," came the answer.[12]

The accident with the button notwithstanding, improvement in US-Russian relations led to the signing of a new START treaty by Obama and the new Russian president, Dmitrii Medvedev, reducing the nuclear arsenals of the two superpowers. Moscow and Washington also cooperated on sanctions against Iran. This settling of the "Russian question" allowed the Obama administration to feel quite safe in declaring a "pivot" toward Asia in the fall of 2011. "Once we pressed that reset button in 2009, between then and 2012, we achieved a great deal in cooperation with Russia to advance our mutual interests and I would argue the interests of Europe," declared Joe Biden in February 2015. By that time, new clouds were not just on the horizon but fully obscuring the sky above Russo-American relations.[13]

The main cloud maker was Vladimir Putin, who returned to presidential office for a third term in May 2012. Putin had convinced himself that the mass protests in Moscow at the end of 2011, on the eve of Russian parliamentary elections and his return to office, had been orchestrated by the United States. He held Hillary Clinton personally responsible for that alleged interference in Russia's internal affairs, as she had issued an official statement questioning the fairness of the Russian parliamentary elections. The Russian people, read the statement, "deserve to have their voices heard and their votes counted, and that means they deserve fair, free transparent elections and leaders who are accountable to them." Putin accused Clinton of provoking the protests.[14]

Russia's annexation of the Crimea in March 2014 and the beginning of its hybrid war in the Donbas led to US-led sanctions against Russia to punish it for unprovoked aggression. That ended the "reset" of relations between Washington and Moscow with an "overload," leading Russia to meddle in the American presidential elections of 2016. According to US intelligence, Putin had personally ordered the cyber-hacking of the Democratic National Committee's computer servers and those of affiliated Democratic Party institutions and campaign officials. Eleven Russian intelligence officers would be charged with hacks targeting the Clinton presidential campaign's servers and with releasing hundreds of stolen emails that undermined her bid for the presidency. A Russian troll farm in St. Petersburg, Putin's hometown, created thousands of social media accounts and spread disinformation to millions of American voters, all in a generally successful attempt to embarrass Hillary Clinton and discredit American democracy.[15]

The main beneficiary of Russian interference was the successful Republican presidential nominee, Donald John Trump. In the course of his electoral campaign and tenure in the Oval Office, he never once attacked Vladimir Putin or criticized Russian actions or the Kremlin's "sovereign democracy." Like Obama, Trump sought to make the Asia-Pacific region his foreign-policy priority, but his pivot toward Asia was quite different from that of his predecessor. Trump withdrew from the Trans-Pacific Trade Agreement negotiated by Obama and began a trade war with China, imposing tariffs on hundreds of billions of dollars' worth of Chinese imports to the United States.

Long and complex negotiations led to the conclusion of a new US trade deal with Beijing, allowing Trump to claim victory in the trade war and leaving him free to attack China on a number of fronts, from causing the COVID outbreak to unfair trade practices. In 2020, Trump's last year in office, the United States sanctioned ninety Chinese corporations and individuals, creating a situation in which every tenth American sanction imposed at the time targeted the Chinese. Trump and his advisers clearly saw China as an immediate threat to US interests, relegating Russia, whose economy was not even counted among the world's ten largest, to secondary status.[16]

While Trump found it difficult to hide his admiration for Putin and his authoritarian rule, his administration took a stronger position vis-à-vis Russia and provided more support to Ukraine in its hybrid war with Moscow than did their predecessors. Obama had refused to provide Ukraine with lethal weapons despite bipartisan congressional support for such a measure. Trump approved the sale of $47 million worth of weapons to Ukraine, including anti-tank Javelin missiles. Ironically, it would be US military assistance to Ukraine that became the background to the House of Representatives' first impeachment of Trump in December 2019. Earlier that year, Trump had attempted to use congressional approval of weapons supply to Ukraine as leverage to make Ukraine's newly elected president, Volodymyr Zelensky, launch an investigation into Joe Biden's son, Hunter, and his allegedly questionable business activities in Ukraine.[17]

In 2019, influential RAND Corporation experts advised Washington to focus on China, not Russia, as the main threat to the United States. Upon moving into the White House in January 2021, President Biden and his administration took that advice seriously. In fact, they continued key Trump policies toward China, and on Biden's watch, with the United States declaring a political boycott of the 2022 Winter Olympic Games, hosted by China, relations with Beijing did not improve much. But Washington's relations with Moscow deteriorated even further than the low point reached during Trump's presidency.

Biden's advisers defined the administration's policy toward Russia as the achievement of "stable and predictable relations." "The entire premise of the sort of mantra of 'stable and predictable relations' is that Russia gets off the top of the agenda," said Samuel Charap, a Russia adviser in President Obama's administration, in an interview with NPR in December 2021. "It doesn't cause the U.S. problems and stops taking senior decision-makers' time." He then added: "And that hasn't worked out." The Biden administration's policy failed in that regard because of Putin's increasingly aggressive posture. By the fall of 2021, Russia had replaced China as the main challenger of the United States and the international order that it favored. A pivot to the Asia-Pacific region would have to wait while the administration was compelled to focus its attention on Russia.[18]

The Eastern Partnership

In early February, having already made up his mind to invade Ukraine, Putin flew to Beijing, there to figure as a guest of honor at the opening ceremonies of the Winter Olympic Games hosted by Xi Jinping.

The two met and released a photo in which Putin did not keep his distance from his Chinese counterpart, as he had been doing in meetings with Western leaders during the previous few weeks. Xi and Putin also released a 5,000-word statement declaring friendship and cooperation with "no limits" or "forbidden areas of cooperation" between their countries, which suggested military cooperation. Even so, the declaration fell short of a formal alliance, since China still considers the international order hierarchical and has not regarded Russia as its equal historically and culturally, let alone in terms of economic power and potential. The document called the new agreement "superior to political and military alliances of the cold war era."

There were no specifics on how the partnership would work, but there were particular statements about geopolitics. Xi had publicly supported Putin's opposition to the eastward expansion of NATO—the key reason that the master of the Kremlin had provided to justify his imminent aggression. Putin in turn supported China's claims on Taiwan, and both leaders declared their opposition to "the advancement of US plans to develop global missile defense and deploy its elements in various regions of the world, combined with capacity building of high-precision non-nuclear weapons for disarming strikes and other strategic objectives."[19]

It is not clear to what extent the coming war in Ukraine was discussed at the summit, but Putin could not afford not to mention the war at all, otherwise he would have killed the "no-limits friendship" before it began. Western intelligence found out that Xi did not want the war to start before the closing ceremonies of the Olympic Games, so as not to distract world attention from his great achievement. Indeed, Putin's highly publicized decision to withdraw from the Minsk Agreements with Ukraine was presented to the world on February 21, the day after the end of the Olympics. The Chinese apparently expected a short-term police operation of the kind declared by Putin at the start of his aggression, rather than an all-out invasion, as they advised their nationals in Kyiv not to travel or stock up on supplies, while Western embassy personnel were leaving the city and the country altogether. Taken by surprise at the scope of the invasion, China began to evacuate its citizens from Kyiv only on the fourth day of the war and would not be done until two weeks into the hostilities.[20]

Putin must have returned from Beijing with high hopes for China's neutrality and potential support in the forthcoming confrontation with the West. Indeed Beijing declared neutrality with regard to the war. According to a statement released by the Chinese foreign ministry, Xi told Putin during a telephone conversation in response to his complaints about NATO and the United States ignoring "Russia's legitimate security concerns" that it was necessary to "respect the reasonable security concerns of all countries and reach a balanced, effective and sustainable European security mechanism," and added that it would have to be done through negotiations. He clearly wanted the "military operation" to end quickly. Xi continued: "China supports Russia in resolving the issue through negotiation with Ukraine." He reminded his counterpart that "China has long held the basic position of respecting all countries' sovereignty and territorial integrity, and abiding by the purposes and principles of the UN Charter."[21]

China, having invested heavily in Ukraine before the war, refused to recognize the Russian annexation of the Crimea in 2014 and had little reason to support Russia in its attack on Kyiv, as it indeed valued the sovereignty and territorial integrity of states—the key argument in its claim to Taiwan. Besides, China's foreign policy was based on using economic leverage to project its power, treating military intervention as a last resort. The Russians, for their part, had little more than military means to assert themselves as a great power, and, as the early phase of their invasion of Ukraine would show, even those means were less than effective.

Still, if the war were to go according to Putin's plan, China stood to benefit from his victory in several ways. The fall of Ukraine would further diminish the standing of the United States in the world, create cracks in the Euro-Atlantic alliance, and refocus Western attention on dealing with Moscow. That would allow China to work away from constant American surveillance and criticism, while further developing its economic and military capabilities and strengthening its positions abroad.[22]

But things did not go as planned for Putin or, by extension, for Xi. Successful Ukrainian resistance gave the West reason, opportunity, and time to unite as never before—bad news for the Chinese leadership, which had been counting on disunity not only between the United States and Europe but within Europe itself. The impact of the war on the global economy, with the rise of energy prices and the slowing of the post-COVID recovery, was a major blow to Beijing. China's prestige also took a hit, given Xi's close and public association with Putin, who turned out to be a reckless disrupter of world order with an army incapable of fighting a modern war. Russia's inability to achieve its war aims was also a warning signal to Xi about the prospects of successfully invading Taiwan. In short, the results of Putin's "special military operation" were all bad for China.[23]

The shift in Beijing's attitude toward the war was reflected in Chinese media coverage. At the beginning, after some uncertainty and hesitation, state media adopted the Russian narrative of the war as a special operation that was nothing but a response to the West's aggressive posture and was going according to plan. The media refused to refer to the war as an "invasion" and stuck to that line with some minor deviations. But as the war progressed, with no sign of a speedy victory for Russia, the Chinese media began to entertain opinions critical of the invasion.

On April 30, 2022, the state news agency Xinhua distributed a statement by the Ukrainian foreign minister, Dmytro Kuleba, who made a case against the war from the Chinese perspective. "Russia is jeopardizing the Chinese leaders' Belt and Road Initiative," declared Kuleba, going on to say that "This war is not in line with China's interests. The global food crisis and economic problems . . . will pose a serious threat to the Chinese economy." He wanted China to rein Russia in.[24]

Meanwhile, after the setback to his military effort during the first weeks of the war, Putin was once again knocking on Xi Jinping's door, asking for military equipment and economic assistance. Xi was hardly in a position to turn Putin down completely, as he wanted to keep Russia, with its vast natural resources, in his orbit, but he also could not ignore the United States and Europe, China's largest markets, which had imposed sanctions on Russia and, by extension, on any country that violated their sanctions regime. The Chinese foreign minister, Wang Yi, made it known that China condemned the Western sanctions against Russia. The problem was that China could not ignore them.[25]

On March 18, in an online meeting with Xi, President Biden warned the Chinese leader about the "implications and consequences if China provides material support to Russia as it conducts brutal attacks against Ukrainian cities and civilians." Xi fought back, suggesting that the war was not something the Chinese wanted to see, and reminded Biden of their common "international responsibilities." But the message was received. Beijing's economic growth continued to depend on the international security and economic and financial order underwritten by Washington. Xi allegedly ordered his officials to find a way to help Russia without violating the sanctions. "We understand [Moscow's] predicament. But we cannot ignore our own situation in this dialogue," stated an unnamed Chinese official.[26]

The Return of the Ottomans

On July 18, 2022, Vladimir Putin made his first foreign trip since the beginning of the war, visiting clients and allies in Central Asia. He then headed for Teheran—a clear indication of his isolation on the world stage, as well as a symbol of his pivot to the East.[27]

Putin's trip was meant to strengthen anti-Western solidarity with Iran, a country sanctioned for decades by the United States and the European Union, but it also concerned his war effort in Ukraine. Losing in high-tech warfare in Ukraine to American HIMARS as well as American and Turkish drones, Moscow was now looking to the Middle East for a new generation of arms—a humiliating turn of events after decades of Russia's supplying the region with weapons. The Russians were eyeing the Iranian Shahed 129 and Shahed 191 drones. Putin also discussed drones with another visitor to the Iranian capital, Prime Minister Recep Tayyip Erdogan of Turkey. They met in the company of Iran's Supreme Leader, Ayatollah Ali Khamenei, and had a separate meeting that attracted more media and public attention than any other part of the summit.[28]

A minute or so before the meeting began, Putin's unhappy expression was caught on a video that went viral. If only for 50 seconds, Putin was made to wait in view of television cameras for his Turkish counterpart to enter the room. The Russian president looked morose and humiliated: normally it was he who kept other leaders waiting. "Those 50 seconds that Erdogan made Putin wait, looking frazzled in front of cameras, say plenty of how much has changed after Ukraine," tweeted Joyce Karam, a senior American correspondent for the Abu Dhabi–based newspaper *The National*. "It's also a sweet payback for Erdogan, who in 2020 was humiliated by Putin as he made him wait 2 minutes in a power game play in Russia," added Karam in a comment on her tweet that received 3 million views in the first hours after posting and another 3 million in the next few days.[29]

In March 2020, Putin had made Erdogan and dozens of Turkish officials and aides accompanying him to Moscow wait for two minutes, filmed by cameras, in the anteroom of the Kremlin meeting hall. The video of the humiliated Turks standing in front of the closed doors was then shown on Russian television. This was Putin's way of publicly flaunting his victory in Syria: Erdogan had come to Moscow to ask Putin for a ceasefire in the fighting between the Russia-backed forces of President Bashar al-Assad and Turkish-backed rebels in the province of Idlib.

Putin gave Erdogan what he wanted, halting al-Assad's advance in the region strategically important to Turkey, but not without submitting him to further humiliation. The anteroom where the Turkish delegation was waiting featured portraits of Russian generals, including Aleksandr Suvorov, who had been victorious in the Russian Empire's wars against the Ottoman Turks in the second half of the eighteenth century. The meeting hall that Erdogan was eventually allowed to enter contained a huge statue of Catherine the Great, who had waged those wars, and behind the chairs of the two leaders as they posed for a joint photo was an imperial-era clock decorated with bronze work depicting a scene from another war in which Russia had triumphed over Turkey, that of 1877–78.[30]

The Russians denied any ill intent in making Erdogan's party wait or choosing the venue for his meeting with Putin, but the Turkish prime minister and his delegation had to work hard to convince the Turkish media that there was nothing unusual in the diplomatic protocol to which they were subjected in Russia, and that they had not taken offense. Now, in July 2022, it was Putin's turn to pretend equanimity concerning his reception in Teheran, although the faces he pulled on the video and his body language suggested otherwise. Erdogan had come to Teheran, among other things, to ask Russia and Iran to back up his planned military operation in Syria intended to create a buffer zone between Turkey and the Syrian rebels. This time, however, he was not just a petitioner; he was also being asked for favors.

Putin thanked Erdogan for his role in the Russo-Ukrainian negotiations on exporting Ukrainian grain from Odesa ports. He was also intent on obtaining Turkish armed drones, called Bayraktar TB2. They had performed exceptionally well in Ukrainian hands against Russian troops, and now the Russian leader wanted Erdogan to build a drone factory in Russia. The Bayraktars were produced and shipped to Ukraine by Baykar, a company owned by Erdogan's son-in-law and an inventor and entrepreneur, Selcuk Bayraktar. In 2020, during Erdogan's trip to Moscow, the Russian media had ridiculed the performance of Turkish drones in the Syrian war, but now Putin, denied drones by Israel, wanted the Turkish products for himself. Erdogan was not prepared to comply. One day earlier Haluk Bayraktar, Selcuk's brother and CEO of the Baykar company, had stated that his firm would "never supply" his drones to Russia.[31]

Erdogan, who had previously ignored Russia's complaints about his country's supplying drones to Ukraine, was not about to cave in now. He had no interest in seeing Russia prevail in Ukraine. Istanbul and Moscow, and later St. Petersburg and then Moscow again, had been rivals in the northern Black Sea region for centuries, and it was not always Russia that had emerged victorious. Putin had been eager to suggest otherwise by selecting Moscow as the venue for his meeting with Erdogan in 2020. In the sixteenth century, Khan Devlet I Giray with Crimean Tatars, the Ottomans' regional vassals, had attacked and burned Moscow, forcing Ivan the Terrible to flee the capital. In the seventeenth century the Ottomans had fought Muscovite troops in Ukraine, siding with Ukrainian Cossacks who had rebelled against both Warsaw and Moscow. In the nineteenth century the Ottomans, in coalition with the British and French, had defeated Russia in the Crimean War and forced the demilitarization of the peninsula.[32]

Russo-Turkish rivalry in the region was not just a matter of the past. The Crimean Tatars, the indigenous population of the Crimea, shared with Muslim Turkey not only parts of their history but also their religion. They had a diaspora about a million strong in Turkey—the result of an exodus from the Crimea after Russia's annexation of the peninsula in the eighteenth century and then the Crimean War of the nineteenth. Istanbul did not recognize Russia's annexation of the Crimea in 2014 and supported Crimean Tatar leaders who found refuge in

Kyiv. Turkey also pledged to stand by the Crimean Tatars at the start of the new war. Furthermore, in 2020, Istanbul established itself as a power to reckon with in the Caucasus when an Azeri army supplied and trained by Turkey defeated Russia-backed Armenian forces in Nagorno-Karabakh. The Russians sent peacekeepers to establish their presence in the region, but now they had to deal with growing Turkish influence in what had been considered Moscow's backyard for decades.[33]

If Ukraine were to be defeated at the hands of Russia, then Turkish interests would be undermined not only in the post-Soviet space but also in the Black Sea region, where Istanbul had been busy developing good relations with Georgia, Bulgaria, and Romania—all in an effort to check the ever more assertive Russia. To create an obstacle for Putin, Turkey used its powers under the 1936 Montreux Convention to deny Russian warships entrance from the Atlantic via the Mediterranean into the Black Sea. The supply of Bayraktars was another symbolic and practical gesture that made Turkey and Erdogan valued allies of Kyiv.[34]

But while supporting Kyiv, Erdogan did not want to damage his country's relations with Russia, which supplied gas to Turkey and, through Turkey, to the Balkans and the rest of southeastern Europe. Millions of Russian visitors were important to Turkey's tourist industry, which brought in $30 billion annually, and Russia was a significant market for Turkish business. Erdogan offered Putin a form of neutrality that no other NATO country could duplicate and a platform for negotiations with the world that he otherwise lacked. Turkey refused to join the rest of its NATO allies in imposing sanctions on Russia and attempted to block the admission of Sweden and Finland to the alliance. Erdogan was more than discreet in his public criticism of Putin and Russia's actions. He managed all that without spoiling his country's relations with the United States, Europe, or Ukraine.[35]

Since Erdogan could offer advantages to both Russia and Ukraine, he soon emerged as a key mediator in relations between the two countries, but also between them and the rest of the world. In late March, Erdogan hosted a key round of talks between Ukrainian and Russian representatives in Istanbul's Dolmabahçe Palace, which Russia used to announce its withdrawal from the Kyiv area. The Ukrainian delegation showed readiness to abandon the country's efforts to join NATO in exchange for a collective agreement in which eight countries would guarantee its sovereignty and territorial integrity. Subsequent talks were stalled by the revelations of Russian war crimes in Bucha and other towns near the Ukrainian capital, but Turkey remained the place where the two warring sides felt most comfortable meeting for diplomatic exchanges.[36]

In June, Erdogan achieved something at which Emmanuel Macron and Olaf Scholz had failed. He helped to negotiate a Russo-Ukrainian deal on the resumption of Ukrainian grain shipments from the ports of Odesa, which Russia had blocked.[37] The agreement was finalized on July 22, making it possible to ship 20 million tons of grain from the previous year's harvest and millions of tons from the new one. Ukraine was to earn close to $10 billion from the deal. Russia was rewarded by the United States and the European Union with easement of sanctions on its agricultural and agriculture-related exports. But Erdogan was the main winner. His take was the right to buy grain exported from Ukraine at a 25 percent discount—quite a deal for the leader of a country with its economy in a tailspin and inflation reaching 80 percent. But his principal achievement was that of saving many people from hunger and starvation—a number of African countries relied on Ukrainian grain to avoid famine, and Europe relied on it to prevent another humanitarian catastrophe and refugee crisis near its shores.[38]

Russia hit the Odesa ports with a missile strike the day after its minister of defense, Sergei Shoigu, signed the grain agreement in Istanbul—perhaps payback for the 50 seconds that Putin had had to wait before the meeting with Erdogan in Teheran. But the deal negotiated by Erdogan survived that missile attack and several others. Turkey, working with the United Nations, emerged as the guarantor of the agreement, and the Ukrainians welcomed the entrance of two Turkish naval ships and a submarine from the Mediterranean into the Black Sea to protect the grain shipments. The first Ukrainian ship, loaded with 25,000 tons of corn, left Odesa for Istanbul on August 1. In early

November, when Russia withdrew from the agreement, citing a Ukrainian attack on the Russian navy in the Black Sea, Erdogan declared that the export of the Ukrainian grain would continue with or without Russia's consent. Putin had to make a U-turn and return to the agreement after a telephone conversation with the Turkish president.[39]

The war, which potentially threatened to weaken Turkey and involve it in multiple international quarrels, was skillfully used by Erdogan as a steppingstone toward establishing himself and his country as a regional leader, now not only in the Muslim Middle East but also in the post-Soviet space, and as a political actor in the global arena. Turkey's rise to that role was accelerated by the war and made possible by the multiple setbacks that Russia had suffered in the first month, both on the battlefield and in the diplomatic arena. The rise of Turkey further weakened Russia and obliged Putin, as in the case of his visit to Teheran, to wait for those whom he had previously kept waiting.

The Closing of the West

Moscow's expectations with regard to Western reaction to the "military operation" that Putin was about to initiate were summarized by the former Russian president, Dmitrii Medvedev, on February 21, 2022. He made his remarks in the course of the Russian Security Council's televised discussions of Russia's withdrawal from the Minsk Agreements.

"It will be difficult," said Medvedev, "but after some time, given able management of the situation—and, it seems to me, under the president's leadership we have mastered that—the tension that is now simply vibrating around our country will dissipate one way or another. Not quickly, not in one moment, but human history is so ordered that sooner or later people will tire of the matter and will ask us to return to discussions and negotiations about all problems of ensuring strategic security."[40]

Vladimir Putin and those in his entourage involved in making the key decision to initiate all-out war on Ukraine were surprised by the West's united reaction, but the sanctions introduced by the United

States and Europe had little immediate effect on Russia's ability to prosecute the war, partly because Europe continued to purchase Russian natural gas. In slightly more than two months after the invasion, Europeans bought $46 billion worth of energy, mainly gas, from the Russian Federation. Europe depended on Russia for 40 percent of its gas consumption, and the best that the EU could do under the circumstances was to cut two-thirds of that figure within a year. An immediate cutoff would have produced major economic and social problems. In Germany alone, such a measure would have caused the loss of 400,000 jobs and led to social upheaval.[41]

Rising energy prices increased by war concerns and disruptions, as well as by sanctions on the import of Russian gas and oil, resulted in higher energy profits and greater revenue for Moscow. Consumers faced higher prices at home and at the gas pumps: in Europe, the cost of natural gas increased by 20 percent. As oil prices rose, so did those of gasoline. In Spain, the price of a liter of diesel shot up more than 50 percent, from €1.20 to €1.90, in the course of a year. In the United States, the price of gasoline increased by 55 cents in one week of March 2022, breaking the thirteen-year-old record of $4.10 per gallon.[42]

High prices for oil and gas were good, in fact great, news for Russia and its ability to withstand sanctions, at least in the short run. According to some estimates, the country's account surplus for 2022 might potentially reach $250 billion, offsetting a good part of the assets frozen by the West at the beginning of the war. Russia also managed to withstand the financial shock of the sanctions. The ruble, which initially depreciated by 60 percent, recovered by late March thanks to measures taken by the now sanctioned Central Bank, which doubled interest rates and closed the stock market for a month. In an attempt to generate demand for its currency, Moscow insisted on payment in rubles for its gas and cut off supplies to Poland and Bulgaria when they refused to comply. Others were spared as Putin apparently tried to punish Poland and create divisions within the European sanctions alliance. He did the same with Finland in May, now also as payback for its decision to join NATO.[43]

Rising gas prices hurt not only Europe but also the United States. To deal with the increase, President Biden ordered the release of 180 million barrels of oil from the national stockpile, but it proved a temporary and insufficient measure. The situation required influence on the world's largest oil producers, such as Iran, Venezuela, and Saudi Arabia. But the first two were under sanctions, and the Saudis had become uncooperative after US intelligence implicated Crown Prince Mohammed bin Salman in the order to kill the exiled Saudi journalist Jamal Khashoggi. In July, Biden had little choice but to visit Saudi Arabia, to the dismay of many of his supporters, in an attempt to ease the energy crisis caused by the war. But the Saudis refused to increase output, causing an immediate spike in oil prices. It was only in late November, with the Biden administration taking a position that the Crown Prince should be granted sovereign immunity in the Khashoggi civil case against him, that the Saudis supported the production increase by the OPEC countries.[44]

The inability of sanctions to end the war and their tendency to cause pain not just to Russia but also to the countries that introduced them obscured the major geopolitical shift that they accomplished with regard to Russia's economic and, consequently, political relations with the collective West. While the need for consensus made it difficult for EU member nations to agree on the imposition of sanctions, the same factor made it difficult to remove them. They were therefore likely to remain in place for years, if not decades. And their impact on the Russian economy became obvious from the very start of the war. In its first months, more than 1,000 international companies, representing 40 percent of Russia's GDP, left the Russian Federation, some under pressure of sanctions and others voluntarily in order to avoid reputational risks.[45]

Russian enterprises, including those producing for the military, were reported to be stopping their assembly lines for lack of microchips and components traditionally imported from countries now participating in the sanctions. Seventy percent of commercial aircraft were grounded, as they could not obtain spare parts from Boeing and Airbus. Russian imports fell dramatically, with imports of manufactured goods from the world's nine largest economies falling by 51 percent. The microchip imports dropped by a staggering 90 percent, while car production fell by 64 percent. By October the production of natural gas in comparison to October 2021 fell by 20 percent and so did the revenue from the non-energy sector. According to the Russian Central Bank, the GDP fell by 4.1 percent and 4 percent in the second and third quarters of the year and was poised to drop 7.1 percent in the fourth quarter. The Russian economy was contracting, diminishing the Kremlin's ability to fight the war and contributing to the social tensions inside the country.[46]

Europe's turn away from Russian oil and pledge to drastically cut its consumption of Russian gas began to close the European market for Russian energy much earlier than proponents of Europe's long-term strategy—the achievement of zero net greenhouse emissions by 2050—had expected. Loss of the most lucrative European markets promised nothing good for a country 60 percent of whose government revenues were generated by energy exports. Germany, dependent on Russian gas for 55 percent of its energy before the war, reduced that share to slightly more than one-third of its supply in the first months of the war. It also made plans to build new LNG terminals for American liquefied gas. By July 2022, Europe was already importing more LNG from the United States than the amount of natural gas it had previously bought from Russia.[47]

These European developments produced considerable frustration in the Kremlin. In May, speaking at a meeting on the development of the Russian oil industry, which was bracing itself for hard times without Western technological assistance, Putin called the EU energy policy suicidal. "Obviously, with the diversion of Russian energy resources to other regions of the world, Europe will also lose its potential to increase economic activity. Such an economic auto-da-fé is suicide," declared Putin. Few doubted, in Russia or elsewhere, that the "other region" to which Russian energy could go was China. The path for such Russian exports had broadened before the war, when, as part of Putin's visit to Beijing, the Russian state gas giant Gazprom made a deal with its Chinese counterpart to supply 10 billion cubic meters (over 350 billion cubic feet) of natural gas per annum from the Russian Far East. The overall value of the oil and gas deals reached as part of the visit was estimated at $117.5 billion.[48]

With the outbreak of war, not only China but also India emerged as a beneficiary of Russia's eastward turn for its exports of oil and gas. Like China, India reaffirmed its commitment to the principles of state sovereignty and the inviolability of international borders but refused to condemn or criticize Russia publicly for its aggression against Ukraine. Thus, the world's largest democracy sided with the authoritarian Russian government and complicated relations with its key ally, the United States.

The policy of "strategic ambiguity" adopted by New Delhi was deeply rooted in history, as India had considered Moscow a strategic partner since the times of the Cold War, when it refused to condemn the Soviet suppression of the Hungarian uprising in 1956 and its invasions of Czechoslovakia in 1968 and Afghanistan in 1979. But there was more than history involved when it came to India's formally neutral but essentially pro-Moscow attitude. Russian arms supplies were one of the factors influencing New Delhi's position; the desire not to push Russia closer to China and Pakistan—India's main rivals in the area— was another; and finally there was the tempting economic opportunity of access to Russian energy resources at fire-sale prices.[49]

By May 2022, China and India were buying 2.4 million barrels of Russian oil per day—half of Moscow's oil exports—at discounts up to 30 percent. India increased its purchases of oil from Russia from 33,000 barrels in June 2021 to 1.15 million barrels in June 2022, declining more expensive Iraqi oil. New Delhi stopped importing oil from Mexico and reduced its purchases of American, Nigerian, and Saudi Arabian oil. In June 2022, Russia surpassed Saudi Arabia as the main supplier of oil to China. China's natural gas imports from Russia were discounted by 22 percent in 2021 and had to be further discounted with the start of the war, making it possible for China to all but terminate

LNG purchases from the United States and switch to Russian suppliers. Europe saw a silver lining in the realignment of world energy supply: Russian natural gas supplies to China were expected to reduce the country's demand for LNG, making it cheaper and easier for Europeans to purchase liquefied gas.[50]

During the first ten months of 2022 Russia's energy exports to China grew by 64 percent in value and 10 percent in volume, but in November China began to slow down its purchases of Russian oil, being concerned about the coming EU ban on the import of Russian crude. There are limits on the amount of Russian oil and gas that China will be willing to buy without endangering its energy security and becoming too reliant on Moscow, as happened with Germany and other members of the European Union. Still, China is poised to emerge as the main beneficiary of Moscow's turn toward the East. With nowhere else to go, Putin has become much more vulnerable to traditional Chinese requests to curtail Russian military sales to India, Russia's main arms market, and would have to offer ever greater discounts to convince China to buy more of his oil.[51]

Indeed, in mid-September 2022, when Putin and Xi attended a meeting of the Shanghai Cooperation Organization in Samarkand, Uzbekistan, it was clear that the war in Ukraine and the Russian Army's recent defeat in Kharkiv had strengthened the Chinese position in the so-called "no limits" alliance and weakened the Russian one. When Putin and Xi met, the Russian president had to acknowledge China's "questions and concerns" with regard to the war in Ukraine. To see Xi, Putin had to go to the Samarkand hotel where the Chinese delegation was staying for the summit—a clear indication that China was not only the senior partner in the relationship but also calling the shots in Russia's Central Asian backyard. Prior to the summit, Xi visited Kazakhstan, a long-time Russian ally that felt threatened by the Kremlin's aggression against Ukraine. Xi assured the Kazakh leadership of China's support for its territorial integrity. Russia was the only country against which such a guarantee made any sense.[52]

When the leaders of the countries comprising the G-20 group of the world's largest economies met in mid-November in Bali, Indonesia, Putin was conspicuously absent from the meeting. He knew he would be confronted by leaders such as Britain's new prime minister Rishi Sunak over his aggression against Ukraine. Zelensky instead was present via a video link, and Biden and Xi had a prolonged meeting before the start of the summit. They seemed to agree on two matters: the confrontation between the two largest economies should be avoided, and Putin should be stopped from using nuclear weapons in Ukraine. "The world is big enough for the two countries to develop themselves and prosper together," tweeted Hua Chunying, the spokesperson for the Chinese Ministry of Foreign Affairs. According to the US readout of the meeting, the two leaders agreed that "a nuclear war should never be fought and can never be won." The Chinese neither confirmed nor denied that statement, suggesting that it was correct.[53]

Russia's aggression against Ukraine shook the Russo-Chinese alliance, making it more unequal than ever before. In June 2022, a few months before the Samarkand summit and Putin's no-show in Bali, *Politico* already referred to Putin as "China's new vassal." In an interview with the website, the American security strategist Matthew Kroenig suggested that "in a reverse from the Cold War pattern, Russia will be the junior partner to a more powerful China." History was repeating itself in a new and unpredictable way.[54]

Afterword

THE NEW WORLD ORDER

This book was written between March 2022 and February 2023, the first full year of Russia's all-out war on Ukraine. Many important developments have taken place on the front lines of the war and in the international arena between then and February 2024, when I completed revisions to the paperback edition of this book. None of these developments changed the course of the war, as they reinforced trends already apparent: on the one hand, Russia's determination despite numerous setbacks to achieve its original goals and crush Ukrainian independence; on the other hand, Ukraine's resolve to defend its sovereignty and keep fighting. The new questions that emerged in early 2024 were whether the United States would continue to lead the Western alliance and whether Ukraine would be able to fight without US support.

The year 2023 began in the midst of Russian missile attacks on the Ukrainian energy infrastructure with the goal of freezing the Ukrainians into surrender. The drastic reduction or termination of Russian energy supplies to Europe threatened to undermine European resolve to support Ukraine. On the snow-covered fields of eastern Ukraine, the Russian winter offensive was under way, reaching its peak in February. It was becoming more and more obvious with every passing day that the main questions about the further course of the war would be answered on the battlefield rather than at the negotiation table.

The developments of winter and spring 2023 demonstrated that Western and Ukrainian resolve to fight Russian aggression survived the cold of the winter months. Europe did not freeze in despair, nor did Ukraine, assisted by the Western supply of anti-aircraft and anti-missile systems, including the U.S. Patriot surface-to-air systems that helped protect the electricity-generating facilities and power grids of Ukrainian cities. During those months, Ukraine suffered significant losses in infrastructure and human capital. Millions of people remained abroad as refugees, while intensive fighting in eastern and then southern Ukraine produced mounting casualties among military personnel. Nevertheless, the morale of the country and the armed forces remained high.

On the front lines, the Russian winter offensive produced negligible results, its main achievement being first the destruction and then the capture of the city of Bakhmut in eastern Ukraine. It turned out to be not only a limited victory but also a pyrrhic one. The battle for the city lasted from August 2022 until late May 2023, costing the Russian army tens of thousands of soldiers killed and wounded. The mercenaries of the Wagner Group alone, under the overall command of Putin's client Yevgenii Prigozhin, had more than 22,000 of their fighters killed and over 40,000 wounded. Their ranks were composed mostly of former convicts recruited from the Russian penitentiary system with the promise of presidential pardon. Other Russian units suffered massive losses as well.

The failed winter counteroffensive served as background for the June mutiny by the Wagner Group under Prigozhin's command. Because his troops had not proved as effective as the Kremlin hoped, the decision was made to integrate them into the regular Russian army, leading Prigozhin to rebel. His mercenaries took over Russian military headquarters in the southern city of Rostov-on-Don without any resistance, and proceeded to march on Moscow. Prigozhin unexpectedly ordered them to halt and forced President Vladimir Putin to make a deal exempting them from prosecution. The mutiny and Putin's response to it demonstrated the weakness of the regime and exposed cracks in the Russian military establishment. Key Russian officers, including the former commander of Russian forces in Ukraine, General Sergei Surovikin, and the "butcher" of Mariupol, General Mikhail Mizintsev, were reportedly suspended and investigated for possible participation in the mutiny.

As the Ukrainian counteroffensive began in early June 2023, with the goal of severing the Russian land corridor to the Crimea, the Russian military blew up the Kakhovka Dam on the lower Dnieper River, flooding about 600 square kilometers, or 230 square miles of territory. This was an apparent effort to stop the Ukrainians from crossing the Dnieper from its right (western) bank to the Russian-held left bank. The Surovikin Line, a system of Russian fortifications in southern Ukraine, significantly retarded the Ukrainian advance. Although Ukraine received long promised tanks and armored vehicles from its Western allies, its counteroffensive proceeded slowly because it lacked modern military aviation and long-range missile systems that the West was reluctant to supply for fear of escalating the conflict. Ukrainian forces had to deal with extensive mining of the front lines conducted by well-entrenched Russian troops without the right tools to accomplish the task. The Ukrainian counteroffensive did not achieve the results expected of it, disappointing and discouraging many in Ukraine and abroad.

The Ukrainians fought with what they had. In the spring and summer of 2023, Ukrainian air drones began making regular attacks on Moscow, St. Petersburg, and Russian military targets as far as the Volga region. Warfare extended to territory deep behind the Russian front lines, demonstrating that the Kremlin itself was vulnerable. The Ukrainians used sea drones to damage the Kerch Bridge, making it more difficult for Russia to supply its troops north of the Crimean Peninsula. The Ukrainians used similar drones to attack Russian ships as far away as the port of Novorossiysk. By the end of 2023, Ukraine, a country without a navy, managed to defeat the Russian Black Sea Fleet, forcing it to seek safe harbor at the eastern end of the sea and restoring Ukraine's maritime trade from the port of Odesa to 75 percent of its prewar volume.

Concerned about growing discontent among the population, the Russian authorities increased their repressive measures, arresting nationalist critics such as Igor Girkin and imposing twenty-five-year sentences on liberal opponents such as Vladimir Kara-Murza. A key leader of the Russian opposition, the imprisoned anti-corruption crusader Aleksei Navalny had his already lengthy nine-year sentence extended by another nineteen years. He was moved to a remote penal colony beyond the Arctic Circle, where he died under suspicious circumstances in February 2024, a few weeks before the start of the Russian presidential election. It was a devastating blow to the Russian political opposition, most of whose leaders were now in prison or abroad.

On the international arena, Russian attempts to break out of isolation produced mixed results. The arrest warrant for Vladimir Putin issued in March 2023 by the International Criminal Court because of his role in the unlawful deportation of Ukrainian children delivered a major blow to the international standing of Russia and its president, making it difficult if not impossible for him to travel abroad. China maintained its posture of official neutrality, refusing to supply Moscow with weapons and helping its troubled ally in ways that would not make the shaky Chinese economy vulnerable to international sanctions. The Kremlin's attempts to court the "Global South" were undermined by Putin's withdrawal from the deal, which had allowed the export of Ukraine's grain through its Black Sea ports in July 2023. The sanctions imposed by the West in 2022 began to bite, with the Russian ruble falling to a sixteen-month low in August 2023. But Putin managed to stabilize the Russian economy by militarizing it, with 35 percent of total government spending devoted to financing the war in 2024. He also arranged a continuing supply of drones and other weapons from Iran, and secured weaponry from North Korea.

Meanwhile, Ukraine's Western allies struggled to maintain their

unity and commitment to the country's war effort. To the disappointment of President Volodymyr Zelensky, the NATO summit in July
did not invite Ukraine to join the alliance. It did, however, confirm
the NATO members' commitment to bring Ukraine eventually into
its ranks and promised to accept it without the otherwise obligatory
Membership Action Plan. More importantly, the summit initiated the
process of signing bilateral agreements between Ukraine and NATO
member states outlining plans to provide weapons and other forms
of assistance on a long-term basis. Among the countries agreeing to
enter into such agreements was Japan, whose government broke a long-
standing taboo on providing military support to foreign states.

But as allies of the United States increased their support for
Ukraine, the U.S. Congress failed to put to vote a $60 billion aid pack-
age for that country, raising uncomfortable questions about America's
ability to stand by its allies and maintain its status as a leading world
power. European heads of state, led by France, Poland, and other East
European countries, made important commitments to increase military and financial assistance for Ukraine and boost their production
of armaments badly needed on the Ukrainian front lines. But with the
United States in the midst of a presidential campaign, and Congress
unable to approve the Ukraine aid package because of opposition from
right-wing members of the Republican Party, the issue of Ukraine's
ability to survive the Russian assault reappeared on the political agenda
of world leaders.

As I write these words in late February 2024, it is hard to predict
whether aid from the United States will arrive in time for Ukrainians to
hold the current front line. It has become considerably more difficult to
predict either the outcome of the war or the time and manner in which
it may end. But the first two years of the war have already provided sufficient clues to discern the local and global changes that will influence
and probably define the future of Ukraine, Russia, Europe, and the rest
of the world.

The Russo-Ukrainian War has become the latest military conflict
in the long history of wars of national liberation, which can be traced

back to the American Revolution. It also belongs to the long list of wars that accompanied the decline and disintegration of world empires from the Spanish to the Ottoman and Austro-Hungarian, and then from the British and French to the Dutch, Belgian, and Portuguese. We know how those wars ended—with the political sovereignty of former colonies and dependencies and the concomitant devolution of former empires into post-imperial nation-states.

By repelling the Russian assault and mobilizing itself and half the world in defense of its sovereignty and territorial integrity, Ukraine has ensured its continuing existence as an independent state and nation. The war, often characterized as a Russian war in or against Ukraine, actually became a Russo-Ukrainian war in which the invaders faced resistance not merely from partisan groups but from a strong regular army. The Ukrainian state proved itself capable of surviving and functioning under continuing warfare to a degree matched by few states in Ukraine's European neighborhood during the wars of the twentieth century.

There are reasons to believe that the Ukrainian nation will emerge from this war more united and certain of its identity than at any other point in its modern history. Moreover, Ukraine's successful resistance to Russian aggression is destined to promote Russia's own nation-building project. Russia and its elites will have little choice but to reimagine their country's identity by parting ways not only with the imperialism of the tsarist past but also with the anachronistic model of a Russian nation consisting of Russians, Ukrainians, and Belarusians. By paying an enormous price in wealth and the blood of its citizens, Ukraine can terminate the era of Russian dominance in a good part of eastern Europe and challenging Moscow's claim to primacy in the rest of post-Soviet space.

The impact of the Russo-Ukrainian war has already been felt far beyond the former possessions of the Romanovs and commissars. Ukraine survived the Russian assault and defended itself thanks to the unprecedented solidarity of the international community, which provided the Ukrainian government and people with political, economic, and military support on a scale not seen in decades. For many of Ukraine's friends, this war became not only the largest and deadliest military conflict in Europe since the end of World War II, but also the first major war since the victory over Nazism in which there were few shades of gray when it came to its moral dimensions. It was the first "good war" since the global conflict of 1939–45, in which it was very clear from the start who was the aggressor and who the victim, who was the villain and who the hero, and whose side one wanted to be on.

Russia's aggression against Ukraine produced a nineteenth-century war fought with twentieth-century tactics and twenty-first-century weaponry. Its ideological underpinnings came from the visions of territorial expansion that characterized the Russian imperial era; its strategy was borrowed by the Kremlin from World War II and postwar-era manuals of the Soviet Army; and its key features were not only precision-guided missiles but also intelligence-gathering satellites and cyber warfare used to different degrees by both sides. The war posed a nuclear threat to the world from its very inception. Russia's takeover of the Chernobyl nuclear site and the Zaporizhia nuclear power plant in the first days of the all-out conflict constituted a clear and present danger to part of Europe and the Middle East, as well as a challenge to the safety of nuclear installations worldwide.

For many, Russia's aggression against Ukraine and the mobilization of the West and its allies to fight that aggression brought back images of the Cold War. Indeed, the new war revived old animosities, restored flagging alliances, reestablished old fault lines. The Cold War also provided a language and explanatory frame to describe and understand the new global conflict. There is little doubt, however, that despite numerous parallels with the past, today the world is entering a new era. The peace dividend that came with the end of the Cold War has been fully spent if not squandered over the last thirty years. The world is returning to the era of great-power rivalries on a scale unseen since the fall of the Berlin Wall in 1989. The Russo-Ukrainian war, like nothing else, undermined the foundations of the post–Cold War order, triggering processes that would lead to the formation of the new international order.

The unipolar American world that replaced the bipolar Soviet-American one of the Cold War era never lacked critics, denouncers, and challengers. They emerged soon after the disintegration of the Soviet Union but came to the fore with the start of the twenty-first century and included both governmental and nongovernmental actors. Radical Islam fueled the revolt against American dominance in the Middle East, championed by leaders ranging from those of Al Qaeda to the Islamic State of Iraq and the Levant. Nationalism, coupled with anti-Westernism and a crusade to protect "traditional values," provided grounds for open challenges to the international order by an ever more totalitarian Russia and more subtle challenges by still-communist China, whose leaders learned to use the existing order to their benefit but intended to replace the United States as its leader and guardian, which would allow them to rewrite the rules of engagement.

The ideal shared by all challengers was that of a multipolar world based not so much on Westphalian principles of state sovereignty as on the great-power model of spheres of influence. A return to the world allegedly divided into spheres of influence by the Yalta Conference of 1945 became the demand of both Moscow and Beijing. Ironically, the view that the Yalta Conference had established spheres of influence was mistaken: at the conference, President Franklin Roosevelt rejected not only the principle of spheres of influence, but also Stalin's claim to exclusive control of Eastern Europe.

Washington resisted the challenge, refusing to recognize the post-Soviet space as Russia's sphere of influence and the South China Sea as a Chinese sea. The Russian invasion of Georgia in 2008 and its war on Ukraine, which led to the annexation of the Crimea and the creation of puppet states in the Donbas region of Ukraine, turned a purely diplomatic and economic contest between Russia and the West into a military conflict. The United States was too busy either fighting wars in the Middle East or extricating itself from them to counteract Russia's challenge to the established international order with anything more than economic sanctions.

The botched American withdrawal from Afghanistan in 2021 projected the image of an indecisive and significantly weakened United States, encouraging Putin to try his luck in Ukraine. But the American withdrawal also freed the United States to deal with the new challenge from Russia. Putin's all-out invasion of Ukraine in February 2022 and, most importantly, Ukraine's stubborn resistance, presented the United States with time and opportunity to mobilize domestic and international resources in order to beat back the Russian challenge, not only with much stronger sanctions but also with military support of Ukraine.

The original American reaction to the war showed that the US could maintain its status as the preeminent world power, capable of reviving and creating its own alliances and preventing the formation of competitive ones by using its financial and economic instruments. Washington managed to gather a formidable coalition against Russia's aggression even before it began, capitalizing on support from the United Kingdom and the countries of the eastern flank of NATO and the EU, led by Poland. That coalition helped to convince even nations of the old Europe, primarily Germany, France, and Italy, traditionally reluctant to upset Russia, to join. The decisions of Finland and Sweden to apply for NATO membership made American influence in Europe even stronger than it had been before the war.

The war undermined Russia's hopes of becoming a new global center in the multipolar world envisioned by Russian politicians and diplomats since the 1990s. It exposed weaknesses not only in Russia's clearly overrated and overpromoted army but also in its economic potential. In that context, the decisions of Sweden and Finland to join NATO were not just reactions to the threat posed by Putin's rogue regime but also realizations that a significantly weakened Russia was in no condition to prevent their move.

Russia, for its part, was left with few allies. It forced the Belarusian strongman Aliaksandr Lukashenka, whom it had saved in 2020 from the revolt of his own people, to allow the use of Belarusian territory for its attack on Ukraine but failed to persuade him to join the war. There was even less support from the members of the CSTO (Collective Security Treaty Organization), the Russia-led military alliance of the former Soviet republics of Armenia, Kazakhstan, Kyrgyzstan, Tajikistan, and Uzbekistan. Outside the former Soviet Union, Russia's main diplomatic achievement was alliance with Iran and North Korea. Turkey seized the opportunity afforded by the isolation and weakening of Russia to establish itself as a regional power beyond the Middle East.

China put limits on its "no limits" agreement to cooperate with Russia within weeks of having signed it. While publicly expressing the concern that it shared with Russia about NATO's posture in Europe, Beijing provided Moscow with limited political and economic support and, to the best of current knowledge, no military assistance. This allowed China to continue to benefit from the existing international order and avoid American financial and economic sanctions, which could have disrupted international trade and hurt China's economy. China could hardly avoid being disturbed by the obvious weakness of its Russian fellow-traveler, but it was more concerned by the forceful return of the United States to the international arena and the new spirit of unity within the European Union and between the United States and the EU. China now has the best chance of any country to emerge as a key beneficiary of the current war and the enmity between Russia and the West that the conflict has created.

The war has erected a political and economic Great Wall between Europe and Russia that will grow even taller as the United States and the European Union continue to divest Europe of Russian oil and gas. Beijing has already benefited from the start of European diversification and the reorientation of Russia's energy exports toward the East. It will benefit even more as Russia, eager to secure the Chinese market in order to replace lost revenue from Europe, finds it hard to negotiate favorable prices for its oil and gas. China will not have an economically strong Russian ally in its rivalry with the United States, but it will acquire plenty of cheap oil and gas to fuel that rivalry.

Given the likely continuation of Russia's economic isolation and its increasing dependence on the East, as well as the ongoing rapprochement between Europe and the United States, the war in Ukraine has contributed to the polarization of the world between the two economic superpowers, the United States and China, and between the two camps of countries oriented toward them. The West has been rebuilding its Cold War alliance, now strengthened by new members in eastern Europe, the Baltics, and Scandinavia, while in the East there is a tendency toward reestablishing the Sino-Russian alliance that existed in the 1950s, at the most dangerous stage of the Cold War.

If the United States remains the center of the Western world, there has been a change of roles in the East, with China taking the driver's seat and Russia becoming the poorer and more reckless member of the alliance—the role originally played by China. Ukraine emerges on that map as a new Cold War Germany, its territories divided not just between two countries, but two global spheres and economic blocs. As in the past, there are countries in between, notably India, nonaligned for now but possibly compelled by its troubled relations with China to take sides in the future.

There are clear signs that Russia's turn away from the West is not a passing phase. It is more difficult to say how lasting or permanent that trend might be, given the uncertainty of Russia's relations with Europe and the United States on the one hand, and with China on the other. Russo-Chinese relations were not simple or easy during the Cold War, varying from the close alliance of the early 1950s to the Soviet threat of nuclear attack on China in the 1960s, and the establishment of America's special relations with China in the 1970s.

Technological rivalry between Russia and China, their competition for influence in Central Asia, and China's never forgotten claims to parts of what are now Russia's Siberia and Far East, coupled with the influx of Chinese nationals into those sparsely inhabited territories, portend friction and possible future conflict. But whether Russia ultimately sides with one emerging center of power or the other, the general trend toward a bipolar world order probably will not be affected.

The world order that had been in place on the morning of February 24, 2022, when Russia's invasion began, survived the assault, but the all-out Russo-Ukrainian war demonstrated as never before the imminent trend toward its transformation. Instead of the multipolar world that Russia was hoping for, the conflict presaged a return to the bipolar world of the Cold War, now centered not on Washington and Moscow, but on Washington and Beijing. Whether that new bipolar world will come into existence or not will depend to a great degree on the US and its willingness and ability to continue to perform the role of the leader of the West and the world's democratic pole.

ACKNOWLEDGMENTS

This book came out of the shock, pain, frustration, and anger caused by the start of all-out Russian aggression against Ukraine on February 24, 2022. I would like to thank everyone who helped to transform the emotions aroused in me by the war and channel them into the energy required to write this volume.

My agent, Sarah Chalfant, was the first to suggest that I write about the war unfolding before our eyes. She was seconded by John Glusman of W. W. Norton, and the idea was strongly supported by Casiana Ionita and the editorial team at Penguin. Andrew Wylie provided exceptionally useful advice on the scope and content of the book. My research and writing were influenced by the discussions I had during my sabbatical at the Institut für die Wissenschaften vom Menschen, where I arrived as the Andrei Sheptyts'kyi Senior Fellow in the "Ukraine in European Dialogue" program in February 2022, a few weeks before the start of the all-out invasion.

I thank Timothy Snyder, who was the first to suggest that I spend my Harvard sabbatical in Vienna; the rector of the Institute, Misha

Glenny; and the permanent fellows Ivan Krastev, Ivan Vejvoda, Dariusz Stola, and, last but not least, Kate Younger, for their insights. As research director of the "Ukraine in European Dialogue" program, Kate, together with her wonderful assistant, Lidiia Akryshora, helped me to feel at home in Vienna and initiated a number of projects to help scholars in Ukraine in which I and my colleagues at Harvard were happy to participate.

While the histories of Ukraine and Russia are my lifelong preoccupation, this book required a great deal of new research that, by a historian's standards, had to be done in record time. I would like to thank my wife, Olena, for enduring my long European sabbatical and then for allowing me to concentrate fully on this book upon my return from Vienna. I also thank my friend and veteran editor of my earlier works, Myroslav Yurkevich, for editing the text of this book, and my publishers for being willing to adjust their publication schedules and issue this book sooner than it would otherwise have appeared.

On July 10, 2022, as I was working on the chapters describing warfare in the Donbas, Andriy Shevchenko, a prominent Ukrainian politician and former ambassador of Ukraine to Canada, sent me an email with a photo attached. It was an image of a young man in military uniform reading the Ukrainian translation of my book *Forgotten Bastards of the Eastern Front*, which chronicles the experiences of American pilots on Ukrainian airbases in World War II. Andriy told me in his message that the man in the photo was his younger brother, Lieutenant Yevhen Olefirenko, who had fallen in battle near the city of Bakhmut in the Donbas a few days earlier. The photo of Yevhen holding my book was one of the last ever taken of him. I wrote back to Andriy, struggling to find the right words. I did not find any: there were none.

In mid-October more tragic news came from Bakhmut. My cousin Andriy Kholopov, who had been mobilized a few months earlier, was killed by enemy fire near that city. Once again, I failed to find the right words to console my cousin's family and his children. In my correspondence with Yevhen's brother, Andriy Shevchenko, I promised to do whatever I could to make sure that the heroes of the new Eastern Front would not be forgotten. I dedicate this book to the memory of Andriy and Yevhen, and the many thousands of Ukrainians who sacrificed their lives defending their country and the freedom of many millions of people in Ukraine and abroad.

NOTES

Preface: Making Sense of War

1. Ivo Mijnssen, "Putin will das Russische Reich wiederaufleben lassen—eine Loslö-sung der Ukraine akzeptiert er nicht," *Neue Zürcher Zeitung*, March 5, 2022, https://www.nzz.ch/international/krieg-gegen-die-ukraine/putin-will-das-russische-reich-wieder-aufleben-lassen-ld.1672561?reduced=true; Isaac Chotiner, "Vladimir Putin's Revisionist History of Russia and Ukraine," *New Yorker*, February 23, 2022, https://www.newyorker.com/news/q-and-a/vladimir-putins-revisionist-history-of-russia-and-ukraine.

1. Imperial Collapse

1. Serhii Plokhy, *The Last Empire: The Final Days of the Soviet Union* (New York, 2015), 374–77.
2. Mikhail Gorbachev, *Zhizn' i reformy*, 2 vols. (Moscow, 1995), 1: 5–8; "Obrash-chenie k sovetskim grazhdanam. Vystuplenie po televideniiu prezidenta SSSR," in *1000(0) kliuchevykh dokumentov po sovetskoi i rossiiskoi istorii*, https://www.1000dokumente.de/index.html?c=dokument_ru&dokument=0020_rue&object=translation&l=ru.
3. "Independence—over 90% vote yes in referendum; Kravchuk elected president of Ukraine," *Ukrainian Weekly*, December 8, 1991; Pål Kolstø, *Russians in the Former Soviet Republics* (Bloomington, IN, 1995), 191.
4. Vladislav M. Zubok, *Collapse: The Fall of the Soviet Union* (New Haven and London, 2021), 386–87.
5. Plokhy, *The Last Empire*, 295–318.
6. Anatolii Cherniaev, *1991 god. Dnevnik pomoshchnika prezidenta SSSR* (Moscow, 1997), 98, https://nsarchive.gwu.edu/rus/text_files/Chernyaev/1991.pdf.
7. Zbigniew Brzezinski, "The Premature Partnership," *Foreign Affairs*, March/April 1994, https://www.foreignaffairs.com/articles/russian-federation/1994-03-01/premature-partnership.
8. Simon Franklin and Jonathan Shepard, *The Emergence of Rus, 750–1200* (London, 2014); Mykhailo Hrushevsky, *History of Ukraine-Rus'*, ed. Frank Sysyn et al., vols. 1, 2 (Edmonton and Toronto, 1997, 2021).

9. Aleksei Tolochko, *Kievskaia Rus' i Malorossiia v XIX veke* (Kyiv, 2012).

10. Serhii Plokhy, *The Lost Kingdom: The Quest for Empire and the Making of the Russian Nation from 1470 to the Present* (New York, 2017), 3–18.

11. Isabel de Maradiaga, *Ivan the Terrible* (New Haven and London, 2006); Charles Halperin, *Ivan the Terrible: Free to Reward and Free to Punish* (Pittsburgh, PA, 2019).

12. Chester S. L. Dunning, *Russia's First Civil War: The Time of Troubles and the Founding of the Romanov Dynasty* (University Park, PA, 2001).

13. Robert Frost, *The Oxford History of Poland-Lithuania*, vol. 1, *The Making of the Polish-Lithuanian Union, 1385–1569* (Oxford, 2018), 405–94.

14. Serhii Plokhy, *The Cossacks and Religion in Early Modern Ukraine* (Oxford, 2011), 176–333; Mykhailo Hrushevsky, *History of Ukraine-Rus'*, ed. Frank Sysyn et al., vols. 7–10 (Edmonton and Toronto, 1999–2010).

15. Serhii Plokhy, "Empire or Nation?," in Plokhy, *Ukraine and Russia: Representations of the Past* (Toronto, 2008), 19–20.

16. Tatiana Tairova-Yakovleva, *Ivan Mazepa and the Russian Empire* (Montreal, 2020).

17. Zenon Kohut, *Russian Centralism and Ukrainian Autonomy: Imperial Absorption of the Hetmanate, 1760s–1830s* (Cambridge, MA, 1989); Plokhy, *Lost Kingdom*, 55–70.

18. Andreas Kappeler, *The Russian Empire: A Multi-Ethnic History* (London, 2001), 213–46.

19. Alexei Miller, "'Official Nationality'? A Reassessment of Count Sergei Uvarov's Triad in the Context of Nationalism Politics," in Miller, *The Romanov Empire and Nationalism: Essays in the Methodology of Historical Research* (Budapest, 2008).

20. Plokhy, *Lost Kingdom*, 81–91.

21. Plokhy, *Lost Kingdom*, 105–36.

22. Alexei Miller, *The Ukrainian Question: Russian Empire and Nationalism in the Nineteenth Century* (Budapest, 2003), 117–210.

23. John-Paul Himka, "The Construction of Nationality in Galician Rus': Icarian Flights in Almost All Directions," in *Intellectuals and the Articulation of the Nation*, ed. Ronald G. Suny and Michael D. Kennedy (Ann Arbor, 1999), 109–64; Yaroslav Hrytsak, "'Icarian Flights in Almost All Directions' Reconsidered," *Journal of Ukrainian Studies* 35–36 (2010–11): 81–89.

24. Miller, *The Ukrainian Question*, 211–19; Thomas Prymak, *Mykhailo Hrushevsky: The Politics of National Culture* (Toronto, 1987).

25. Kirill A. Fursov, "Russia and the Ottoman Empire: The Geopolitical Dimension," *Russian Studies in History* 57, no. 2 (2018): 99–102; Jonathan E. Ladinsky, "Things Fall Apart: The Disintegration of Empire and the Causes of War," PhD diss., Massachusetts Institute of Technology, Dept. of Political Science, 2001, 70–219, https://dspace.mit.edu/handle/1721.1/8758.

26. Jane Burbank and Frederick Cooper, *Empires in World History: Power and the Politics of Difference* (Princeton, NJ, 2010), 375–79.

27. Laura Engelstein, *Russia in Flames: War, Revolution, Civil War 1914–1921* (Oxford, 2017), 29–100, 361–582.

28. Vladimir Putin, "Obrashchenie prezidenta Rossiiskoi Federatsii," February 21, 2022, http://kremlin.ru/events/president/news/67828.

29. Viktor Savchenko, *Avantiuristy grazhdanskoi voiny* (Kharkiv, 2000), 53.

30. Serhii Plokhy, *The Gates of Europe: A History of Ukraine* (New York, 2021), 201–28.

31. Terry Martin, *The Affirmative Action Empire: Nations and Nationalism in the Soviet Union, 1923–1939* (Ithaca, NY, 2001), chaps. 1–3; Roman Szporluk, "Lenin, 'Great Russia,' and Ukraine," *Harvard Ukrainian Studies* 28, no. 1 (2006): 611–26.

32. Plokhy, *Lost Kingdom*, 211–44.

33. Martin, *The Affirmative Action Empire*, chaps. 3, 6–9.

34. Serhii Plokhy, "Government Propaganda and Public Response to the Soviet Entry into World War II," in Plokhy, *The Frontline: Essays on Ukraine's Past and Present* (Cambridge, MA, 2021), chap. 9; "U Chervonii armii voiuvalo blyz'ko 6 mil'ioniv ukraïntsiv—istoryky," *Ukraïns'ka pravda*, May 5, 2014, https://www.istpravda.com.ua/short/2014/05/6/142776/.

35. Paul R. Magocsi, *The History of Ukraine: The Land and Its Peoples*, 2d ed. (Toronto, 2010), 666–83; John-Paul Himka, "The Organization of Ukrainian Nationalists, the Ukrainian Police, and the Holocaust," https://www.academia.edu/1071550/The_Organization_of_Ukrainian_Nationalists_the_Ukrainian_Police_and_the_Holocaust; Aleksandr Solzhenitsyn, *Arkhipelag Gulag, 1918–1956*, in *Sobranie sochinenii v 30-ti tomakh* (Moscow, 2006), vol. 6, bk. 3, chap. 2.

36. William Taubman, *Khrushchev: The Man and His Era* (New York, 2012), 208–324.

37. Mark Kramer, "Why Did Russia Give Away Crimea Sixty Years Ago?" *Cold War International History Project*, https://www.wilsoncenter.org/publication/why-did-russia-give-away-crimea-sixty-years-ago; "Vkhodzhennia Kryms'koï oblasti do skladu URSR," *Mynule i teperishnie*, https://mtt.in.ua/ist-ukr_1953–1964_vhodzhennya-krymu-do-ursr/.

38. John P. Willerton, Jr., "Patronage Networks and Coalition Building in the Brezhnev Era," *Soviet Studies* 39, no. 2 (April 1987): 175–204; Ben Fowkes, "The National Question in the Soviet Union under Leonid Brezhnev: Policy and Response," in *Brezhnev Reconsidered*, eds. Edwin Bacon and Mark Sandle (New York, 2002), 68–89.

39. "Osnovnye pokazateli razvitiia narodnogo khoziaistva soiuznykh respublik," pt. 1, in *Strana Sovetov za 50 let. Sbornik statisticheskikh materialov* (Moscow, 1967), https://istmat.org/node/17051.

40. "Osnovnye pokazateli razvitiia narodnogo khoziaistva soiuznykh respublik."

41. "Vsesoiuznaia perepis' naseleniia 1959 goda. Natsional'nyi sostav naseleniia po respublikam SSSR," *Demoskop* Weekly, http://www.demoscope.ru/weekly/ssp/sng_nac_59.php?reg=1; "Material'no-tekhnicheskaia baza narodnogo khoziaistva i ee tekhnicheskoe perevooruzhenie i rekontsruktsiia," in *Narodnoe khoziaistvo SSSR za 70 let*, https://istmat.org/node/9264.

42. Vasyl Markus and Roman Senkus, "Shelest, Petro," Internet Encyclopedia of Ukraine, http://www.encyclopediaofukraine.com/display.asp?linkpath=pages%5CS%5CH%5CShelestPetro.htm; Lowell Tillett, "Ukrainian Nationalism and the Fall of Shelest," *Slavic Review* 34, no. 4 (December 1975): 752–68.

43. Archie Brown, *The Gorbachev Factor* (Oxford, 1996), 260–69; Zubok, *Collapse*, 98–125.

44. Mark R. Beissinger, *Nationalist Mobilization and the Collapse of the Soviet State* (Cambridge, UK, 2002), 1–146.

45. Bohdan Nahaylo, *The Ukrainian Resurgence* (London, 1999).

46. Plokhy, *The Last Empire*, 275–316.

47. Zubok, *Collapse*, 365–426; Plokhy, *The Last Empire*, 220, 326.

48. Yegor Gaidar, *Collapse of an Empire: Lessons for Modern Russia* (Washington, DC, 2007), 1–7; Jack Matlock, *Autopsy on an Empire: The American Ambassador's Account of the Collapse of the Soviet Union* (New York, 1995).

49. George F. Kennan, "Witness to the Fall," *New York Review of Books*, November 16, 1995, https://www.nybooks.com/articles/1995/11/16/witness-to-the-fall/.

50. Dominic Lieven, *The Russian Empire and Its Rivals* (New Haven and London, 2001), 366–67.

51. Burbank and Cooper, *Empires in World History*, 404–30; Lieven, *The Russian Empire*, 343–412.

52. Misha Glenny, *The Fall of Yugoslavia* (London, 1996); Michael Ignatieff, *Virtual War: Kosovo and Beyond* (New York, 2000); Catherine Baker, *The Yugoslav Wars of the 1990s* (New York, 2015).

2. Democracy and Autocracy

1. Jonathan Steele and David Hearst, "Yeltsin Crushes Revolt," *Guardian*, October 5, 1993, https://www.theguardian.com/world/1993/oct/05/russia.davidhearst; "History in REAL TIME: Relive the #1993 Russian Parliament siege," *RT*, October 3, 2013, https://www.rt.com/news/parliament-siege-yeltsin-timeline-691.

2. *Moskva. Osen'–93. Khronika protivostoianiia* (Moscow, 1995), 530–33; "25 Years Ago: The Day The Russian White House Was Shelled," https://www.youtube.com/watch?v=3PJuIVIZ72k.

3. Timothy J. Colton, *Yeltsin: A Life* (New York, 2008), 393–444.

4. Mykhailo Minakov, Georgiy Kasianov, and Matthew Rojansky, eds., *From "the Ukraine" to Ukraine: A Contemporary History, 1991–2021* (Stuttgart, 2021), 169–206, 321–58.

5. Paul D'Anieri, *Ukraine and Russia: From Civilized Divorce to Uncivil War* (Cambridge, UK, 2019), 3–4, 15; Andrew Wilson, *Ukraine's Orange Revolution* (New Haven and London, 2005).

6. Natal'ia Rimashevskaia, "Sotsial'nye posledstviia ėkonomicheskikh transformatsii v Rossii," *Sotsiologicheskie issledovaniia*, no. 6 (1997): 55–65; Branko Milanovic, *Income, Inequality, and Poverty during the Transformation from Planned to Market Economy* (Washington, DC, 1998), 186.

7. David M. Kotz and Fred Weir, *Russia's Path from Gorbachev to Putin: The Demise of Soviet System and the New Russia* (London and New York, 2007), 155–210.

8. Colton, *Yeltsin*, 272–77.

9. Petr Aven and Alfred Kokh, *Gaidar's Revolution: The Inside Account of the Economic Transformation of Russia* (London and New York, 2013), 325–27. Cf. "Russian Defense Minister Pavel Grachev Oral History Excerpt," National Security Archive, https://nsarchive.gwu.edu/document/16854-document–12-russian-defense-minister-pavel.

10. "Memorandum of Telephone Conversation: Telcon with President Boris Yeltsin of Russian Federation," October 5, 1993, National Security Archive, https://nsarchive.gwu.edu/document/16847-document-05-memorandum-telephone-conversation.

11. Svetlana Savranskaya, "A Quarter Century after the Storming of

the Russian White House," National Security Archive, https://nsarchive.gwu.edu/briefing-book/russia-programs/2018-10-04/yeltsin-shelled-russian-parliament–25-years-ago-us-praised-superb-handling.

12. Boris Yeltsin, "Prezident Rossii otvechaet na voprosy gazety 'Izvestiia,'" *Izvestiia*, November 16, 1993.

13. "Rezul'taty vyborov v Dumu 1-go sozyva, December 12, 1993," *Federal'noe sobranie. Sovet Federatsii. Fond razvitiia parlamentarizma v Rossii, 1994–1996*. Electronic version, 2000, http://www.politika.su/fs/gd1rezv.html.

14. Colton, *Yeltsin*, 280–81.

15. Timothy J. Colton, "Superpresidentialism and Russia's Backward State," *Post-Soviet Affairs* 11, no. 2 (1995): 144–48; M. Steven Fish, *Democracy Derailed in Russia: The Failure of Open Politics* (New York, 2005), 114–245.

16. Milanovic, *Income, Inequality, and Poverty*, 186; Gwendolyn Sasse, "Ukraine: The Role of Regionalism," *Journal of Democracy* 21, no. 3 (July 2010): 99–106; Andrew Wilson, *Ukrainian Nationalism in the 1990s: A Minority Faith* (Cambridge, UK, 1997).

17. Lucan Way, *Pluralism by Default: Weak Autocrats and the Rise of Competitive Politics* (Baltimore, MD, 2015), 43–44; Wilson, *Ukrainian Nationalism*.

18. Yitzhak M. Brudny and Evgeny Finkel, "Why Ukraine Is Not Russia: Hegemonic National Identity and Democracy in Russia and Ukraine," *East European Politics and Societies and Cultures* 25, no. 4 (December 2011): 813–33.

19. Serhii Plokhy, *The Last Empire: The Final Days of the Soviet Union* (New York, 2014), 24–72.

20. Paul Robert Magocsi, *A History of Ukraine: The Land and Its Peoples*, 2d ed. (Toronto, 2010), 725–50.

21. Taras Kuzio, *Ukraine: State and Nation Building* (London and New York, 1998).

22. Brudny and Finkel, "Why Ukraine Is Not Russia."

23. "Russia GDP Growth Rate 1990–2022," *Macrotrends*, https://www.macrotrends.net/countries/RUS/russia/gdp-growth-rate; "Ukraine GDP 1987–2022," *Macrotrends*, https://www.macrotrends.net/countries/UKR/ukraine/gdp-gross-domestic-product; Volodymyr Holovko and Larysa Iakubova, *Ukraïna i vyklyky posttotalitarnoho tranzytu, 1990–2019* [=*Ukraïna: Narysy istoriï*, ed. Valerii Smolii, vol. 3] (Kyiv, 2021), 51–55; D'Anieri, *Ukraine and Russia*, 37–38.

24. D'Anieri, *Ukraine and Russia*, 45.

25. Holovko and Iakubova, *Ukraïna i vyklyky*, 59–65; D'Anieri, *Ukraine and Russia*, 71–72.

26. Constitution of Ukraine with amendments by the Law of Ukraine No. 2222-IV from December 8, 2004, Venice Commission, https://web.archive.org/web/20120427012054/http://www.venice.coe.int/docs/2006/CDL   percent282006 percent29070-e.pdf; Serhiy Kudelia and Georgiy Kasianov, "Ukraine's Political Development after Independence," in Minakov et al., eds., *From "the Ukraine" to Ukraine*, 9–52; Mykhailo Minakov and Matthew Rojansky, "Democracy in Ukraine," ibid., 321–58.

27. Brudny and Finkel, "Why Ukraine Is Not Russia."

28. Colton, *Yeltsin*, 282, 356.

29. Kotz and Weir, *Russia's Path from Gorbachev to Putin*, 259–64; Colton, *Yeltsin*, 351.

30. Colton, *Yeltsin*, 356–57; Johanna Granville, "Dermokratizatsiya and Prikh-

vatizatsiya: The Russian Kleptocracy and Rise of Organized Crime," *Demokratizatsiya* (Summer 2003): 448–57.

31. Michael McFaul, *Russia's 1996 Presidential Election: The End of Polarized Politics* (Stanford, CA, 1997).

32. Colton, *Yeltsin*, 409–10, 414; Abigail J. Chiodo and Michael T. Owyang, "A Case Study of a Currency Crisis: The Russian Default of 1998," *Federal Reserve Bank of St. Louis Review* 84, no. 6 (November/December 2002): 7–18, https://research.stlouisfed.org/publications/review/2002/11/01/a-case-study-of-a-currency-crisis-the-russian-default-of-1998.

33. Colton, *Yeltsin*, 421–22, 425–26.

34. Colton, *Yeltsin*, 430–31.

35. Steven Lee Myers, *The New Tsar: The Rise and Reign of Vladimir Putin* (New York, 2015), 136–42.

36. John B. Dunlop, *Russia Confronts Chechnya: Roots of a Separatist Conflict* (Cambridge, UK, 1998); James Hughes, *Chechnya: From Nationalism to Jihad* (Philadelphia, PA, 2011), 1–93; Fiona Hill and Clifford G. Gaddy, *Mr. Putin: Operative in the Kremlin* (Washington, DC, 2015), 29–31.

37. Hughes, *Chechnya: From Nationalism to Jihad*, 94–161.

38. "Russian bomb scare turns out to be anti-terror drill," CNN, September 24, 1999, http://edition.cnn.com/WORLD/europe/9909/24/russia.bomb.01/; Myers, *The New Tsar*, 154–76, 184–87.

39. Olga Oliker, *Russia's Chechen Wars 1994–2000: Lessons from Urban Combat* (Santa Monica, CA, 2000), 41–79.

40. Myers, *The New Tsar*, 164–88; "Russia, Presidential Elections, 2000," *Electoral Geography*, https://www.electoralgeography.com/en/countries/r/russia/2000-president-elections-russia.html.

41. Sarah Whitmore, *State Building in Ukraine: The Ukrainian Parliament, 1990–2003* (London and New York, 2004), 66–91, 106; Holovko and Iakubova, *Ukraïna i vyklyky*, 72–74.

42. Holovko and Iakubova, *Ukraïna i vyklyky*, 77–79; Wilson, *Ukraine's Orange Revolution*, 42–45.

43. Serhii Plokhy, *The Gates of Europe: A History of Ukraine* (New York, 2015), 332–35; Wilson, *Ukraine's Orange Revolution*, 45–50; Holovko and Iakubova, *Ukraïna i vyklyky*, 76.

44. Holovko and Iakubova, *Ukraïna i vyklyky*, 80, 82; Dieter Nohlen and Philip Stöver, eds., *Elections in Europe: A Data Handbook* (Baden-Baden, 2010), 1976, 1969, 1985–86; Serhy Yekelchyk, *The Conflict in Ukraine: What Everyone Needs to Know* (New York, 2015), 87–89.

45. Holovko and Iakubova, *Ukraïna i vyklyky*, 84–85; Wilson, *Ukraine's Orange Revolution*, 51–60; J. V. Koshiw, *Beheaded: The Killing of a Journalist* (Reading, UK, 2003).

46. D'Anieri, *Ukraine and Russia*, 104–13; Holovko and Iakubova, *Ukraïna i vyklyky*, 87.

47. Koshiw, *Beheaded*; Wilson, *Ukraine's Orange Revolution*, 51–60, 93–96; D'Anieri, *Ukraine and Russia*, 107–13.

48. D'Anieri, *Ukraine and Russia*, 127–28; Wilson, *Ukraine's Orange Revolution*, 70–93; Holovko and Iakubova, *Ukraïna i vyklyky*, 87–89.

49. Wilson, *Ukraine's Orange Revolution*, 93–104; Holovko and Iakubova, *Ukraïna i vyklyky*, 98–99.

50. Wilson, *Ukraine's Orange Revolution*, 105–21; Holovko and Iakubova, *Ukraïna i vyklyky*, 101–2.

51. Taras Kuzio, "Nationalism, Identity and Civil Society in Ukraine: Understanding the Orange Revolution," *Communist and Post-Communist Studies* 43, no. 3 (September 2010): 285–96; Mark R. Beissinger, "The Semblance of Democratic Revolution: Coalitions in Ukraine's Orange Revolution," *American Political Science Review* 107, no. 3 (August 2013): 574–92; Wilson, *Ukraine's Orange Revolution*, 122–38; Holovko and Iakubova, *Ukraïna i vyklyky*, 102–6.

52. Wilson, *Ukraine's Orange Revolution*, 138–55; Holovko and Iakubova, *Ukraïna i vyklyky*, 109.

53. Leonid Kuchma, *Ukraina—ne Rossiia* (Moscow, 2003); Vystuplenie prezidenta Ukrainy Leonida Kuchmy na prezentatsii knigi "Ukraina—ne Rossiia" v Moskve, September 3, 2003, http://supol.narod.ru/archive/books/cuchma.htm.

3. Nuclear Implosion

1. Serhii Plokhy and M. E. Sarotte, "The Shoals of Ukraine: Where American Illusions and Great Power Politics Collide," *Foreign Affairs* 99, no. 1 (2020): 81–95, here 84.

2. "Deklaratsiia pro derzhavnyi suverenitet Ukraïny," *Vidomosti Verkhovnoï Rady URSR*, 1990, no. 31, p. 429, https://zakon.rada.gov.ua/laws/show/55-12#Text; Mariana Budjeryn, "Looking Back: Ukraine's Nuclear Predicament and the Nonproliferation Regime," *Arms Control Today* 44 (December 2014): 35–40.

3. Paul D'Anieri, *Ukraine and Russia: From Civilized Divorce to Uncivil War* (Cambridge, UK, 2019), 48–49; Deborah Sanders, *Security Cooperation between Russia and Ukraine in the Post-Soviet Era* (New York, 2001), 43–44.

4. "Zaiava pro bez'iadernyi status Ukraïny," Verkhovna Rada Ukraïny, https://zakon.rada.gov.ua/laws/show/1697-12#Text; Yuri Kostenko, *Ukraine's Nuclear Disarmament: A History* (Cambridge, MA, 2021), 41; Sanders, *Security Cooperation*, 43–44.

5. Stanislav Smagin, "Memorandum Voshchanova. Kak El'tsin napugal Ukrainu i Kazakhstan," *Ukraina.ru*, August 26, 2020, https://ukraina.ru/history/20200826/1028666047.html.

6. Smagin, "Memorandum Voshchanova"; Aleksandr Solzhenitsyn, "Kak nam obustroit' Rossiiu," *Komsomol'skaia pravda*, September 18, 1990.

7. Serhii Plokhy, *The Last Empire: The Final Days of the Soviet Union* (New York, 2014), 178–82; Taras Kuzio, *Ukraine—Crimea—Russia: Triangle of Conflict* (Stuttgart, 2014), 7; Vsevolod Vladimirov, "Zabytyi ul'timatum," *Sovershenno sekretno*, August 10, 2022, https://www.sovsekretno.ru/articles/zabytyy-ultimatum/.

8. "Pavel Voshchanov: kak ia ob"iavlial voinu Ukraine," *Viperson*, October 23, 2003, http://viperson.ru/articles/pavel-voschanov-kak-ya-ob-yavlyal-voynu-ukraine.

9. "Ethnic Composition of Crimea," International Committee for Crimea, https://iccrimea.org/population.html.

10. Jeff Berliner, "Yeltsin Turns Up on Black Sea," UPI, January 28, 1992, https://www.upi.com/Archives/1992/01/28/Yeltsin-turns-up-on-Black-Sea/7315696574800;

Victor Zaborsky, "Crimea and the Black Sea Fleet in Russian-Ukrainian Relations," Discussion Paper, Belfer Center for Science and International Affairs, September 1995, https://www.belfercenter.org/publication/crimea-and-black-sea-fleet-russian -ukrainian-relations.

11. Gwendolyn Sasse, *The Crimea Question: Identity, Transition and Conflict* (Cambridge, MA, 2007); Serhii Plokhy, "History and Territory," in Sasse, *Ukraine and Russia: Representations of the Past* (Toronto, 2008), 165–67, 326.

12. Serhii Plokhy, "The City of Glory," in Sasse, *Ukraine and Russia*, 182–95; Plokhy, "The Ghosts of Pereiaslav," ibid., 196–212.

13. Zaborsky, "Crimea and the Black Sea Fleet in Russian-Ukrainian Relations"; Alexander J. Motyl, *Dilemmas of Independence: Ukraine after Totalitarianism* (New York, 1993), 106; Sasse, *The Crimea Question*, 227–31; Natalya Belitser, "The Transnistrian Conflict," in *Frozen Conflicts in Europe*, ed. Anton Bebler (Opladen, Berlin, and Toronto, 2015), 45–56.

14. Evgeniia Koroleva, "Khronika anneksii. Kak s posiagatel'stvami na Krym stalkivalis' poocheredno vse prezidenty Ukrainy," *Fokus*, February 28, 2021, https://focus .ua/politics/475914-hronika-anneksii-kak-s-posyagatelstvami-na-krym-stalkivalis -poocheredno-vse-prezidenty-ukrainy; V. Bezkorovainyi, "Masandrivs'kyi protokol. Dzherela i naslidky," *Universum*, nos. 3/4 (2011), https://zakon.rada.gov.ua/ laws/show/643_054#Text; D'Anieri, *Ukraine and Russia*, 40–41.

15. "Uhoda mizh Ukraïnoiu ta Rosiis'koiu Federatsiieiu pro poetapne vrehuliuvannia problem Chornomors'koho flotu," April 15, 1994, https://zakon.rada.gov.ua/ laws/show/643_128#Text; D'Anieri, *Ukraine and Russia*, 78–79.

16. Zaborsky, "Crimea and the Black Sea Fleet in Russian-Ukrainian Relations," https://www.belfercenter.org/publication/crimea-and-black-sea-fleet-russian -ukrainian-relations; D'Anieri, *Ukraine and Russia*, 80.

17. Sergei Shargorodsky, "Ukraine Suspends Removal of Tactical Nuclear Weapons with Am-Soviet-Unrest," *Associated Press*, March 12, 1992, https://apnews.com/ f040f8c662d7eb5cc26b7056aafc2dac; Steven Pifer, *The Eagle and the Trident: U.S.-Ukraine Relations in Turbulent Times* (Washington, DC, 2017), 11.

18. D'Anieri, *Ukraine and Russia*, 50–51.

19. John J. Mearsheimer, "The Case for a Ukrainian Nuclear Deterrent," *Foreign Affairs* 72, no. 3 (Summer 1993): 50–66.

20. D'Anieri, *Ukraine and Russia*, 52–53; Budjeryn, "Looking Back"; "Nuclear Disarmament. Ukraine," Nuclear Threat Initiative, https://www.nti.org/analysis/ articles/ukraine-nuclear-disarmament/; Eugene M. Fishel, *The Moscow Factor: US Policy toward Sovereign Ukraine and the Kremlin* (Cambridge, MA, 2022), 85–114.

21. Budapest Memorandums on Security Assurances, 1994, Council on Foreign Relations, https://web.archive.org/web/20140317182201/http://www.cfr.org/arms -control-disarmament-and-nonproliferation/budapest-memorandums-security -assurances-1994/p32484#.

22. Lara Jakes, Edward Wong, and Michael Crowley, "America's Road to the Ukraine War," *New York Times*, April 24, 2022, https://www.nytimes.com/ 2022/04/24/us/politics/russia-ukraine-diplomacy.html; Jane Perlez, "Economic Collapse Leaves Ukraine with Little to Trade but Its Weapons," *New York Times*, January 13, 1994; "Ukraine Inflation Rate, 1993–2022," *Macrotrends*, https://

www.macrotrends.net/countries/UKR/ukraine/inflation-rate-cpi; Serhii Plokhy, *The Gates of Europe: A History of Ukraine* (New York, 2016), 328–29.

23. Dieter Nohlen and Philip Stöver, eds., *Elections in Europe: A Data Handbook* (Baden-Baden, 2010), 1976.

24. Andrew D. Sorokowski, "Treaty on Friendship, Cooperation, and Partnership between Ukraine and the Russian Federation," *Harvard Ukrainian Studies* 20 (1996): 319–29, http://www.jstor.org/stable/41036701; Spencer Kimball, "Bound by Treaty: Russia, Ukraine and Crimea," *DW*, November 11, 2014, https://www.dw.com/en/bound-by-treaty-russia-ukraine-and-crimea/a-17487632.

25. "Nuclear Disarmament. Ukraine," Nuclear Threat Initiative, https://www.nti.org/analysis/articles/ukraine-nuclear-disarmament/; "Tretia pislia Rosiï ta SShA. Iak vyhliadav iadernyi potentsial Ukraïny," https://www.youtube.com/watch?v=Kedw7IhwnCc; Postanovlenie Gosudarstvennoi Dumy federal'nogo sobraniia Rossiiskoi Federatsii ot 25.12.1998 no. 3459 II GD, O federal'nom zakone "O ratifikatsii Dogovora o druzhbe, sotrudnichestve i partnerstve mezhdy Rossiiskoi Federatsiei i Ukrainoi," *Sbornik zakonov*, http://sbornik-zakonov.ru/184970.html.

26. "The Accession of Poland, the Czech Republic and Hungary to NATO," Warsaw Institute, March 29, 2021, https://warsawinstitute.org/accession-poland-czech-republic-hungary-nato/#:~:text=During%20the%20NATO%20summit%20in,countries%20officially%20began%20accession%20talks.

27. Bill Clinton, "Remarks at a Reception for the Opening of the United States Holocaust Memorial Museum," April 21, 1993, The American Presidency Project, https://www.presidency.ucsb.edu/documents/remarks-reception-for-the-opening-the-united-states-holocaust-memorial-museum.

28. "'Banal Conversation': What Is Behind the Historical Dialogue between Lech Walesa and Bill Clinton about the 'Danger' of Russia," *Teller Report*, February 13, 2020, https://www.tellerreport.com/news/2020-02-13---%E2%80%9Cbanal-conversation%E2%80%9D--what-is-behind-the-historical-dialogue-between-lech-walesa-and-bill-clinton-about-the-%E2%80%9Cdanger%E2%80%9D-of-russia-.HklyX8XQ8.html; M. E. Sarotte, *Not One Inch: America, Russia, and the Making of Post–Cold War Stalemate* (New Haven and London, 2021), 161.

29. Sarotte, *Not One Inch*, 55.

30. Sarotte, *Not One Inch*, 11; Sarotte, "The Betrayal Myth behind Putin's Brinkmanship," *Wall Street Journal*, January 7, 2022, https://www.wsj.com/articles/the-betrayal-myth-behind-putins-brinkmanship-11641568161; D'Anieri, *Ukraine and Russia*, 61.

31. Sarotte, *Not One Inch*, 161.

32. Sarotte, *Not One Inch*, 142, 163–66.

33. Sarotte, *Not One Inch*, 165; Samuel Charap and Timothy J. Colton, *Everyone Loses: The Ukraine Crisis and the Ruinous Contest for Post-Soviet Eurasia* (New York, 2016), 41.

34. Charap and Colton, *Everyone Loses*, 42; Sarotte, *Not One Inch*, 166; John Borawski, "Partnership for Peace and Beyond," *International Affairs* 71, no. 2 (April 1995): 233–46.

35. D'Anieri, *Ukraine and Russia*, 65–66, 92.

36. NATO Summit, Madrid, Spain, July 8–9, 1997, https://www.nato.int/docu/comm/1997/970708/home.htm; Bill Clinton, "Memorandum of Conversation—

President Leonid Kuchma of Ukraine," June 5, 2000, Clinton Digital Library, https://clinton.presidentiallibraries.us/items/show/101663; Sarotte, "The Betrayal Myth behind Putin's Brinkmanship."

37. "March 24, 1999: NATO Bombs Yugoslavia," This Day in History, https://www.history.com/this-day-in-history/nato-bombs-yugoslavia.

38. Thomas W. Lippman, "Russian Leader Cancels Trip in Protest," *Washington Post*, March 24, 1999, A 22, https://www.washingtonpost.com/wp-srv/inatl/daily/march99/russia032499.htm; Charap and Colton, *Everyone Loses*, 47–48.

4. The New Eastern Europe

1. Vladimir Putin, "Speech to Representatives of the US Public and Political Leaders," November 14, 2001, President of Russia, http://www.en.kremlin.ru/events/president/transcripts/21398.

2. Angela Stent, "The Impact of September 11 on US-Russian Relations," *Brookings*, September 8, 2021, https://www.brookings.edu/blog/order-from-chaos/2021/09/08/the-impact-of-september–11-on-us-russian-relations/; Samuel Charap and Timothy J. Colton, *Everyone Loses: The Ukraine Crisis and the Ruinous Contest for Post-Soviet Eurasia* (New York, 2016), 67–68.

3. Wade Boese, "Russia Declares Itself No Longer Bound by START II," *Arms Control Association*, July/August 2002, https://www.armscontrol.org/act/2002-07/news/russia-declares-itself-longer-bound-start-ii; Susan B. Glasser, "Tensions with Russia Propel Baltic States toward NATO," *Washington Post*, October 7, 2002; Simon Lunn, "The NATO-Russia Council: Its Role and Prospects," European Leadership Network, Policy Brief, November 2013.

4. Paul D'Anieri, *Ukraine and Russia: From Civilized Divorce to Uncivil War* (Cambridge, UK, 2019), 129, 133; Volodymyr Holovko and Larysa Iakubova, *Ukraïna i vyklyky post-totalitarnoho tranzytu, 1990–2019* [=*Ukraïna: Narysy istoriï*, ed. Valerii Smolii, vol. 3] (Kyiv, 2021), 100.

5. Steven Lee Myers, *The New Tsar: The Rise and Reign of Vladimir Putin* (New York, 2015), 231–46; Dieter Nohlen and Philip Stöver, eds., *Elections in Europe: A Data Handbook* (Baden-Baden, 2010), 1642; Dov Lynch, " 'The Enemy is at the Gate': Russia after Beslan," *International Affairs* 81, no. 1 (January 2002): 141–61.

6. Myers, *The New Tsar*, 263–303; D'Anieri, *Ukraine and Russia*, 148–50; Andrew Wilson, *Ukraine's Orange Revolution* (New Haven and London, 2005), 174–83; Lincoln A. Mitchell, *The Color Revolutions* (Philadelphia, PA, 2012).

7. Askold Krushelnycky, "Ukraine: A Look at Kyiv's Motives for Seeking NATO Membership," Radio Free Europe/Radio Liberty, May 30, 2002, https://www.rferl.org/a/1099856.html; Jakob Hedenskog, *Ukraine and NATO: Deadlock or Re-Start?* Swedish Research Agency, December 2006, 59–63; Grigoriy M. Perepelytsia, "NATO and Ukraine: At the Crossroads," *NATO Review*, April 1, 2007, https://www.nato.int/docu/review/articles/2007/04/01/nato-and-ukraine-at-the-crossroads/index.html.

8. "Opening statement by Viktor Yushchenko, President of Ukraine at the press conference following the meeting of the NATO-Ukraine Council at the level of Heads of State and Government," NATO summit, February 22, 2005, https://www.nato.int/docu/speech/2005/s050222g.htm (edited for clarity); "NATO-Russia Relations: The Background," Media backgrounder, NATO,

March 2020, https://www.nato.int/nato_static_fl2014/assets/pdf/2020/4/pdf/2003-NATO-Russia_en.pdf.

9. Paul D'Anieri, *Ukraine and Russia*, 12–13.

10. Rajan Menon and Eugene Rumer, *Conflict in Ukraine: The Unwinding of the Post–Cold War Order* (Cambridge, MA, and London, 2015), 41–44; D'Anieri, *Ukraine and Russia*, 155–57; Margarita M. Balmaceda, *Russian Energy Chains: The Remaking of Technopolitics from Siberia to the European Union* (New York, 2021), 91–104.

11. Vladimir Putin, "Speech and the Following Discussion at the Munich Conference on Security Policy," February 10, 2007, President of Russia, http://en.kremlin.ru/events/president/transcripts/24034 (edited for clarity).

12. Rob Watson, "Putin's Speech: Back to Cold War?" BBC, February 10, 2007, http://news.bbc.co.uk/2/hi/europe/6350847.stm; Luke Harding, "Bush Backs Ukraine and Georgia for Nato Membership," *Guardian*, April 1, 2008, https://www.theguardian.com/world/2008/apr/01/nato.georgia; Charap and Colton, *Everyone Loses*, 88; D'Anieri, *Ukraine and Russia*, 162.

13. Illya Labunka, "Ukraine Seeks NATO Membership Action Plan," *Ukrainian Weekly*, January 27, 2008; "Joint Address to the NATO Secretary General," ibid., p. 3, http://www.ukrweekly.com/archive/pdf3/2008/The_Ukrainian_Weekly_2008-04.pdf.

14. D'Anieri, *Ukraine and Russia*, 162–63; Labunka, "Ukraine Seeks NATO Membership Action Plan."

15. Charap and Colton, *Everyone Loses*, 87.

16. "Bucharest Summit Declaration." Issued by the Heads of State and Government Participating in the Meeting of the North Atlantic Council in Bucharest on April 3, 2008, NATO, https://www.nato.int/cps/en/natolive/official_texts_8443.htm.

17. Jan Maksymiuk, "Is Ukraine Prepared To Maintain Its Tough Stand Against Russia?" Radio Free Europe/Radio Liberty, August 15, 2008, https://www.rferl.org/a/Is_Ukraine_Prepared_To_Maintain_Its_Tough_Stand_Against_Russia/1191251.html; Charap and Colton, *Everyone Loses*, 91–94; Svante E. Cornell and Frederick S. Starr, *The Guns of August 2008: Russia's War in Georgia* (Armonk, NY, 2009); Ronald D. Asmus, *A Little War That Shook the World: Georgia, Russia, and the Future of the West* (New York, 2010).

18. Ivan Watson and Maxim Tkachenko, "Russia, Ukraine agree on naval-base-for-gas deal," CNN, April 21, 2010, http://www.cnn.com/2010/WORLD/europe/04/21/russia.ukraine/index.html; Menon and Rumer, *Conflict in Ukraine*, 44–52.

19. Vladimir Putin, "Novyi integratsionnyi proekt dlia Evrazii—budushchee, kotoroe rozhdaetsia segodnia," *Izvestiia*, October 3, 2011, https://sroportal.ru/publications/novyj-integracionnyj-proekt-dlya-evrazii-budushhee-kotoroe-rozhdaetsya-segodnya/.

20. Putin, "Novyi integratsionnyi proekt dlia Evrazii."

21. Fiona Hill and Clifford G. Gaddy, *Mr. Putin: Operative in the Kremlin* (Washington, DC, 2015), 358–62.

22. Serhii Plokhy, *The Gates of Europe: A History of Ukraine*, rev. ed. (New York, 2021), 338; D'Anieri, *Ukraine and Russia*, 184.

23. D'Anieri, *Ukraine and Russia*, 92; Plokhy, *The Gates of Europe*, 340.

24. D'Anieri, *Ukraine and Russia*, 204–5.

25. "Eased Russian customs rules to save Ukraine $1.5 bln in 2014, says minister," *Inter-*

fax, December 18, 2013, https://en.interfax.com.ua/news/economic/182691.html; D'Anieri, *Ukraine and Russia*, 200–203; Plokhy, *The Gates of Europe*, 340.

26. Hennadii Moskal interviewed on the "Gordon" television program, January 21, 2018, https://www.youtube.com/watch?v=ZSer846Yi_8&t=0s.

27. "Meeting with President of Ukraine Viktor Yanukovych," December 17, 2013, President of Russia, http://kremlin.ru/events/president/news/19849; "Dekabr' 2013 goda, rabochii vizit Prezidenta Ukrainy v Moskvu," *Levyi Bereg*, December 17, 2013, https://lb.ua/news/2013/12/17/247980_dekabr_2013t_goda_rabochiy_vizit.html.

28. Plokhy, *The Gates of Europe*, 339; "Shturm barykad. 11 hrudnia. Nich ta ranok suprotyvu," *Ukraïns'ka pravda*, December 11, 2013, https://www.pravda.com.ua/articles/2013/12/11/7005267/; "Top U.S. official visits protesters in Kiev as Obama admin. ups pressure on Ukraine president Yanukovich," *CBS News*, December 11, 2013, https://www.cbsnews.com/news/us-victoria-nuland-wades-into-ukraine-turmoil-over-yanukovich/.

29. Serhii Leshchenko, "Taiemna zustrich Ianukovycha z Putinym ta inshi sekrety z mizhyhirs'koho notatnyka," *Ukraïns'ka pravda*, March 11, 2014, https://www.pravda.com.ua/articles/2014/03/11/7018404/; "Ianukovych zibravsia do Rosiï—dzherelo. Povidomliaiut', shcho prezydent 8 sichnia taiemno zustrichavsia z Putinym," *Livyi bereh*, January 31, 2014, https://lb.ua/news/2014/01/31/253927_yanukovich_sobralsya_rossiyu.html.

30. D'Anieri, *Ukraine and Russia*, 216–18; "Mizh nevoleiu i nezalezhnistiu, 18–22 liutoho 2014," *Ukraïns'ka pravda*, February 18, 2015, https://www.istpravda.com.ua/articles/2015/02/18/147385/.

31. "Mizh nevoleiu i nezalezhnistiu, 18–22 liutoho 2014."

32. D'Anieri, *Ukraine and Russia*, 217, 219–20.

33. "Mizh nevoleiu i nezalezhnistiu, 18–22 liutoho 2014"; Dmytro Ievchyn, Inna Anitova, and Nataliia Nedel'ko, "Iak Ianukovych utikav do Krymu: svidchennia ochevydtsiv," *Krym.realiï*, March 1, 2018, https://ua.krymr.com/a/29070914.html.

34. "Mizh nevoleiu i nezalezhnistiu, 18–22 liutoho 2014"; "Rada skynula Ianukovycha, iakyi unochi vtik do Rosiï, Khronika revoliutsii hidnosti," *Ukrinform*, February 22, 2021, https://www.ukrinform.ua/rubric-society/3193991-rada-skinula-anukovica-akij-unoci-vtik-do-rosii.html;"Vtechaeksharanta: iak Ianukovych u 2014 rotsi tikav z Ukraïny," *UNIAN*, February 21, 2020, https://www.unian.ua/politics/10883561-vtecha-eks-garanta-yak-yanukovich-u–2014-roci-tikav-z-ukrajini.html.

5. The Crimean Gambit

1. Aleksandr Solzhenitsyn, "Russkii vopros v kontse XX veka," *Novyi mir*, no. 7 (1994); Vladimir Putin, "Message to the Federal Assembly of the Russian Federation," April 25, 2005, http://kremlin.ru/events/president/transcripts/22931; Serhii Plokhy, *Lost Kingdom: The Quest for Empire and the Making of the Russian Nation from 1470 to the Present* (New York, 2017), 312–15.

2. Ernest Gellner, *Nations and Nationalism* (Ithaca, NY, 1983), 1.

3. Julia Rubin, "Meditations on Russia: Yeltsin Calls for New National 'Idea,'" *AP*, August 2, 1996, https://apnews.com/article/122cd732a8cf8b35989afeec4db69dcd; Vera Tolz, "The Search for a National Identity in the Russia of Yeltsin and

Putin," in Yitzhak Brudny, Jonathan Frankel, and Stefani Hoffman, eds., *Restructuring Post-Communist Russia* (Cambridge, UK, 2004), 160–78.

4. Timothy Snyder, *The Road to Unfreedom: Russia, Europe, America* (New York, 2019), 88–91; Marlene Laruelle, "Scared of Putin's Shadow: In Sanctioning Dugin, Washington Got the Wrong Man," *Foreign Affairs*, March 25, 2015, https://www.foreignaffairs.com/articles/russian-federation/2015-03-25/scared-putins-shadow; http://newfascismsyllabus.com/contributions/into-the-irrational-core-of-pure-violence-on-the-convergence-of-neo-eurasianism-and-the-kremlins-war-in-ukraine/.

5. Plokhy, *Lost Kingdom*, 121–53; Alexei Miller, *The Ukrainian Question: Russian Empire and Nationalism in the 19th Century* (Budapest, 2003), 24–26.

6. Snyder, *The Road to Unfreedom*, 16–35.

7. Aleksandr Solzhenitsyn, *Kak nam obustroit' Rossiiu?* (Paris, 1990); Solzhenitsyn, "Russkii vopros v kontse XX veka" (1994); Solzhenitsyn, *Rossiia v obvale* (Moscow, 1998), 79.

8. "Putin vozlozhil tsvety k nadgrobiiam Denikina, Il'ina i Shmeleva," *Vesti.ru*, May 24, 2009, https://www.vesti.ru/article/2180162.

9. Plokhy, *Lost Kingdom*, 326.

10. "Putin vozlozhil tsvety k nadgrobiiam Denikina, Il'ina i Shmeleva."

11. "Putin: Krym prisoedinili, chtoby ne brosat' natsionalistam," *BBC News*, March 9, 2015, https://www.bbc.com/russian/international/2015/03/150309_putin_crimea_annexion_film.

12. Antonina Dolomanzhi, "Ianukovych II raziv hovoryv z Putinym pid chas naikryvavishykh podii Maidanu—prokuror," *UNIAN*, November 17, 2021, https://www.unian.ua/politics/yanukovich—II-raziv-govoriv-z-putinim-pid-chas-naykrivavishih-podiy-maydanu-prokuror-novini-ukrajina—1161286o.html; "Uhoda pro vrehuliuvannia kryzy v Ukraïni," *Ukraïns'ka pravda*, February 21, 2014, https://www.pravda.com.ua/articles/2014/02/21/7015533/; Valerii Kal'nysh, Kirill Mikhailov, Sergei Minenko, and Boris Iunakov, "21 fevralia 2014 goda, piatnitsa," *Novoe vremia*, no. 5 (February 16, 2015), https://newtimes.ru/articles/detail/94681.

13. "Putin rasskazal, kak pomog Ianukovichu vyekhat' iz Ukrainy," *ATN*, October 24, 2014, https://atn.ua/world/putin-rasskazal-kak-pomog-janukovichu-vyehat-iz-ukrainy–151693/; Konstantin Remchukov, "What Vladimir Putin is Really Thinking. The person who has had to deal with Russia's new challenge is Putin and Putin alone," *National Interest*, July 6, 2022, https://nationalinterest.org/feature/what-vladimir-putin-really-thinking–203422?page=0%2C1; Ben Rhodes, *The World as It Is: A Memoir of the Obama White House* (New York, 2019), 270–71.

14. "Putin rasskazal, kak pomog Ianukovichu vyekhat' iz Ukrainy."

15. "V Khar'kov edut boeviki, a v Krymu snimaiut ukrainskie flagi. V regionakh Ukrainy nastupilo napriazhennoe ozhidanie," *Mangazeia. Informatsionnoe agentstvo*, February 26, 2014, https://www.mngz.ru/russia-world-sensation/366198-v-harkov-edut-boeviki-a-v-krymu-snimayut-ukrainskie-flagi-v-regionah-ukrainy-nastupilo-napryazhennoe-ozhidanie.html; "Ofitsiine vidstoronennia Ianukovycha vid vlady: khronika podii," *5 kanal*, February 22, 2018, https://www.5.ua/suspilstvo/ofitsiine-vidstoronennia-yanukovycha-vid-vlady–165461.html; "V gostiakh u Gordona: Dobkin, Kernes, Avakov, zhaba Poroshenko, ubiistvo Kush-

nareva," October 6, 2020, https://www.youtube.com/watch?v=xcdcdDR8toc; "Vystup Ianukovycha na z'ïzdi v Kharkovi 22 liutoho 2014 roku mih vidkryty shliakh tankam Putina na Kyïv—Turchynov," *Hordon*, February 22, 2019, https://gordonua.com/ukr/news/maidan/vistup-janukovicha-na-z-jizdi-v-harkovi-22-ljutogo-2014-roku-moglo-vidkriti-shljah-tankam-putina-na-kijiv-turchinov-759148.html; "Kharkivs'kyi z'ïzd oholosyv pro kontrol' nad chastynoiu Pivdnia i Skhodu," *BBC News*, February 22, 2014, https://www.bbc.com/ukrainian/politics/2014/02/140222_kharkiv_nk; "Z'ïzd u Kharkovi: my proty separatyzmu, my za iedynu Ukraïnu," *Krym.realiï*, February 22, 2014, https://ua.krymr.com/a/25348311.html.

16. "'Ego by prosto unichtozhili,' Vladimir Putin rasskazal o spasenii Ianukovicha," *Vesti.ru*, March 15, 2015, https://www.vesti.ru/article/1720038; "Putin rasskazal, kak pomog Ianukovichu vyekhat' iz Ukrainy."

17. "Putin dal ukazanie anneksirovat' Krym v noch' na 23 fevralia—Ponomarev," *Ukraïns'ka pravda*, February 13, 2018, https://www.pravda.com.ua/rus/news/2018/02/14/7171592/.

18. "'Ego by prosto unichtozhili,' Vladimir Putin rasskazal o spasenii Ianukovicha"; "Telokhranitel' rasskazal sudu v Kieve, kak Ianukovich bezhal v Rossiiu," *BBC News*, January 18, 2018, https://www.bbc.com/russian/news-42740229.

19. "'Ego by prosto unichtozhili,' Vladimir Putin rasskazal o spasenii Ianukovicha"; "Telokhranitel' rasskazal sudu v Kieve, kak Ianukovich bezhal v Rossiiu"; "Ianukovicha v Khar'kove i Donetske presledovali 'vooruzhennye boeviki,'—okhrannik," *BBC News*, July 16, 2018, https://www.bbc.com/ukrainian/news-russian-44847511.

20. "'Ego by prosto unichtozhili,' Vladimir Putin rasskazal o spasenii Ianukovicha"; "Ianukovicha v Khar'kove i Donetske presledovali 'vooruzhennye boeviki'"; "'Putin rasskazal, kak pomog Ianukovichu vyekhat' iz Ukrainy"; "Telokhranitel' rasskazal sudu v Kieve, kak Ianukovich bezhal v Rossiiu."

21. "V gostiakh u Gordona: Dobkin, Kernes, Avakov, zhaba Poroshenko, ubiistvo Kushnareva."

22. Paul D'Anieri, *Ukraine and Russia: From Civilized Divorce to Uncivil War* (Cambridge, UK, 2019), 226.

23. "Ukraine Crimea: Rival rallies confront one another," *BBC News*, February 26, 2014, https://www.bbc.com/news/world-europe-26354705; "V Khar'kov edut boeviki, a v Krymu snimaiut ukrainskie flagi"; Viktoriia Veselova, "Plenki Glaz'eva: kto i kak koordiniroval iz Rossii sobytiia 'krymskoi vesny,'" *Krym.realii*, December 26, 2017, https://ru.krymr.com/a/28933736.html; Sergei Chasovskikh, *Novorossiia. God voiny* (Moscow, 2018).

24. "Stenohrama zasidannia RNBO Ukraïnu u zv'iazku z pochatkom rosiis'koï ahresiï v Krymu," *Ukraïns'ka pravda*, February 22, 2016, https://www.pravda.com.ua/articles/2016/02/22/7099911/.

25. "Stenohrama zasidannia RNBO Ukraïny."

26. D'Anieri, *Ukraine and Russia*, 227; "Ianukovych prosyv Putina vvesty viis'ka v Ukraïnu," *Livyi bereh*, March 3, 2014, https://lb.ua/news/2014/03/03/258044_yanukovich_poprosil_putina_vvesti.html; "Ianukovych vyznav, shcho prosyv Putina vvesty viis'ka v Ukraïnu," *Livyi bereh*, March 2, 2018, https://lb.ua/news/2018/03/02/391645_yanukovich_priznal_prosil_putina.html.

27. "Putin dumaet, chto v Ukraine Ianukovicha mogli ubit'," *Segodnia*, March 4, 2014, https://politics.segodnya.ua/politics/putin-dumaet-chto-v-ukraine-yanukovicha -mogli-ubit-500420.html; "Putin: My ne rassmatrivaem variant prisoedineniia Kryma," *Vedomosti*, March 4, 2014, https://www.vedomosti.ru/politics/articles/2014/ 03/04/putin-nachal-press-konfernenciyu.
28. D'Anieri, *Ukraine and Russia*, 228–29; Carol Morello, Pamela Constable, and Anthony Faiola, "Crimeans vote in referendum on whether to break away from Ukraine, join Russia," *Washington Post*, March 17, 2014; Jason Samuel, "The Russian Constitutional Path to the Annexation of Crimea," *Jurist*, May 25, 2014, https://www.jurist.org/commentary/2014/05/jason-samuel-russia-crimea/.
29. Andrei Zubov, "Ėto uzhe bylo," *Vedomosti*, March 1, 2014; "Iz MGIMO uvolen professor Andrei Zubov," *BBC News*, March 24, 2014, https://www.bbc.com/ russian/rolling_news/2014/03/140324_rn_professor_mgimo_fired.
30. Gellner, *Nations and Nationalism*, 1; "Anschluss and World War II," *Britannica*, https://www.britannica.com/place/Austria/Anschluss-and-World-War-II; Keren Yarhi-Milo, *Knowing the Adversary: Leaders, Intelligence, and Assessment of Intentions in International Relations* (Princeton, NJ, 2014), 69–98; Rick Noack, "Why do nearly 40 percent of Germans endorse Russia's annexation of Crimea?" *Washington Post*, November 28, 2014.

6. The Rise and Fall of the New Russia

1. Serhii Plokhy, "The Empire Strikes Back," in Plokhy, *The Frontline: Essays on Ukraine's Past and Present* (Cambridge, MA, 2020), 231; Rajan Menon and Eugene Rumer, *Conflict in Ukraine: The Unwinding of the Post–Cold War Order* (Cambridge, MA, and London, 2015), 81–85; Serhy Yekelchyk, *The Conflict in Ukraine: What Everyone Needs to Know* (New York, 2015), 128–31.
2. Vladimir Putin, "Address by President of the Russian Federation," March 18, 2014, http://en.kremlin.ru/events/president/news/20603; Fiona Hill and Clifford G. Gaddy, *Mr. Putin: Operative in the Kremlin* (Washington, DC, 2015), 368–69.
3. "Putin sozdal krymskii federal'nyi okrug," *BBC News*, March 21, 2014, https:// www.bbc.com/russian/russia/2014/03/140321_crimea_putin_federal_district.
4. "MID Rossii predlozhil sdelat' Ukrainu federatsiei," *Vedomosti*, March 17, 2014, https://www.vedomosti.ru/politics/articles/2014/03/17/mid-rossii-predlozhil -sdelat-ukrainu-federaciej.
5. "Lavrov nastaivaet na federalizatsii Ukrainy," *Polit.ru*, March 31, 2014, https://m .polit.ru/news/2014/03/31/lavrov/; "MID Ukrainy zaiavil ob otkaze vlastei ot federalizatsii strany," *Polit.ru*, April 1, 2014, https://m.polit.ru/news/2014/04/01/ federalization/; Julian Borger and Alec Luhn, "Ukraine crisis: Geneva talks produce agreement on defusing conflict," *Guardian*, April 17, 2014, https://www .theguardian.com/world/2014/apr/17/ukraine-crisis-agreement-us-russia-eu; "Ukraine crisis: Deal to 'de-escalate' agreed in Geneva," *BBC News*, April 17, 2014, https://www.bbc.com/news/world-europe-27072351.
6. Lidia Kelly, "Russian politician proposes new divisions of Ukraine," Reuters, March 24, 2014, https://www.reuters.com/article/ukraine-crisis -partition-letter/russian-politician-proposes-new-divisions-of-ukraine -idUSL5N0ML1LO20140324; "Former Polish FM Says Putin Offered to Divide

Ukraine With Poland," *Radio Free Europe/Radio Liberty*, October 21, 2014, https://www.rferl.org/a/26647587.html.

7. Kelly, "Russian politician proposes new divisions of Ukraine"; "President Vladimir Putin met with Polish Prime Minister Donald Tusk," President of Russia, February 8, 2008, http://en.kremlin.ru/events/president/news/43774; Marcel H. Van Herpen, *Putin's Wars: The Rise of Russia's New Imperialism* (Lanham, Boulder, New York, and London, 2015), 4–5.

8. Linda Kinstler, "In eastern Ukraine, protestors are chanting 'New Russia'—an old term that's back in fashion," *New Statesman*, April 8, 2014, https://www.newstatesman.com/politics/2014/04/eastern-ukraine-protestors-are-chanting-new-russia-old-term-s-back-fashion; Veselova, "Plenki Glaz'eva: kto i kak koordiniroval iz Rossii sobytiia 'krymskoi vesny'"; "Direct Line with Vladimir Putin," President of Russia, April 17, 2014, http://kremlin.ru/events/president/news/20796.

9. Marlene Laruelle, *Russian Nationalism: Imaginaries, Doctrines, and Political Battlefields* (London and New York, 2019), 196.

10. Paul D'Anieri, *Ukraine and Russia: From Civilized Divorce to Uncivil War* (Cambridge, UK, 2019), 234–35, 240–41; Michael Kofman, Katya Migacheva, Brian Nichiporuk, Andrew Radin, Olesya Tkacheva, and Jenny Oberholtzer, *Lessons from Russia's Operations in Crimea and Eastern Ukraine* (Santa Monica, CA, 2019), 39–40.

11. Plokhy, *The Gates of Europe*, 342; Yuri Zhukov, "Trading Hard Hats for Combat Helmets: The Economics of Rebellion in Eastern Ukraine," *Journal of Comparative Economics* 44, no. 1 (October 2015): 1–15; cf. Zhukov, "The Economics of Rebellion in Eastern Ukraine," *Vox Ukraine*, November 10, 2015, https://voxukraine.org/en/the-economics-of-rebellion-in-eastern-ukraine/.

12. Laruelle, *Russian Nationalism*, 196–206; Laruelle, "Back from Utopia: How Donbas Fighters Reinvent Themselves in a Post-Novorossiya Russia," *Nationalities Papers* 47, no. 5 (2019): 719–33.

13. Paul Sonne and Philip Shishkin, "Pro-Russian Commander in Eastern Ukraine Sheds Light on Origin of Militants," *Wall Street Journal*, April 26, 2014, https://www.wsj.com/articles/SB10001424052702304788404579526160643349256.

14. "Poroshenko: 'No negotiations with separatists,'" *DW*, May 8, 2014, https://www.dw.com/en/poroshenko-no-negotiations-with-separatists/a-17619764; Alec Luhn and Shaun Walker, "Poroshenko promises calm 'in hours' amid battle to control Donetsk airport," *Guardian*, March 26, 2015.

15. "Donetsk militants send 34 pro-Russian separatist bodies to Russia leader," *Kyiv Post*, May 30, 2014, https://www.kyivpost.com/article/content/war-against-ukraine/donetsk-militants-send-34-pro-russian-separatists-bodies-to-russia-leader-350016.html; Christopher Miller, "Ukrainian Forces Seize Crucial Port City from Pro-Russia Separatists," *Mashable*, June 13, 2014, https://mashable.com/archive/ukraine-seize-port-city-russia-separatists.

16. "Ukraine crisis: Rebels abandon Sloviansk stronghold," *BBC News*, July 5, 2014, https://www.bbc.com/news/world-europe-28174104; Karoun Demirjian and Michael Birnbaum, "Russia warns Ukraine of 'irreversible consequences' after cross-border shelling," *Washington Post*, July 13, 2014, https://www.washingtonpost.com/world/russia-warns-ukraine-of-irreversible

-consequences-after-cross-border-shelling/2014/07/13/
d2be1bb0-0a85-11e4-8341-b8072b1e7348_story.html; "Ukrainian Troops Were
Likely Shelled from Russian MRLS Tornado in Zelenopillia," *Censor.net*, July
15, 2014, https://censor.net/en/news/293840/ukrainian_troops_were_likely_
shelled_from_russian_mrls_tornado_in_zelenopillia.

17. "Update in criminal investigation MH17 disaster," Openbaar Ministe-
rie, May 24, 2018, https://web.archive.org/web/20180524222602/https://
www.om.nl/onderwerpen/mh17-crash/@103196/update-criminal-o/; Michael
Walsh and Larry McShane, "Malaysia Airlines Flight 17 shot down by surface-
to-air missile in what Ukrainian president calls 'act of terrorism,'" *New
York Daily News*, July 18, 2014, https://www.nydailynews.com/news/world/
malaysian-airlines-plane-crashes-ukraine-russian-border-article-$21870413;
"MH17 plane crash: EU to widen Russia sanctions," *BBC News*, 22 July 2014,
https://www.bbc.com/news/uk-28415248.

18. "Sylam ATO nareshti vdalosia rozdilyty terorystiv na Donbasi na dvi hrupy," *TSN*,
August 3, 2014, https://tsn.ua/ukrayina/silam-ato-nareshti-vdalosya-rozdiliti
-teroristiv-na-donbasi-na-dvi-grupi-361740.html.

19. "V Amvrosievku voshli rossiiskie voiska bez znakov otlichiia," *Liga.novyny*, August
24, 2014, https://news.liga.net/politics/news/v_amvrosievku_voshli_rossiyskie_
voyska_istochnik; "Captured Russian troops in Ukraine by accident,'" *BBC
News*, August 26, 2014, https://www.bbc.com/news/world-europe-28934213;
"Fears of massacre after accusations Russians reneged on safe passage for Ukrainian forces," *Daily Telegraph*, August 31, 2014; Taras Kuzio, *Putin's War against
Ukraine: Revolution, Nationalism, and Crime* (Toronto, 2017), 253.

20. "Protokol po itogam konsul'tatsii Trekhstoronnei kontaktnoi gruppy," chrome-
extension://efaidnbmnnnibpcajpcglclefindmkaj/https://www.osce.org/files/f/
documents/a/a/123258.pdf; D'Anieri, *Ukraine and Russia*, 247.

21. Shaun Walker and Oksana Grytsenko, "Ukraine forces admit loss of Donetsk
airport to rebels," *Guardian*, January 21, 2015, https://www.theguardian
.com/world/2015/jan/21/russia-ukraine-war-fighting-east; "Debal'tseve battle:
Pro-Russian and Ukrainian forces agree to humanitarian corridor for civilians,"
International Business Times, February 6, 2015; "Ukraine troops, pro-Russia rebels
intensify clashes," *CBS News*, February 10, 2015, https://www.cbsnews.com/news/
ukraine-troops-pro-russia-rebels-intensify-clashes/; Kuzio, *Putin's War*, 256.

22. "Minsk agreement on Ukraine crisis: text in full," *Daily Telegraph*, February 12,
2015.

23. Laruelle, "Back from Utopia: How Donbas Fighters Reinvent Themselves in a Post-Novorossiya Russia"; Donbas Doubles: The Search for Girkin and Plotnitsky's Cover Identities," *Bellingcat*, July 18, 2022, https://
www.bellingcat.com/news/2022/07/18/donbas-doubles-the-search-for-girkin-and
-plotnitskys-cover-identities/;__"GRU-shnik Girkin zaiavil," https://www
.youtube.com/shorts/6RHeRkTzjmo.

24. Sviatoslav Khomenko, "Kto za kogo golosoval: elektoral'naia geografiia pre-
zidentskikh vyborov," *BBC News*, May 28, 2014, https://www.bbc.com/
ukrainian/ukraine_in_russian/2014/05/140528_ru_s_electoral_geography;
"Obrobleni 100% biuleteniv: Poroshenko peremih u pershomu turi," *BBC News*, May
29, 2014, https://www.bbc.com/ukrainian/politics/2014/05/140529_poroshenko_

vote_count_dt; Serhii Plokhy, *The Gates of Europe: A History of Ukraine*, rev. ed. (New York, 2021), 343–44.

25. "Kazhdyi sam po sebe: Boiko i Medvedchuk idut v radu otdel'no ot Akhmetova i Novinskogo," *Kyivvlada*, June 6, 2019, https://kievvlast.com.ua/vybory/kazhdyj-sam-po-sebe-bojko-i-medvedchuk-idut-v-radu-otdelno-ot-ahmetova-i-novinskogo.

26. Oxana Shevel, "Decommunization in Post-Euromaidan Ukraine: Law and Practice," *Ponaris Eurasia, Policy Memos*, January 11, 2016, https://www.ponarseurasia.org/decommunization-in-post-euromaidan-ukraine-law-and-practice/; Serhii Plokhy, *The Frontline: Essays on Ukraine's Past and Present* (Cambridge, MA, 2021) 257–79.

27. Pavel Polityuk, "Ukraine passes language law, irritating president-elect and Russia," Reuters, April 25, 2019, https://www.reuters.com/article/us-ukraine-parliament-language-idUSKCN1S111N; "Language, Revolution of Dignity Project, Contemporary Atlas, Digital Atlas of Ukraine," Harvard Ukrainian Research Institute, https://gis.huri.harvard.edu/language-module.

28. Marina Presenti, "Ukraine's cultural revival is a matter of national security," *Atlantic Council*, January 19, 2021, https://www.atlanticcouncil.org/blogs/ukrainealert/ukraines-cultural-revival-is-a-matter-of-national-security/l.

29. Andriy Mykhaleyko, "The New Independent Orthodox Church in Ukraine," *Comparative Southeast European Studies* 67, no. 4 (2019): 476–99, https://www.degruyter.com/document/doi/10.1515/soeu-2019-0037/html; "Transfer of Parishes," Religious Revolution, Revolution of Dignity Project, Contemporary Atlas, MAPA: Digital Atlas of Ukraine, https://gis.huri.harvard.edu/transfer-parishes.

30. Plokhy, *The Gates of Europe*, 348–49.

31. Steven Pifer, "Poroshenko Signs EU-Ukraine Association Agreement," *Brookings*, June 27, 2014, https://www.brookings.edu/blog/up-front/2014/06/27/poroshenko-signs-eu-ukraine-association-agreement/; "Visas: Council confirms agreement on visa liberalisation for Ukrainians," European Council, Council of the European Union, March 2, 2017, https://www.consilium.europa.eu/en/press/press-releases/2017/03/02/visa-liberalisation-ukraine/; Plokhy, *The Gates of Europe*, 350–51.

7. Putin's War

1. "Putin u menia sprashival, chto o nem napishut v uchebnikakh: glavred 'Ëkha' o lichnom razgovore s prezidentom RF," *Pervyi Russkii*, August 20, 2019, https://tsargrad.tv/news/putin-u-menja-sprashival-chto-o-nem-napishut-v-uchebnikah-glavred-jeha-o-lichnom-razgovore-s-prezidentom-rf_213278.

2. Fiona Hill and Clifford G. Gaddy, *Mr. Putin: Operative in the Kremlin* (Washington, DC, 2015), 64–66.

3. Putin, "On the Historical Unity of the Russians and Ukrainians," President of Russia, http://en.kremlin.ru/events/president/news/66181.

4. Serhii Plokhy, *Lost Kingdom: The Quest for Empire and the Making of the Russian Nation from 1470 to the Present* (New York, 2017), 89–91.

5. Putin, "On the Historical Unity of the Russians and Ukrainians."

6. Putin, "On the Historical Unity of the Russians and Ukrainians," 1.

7. Serhii Rudenko, *Zelensky: A Biography* (Cambridge, UK, 2022).

8. Katya Gorchinskaya, "A brief history of corruption in Ukraine: the Poroshenko Era. The candyman can't confect a system to contain graft," *Eurasianet*, June 11, 2020.

9. "How Volodymyr Zelenskiy beat Petro Poroshenko in Ukraine," *DW*, April 24, 2019, https://www.dw.com/en/how-volodymyr-zelenskiy-beat-petro-poroshenko -in-ukraine/a-48437457.

10. Taras Kuzio, "Russia is quietly occupying Ukraine's information space," *Atlantic Council*, June 27, 2020, https://www.atlanticcouncil.org/blogs/ukrainealert/ russia-is-quietly-occupying-ukraines-information-space/; "Ukraine election: Comedian Zelensky wins presidency by landslide," *BBC News*, April 22, 2019, https://www.bbc.com/news/world-europe-48007487; Leonid Nevzlin, Interview with Dmitrii Gorgon, *V gostiakh u Gordona*, August 1, 2022, https:// www.youtube.com/watch?v=Iw6A_b7p_2s&t=2956s.

11. Andrei Bogdan, *V gostiakh u Gordona*, December 14, 2022, https:// www.youtube.com/watch?v=QBZM_LBToQM; Oksana Torop, "Chy nablyzyvsia Zelens'kyi do myru na Donbasi?" *BBC News*, May 19, 2020, https://www.bbc.com/ ukrainian/features-52542365.

12. "Ukraine hopes to get MAP at NATO summit next year—Taran," *Ukrinform*, December 1, 2020, https://www.ukrinform.net/rubric-defense/3146549-ukraine -hopes-to-get-map-at-nato-summit-next-year-taran.html.

13. Yuras Karmanau, "Ukraine shuts TV channels owned by Russia-friendly tycoon," *ABC News*, February 3, 2021, https://abcnews.go.com/Business/wireStory/ ukraine-shuts-tv-channels-owned-russia-friendly-tycoon-75661067.

14. Aleksei Titov, "Putin vpervye prokomentiroval zakrytie kanalov Medved-chuka," *Obozrevatel'*, February 17, 2022, https://news.obozrevatel.com/russia/ putin-vpervyie-prokommentiroval-zakryitie-kanalov-medvedchuka.htm.

15. Dan Sabbagh, "Ukraine urges Nato to hasten membership as Russian troops gather," *Guardian*, April 6, 2021, https://www.theguardian.com/world/2021/apr/06/ ukraine-pressures-nato-for-membership-as-russia-amasses-troops-at-border; Amy Mackinnon, Jack Detsch, and Robbie Gramer, "Near Ukraine Puts Team Biden on Edge: Is Russia Testing the Waters or Just Testing Biden?," *Foreign Policy*, April 2, 2021, https://foreignpolicy.com/2021/04/02/russia-ukraine-military-biden/; Mykola Bielieskov, "The Russian and Ukrainian Spring 2021 War Scare," Center for Strategic and International Studies, September 21, 2021, https://www.csis.org/ analysis/russian-and-ukrainian-spring-2021-war-scare.

16. Gordon Corera, "Ukraine: Inside the spies' attempts to stop the war," *BBC News*, April 9, 2022, https://www.bbc.com/news/world-europe-61044063; Holly Ellyatt, "Biden and Putin conclude high-stakes diplomacy at Geneva summit," *CNBC News*, June 16, 2021, https://www.cnbc.com/2021/06/16/ putin-biden-summit-in-geneva-2021.html.

17. Shane Harris, Karen DeYoung, Isabelle Khurshudyan, Ashley Parker, and Liz Sly, "Road to war: U.S. struggled to convince allies, and Zelensky, of risk of invasion," *Washington Post*, August 16, 2022, https://www.washingtonpost.com/national-security/ interactive/2022/ukraine-road-to-war/?itid=hp-top-table-main.

18. Harris et al., "Road to war: U.S. struggled to convince allies, and Zelensky, of risk of invasion"; Corera, "Ukraine: Inside the spies' attempts to stop the war";

"Russia planning massive military offensive against Ukraine, involving 150,000 troops," *Washington Post*, December 3, 2021, https://www.washingtonpost.com/national-security/russia-ukraine-invasion/2021/12/03/98a3760e–546b–11ec–8769–2f4ecdf7a2ad_story.html.

19. Andrew Roth, "Russia issues list of demands it says must be met to lower tensions in Europe," *Guardian*, December 17, 2021, https://www.theguardian.com/world/2021/dec/17/russia-issues-list-demands-tensions-europe-ukraine-nato.

20. Harris et al., "Road to war: U.S. struggled to convince allies, and Zelensky, of risk of invasion."

21. Aishvarya Kavi, "Biden Warns U.S. Won't Send Troops to Rescue Americans in Ukraine," *New York Times*, February 10, 2022, https://www.nytimes.com/2022/02/10/us/biden-ukraine.html; Julian Borger, "Biden threatens Putin with personal sanctions if Russia invades Ukraine," *Guardian*, January 26, 2022, https://www.theguardian.com/world/2022/jan/26/biden-threatens-putin-with-personal-sanctions-if-russia-invades-ukraine; Dan Sabagh, "US and UK intelligence warnings vindicated by Russian invasion," *Guardian*, February 24, 2022, https://www.theguardian.com/us-news/2022/feb/24/us-uk-intelligence-russian-invasion-ukraine.

22. Illia Ponomarenko, "US delivers 300 more Javelins to Ukraine," *Kyiv Independent*, January 26, 2022, https://kyivindependent.com/national/us-delivers-300-more-javelins-to-ukraine/; Zach Dorfman, "CIA-trained Ukrainian paramilitaries may take central role if Russia invades," *Yahoo!News*, January 13, 2022, https://news.yahoo.com/cia-trained-ukrainian-paramilitaries-may-take-central-role-if-russia-invades–185258008.html; Eliot A. Cohen, "Arm the Ukrainians Now!" *Atlantic*, February 2022, https://www.theatlantic.com/ideas/archive/2022/02/putin-russia-invasion-ukraine-war/621182/.

23. Readout of President Biden's Video Call with President Vladimir Putin of Russia, December 7, 2021, https://www.whitehouse.gov/briefing-room/statements-releases/2021/12/07/readout-of-president-bidens-video-call-with-president-vladimir-putin-of-russia/; Readout of President Biden's Video Call with European Leaders on Russia and Ukraine, January 24, 2022, https://www.whitehouse.gov/briefing-room/statements-releases/2022/01/24/readout-of-president-bidens-video-call-with-european-leaders-on-russia-and-ukraine/; Michael Crowley and David E. Sanger, "U.S. and NATO Respond to Putin's Demands as Ukraine Tensions Mount," *New York Times*, January 26, 2022, https://www.nytimes.com/2022/01/26/us/politics/russia-demands-us-ukraine.html; Serhii Plokhy, "The empire returns: Russia, Ukraine and the long shadow of the Soviet Union," *Financial Times*, January 28, 2022, https://www.ft.com/content/0cbbd590–8e48–4687-a302-e74b6f0c905d.

24. Anton Troianovski and David E. Sanger, "Russia Issues Subtle Threats More Far-Reaching Than a Ukraine Invasion," *New York Times*, January 16, 2022, https://www.nytimes.com/2022/01/16/world/europe/russia-ukraine-invasion.html; Rafael Bernal, "Russia suggests military deployments to Cuba, Venezuela an option," *The Hill*, January 13, 2022, https://thehill.com/policy/defense/589595-russia-suggests-military-deployments-to-cuba-venezuela-an-option/.

25. Manohla Dargis, "'Munich: The Edge of War' Review: 'Well Navigated, Sir' (Not!),"

New York Times, January 20, 2022, https://www.nytimes.com/2022/01/20/movies/munich-the-edge-of-war-review.html.

26. Harris et al., "Road to war: U.S. struggled to convince allies, and Zelensky, of risk of invasion."

27. Harris et al., "Road to war: U.S. struggled to convince allies, and Zelensky, of risk of invasion"; Readout of President Biden's Call with President Zelenskyy of Ukraine, January 27, 2022, https://www.whitehouse.gov/briefing-room/statements-releases/2022/01/27/readout-of-president-bidens-call-with-president-zelenskyy-of-ukraine-2/; "Zelens'kyi: panika koshtuvala Ukraïni 15,5 mlrd," *BBC News*, January 28, 2022, https://www.bbc.com/ukrainian/news-60171082; Christo Grozev interview, https://m.youtube.com/watch?v=ekQB8pOwsC4.

28. Matthew Luxmoore and Bojan Pancevski, "Russia, Ukraine Talks Falter as Scope for Diplomatic Solution Narrows," *Wall Street Journal*, February 10, 2022; "Exclusive: As war began, Putin rejected a Ukraine peace deal recommended by aide," Reuters, September 14, 2022, https://www.reuters.com/world/asia-pacific/exclusive-war-began-putin-rejected-ukraine-peace-deal-recommended-by-his-aide-2022-09-14/.

29. Harris et al., "Road to war: U.S. struggled to convince allies, and Zelensky, of risk of invasion"; "Ukraine's president told Biden to 'calm down' Russian invasion warnings, saying he was creating unwanted panic: report," *Business Insider*, January 28, 2022, https://www.businessinsider.com/ukraine-president-told-biden-calm-down-russian-invasion-warnings-report-2022-1; Marta Bondarenko, "Dosyt' siiaty paniku cherez viinu," *Fakty*, January 29, 2022, https://fakty.com.ua/ua/ukraine/polituka/20220129-dosyt-siyaty-paniku-cherez-vijnu-zelenskyj-dorikaye-zahidnym-lideram-shho-pyshut-zakordonni-zmi-pro-preskonferencziyu-prezydenta/.

30. "Vystup Prezydenta Ukraïny na 58-i Miunkhens'kii konferentsiï z pytan' bezpeky," Prezydent Ukraïny, February 19, 2022, https://www.president.gov.ua/news/vistup-prezidenta-ukrayini-na-58-j-myunhenskij-konferenciyi-72997.

31. "Zelensky's full speech at Munich Security Conference," *Kyiv Independent*, February 19, 2022, https://kyivindependent.com/national/zelenskys-full-speech-at-munich-security-conference/; Patrick Wintour, "Memory of 1938 hangs heavy in Munich as Ukrainian president calls for action," *Guardian*, February 20, 2022, https://www.theguardian.com/world/2022/feb/20/memory-of-1938-munich-ukrainian-president-zelenskiy-russia.

32. Roman Romaniuk, "From Zelenskyy's 'surrender' to Putin's surrender: how the negotiations with Russia are going," *Ukraïns'ka pravda*, May 5, 2022, https://www.pravda.com.ua/eng/articles/2022/05/5/7344096/.

33. Sergei Markov, "Putin ne mozhet uiti ot vlasti, ostaviv Ukrainu okkupirovannoi," Sovet po vneshnei i oboronnoi politike, December 27, 2021, http://svop.ru/main/40348/; "Putin's worsening health set to be a determining factor in Russia's policy over the next four years," Robert Lansing Institute, September 29, 2021, https://lansinginstitute.org/2021/09/29/putins-worsening-health-set-to-be-a-determining-factor-in-russias-policy-over-the-next-four-years/.

34. Plokhy, *Lost Kingdom*, 331–32; Paul D'Anieri, *Russia and Ukraine: From Civilized Divorce to Uncivil War* (Cambridge, UK, 2019), 193–94.

35. Jeffrey Edmonds, "Start with the Political: Explaining Russia's Bungled Inva-

sion of Ukraine," *War on the Rocks*, April 28, 2022, https://warontherocks
.com/2022/04/start-with-the-political-explaining-russias-bungled-invasion-of
-ukraine/; "Otkrytoe pis'mo generala Ivashova—Putinu," https://proza.ru/2022
/02/07/189.

36. *Russia's War in Ukraine: Military and Intelligence Aspects*, 1; "Oh, How They
Lied. The Many Times Russia Denied Ukraine Invasion Plans," *Polygraph.Info*,
March 9, 2022, https://www.polygraph.info/a/fact-check-russia-lies-ukraine
-war/31745164.html; "Putin vral, chto voiny s Ukrainoi ne budet. Khronolo-
giia obmana prezidenta RF," *DW*, February 24, 2022, https://www.dw.com/ru/
putin-vral-chto-vojny-s-ukrainoj-ne-budet-hronologija-obmana/a—60904218.

37. "Bol'shoe zasedanie Soveta bezopasnosti Rossii. Priamaia transliatsiia," February 21, 2022, https://www.1tv.ru/shows/vystupleniya-prezidenta-rossii/
vneocherednoe-zasedanie-soveta-bezopasnosti-rossii/bolshoe-zasedanie-soveta
-bezopasnosti-rossii-pryamaya-translyaciya.

38. Aleksandr Iuzovskii, "Khristo Grozev: dazhe Lavrov byl shokirovan nachalom
voiny v Ukraine," MINEWSS, May 6, 2022, https://mignews.com/news/politic/
hristo-grozev-dazhe-lavrov-byl-shokirovan-nachalom-vojny-v-ukraine.html.

39. Address by the President of the Russian Federation, February 21, 2022, 22:35.
The Kremlin, Moscow, http://en.kremlin.ru/events/president/news/20603.

40. Serhii Plokhy, "Casus Belli: Did Lenin Create Modern Ukraine?" Harvard Ukrainian Research Institute, February 27, 2022, https://huri.harvard.edu/news/
serhii-plokhii-casus-belli-did-lenin-create-modern-ukraine.

41. "Address by the President of the Russian Federation," President of Russia, February 24, 2022, http://en.kremlin.ru/events/president/news/67843.

42. Dan Sabbagh, "Russia is creating lists of Ukrainians 'to be killed or
sent to camps,' US claims," *Guardian*, February 21, 2022, https://www
.theguardian.com/world/2022/feb/21/us-claims-russia-creating-lists-of-ukrainians
-to-be-killed-or-sent-to-camps-report.

43. "Address by the President of the Russian Federation," President of Russia, February 24, 2022; Magdalena Kaltseis, "Russia's invasion of Ukraine:
The first day of the war in Russian TV talk shows," Forum for Ukrainian Studies, May 11, 2022, https://ukrainian-studies.ca/2022/05/11/
russias-invasion-of-ukraine-the-first-day-of-the-war-in-russian-tv-talk-shows/;
"Russia won't invade Ukraine, intends to protect DPR, LPR within their borders, MP says," *TASS Russian News Agency*, February 24, 2022, https://tass.com/
politics/1409525?utm_source=google.com&utm_medium=organic&utm_
campaign=google.com&utm_referrer=google.com.

44. Ol'ha Hlushchenko, "U mistakh Ukraïny chutni vybukhy," *Ukraïns'ka pravda*, February 24, 2022, 05:37, https://www.pravda.com.ua/news/2022/02/24/7325223/; "U
Kyievi i Kharkovi pochalysia raketni udary," *Ukraïns'ka pravda*, February 24, 2022,
05:53, https://www.pravda.com.ua/news/2022/02/24/7325224/; "Rosiiany ataku-
valy kordon u 5 oblastiakh i z Krymu," *Ukraïns'ka pravda*, February 24, 2022, 07:17,
https://www.pravda.com.ua/news/2022/02/24/7325234/.

45. *Russia's War in Ukraine: Military and Intelligence Aspects*, Updated April 27, 2022,
Congressional Research Service, 3–4, https://crsreports.congress.gov R47068.

46. Al Jazeera Staff, "Russia facing setbacks in Ukraine, US intelligence officials say,"
Aljazeera, March 8, 2022, https://www.aljazeera.com/news/2022/3/8/russia

-facing-setbacks-in-ukraine-us-intelligence-officials-say; "Budut antifashistskie vosstaniia: Sergei Markov o planakh Rossii v konflikte s Ukrainoi."

47. "Budut antifashistskie vosstaniia: Sergei Markov o planakh Rossii v konflikte s Ukrainoi."

8. The Gates of Kyiv

1. Simon Shuster, "Inside Zelensky's World," *Time*, April 28, 2022, https://time.com/6171277/volodymyr-zelensky-interview-ukraine-war/; Christo Grozev interview @*Prodolzhenie sleduet*, June 16, 2022, https://m.youtube.com/watch?v=ekQB8pOwsC4, 24.00.

2. Sevgil' Musaieva, "Oleksii Danilov: Rosiia rozpadet'sia shche pry nashomu zhytti," *Ukraïns'ka pravda*, April 22, 2022, https://www.pravda.com.ua/articles/2022/04/22/7341267/.

3. Paul Sonne, Isabelle Khurshudyan, Serhiy Morgunov, and Kostiantyn Khudov, "Battle for Kyiv: Ukrainian valor, Russian blunders combined to save the capital," *Washington Post*, August 24, 2022, https://www.washingtonpost.com/national-security/interactive/2022/kyiv-battle-ukraine-survival/; Roman Kravets' and Roman Romaniuk, "Try naidovshi dni liutoho. Iak pochalasia velyka viina, v iaku nikhto ne viryv," *Ukrains'ka Pravda*, September 5, 2022, https://www.pravda.com.ua/articles/2022/09/5/7366059/.

4. "Rosiia napala na Ukraïnu," *Ukraïns'ka pravda*, February 24, 2022, https://www.pravda.com.ua/articles/2022/02/24/7325239/.

5. Valentyna Romanenko, "Viis'kovi do ostann'oho spodivalysia, shcho RF pide v nastup til'ky cherez Donbas—bryhadnyi heneral," *Ukraïns'ka pravda*, June 4, 2022, https://www.pravda.com.ua/news/2022/06/4/7350496/.

6. "Budut antifashistskie vosstaniia: Sergei Markov o planakh Rossii v konflikte s Ukrainoi," *Biznes.Onlain*, February 25, 2022, https://www.business-gazeta.ru/article/540893.

7. Avid M. Herszenhorn and Paul McLeary, "Ukraine's 'iron general' is a hero, but he's no star," *Politico*, April 8, 2022; Simon Shuster and Vera Bergengruen, "Inside the Ukrainian Counterstrike that Turned the Tide of the War," *Time*, September 26, 2022, https://time.com/6216213/ukraine-military-valeriy-zaluzhny/; Sonne et al., "Battle for Kyiv: Ukrainian valor, Russian blunders combined to save the capital."

8. "Rosiis'ki viis'ka z Bilorusi uviishly do Chornobyl's'koï zony—Herashchenko," *Ukraïns'ka pravda*, February 24, 2022, 16:40, https://www.radiosvoboda.org/a/news-rosiiski-viiska-bilorus-chornobylska-zona/31721085.html; Ari Saito and Maria Tsvetkova, "The Enemy Within," Reuters, July 28, 2022, https://www.reuters.com/investigates/special-report/ukraine-crisis-russia-saboteurs/.

9. Erin Doherty and Ivana Saric, "Russian military forces seize Chernobyl nuclear plant," *Axios*, February 24, 2022, https://www.axios.com/2022/02/24/ukraine-zelensky-chernobyl-nuclear-power-plant; Meghan Kruger, "15 new Chernobyls: A Survivor's Fears about Putin's War," *Washington Post*, March 2, 2022, https://www.washingtonpost.com/opinions/2022/03/02/ukraine-war-nuclear-chernobyl-zaporizhia-reactor/; Tobin Harshaw, "Another Chernobyl Disaster? Russian Invaders Are Taking the Risk. A Q&A with atomic energy expert Serhii Plokhii on Putin's new form of 'nuclear terrorism,'" Bloomberg, March

11, 2022; Serhii Plokhy, "Poisoned legacy: why the future of power can't be nuclear," *Guardian*, May 14, 2022; "Nuclear plants could become dirty bombs in Ukraine, warns Serhii Plokhy," *Economist*, June 16, 2022, https://www.economist.com/by-invitation/2022/06/16/nuclear-plants-could-become-dirty-bombs-in-ukraine-warns-serhii-plokhy.

10. *Russia's War in Ukraine: Military and Intelligence Aspects*, 4; Mykhailo Zhyrokhov, "Bytva za Kyïv: iak kuvalasia peremoha ukraïns'koï armiï," *Apostrof*, April 7, 2022, https://apostrophe.ua/ua/article/society/2022-04-07/bitva-za-kiev-kak-kovalas-pobeda-ukrainskoy-armii/45241; "ZSU znyshchyly kadyrivtsiv, iaki planuvaly vbyty Zelens'koho—rozvidka," *Ukraïns'ka pravda*, March 1, 2022, https://www.pravda.com.ua/news/2022/03/1/7327224/.

11. Zhyrokhov, "Bytva za Kyïv: iak kuvalasia peremoha ukraïns'koï armiï"; Sebastian Roblin, "Pictures: In Battle for Hostomel, Ukraine Drove Back Russia's Attack Helicopters and Elite Paratroopers," *1945*, February 25, 2022, https://www.19fortyfive.com/2022/02/pictures-in-battle-for-hostomel-ukraine-drove-back-russias-attack-helicopters-and-elite-paratroopers/; James Marson, "Putin Thought Ukraine Would Fall Quickly. An Airport Battle Proved Him Wrong," *Wall Street Journal*, March 3, 2022, https://www.wsj.com/articles/putin-thought-ukraine-would-fall-quickly-an-airport-battle-proved-him-wrong–11646343121; "Hostomel's'kyi kapkan: iak ukraïns'ki voïny znyshchuvaly 'slavnozvisnyi' rosiis'kyi desant pid Kyievom," June 3, 2022, https://www.youtube.com/watch?v=iB1vApynTiE; Sonne et al. "Battle for Kyiv: Ukrainian valor, Russian blunders combined to save the capital."

12. Zhyrokhov, "Bytva za Kyïv: iak kuvalasia peremoha ukraïns'koï armiï;" "Terminovo. Okupanty namahaiut'sia vysadyty desant u Vasyl'kovi, idut' boï," *Ukrinform*, February 26, 2022, 01:35, https://www.ukrinform.ua/rubric-ato/3413199-okupanti-namagautsa-visaditi-desant-u-vasilkovi-jdut-boi.html; "Vasyl'kiv pid kontrolem ukraïns'kykh viis'kovykh, boï zakinchuit'sia—vlada," Radio Liberty, February 26, 2022, 07:38, https://www.radiosvoboda.org/a/news-vasylkiv-boyi/31724428.html; "Russian-Belarusian maneuvers: Concern and mistrust near the Ukrainian border," *DW*, February 15, 2022, https://www.dw.com/en/russian-belarusian-maneuvers-concern-and-mistrust-near-the-ukrainian-border/a–60791583.

13. Zhyrokhov, "Bytva za Kyïv: iak kuvalasia peremoha ukraïns'koï armiï"; Romanenko, "Viis'kovi do ostann'oho spodivalysia, shcho RF pide v nastup til'ky cherez Donbas."

14. Mykhaylo Zabrodskyi, Dr. Jack Watling, Oleksandr V. Danylyuk, and Nick Reynolds, *Preliminary Lessons in Conventional Warfighting from Russia's Invasion of Ukraine: February–July 2022* (London: Royal United Services Institute for Defence Studies, 2022), 1; "Brytans'ka rozvidka nazvala kliuchovyi factor ostannikh taktychnykh uspikhiv RF na Donbasi," *Ukraïns'ka pravda*, June 4, 2022, https://www.pravda.com.ua/news/2022/06/4/7350474/; Yaroslav Trofimov, "Ukrainian Forces Repel Russian Attack on Kyiv, Prepare for Next Assault," *Wall Street Journal*, February 26, 2022, https://www.wsj.com/articles/russias-assault-on-ukraine-presses-forward-as-street-battles-rage-in-kyiv–11645864200; Zhyrokhov, "Bytva za Kyïv: iak kuvalasia peremoha ukraïns'koï armiï;" Iryna Balachuk, "Pid Kyievom pidirvaly mosty, shchob

zupynyty voroha," *Ukraïns'ka pravda*, February 25, 2022, https://www.pravda
.com.ua/news/2022/02/25/7325670/; Anjali Singhvi, Charlie Smart, Mika Grön-
dahl and James Glanz, "How Kyiv Has Withstood Russia's Attacks," *New York
Times*, April 2, 2022, https://www.nytimes.com/interactive/2022/04/02/world/
europe/kyiv-invasion-disaster.html.

15. "Brytans'ka rozvidka nazvala kliuchovyi faktor ostannikh taktychnykh uspikhiv
RF na Donbasi."

16. "Putin prizval ukrainskikh voennykh vziat' vlast' v svoi ruki," *Vedomosti*, February 25, 2022, https://www.vedomosti.ru/politics/news/2022/02/25/911011-putin
-prizval-ukrainskih-voennih-vzyat-vlast; Christo Grozev, interview with @Prodol-
zhenie sleduet, June 16, 2022, https://m.youtube.com/watch?v=ekQB8pOwsC4,
14:16; Mykhaylo Zabrodskyi, Dr. Jack Watling, Oleksandr V. Danylyuk, and Nick
Reynolds, *Preliminary Lessons in Conventional Warfighting from Russia's Invasion of
Ukraine: February–July 2022* (London: Royal United Services Institute for Defence
Studies, 2022), 25.

17. Jeffrey Edmonds, "Start with the Political: Explaining Russia's Bungled Invasion of
Ukraine," *War on the Rocks*, April 28, 2022, https://warontherocks.com/2022/04/
start-with-the-political-explaining-russias-bungled-invasion-of-ukraine/.

18. Sharon Braithwaite, "Zelensky refuses US offer to evacuate, saying 'I need
ammunition, not a ride,'" *CNN*, February 26, 2022, https://edition.cnn
.com/2022/02/26/europe/ukraine-zelensky-evacuation-intl/index.html.

19. "Zelens'kyi maie naivyshchyi reitynh doviry hromadian sered politykiv—
opytuvannia," *Interfax-Ukraina*, February 23, 2022, https://ua.interfax.com.ua/
news/political/800817.html%2041/57.

20. "Vira ukraïntsiv u peremohu shchodnia zrostaie i zaraz siahnula
88%—opytuvannia," *Khmarochos*, March 2, 2022, https://hmarochos.kiev
.ua/2022/03/02/vira-ukrayinciv-u-peremogu-shhodnya-zrostaye-j-zaraz
-syagnula–88-opytuvannya/; "Doslidzhennia: Maizhe 80% ukraïntsiv viriat'
u peremohu Ukraïny u viini z Rosiieiu," *Detektor.media*, March 8, 2022,
https://detector.media/infospace/article/197289/2022-03-08-doslidzhennya
-mayzhe–80-ukraintsiv-viryat-u-peremogu-ukrainy-u-viyni-z-rosiieyu/.

21. Valentyna Romanova and Andreas Umland, "Kennan Cable No. 44: Ukrainian
Local Governance Prior to Euromaidan: The Pre-History of Ukraine's Decentral-
ization Reform," Kennan Institute, https://www.wilsoncenter.org/publication/
kennan-cable-no-44-ukrainian-local-governance-prior-to-euromaidan-the
-pre-history; "Decentralisation in Ukraine: A Successful Reform," Council of
Europe, Democratic Government Newsroom, Kyiv, Ukraine, July 28, 2021,
https://www.coe.int/en/web/good-governance/-/decentralisation-in-ukraine
-a-successful-reform; Nataliya Gumenyuk, "Russia's Invasion is Making Ukraine
More Democratic," *Atlantic*, July 13, 2022, https://www.theatlantic.com/ideas/
archive/2022/07/russian-invasion-ukraine-democracy-changes/661451/.

22. Trofimov, "Ukrainian Forces Repel Russian Attack on Kyiv"; Ivan Boiko, "Zakhyst
Kyieva: stalo vidomo, chym ozbroïly teroboronu stolytsi," *UNIAN*, March 3, 2022,
https://www.unian.ua/war/oborona-kiyeva-stalo-vidomo-chim-ozbrojili-teroboronu
-stolici-novini-kiyeva–11728030.html.

23. Richard Engel, Lauren Egan, and Phil McCausland, "Ukraine tells Russia 'die or surrender' as its Kyiv counterattack pushes back invaders," *NBC*

News, March 24, 2022, https://www.nbcnews.com/news/world/ukraine-tells
-russia-die-surrender-kyiv-counterattack-drives-invaders-rcna21197; Alex Ver-
shinin, "Lessons From the Battle for Kyiv, *Russia Matters,* April 21, 2022, https://
www.russiamatters.org/analysis/lessons-battle-kyiv.

24. Andrei Soldatov, "Why is a Russian Intelligence General in Moscow Lefortovo
    Prison?" *Moscow Times,* April 12, 2022, https://www.themoscowtimes
    .com/2022/04/11/why-is-a-russian-intelligence-general-in-moscow-lefortovo
    -prison-a77301; Reid Sandish, "Interview: Why The 'Failure' Of Rus-
    sian Spies, Generals Is Leading To 'Apocalyptic' Thinking in the Kremlin,"
    Radio Free Europe/Radio Liberty, May 8, 2022, https://www.rferl.org/a/russia
    -ukraine-war-setbacks-strategy-generals-putin/31839737.html; Roman Anin, "Kak
    Putin prinial reshenie o voine," *Vazhnye istorii,* May 16, 2022, https://istories.media/
    opinions/2022/05/16/kak-putin-prinyal-reshenie-o-voine/.

25. " 'My voobshche-to mirotvortsy. No vam vsem p@zdets . . .' 35 dniv okupatsiï sela
    Obukhovychi—vid trahediï do farsu," *Ukraïns'ka pravda,* May 18, 2022, https://
    www.pravda.com.ua/articles/2022/05/18/7346648/.

26. "Terminovo. Rosiis'ki zaharbnyky zastrelyly mera Hostomelia pid chas roz-
    dachi dopomohy," *Ukrinform,* March 3, 2022, https://www.ukrinform
    .ua/rubric-ato/3422459-rosijski-zagarbniki-zastrelili-mera-gostomela-pid-cas
    -rozdaci-dopomogi.html; Iana Korniichuk, "Pislia vbyvstva rosiiany zaminuvaly
    tilo mera Hostomelia," *Slidstfo.Info,* March 10, 2022, https://www.slidstvo.info/
    warnews/pislya-vbyvstva-rosiyany-zaminuvaly-tilo-miskogo-golovy-gostomelya/;
    Ol'ha Kyrylenko, "Dyiavol nosyt' formu rosiis'koho soldata. Iak katuvaly na
    Kyïvshchyni," *Ukraïns'ka pravda,* April 6, 2022, https://www.pravda.com.ua/
    articles/2022/04/6/7337625/.

27. Svitlana Kizilova, "Bucha pislia vazhkykh boïv: spaleni vorozhi kolony, posh-
    kodzheni khaty. Ie vtraty," *Ukraïns'ka pravda,* February 28, 2022, https://
    www.pravda.com.ua/news/2022/02/28/7326868/; Ol'ha Kyrylenko, "Poch-
    aly rozstriliuvaty, koly zrozumily, shcho Kyïv ïm ne vziaty—mer Buchi Ana-
    tolii Fedoruk," *Ukraïns'ka pravda,* April 8, 2022, https://www.pravda.com.ua/
    articles/2022/04/8/7338142/.

28. Liena Chychenina, "Budennist' zla. Mii dosvid spilkuvannia z rosiis'kymy
    viis'kovymy v Buchi," *Detektor media,* April 12, 2022, https://detector.media/
    infospace/article/198343/2022-04–13-budennist-zla-miy-dosvid-spilkuvannya
    -z-rosiyskymy-viyskovymy-v-buchi/.

29. Svitlana Kizilova, "Vbyvstvo na rozi Vodoprovidnoï ta Iabluns'koï. Rizanyna
    v Buchi," *Ukraïns'ka pravda,* April 18, 2022, https://www.pravda.com.ua/
    articles/2022/04/18/7340436/.

30. "Bucha killings: Satellite image of bodies site contradicts Russian claims," *BBC
    News,* April 11, 2022, https://www.bbc.com/news/60981238; Kyrylenko, "Poch-
    aly rozstriliuvaty, koly zrozumily, shcho Kyïv ïm ne vziaty"; Chychenina, "Buden-
    nist' zla."

31. Vladyslav Verstiuk, *Dumky z pidvalu (Dumky ta refleksiï voiennoï doby, Dia-
    riush istoryka).* Vstupne slovo Hennadiia Boriaka (Kyiv, 2022), http://
    resource.history.org.ua/cgi-bin/eiu/history.exe?&I21DBN=ELIB&P21DBN=ELIB
    &S21STN=1&S21REF=10&S21FMT=elib_all&C21COM=S&S21CNR=20&S21P0
    1=0&S21P02=0&S21P03=ID=&S21COLORTERMS=0&S21STR=0016524.

32. Mariia Stepaniuk, "Radiatsiina panika: Denysenko rozpoviv, chomu viis'ka RF idut' iz Chornobyl's'koï zony," *Fakty*, March 31, 2022, https://www.stopcor.org/ukr/section-suspilstvo/news-vijska-rf-vijshli-z-chornobilskoi -zoni-energoatom–31-03–2022.html; "ChAES Nezstrumlena. Ukraïns'ki enerhetyky vedut' perehovory z viis'kovymy RF," *BBC News*, March 9, 2022, https://www.bbc.com/ukrainian/news–60679062; Wendell Stevenson with Marta Rodionova, "The inside story of Chernobyl during the Russian occupation," *Economist*, https://www.economist.com/1843/2022/05/10/ the-inside-story-of-chernobyl-during-the-russian-occupation.

33. "HUR opryliudnylo spysok rosiis'kykh viis'kovykh, prychetnykh do zvirstv v Buchi," *Ukraïns'ka pravda*, April 4, 2022, https://www.pravda .com.ua/news/2022/04/4/7337048/; Aliona Mazurenko, "U Buchi u brats'kykh mohylakh pokhovaly maizhe 3000 liudei, na vulytsi desiatky trupiv," *Ukraïns'ka pravda*, April 2, 2022, https://www.pravda.com.ua/news/2022/04/2/7336702/; "Ukraine War: Biden accuses Russian troops of committing genocide in Ukraine," *BBC News*, April 13, 2022, https://www.bbc.com/news/world-us-canada–61093300; Iurii Korohods'kyi, "Okupanty vbyly na Kyïvshchyni 1346 tsyvil'nykh—politsiia," *Livyi Bereh*, July 17, 2022, https://lb.ua/society/2022/07/17/523421_okupanti_vbili_ kiivshchini_1346.html.

34. Ukaz Prezidenta Rossiiskoi Federatsii ot 18.04.2022 No 215 "O prisvoenii 64 otdel'noi motostrelkovoi brigade pochetnogo naimenovaniia," http://publication .pravo.gov.ru/Document/View/0001202204180025; Yousur Al-Hlou, Masha Froliak, Dmitriy Khavin, Christoph Koettl, Haley Willis, Alexander Cardia, Natalie Reneau, and Malachy Browne, "Caught on Camera, Traced by Phone: The Russian Military Unit That Killed Dozens in Bucha," *New York Times*, December 22, 2022.

35. Hannah Knowles, Paulina Firozi, Annabelle Timsit, Miriam Berger, Rachel Pannett, Julian Mark, and Dan Lamothe, "Ukraine hopes for cease-fire as Istanbul hosts new talks," *Washington Post*, March 28, 2022, https://www.washingtonpost .com/world/2022/03/28/russia-ukraine-war-news-putin-live-updates/; Kareem Fahim, David L. Stern, Dan Lamothe, and Isabelle Khurshudyan, "Ukraine-Russia talks stir optimism, but West urges caution," *Washington Post*, March 29, 2022, https://www.washingtonpost.com/national-security/2022/03/29/ukraine -russia-turkey-negotiations/; Marco Djurica, "Zelenskiy says Russian war crimes in Ukraine make negotiations harder," Reuters, April 4, 2022, https://www .reuters.com/world/europe/ukraines-president-says-russian-actions-ukraine -make-negotiations-harder–2022-04-04/.

36. "How many Ukrainian refugees are there and where have they gone?" *BBC News*, July 4, 2022, https://www.bbc.com/news/world–60555472; "Cumulative number of people who crossed the Polish border from the war-stricken Ukraine as of July 2022," *Statista*, https://www.statista.com/statistics/1293228/ poland-ukrainian-refugees-crossing-the-polish-border/; Operational Data Portal. Ukraine Refugee Situation, The UN Refugee Agency, August 30, 2022, https:// data.unhcr.org/en/situations/ukraine.

37. Dylan Carter, "Tragedy and utter desolation: Ukraine refugees in Brussels tell their story," *Brussels Times*, March 24, 2022, https://www.brusselstimes.com/212576/ tragedy-and-utter-desolation-ukraine-refugees-in-brussels-tell-their-story.

38. Mark Armstrong, "Ukraine war: Long queues at Polish border as thousands flee the violence," *Euronews*, February 26, 2022, https://www.euronews .com/2022/02/26/ukraine-invasion-long-queues-at-polish-border-as-thousands -flee-the-violence; Agnieszka_Pikulicka-Wilczewska, "'It was hell': Long lines of Ukrainian refugees at Poland border," *Aljazeera*, February 27, 2022, https://www .aljazeera.com/news/2022/2/27/ukraine-poland-border-refugees-medyka-russia -invasion.

39. "Putin Knows What He's Doing With Ukraine's Refugees. This Is the World's Big Test," *New York Times*, April 1, 2022, https://www.nytimes.com/2022/04/01/ opinion/ukraine-russia-war-refugees.html; "UNHCR: A record 100 million peo- ple forcibly displaced worldwide," *UN News*, May 23, 2022, https://news.un.org/ en/story/2022/05/1118772.

9. Eastern Front

1. "Ukraine war exposes Russia military shortcomings: analysts," *France 24*, April 25, 2022, https://www.france24.com/en/live-news/20220425-ukraine -war-exposes-russia-military-shortcomings-analysts; "Investigation: How is the Ukraine war redefining future conflict?" *BBC Newsnight*, May 12, 2022, https://www.youtube.com/watch?v=sTQ5ZGHV9Zs; "War in Ukraine: why is Russia's army so weak?" *Economist*, May 9, 2022, https://www.youtube.com/ watch?v=x8C7aMeunE0.

2. Volodymyr Kravchenko, *The Ukrainian-Russian Borderland: History versus Geog- raphy* (Montreal and Kingston, 2022).

3. Jack Losh, "The Kharkiv Resistance Has Already Begun," *Foreign Policy*, Feb- ruary 24, 2022, https://foreignpolicy.com/2022/02/24/russia-ukraine-war -resistance-kharkiv/; "Center for Countering Misinformation: Russian reports about surrendered 302nd anti-aircraft regiment in Kharkiv region fake," *Interfax-Ukraine*, February 27, 2022, https://ua.interfax.com.ua/news/ general/803053.html; James Verini, "Surviving the Siege of Kharkiv," *New York Times Magazine*, May 19, 2022, https://www.nytimes.com/interactive/ 2022/05/19/magazine/kharkiv-siege.html.

4. Stuart Hughes, "Global cluster bomb ban comes into force," *BBC News*, August 1, 2010, https://www.bbc.com/news/world–10829976.

5. David L. Stern, "Dozens Wounded in Shelling of Kharkiv as Russia Strikes Build- ings with Suspected Cluster Munitions," *Washington Post*, February 28, 2022, https://www.washingtonpost.com/world/2022/02/28/kharkiv-rockets-shelling -russia-ukraine-war/; Lucia Binding, "Ukraine invasion: Three children among nine dead as footage shows Kharkiv apartment block being rocked by series of blasts," *Sky News*, March 1, 2022, https://news.sky.com/story/ukraine-invasion -cluster-munition-strikes-buildings-in-kharkiv-as-dozens-killed-in-mass -shelling–12554056; "Rossiiskoi gruppirovke v Sirii nashli novogo komanduiush- chego," *RBK*, November 2, 2017, https://www.rbc.ru/politics/02/11/2017/59faf4 3e9a7947fe3ef01c99.

6. Ekaterina Novak, Facebook page, https://www.facebook.com/ekaterina.novak .7/videos/475838344031641.

7. Ekaterina Novak, Facebook page; https://suspilne.media/241327-vid-obstriliv -rf-zaginuv-zitel-cirkuniv-e-poraneni-u-harkovi-ta-oblasti/; Maryna Pohorilko,

"U Kharkovi okupanty zavdaly udaru po mis'kradi, televezhi ta skynuly bombu na Palats Pratsi," *Obozrevatel'*, March 2, 2022, https://news.obozrevatel.com/ukr/society/u-harkovi-okupanti-zavdali-udaru-po-televezhi-i-skinuli-snaryad-na-palats-pratsi-foto-i-video.htm.

8. "Ukrainian forces reach Russian border near Kharkiv," May 16, 2022, https://www.youtube.com/watch?v=qZVbN6GGUHs; "U Rosiï zvil'nyly vysokopostavlenykh komandyriv za provaly v Ukraïni—brytans'ka rozvidka," *Ievropeis'ka pravda*, May 19, 2022, https://www.pravda.com.ua/news/2022/05/19/7347143/.

9. "Kharkiv'iany—novi banderivtsi. Stavlennia u misti do Rosiï," June 1, 2022, https://www.youtube.com/watch?v=pw4FN6GrosY.

10. "Military were withdrawn from Mariupol to avoid further aggravation," *Kyiv Post*, May 12, 2014, https://web.archive.org/web/20140512222616/http://www.kyivpost.com/content/ukraine/military-were-withdrawn-from-mariupol-to-avoid-further-aggravation-347355.html; "Ukraine crisis: Kiev forces win back Mariupol," *BBC News*, June 13, 2014, https://www.bbc.com/news/world-europe-27829773.

11. Olena Bilozers'ka, "Batalion 'Azov': Bii za Mariupol'," *Antykor*, June 2014, https://antikor.com.ua/ru/articles/7697-bataljjon_azov._bij_za_mariupolj; Vladislav Davidzon, "The Defenders of Mariupol," *Tablet*, May 17, 2022, https://www.tabletmag.com/sections/news/articles/defenders-of-mariupol-azov.

12. Roman Romaniuk, "'Ostriv nadii.' Iak vyishly i shcho zaraz iz zakhysnykamy 'Azovstali,'" *Ukraïns'ka pravda*, June 9, 2022, https://www.pravda.com.ua/articles/2022/06/9/7351390/; "'My dosyt' mitsni, shchob krov'iu i potom vidvoiuvaty nashu zemliu . . . ,'—Heroi Ukraïny Denys Prokopenko," *ArmiiaInform*, March 23, 2022, https://archive.ph/mPF7U; Aleksandar Vasovic, "Port city of Mariupol comes under fire after Russia invades Ukraine," Reuters, February 24, 2022, https://www.reuters.com/world/europe/strategic-city-mariupol-wakes-blasts-russia-invades-ukraine-2022-02-24/; https://www.maritime-executive.com/article/russian-navy-carries-out-amphibious-assault-near-mariupol.

13. Lee Brown, "Russian 'Butcher of Mariupol' blamed for worst Ukraine war atrocities," *New York Post*, March 24, 2022, https://nypost.com/2022/03/24/butcher-of-mariupol-blamed-for-worst-russia-ukraine-atrocities/; "Russian Offensive Campaign Assessment, April 9," Institute for the Study of War, April 9, 2022, https://www.understandingwar.org/backgrounder/russian-offensive-campaign-assessment-april-9.

14. Will Stewart and Walter Finch, "Russia finally recovers the body of one of its seven dead generals a month after he was killed in Mariupol steel factory," *Daily Mail*, April 13, 2022, https://www.dailymail.co.uk/news/article-10714981/Russia-recovers-body-dead-general-MONTH-killed-Mariupol-steel-factory.html; Joel Gunter, "Siege of Mariupol: Fresh Russian attacks throw evacuation into chaos," *BBC News*, March 5, 2022, https://www.bbc.com/news/world-europe-60629851; Khrystyna Bondarenko, Ivan Watson, Anne Claire Stapleton, Tom Booth, and Alaa Elassar, "Mariupol residents are being forced to go to Russia, city council says," *CNN*, March 19, 2022, https://edition.cnn.com/2022/03/19/europe/mariupol-shelter-commander-ukraine-intl/index.html.

15. "Rosiis'ki viis'ka rozbombyly likarniu ta polohovyi v Mariupoli," *BBC News*, March 9, 2022, https://www.bbc.com/ukrainian/news-60679065; "Ukraine says 1,170 civilians have been killed in Mariupol since Russian invasion,"

Reuters, March 9, 2022, https://www.reuters.com/world/ukraine-says–1170
-civilians-have-been-killed-mariupol-since-russian-invasion–2022-03-09/; Lori
Hinnant, Mstyslav Chernov, and Vasilisa Stepanenko, "AP evidence points to
600 dead in Mariupol theater airstrike," *AP*, May 4, 2022, https://apnews.com/
article/Russia-ukraine-war-mariupol-theater-c321a196fbd568899841b506af
cac7a1; "Russia-Ukraine war: 21,000 civilians killed, mayor of Mariupol estimates," *Jerusalem Post*, April 19, 2022, https://www.jpost.com/international/
article–703925.

16. Romaniuk, "Ostriv nadii."

17. "Russian Offensive Campaign Assessment, April 9," Institute for the Study
of War, April 23, 2022, https://www.understandingwar.org/backgrounder/
russian-offensive-campaign-assessment-april–23; Tim Lister and Olga
Voitoivych, "Mariupol steel plant suffers 'heaviest airstrikes so far,' Ukrainian
official says," *CNN*, April 23, 2022, https://edition.cnn.com/europe/live-news/
russia-ukraine-war-news-04–28–22/h_dd62bedc8e546d2ac1e63fe1f9c5c89e.

18. "What we know about the UN-led Azovstal steel plant evacuation in Mariupol," *ABC News*, May 1, 2022, https://www.abc.net.au/news/2022-05-02/
inside-the-mariupol-azovstal-steel-plan-evacuation/101029722.

19. Romaniuk, "Ostriv nadii."

20. Thomas Kingsley, " 'Don't let them die': Wives of last remaining Azovstal fighters plead with Pope Francis for help," *Independent*, Wednesday, May 11, 2022,
https://www.independent.co.uk/news/world/europe/azovstal-mariupol-pope
-francis-ukraine-b2076587.html; "Zelensky reveals mediators in Azovstal talks,"
Ukrinform, May 21, 2022, https://www.ukrinform.net/rubric-polytics/3488630
-zelensky-reveals-mediators-in-azovstal-talks.html; Faustine Vincent, " 'Ukraine
needs its heroes to be alive': Soldiers from Azovstal evacuated to Moscow-controlled
territory," *Le Monde*, May 18, 2022, https://www.lemonde.fr/en/international/
article/2022/05/18/ukraine-needs-its-heroes-to-be-alive-soldiers-from-azovstal
-evacuated-to-moscow-controlled-territory_5983874_4.html; "Russia says nearly
1,000 Ukrainian soldiers in Mariupol steel plant have surrendered," *Le Monde*,
May 18, 2022, https://www.lemonde.fr/en/international/article/2022/05/18/
nearly–1-000-ukrainian-soldiers-in-mariupol-steel-plant-have-surrendered-says
-russia_5983880_4.html.

21. "Ukraine war: Russia 'takes full control' of Azovstal steelworks in Mariupol," *EuroNews*, May 20, 2022, https://www.euronews.com/2022/05/20/
ukraine-war-live-us-congress-approves–40-billion-aid-package-for-ukraine;
"Russian parliamentarian hints at possible exchange of Azovstal PoWs for
detained Putin ally," *Yahoo!News*, May 21, 2022, https://news.yahoo.com/
russian-parliamentarian-hints-possible-exchange—194019876.html.

22. "Azovstal'—mistse moieï smerti i moho zhyttia—Dmytro Kozats'kyi," *ArmiiaInform*, May 20, 2022, https://armyinform.com.ua/2022/05/20/svitlo-peremozhe
-temryavu-voyin-polku-azov-zrobyv-unikalne-foto-zahysnyka-mariupolya/; "A
Ukrainian soldier uploaded all his photos of Azovstal before he was captured.
Here they are," *Guardian*, May 23, 2022, https://www.theguardian.com/world/
gallery/2022/may/23/inside-the-battle-for-the-azovstal-metalworks?fbclid=IwAR
ot9GytQUHkg7zXlBONIKk6TOWZo1SZg2hhWsl5GbQSNyjpsMQ12twN7Jg.

23. Shaun Walker, "Russia trades Azov fighters for Putin ally in biggest prisoner

swap of Ukraine war," *Guardian*, September 22, 2022; "The author of the photos of the 'Azovstal' fighters received the Prix de la Photographie Paris award,"
Odessa Journal, September 12, 2022, https://odessa-journal.com/the-author-of-the
-photos-of-the-azovstal-fighters-received-the-prix-de-la-photographie-paris-award/;
"Azov fighters who survived Olenivka among those returning home in latest
prisoner swap," YAHOO! September 22, 2022, https://www.yahoo.com/now/
azov-fighters-survived-olenivka-among–100800029.html.

24. Todd Prince, "Russia's Capture of Azovstal: Symbolic Success, 'Pyrrhic' Victory?"
Radio Free Europe/Radio Liberty, May 18, 2022, https://www.rferl.org/a/azovstal
-russia-ukraine-captured/31856565.html; "Stalo vidomo, skil'ky ukraïntsiv
zalyshylos' u blokadnomu Mariupoli," *Slovo i dilo*, April 13, 2022, https://www
.slovoidilo.ua/2022/04/13/novyna/suspilstvo/stalo-vidomo-skilky-ukrayincziv
-zalyshylos-blokadnomu-mariupoli.

25. "Shoigu vpervye za polmesiatsa kommentiruet voinu: glavnaia tsel'—Donbass,
prizyv uvelichivat' ne budut," *BBC News*, March 29, 2022, https://www.bbc.com/
russian/features–60914131; "Lavrov zaiavil o nachale sleduiushchei fazy spetsop-
eratsii na Ukraine," *RBK*, April 19, 2022, https://www.rbc.ru/politics/19/04/202
2/625e7c329a794710da312799.

26. Illia Ponomarenko, "EXPLAINER: What to expect from the Battle of Donbas, Russia's new offensive," *Kyiv Independent*, April 21, 2022, https://kyivindependent.com/
national/explainer-what-to-expect-from-the-battle-of-donbas-russias-new-offensive;
"Ukraine war: Russia bombards cities as eastern offensive begins," *BBC News*, April
19, 2022, https://www.bbc.com/news/world-europe–61145578.

27. "Ukraine troops retreat from Popasna, Luhansk governor confirms," Reuters,
May 8, 2022, https://www.reuters.com/world/europe/chechnyas-kadyrov-says-his
-soldiers-control-popasna-ukraine-disagrees–2022-05-08/;https://edition.cnn.com
/europe/live-news/russia-ukraine-war-news-05–13–22/h_67faa3f08da188441de7
673413e390737; Tim Lister and Julia Kesaieva, "Ukrainian forces lose foothold in
eastern town," *CNN*, May 13, 2022, https://web.archive.org/web/20220516030015/
https://www.nytimes.com/2022/05/15/world/europe/pro-russian-war-bloggers
-kremlin.html.

28. Ponomarenko, "EXPLAINER: What to expect from the Battle of Donbas, Russia's new offensive"; "The Russians drowned the tank company while fleeing from the 'Bilohorivka bridgehead,'" *Militarnyi*, https://web.archive.org/
web/20220514171048/https://mil.in.ua/en/news/the-russians-drowned-the
-tank-company-while-fleeing-from-the-bilohorivka-bridgehead/; Tom Balmforth
and Jonathan Landay, "Ukraine wages counteroffensive against Russian forces
in east," Reuters, May 14, 2022, https://www.reuters.com/world/europe/ukraine
-collects-russian-dead-war-rages-multiple-fronts–2022-05–14/.

29. "Fall of Severodonetsk is Russia's biggest victory since Mariupol," *Aljazeera*, June 25,
2022, https://www.aljazeera.com/news/2022/6/25/fall-of-severodonetsk-is-russias
-biggest-victory-since-mariupol.

30. "Russian Offensive Campaign Assessment, June 23," Institute for the Study of
War, June 23, 2022, https://www.understandingwar.org/backgrounder/russian
-offensive-campaign-assessment-june–23; "20 km on foot, the wounded were carried on their own, Zolote-Girske," *Butusov Plus*, July 14, 2022, https://www.youtube
.com/watch?v=Nyhle2faQ-w; "Russian Offensive Campaign Assessment, July 2,"

Institute for the Study of War, July 2, 2022, https://www.understandingwar.org/backgrounder/russian-offensive-campaign-assessment-july–$2.

31. Mykhaylo Zabrodskyi, Dr. Jack Watling, Oleksandr V. Danylyuk, and Nick Reynolds, *Preliminary Lessons in Conventional Warfighting from Russia's Invasion of Ukraine: February–July 2022* (London: Royal United Services Institute for Defence Studies, 2022), 2; Isobel Koshiv, "We're almost out of ammunition and relying on western arms, says Ukraine," *Guardian*, June 10, 2022, https://www.theguardian.com/world/2022/jun/10/were-almost-out-of-ammunition-and-relying-on-western-arms-says-ukraine; Dan Sabbagh, "Ukraine's high casualty rate could bring war to tipping point," *Guardian*, June 10, 2022, https://www.theguardian.com/world/2022/jun/10/ukraine-casualty-rate-russia-war-tipping-point.

32. "Spetsoperatsiia, 4 iiulia: Shoigu dolozhil Putinu ob osvobozhdenii LNR," *RIA Novosti*, July 4, 2022, https://ria.ru/20220704/spetsoperatsiya–1800226455.html.

33. Gordon Corera, "Russia about to run out of steam in Ukraine—MI6 chief," *BBC News*, July 21, 2022, https://www.bbc.com/news/world-europe–62259179.

34. Jason Lemon, "Ukraine HIMARS Destroy More Than 100 'High Value' Russian Targets: Official," *Newsweek*, July 22, 2022, https://www.newsweek.com/ukraine-himars-destroy-high-value-russian-targets–1727253; Zabrodskyi, Watling, Danylyuk, and Reynolds, *Preliminary Lessons in Conventional Warfighting from Russia's Invasion of Ukraine*, 43.

35. "Shoigu otdal prikaz unichtozhit' amerikanskie HIMARS v Ukraine," *Moscow Times*, July 18, 2022, https://www.moscowtimes.ru/2022/07/18/shoigu-otdal-prikaz-unichtozhit-amerikanskie-himars-v-ukraine-a22357; "Minoborony zaiavilo ob unichtozhenii chetyrekh HIMARS na Ukraine posle prikaza Shoigu," *Kapital strany*, July 22, 2022, https://kapital-rus.ru/news/389029-minoborony_zayavilo_ob_unichtojenii_chetyreh_himars_na_ukraine_posle/; Lemon, "Ukraine HIMARS Destroy More Than 100 'High Value' Russian Targets"; Mia Jankowicz, "Russia hasn't destroyed any of the devastating HIMARS artillery given Ukraine, US says, contradicting Russia's claims," *Business Insider*, July 22, 2022, https://www.businessinsider.in/international/news/russia-hasnt-destroyed-any-of-the-devastating-himars-artillery-given-ukraine-us-says-contradicting-russias-own-claims/articleshow/93053187.cms.

36. Iurii Bratiuk, "U Pereiaslavi demontuvaly pam'iatnyk 'vozz'iednanniu' z Rosiieiu," *Zaxid.net*, July 7, 2022, https://zaxid.net/u_pereyaslavi_demontuvali_pamyatnik_vozzyednannya_z_rosiyeyu_n1545835; Serhii Plokhy, "Vladimir Putin's war is banishing for good the outdated myth that Ukrainians and Russians are the same," *Telegraph*, March 3, 2022, https://www.telegraph.co.uk/authors/s/sa-se/serhii-plokhy/.

37. Margaret Besheer, "Ukraine's Cultural Heritage Under Attack, Official Says," *Voice of America*, July 15, 2022, https://www.voanews.com/a/ukraine-s-cultural-heritage-under-attack-official-says/6661269.html; Andrei Krasniashchikh, "Kak gorit pod bombami russkaia kul'tura," *Ukraïns'ka pravda*, May 3, 2022, https://www.pravda.com.ua/rus/columns/2022/05/3/7343653/.

38. L. P. Shemeta, *Mark Bernes v pesniakh* (Kyiv, 2008), 169; "Kto zhe khochet

voiny?" ZDF Magazine Royale, March 4, 2022, https://www.youtube.com/watch?v=Cmk5-TM6eEw.

39. Krasniashchikh, "Kak gorit pod bombami russkaia kul'tura."
40. "Udar Rosiï po muzeiu Skovorody ie splanovanoiu aktsiieiu—Tkachenko," *Ukrinform*, May 7, 2022, https://www.ukrinform.ua/rubric-culture/3477358-udar-rosii-po-muzeu-skovorodi-e-splanovanou-akcieu-tkacenko.html.
41. Olenka Pevny, "Recreating a Monumental Past: Self-Identity and Ukraine's Medieval Monuments," J. B. Rudnyckyj Memorial Lecture, University of Manitoba, https://www.researchgate.net/publication/337623350_Olenka_Pevny_RECREATING_A_MONUMENTAL_PAST_SELF-IDENTITY_AND_UKRAINE'S_MEDIEVAL_MONUMENTS; "Ukrainian cultural heritage is also under Russian bombing—Olenka Z Pevny," *Breaking Latest News*, March 19, 2022; "Building of Chernihiv Collegium Cossack Baroque Architectural Style Historical Heritage of Ukraine," November 17, 2016, https://www.youtube.com/watch?v=kewDM45N8t4.
42. Ivan Boiko, "U Chernihovi vnaslidok raketnoho udaru zruinovano istorychnu budivliu kintsia 30-kh rokiv XX stolittia," *UNIAN*, February 27, 2022, https://www.unian.ua/war/u-chernigovi-vnaslidok-raketnogo-udaru-zruynovano-istorichnu-budivlyu-kincya-30-h-rokiv-hh-stolittya-video-novini-vtorgnennya-rosiji-v-ukrajinu-11721241.html; John Marone, "They Came, They Shelled, They Left—Russia's Failed Advance in Northern Ukraine," *Kyiv Post*, April 12, 2022, https://www.kyivpost.com/ukraine-politics/they-came-they-shelled-they-left-russias-failed-advance-in-northern-ukraine.html#:~:text=Just%20as%20in%20the%20case,miles%20from%20the%20Russian%20border; "Pislia nal'otiv rosiis'koï aviatsiï u Chernihovi zahynulo 47 osib—OVA," *Espreso*, March 4, 2022, https://espreso.tv/pislya-nalotiv-rosiyskoi-aviatsii-u-chernigovi-zaginulo-47-osib-ova.
43. David Axe, "Ukraine's Best Tank Brigade Has Won the Battle For Chernihiv," *Forbes*, March 31, 2022, https://www.forbes.com/sites/davidaxe/2022/03/31/ukraines-best-tank-brigade-has-won-the-battle-for-chernihiv/?sh=554db4c7db9a.
44. "Iz profesora Hoholevs'koho vyshu peretvoryvsia na voïna ukraïns'koho viis'ka," *Nizhyn.City*, May 17, 2022, https://nizhyn.city/articles/212963/iz-profesora-gogolevogo-vishu-peretvorivsya-na-voina-ukrainskogo-vijska?fbclid=IwAR2wLJtR6bcpyKZ641pFaX4uuGRjH5SgfzcYTIdCj5iXebe_hGgzE_LWrWw.
45. Plokhy, "Vladimir Putin's war is banishing for good the outdated myth that Ukrainians and Russians are the same."
46. Lena Rudenko, "Mitropolit UPTs MP 'poblagodaril' patriarkha Kirilla za prolituiu v Ukraine krov': vy otvetite pered Bogom," *Apostrof*, June 6, 2022, https://apostrophe.ua/news/society/2022-06-06/mitropolit-upts-mp-poblagodaril-patriarha-kirilla-za-prolituyu-v-ukraine-krov-vyi-otvetite-pered-bogom/271059.
47. "Postanova Soboru Ukraïns'koï Pravoslavnoï Tserkvy vid 27 travnia 2022 roku," Ukraïns'ka Pravoslavna Tserkva, https://news.church.ua/2022/05/27/postanova-soboru-ukrajinskoji-pravoslavnoji-cerkvi-vid-27-travnya-2022-roku/; "Eparkhiia UPTs MP v okupirovannykh Roven'kakh reshila ne upominat' Onufriia kak predstoiatelia tserkvi," *Gordonua.com*, May 31, 2022, https://

gordonua.com/news/society/eparhiya-upc-mp-v-okkupirovannyh-rovenkah
-reshila-ne-upominat-onufriya-kak-predstoyatelya-cerkvi–1611113.html; Olena
Roshchina, "Zelenskyy: Ukraine's National Security and Defence Council
requests legislative ban on Ukrainian Orthodox Church of Moscow Patriarchate," *Ukrains'ka pravda*, December 1, 2022, https://www.pravda.com.ua/eng/
news/2022/12/1/7378896/.

48. Plokhy, "Vladimir Putin's war is banishing for good the outdated myth that
Ukrainians and Russians are the same."

10. The Black Sea

1. "U Kyievi vyshykuvalasia velychezna cherha za kul'tovoiu poshtovoiu mar-
koiu," *TSN*, April 15, 2022, https://kyiv.tsn.ua/u-kiyevi-vishikuvalasya
-velichezna-cherga-za-kultovoyu-poshtovoyu-markoyu-foto–2037919.html;
"Rozibraly za try khvylyny: u Rozetka rozpovily, iak prodavaly marku z 'russ-
kim korablem,'" *Ekonomichna etail*, May 7, 2022, https://www.epravda.com
.ua/news/2022/05/7/686775/.

2. Valentyna Romanenko, "Russkii korabl', idi etai.i: zakhysnyky Zmiïnoho vid-
povily vorohovi," *Ukraïns'ka etail*, February 25, 2022, https://web.archive.org/
web/20220225021042/https://www.pravda.com.ua/news/2022/02/25/7325592/;
Andrew Keen, "Go Fuck Yourself." On Putin's Propaganda and the Week in
Ukrainian Resistance," *Literary Hub*, March 4, 2022, https://lithub.com/go
-fuck-yourself-on-putins-propaganda-and-the-week-in-ukrainian-resistance/.

3. "Geroi mema 'Russkii voennyi korabl', idi na . . .' s ostrova Zmeinyi zhivy, no vziaty v
plen," *BBC News*, February 25, 2022, https://www.bbc.com/russian/news–60523774;
"Ukraïna ta rosiia provely pershyi povnotsinnyi obmin viis'kovopolonennymy—
etail," *Slovo i dilo*, March 24, 2022, https://www.slovoidilo.ua/2022/03/24/
novyna/bezpeka/ukrayina-ta-rosiya-provely-pershyj-povnoczinnyj-obmin
-vijskovopolonenymy-detali.

4. Alyona Silchenko, "Why is Crimea called Taurida?," *Holos Krymu. Kul'tura*, July
22, 2020, https://culture.voicecrimea.com.ua/en/why-is-crimea-called-tavrida/.

5. "Pervye chasy voiny: pochemu VSU priniali boi, no otstupili na iuge?," *Krym
realii*, July 16, 2022, https://www.youtube.com/watch?v=oeuVJp-ExPk 10:53;
Ol'ha Kyrylenko, "Mer Novoï Kakhovky pro robotu v okupatsiï: 'Nas trymala
dumka, shcho os'-os' povernut'sia ZSU, i vse bude harazd,'" *Ukraïns'ka pravda*,
July 25, 2022, https://www.pravda.com.ua/articles/2022/07/25/7359983/;
"Na Trypil's'kii TES stavsia vybukh, okupanty zakhopyly Kakhovs'ku HES—
Minenerho," *Liha.Biznes*, February 24, 2022, https://biz.liga.net/ua/ekonomika/
tek/novosti/na-tripolskoy-tes-proizoshel-vzryv-okkupanty-zahvatili-kahovskuyu
-ges-minenergo.

6. Dariia Demianyk, "Okupanty zakhvatili Kakhovskuiu GES i podniali rossiiskii flag
(video)," *Glavkom*, February 24, 2022, https://glavcom.ua/ru/news/okkupanty
-zahvatili-kahovskuyu-ges-i-podnyali-rossiyskiy-flag-video–824677.html.

7. *Russia's War in Ukraine: Military and Intelligence Aspects*, Congressional Research
Service, Updated April 27, 2022, 5, https://crsreports.congress.gov/product/
pdf/R/R47068.

8. Kateryna Tyshchenko, "V Khersonskoi oblasti proshli ucheniia, Zelenskii nab-
liudal," *Ukraïns'ka pravda*, February 12, 2022, https://www.pravda.com.ua/rus/

news/2022/02/12/7323753/; "Pervye chasy voiny: pochemu VSU priniali boi, no otstupili na iuge?" https://www.youtube.com/watch?v=oeuVJp-ExPk 4:48.

9. "Pervye chasy voiny: pochemu VSU priniali boi, no otstupili na iuge?" https://www.youtube.com/watch?v=oeuVJp-ExPk, 6:05, 7:54.

10. Iuliia Zhukova, "Rossiia pustila vodu iz Ukrainy v anneksirovannyi Krym," *Nastoiashchee vremia*, April 22, 2022, https://www.currenttime.tv/a/ukrainskuyu-vodu-siloy-vernuli-v-anneksirovannyy-krym-chtoby-zapolnit-vysohshiy-za–8-let-kanal-voennye-rf-vzorvali-dambu-/31816486.html; Denys Karlovs'kyi, "Henshtab ZSU prokomentuvav chutky pro 'rozminuvannia' peresheiku z Krymom pered viinoiu," *Ukraïns'ka pravda*, April 25, 2022, https://www.pravda.com.ua/news/2022/04/25/7342072/.

11. "Tankist Ievhen Pal'chenko rozpoviv pro proryv cherez Antonivs'kyi mist na Khersonshchyni," *Most*, June 21, 2022, https://most.ks.ua/news/url/tankist_jevgen_palchenko_rozpoviv_pro_proriv_cherez_antonivskij_mist_na_hersonschini; "Pervye chasy voiny: pochemu VSU priniali boi, no otstupili na iuge?" https://www.youtube.com/watch?v=oeuVJp-ExPk, 1322.

12. "Pervye chasy voiny: pochemu VSU priniali boi, no otstupili na iuge?," https://www.youtube.com/watch?v=oeuVJp-ExPk 15:30; Iuliia Kovalysheva, "Zelens'kyi vruchyv 'Zolotu zirku' tankistu z Vinnychchyny," *Suspil'ne*, May 24, 2022, https://suspilne.media/242756-zelenskij-vruciv-zolotu-zirku-tankistu-z-vinniccini/.

13. "Rezantsev Iakov Vladimirovich," *Myrotvorets*, https://myrotvorets.center/criminal/rezancev-yakov-vladimirovich/; Sevgil' Musaieva, "Ihor Kolykhaiev: Ne zabuvaite pro Kherson. Nam zaraz duzhe skladno," *Ukraïns'ka pravda*, April 5, 2022, https://www.pravda.com.ua/articles/2022/04/5/7337193/.

14. "My ne imeli moral/nogo prava napadat' na dryguiu stranu. Rossiiski desantnik napisal knigu o pervykh dniakh voiny," *Meduza*, August 11, 2022, https://meduza.io/feature/2022/08/11/my-ne-imeli-moralnogo-prava-napadat-na-druguyu-stranu.

15. "Enerhodar: liudy ne propuskaiut' kolonu RF v misto," *Militarnyi*, March 2, 2022, https://mil.in.ua/uk/news/energodar-lyudy-ne-puskayut-tanky-v-misto/; "Viis'ka zaharbnyka aktyvizovaly sproby zakhopyty Zaporiz'ku AES v Enerhodari," *Ukrinform*, March 3, 2022, https://www.ukrinform.ua/rubric-ato/3419318-vijska-rosii-aktivizuvali-sprobi-zahopiti-zaporizku-aes.html.

16. Liubov' Velichko, "Mir pod udarom. Kak Rossii grozit iadernoi katastrofoi na ukrainskikh AĖS i pochemu molchit MAGATE," *PGNovosti*, June 8, 2022.

17. Olena Roshchina, "Zaporiz'ka AES pid kontrolem rosiis'kykh okupantiv," *Ukraïns'ka pravda*, March 4, 2022, https://www.pravda.com.ua/news/2022/03/4/7328064/; Olena Roshchina, "V Enerhodari na proshchannia z heroiamy pryishly kil'ka soten' liudei," *Ukraïns'ka pravda*, March 7, 2022, https://www.pravda.com.ua/news/2022/03/7/7329077/.

18. Denys Karlovs'kyi, "Henshtab ZSU prokomentuvav chutky pro 'rozminuvannia' pereshyiku z Krymom pered viinoiu," *Ukraïns'ka pravda*, April 25, 2022, https://www.pravda.com.ua/news/2022/04/25/7342072/.

19. Musaieva, "Ihor Kolykhaiev: Ne zabuvaite pro Kherson"; "Ukrainian law enforcers detain former Crimea SBU department chief," *NV*, July 17, 2022, https://english.nv.ua/nation/ukraine-arrests-former-sbu-department-head-for-treason-ukraine-news–50256965.html; Svetlana Kizilova, "Zelenskii nakazal dvukh generalov SBU—lishil zvaniia za 'antigeroizm,'" *Ukraïns'ka pravda*, April 1, 2022,

https://www.pravda.com.ua/rus/news/2022/04/1/7336190/; Mariia Stepaniuk, "Shvydke zakhoplennia Khersonshchyny stalo mozhlyvym cherez zradu spivrobitnyka SBU Sadokhina," *Fakty*, June 18, 2022, https://fakty.com.ua/ua/ukraine/suspilstvo/20220618-shvydke-zahoplennya-hersonshhyny-stalo-mozhlyvym-cherez-zradu-spivrobitnyka-sbu-sadohina/; "Ukraine parliament removes security chief, Zelenskiy fires another top official," Reuters, July 19, 2022.

20. Kyrylenko, "Mer Novoï Kakhovky pro robotu v okupatsiï," https://www.radiosvoboda.org/a/news-fedorov-melitopol-obmin/31756706.html.

21. Iryna Balachuk, "U Khersoni tysiachi liudei vyishly na mitynh proty okupanta, rosiiany vidkryly vohon'," *Ukraïns'ka pravda*, March 13, 2022, https://www.pravda.com.ua/news/2022/03/13/7330971/; "Khersons'ka oblrada na ekstrennomu zasidanni vidkynula ideiu stvorennia 'KhNR,'" *Ukraïns'ka pravda*, March 12, 2022, https://www.pravda.com.ua/news/2022/03/12/7330824/.

22. Musaieva, "Ihor Kolykhaiev: Ne zabuvaite pro Kherson"; Olena Rishchina, "Kherson: liudy vyishly na mitynh, okupanty rozpylyly sl'ozohonnyi haz," *Ukraïns'ka pravda*, March 22, 2022, https://www.pravda.com.ua/news/2022/03/22/7333593/; "Russian Invaders Abduct Kherson Mayor Kolykhaev—Advisor Liashevska," *Ukrainian News*, June 28, 2022, https://ukranews.com/en/news/865629-russian-invaders-abduct-kherson-mayor-kolykhaev-advisor-liashevska.

23. "Berdiansk, Kherson, Kakhovka. Kak proshli proukrainskie mitingi 20 marta," *BBC News*, March 20, 2022, https://www.bbc.com/russian/media–60814719; "Russia Sending Teachers to Ukraine to Control What Students Learn," *Washington Post*, July 18, 2022, https://www.washingtonpost.com/world/2022/07/18/russia-teachers-ukraine-rewrite-history/.

24. Timofei Sergeitsev, "Chto Rossiia dolzhna sdelat' s Ukrainoi," *RIA Novosti*, April 3, 2022, https://ria.ru/20220403/ukraina–1781469605.html.

25. "Okupanty v Khersoni rozkleïly propahandysts'ki bilbordy: absurdni foto," *24 Kanal*, May 30, 2022, https://24tv.ua/okupanti-hersoni-rozkleyili-propagandistski-bilbordi-absurdni_n1991218?fbclid=IwAR3z28WY9jvrJRRYMYiFZsRlikohErzAtdTZ5zlaYKuSrleRk5EZP_8DFUU; "Kherson region," State Statistics Committee of Ukraine, https://web.archive.org/web/20071104211010/http://www.ukrcensus.gov.ua/eng/regions/reg_khers/.

26. Mariya Petkova, "Russia-Ukraine war: The battle for Odesa," *Aljazeera*, March 9, 2022, https://www.aljazeera.com/news/2022/3/9/russia-ukraine-war-the-battle-for-odesa.

27. "U chomu pomylyvsia Putin i koly peremoha?" *Krym realiï*, June 14, 2022, https://www.youtube.com/watch?app=desktop&v=oUToxyp1mjs; Vira Kasiian, "ZSU razom z teroboronoiu vidstoialy Mykolaïv, komendants'ku hodynu skasuvaly," *LB.ua*, March 2, 2022; "Mykolaïv povnistiu zvil'nyly vid rosiis'kykh okupantiv—holova ODA," *Shpal'ta*, March 5, 2022, https://shpalta.media/2022/03/05/mikolaiv-povnistyu-zvilnili-vid-rosijskix-okupantiv-golova-oda/; https://lb.ua/society/2022/03/02/507677_zsu_razom_z_teroboronoyu_vidstoyali.html; "Heneral Marchenko bil'she ne komanduie oboronoiu Mykolaieva," *Speaker News*, April 7, 2022, https://speakernews.com.ua/suspilstvo/general-marchenko-bilshe-ne-komanduye-oboronoyu-mykolayeva–20286.

28. Yaroslav Trofimov, "Ukrainian Counteroffensive near Mykolaiv Relieves Strategic Port City," *Wall Street Journal*, March 18, 2022; Ol'viia Aharkova, "Mer

Voznesens'ka povidomyv pro vybukh dvokh mostiv u misti: nam dovelosia," *RBK-Ukraïna*, March 2, 2022, https://www.rbc.ua/ukr/news/mer-voznesenska -soobshchil-vzryve-dvuh-mostov–1646246424.html; "Boi za Voznesensk. Kak ostanovili nastuplenie na Odessu," *Inshe.TV*, March 18, 2022, https://inshe.tv/ nikolaev/2022-03-18/665712; "U chomu pomylyvsia Putin i koly peremoha?"

29. Joseph Trevithick and Tyler Rogoway, "Barrage Leaves Russian-Occupied Kherson Airbase in Flames," *The Drive*, March 15, 2022; "Ukraïns'ki voïny znyshchyly 30 helikopteriv voroha na aerodromi Chornobaïvka bilia Khersonu," *Armiia. inform*, March 7, 2022, https://armyinform.com.ua/2022/03/07/ukrayinski -voyiny-znyshhyly–30-gelikopteriv-voroga-na-aerodromi-chornobayivka-bilya -hersonu/; "Nardep soobshchil o gibeli ocherednogo komanduiushchego rossiiskoi armiei i generala," *DonPress*, March 25, 2022, https://donpress.com/ news/25-03–2022-nardep-soobschil-o-gibeli-ocherednogo-komanduyuschego -rossiyskoy-armiey-i-generala; Aleksandr Kovalenko, "Fenomen Chernobaevki kak on est'," *Khartyia'97%*, March 29, 2022, https://charter97.org/ru/ news/2022/3/29/461181/.

30. "Riatuval'ni roboty pislia vluchannia rakety okupantiv u budivliu Mykolaïvs'koi ODA tryvaiut' dosi," *AAM*, March 30, 2022, https://aam.com.ua/2022/03/30/ ryatuvalni-roboty/.

31. "Odes'ke uzberezhzhia obstrilialy dva korabli rf—artyleriia ZSU vidihnala voroha," *Ukrinform*, March 21, 2022, https://www.ukrinform.ua/rubric-ato/3435618 -odeske-uzberezza-obstrilali-dva-korabli-rf-artileria-zsu-vidignala-voroga.html; Aleksandr Vel'mozhko, "Boiovi diï 27 bereznia: voroh namahavsia obstriliaty Odesu raketamy," *Odesskii kur'er*, March 27, 2022, https://uc.od.ua/columns/ alexvelmozhko/1241818.

32. "Guided Missile Cruiser Moskva (ex-Slava), Project 1164/Slava Class," Black Sea Fleet, https://www.kchf.ru/eng/ship/cruisers/slava.htm.

33. Adam Taylor and Claire Parker, "'Neptune' Missile Strike Shows Strength of Ukraine's Homegrown Weapons," *Washington Post*, April 15, 2022; "How Did Ukraine Destroy the Moskva, a Large Russian Warship," *Economist*, April 20, 2022.

34. Peter Suciu, "Moskva: The Story of Russia's Navy Warship That Ukraine Destroyed," *1945*, April 21, 2022, https://www.19fortyfive.com/2022/04/moskva-the-story-of -russias-navy-warship-that-ukraine-destroyed/; Viktoriia Andrieieva, "Znovu cherha: ponad 500 kyian 'poliuiut'' na novu marku z korablem," *Ukraïns'ka pravda*, May 23, 2022, https://life.pravda.com.ua/society/2022/05/23/248764/; "Intelligence Update. Update on Ukraine, May 19, 2022," Defence Intelligence, https://img.pravda.com/ images/doc/1/c/1c9f090–280075714–1488231861575174–1301885241671439071-n -original.jpg; Joe Inwood, "Moskva wreckage declared item of Ukrainian underwater cultural heritage," *BBC News*, April 22, 2022.

35. Ilona Kivva, "Bytva za Chorne more: ukraïns'ka rozvidka poiasnyla navishcho okupantam Zmiïnyi," *Zaborona*, May 14, 2022, https://zaborona.com/bytva-za -chorne-more-ukrayinska-rozvidka-poyasnyla-navishho-okupantam-zmiyinyj/; Max Hunder and Tom Balmforth, "Russia abandons Black Sea outpost of Snake Island in victory for Ukraine," Reuters, June 30, 2022, https://www.reuters.com/ world/europe/russia-steps-up-attacks-ukraine-after-landmark-nato-summit– 2022-06-30/; Joseph Golder, "Ukraine Hoists Flag on Snake Island After Rus-

sian Forces Withdraw," *Newsweek*, July 8, 2022, https://www.newsweek.com/
ukraine-hoists-flag-snake-island-after-russian-forces-withdraw–1722834.

36. Dmitrii Akimov, "Rossiia otmechaet 350 let so dnia rozhdeniia Petra Velikogo,"
Smotrim, June 9, 2022, https://smotrim.ru/article/2789489; "Putin posetil
vystavku o Petre I na VDNKh," *Vesti.ru*, June 9, 2022, https://www.vesti.ru/
article/2790684.

37. "Meeting with young entrepreneurs, engineers and scientists," President of
Russia, June 9, 2022, http://en.kremlin.ru/events/president/news/68606;
"Putin compares himself to Peter the Great in Russian territorial push," June
9, 2022, https://www.youtube.com/watch?v=N2sfJjl7_Zk; "Address by the President of the Russian Federation," President of Russia, February 24, 2022, http://
en.kremlin.ru/events/president/news/67843.

38. Andrew Roth, "Putin compares himself to Peter the Great in quest to take
back Russian lands," *Guardian*, June 10, 2022, https://www.theguardian.com/
world/2022/jun/10/putin-compares-himself-to-peter-the-great-in-quest-to-take
-back-russian-lands.

39. Lawrence Freedman, "Spirits of the Past. The Role of History in the Russo-
Ukraine War," *Comment is Freed*, June 12, 2022, https://samf.substack.com/p/
spirits-of-the-past?s=w&utm_medium=web.

40. "In Ukraine, they announced Zelensky's order to recapture the south of the country,"
West Observer, July 11, 2022, https://westobserver.com/news/europe/in-ukraine
-they-announced-zelenskys-order-to-recapture-the-south-of-the-country/;   Andrii Tsapliienko, "The Ukrainian military hit the Antonovsky bridge in occupied
Kherson, which connects the city with the left bank of the Dnieper," *Odessa
Journal*, July 19, 2022, https://odessa-journal.com/the-ukrainian-military-hit
-the-antonovsky-bridge-in-occupied-kherson-which-connects-the-city-with-the
-left-bank-of-the-dnieper/.

41. Peter Beaumont, "Russian forces dig in as bloody Ukrainian counterattack
anticipated in south," *Guardian*, July 22, 2022, https://www.theguardian.com/
world/2022/jul/22/ukrainian-counter-offensive-may-bring-war-to-bloodiest
-phase-yet-say-analysts.

42. Mauro Orru, "Ukraine's Occupied Kherson Seeks to Join Russia, Moscow-Installed
Leader Says," *Wall Street Journal*, May 11, 2022, https://www.wsj.com/livecoverage/
russia-ukraine-latest-news-2022-05-11/card/ukraine-s-occupied-kherson-seeks-to
-join-russia-moscow-installed-leader-says-WNFl1yxwOEkDVbG2Fpic; "Signs Multi-
ply Russia Seeks Control of South Ukraine," *Moscow Times*, May 19, 2022, https://
www.themoscowtimes.com/2022/05/19/signs-multiply-russia-seeks-control-of
-south-ukraine-a77739.

43. "Novaia administratsiia Zaporozhskoi oblasti anonsirovala referendum o vkhozh-
denii v sostav Rossii 'v tekushchem godu,'" *Meduza*, June 8, 2022, https://meduza
.io/news/2022/06/08/novaya-administratsiya-zaporozhskoy-oblasti-anonsirovala
-referendum-o-vhozhdenii-v-sostav-rossii-v-tekuschem-godu; "Prisoediniat zakh-
vachennye oblasti: v razvedke rasskazali o planakh Rossii po Ukraine," *Fokus*, July
13, 2022, https://focus.ua/voennye-novosti/522002-prisoedinyat-zahvachennye
-oblasti-v-razvedke-rasskazali-o-planah-rossii-po-ukraine'; "RF   pryznachyla
svoho chynovnyka 'holovoiu uriadu' okupovanoï Zaporiz'koï oblasti," *Ukraïns'ka
pravda*, July 18, 2022, https://www.pravda.com.ua/news/2022/07/18/7358827/.

44. White House Daily Briefing, July 19, 2022, https://www.c-span.org/video/?521824–1/ white-house-briefs-russias-plans-annex-ukrainian-territory; Ivan Nechepurenko and Eric Nagourney, "Russia Signals That It May Want a Bigger Chunk of Ukraine," *New York Times*, July 20, 2022, https://www.nytimes.com/2022/07/20/world/europe/putin -ukraine-invasion-russia-war.html.

11. The Counteroffensive

1. Maxim Tucker, "Ukraine has one million ready for fightback to recapture south," *The Times*, July 10, 2022, https://www.thetimes.co.uk/article/ukraine -has-one-million-ready-for-fightback-to-recapture-south–3rhkrhstf.

2. Kseniia Teslenko, "Vereshchuk zaklykaie meshkantsiv pivdennykh oblastei terminovo evakuiuvatysia," *S'ohodni*, July 9, 2022, https://war.segodnya.ua/ ua/war/vtorzhenie/vereshchuk-prizyvaet-zhiteley-yuzhnyh-oblastey-srochno -evakuirovatsya–1629727.html.

3. "Ukraïna vede perehovory z derzhavamy-partneramy shchodo postachannia neob-khidnoï zbroï, ale ne varto rozholoshuvaty podrobytsi—prezydent," *Zelens'kyi. Ofitsiine internet predstavnytstvo*, July 11, 2022, https://www.president.gov.ua/ news/ukrayina-vede-peregovori-z-derzhavami-partnerami-shodo-posta–76417.

4. Bohdan Prykhod'ko, "Velyka kontrataka chy zakhyst Kyieva? Chomu Ukraïna povidomliaie vorohovi pro nastup na Kherson?," *S'ohodni*, July 11, 2022, https://www.segodnya.ua/ua/strana/podrobnosti/bolshaya-kontrataka-ili -zashchita-kieva-pochemu-ukraina-soobshchaet-vragu-o-nastuplenii-na-herson –1630084.html.

5. Roman Adrian Cybrivsky, *Along Ukraine's River: A Social and Environmental History of the Dnipro* (Budapest, 2018), 104.

6. "Na Khersonshchyni zaharbnyky vidnovyly mist na hrebli Kakhovs'ko HES," *Ukrinform*, August 17, 2022, https://www.ukrinform.ua/rubric-ato/3552348-na -hersonsini-zagarbniki-vidnovili-mist-na-grebli-kahovskoi-ges.html.

7. "Antonovskii most," Khersonshchina turisticheskaia, https://khersonregion.com/ antonovskij-most/.

8. "Viis'ka RF zvodiat' fortyfikatsiini sporudy bilia Antonivs'koho mostu na Kher-sonshchyni," *Tsenzor.net*, July 13, 2022, https://m.censor.net/ua/news/3353971/ viyiska_rf_zvodyat_fortyfikatsiyini_sporudy_bilya_antonivskogo_mostu_na_ hersonschyni_ova; Mark Trevelyan, "Russia declares expanded war goals beyond Ukraine's Donbas," Reuters, July 20, 2022, https://www.reuters.com/world/ europe/lavrov-says-russias-objectives-ukraine-now-go-beyond-donbas–2022-07– 20/.

9. "Iak i chomu pochaly zlitaty zbroini sklady v tylu rosiis'kykh viis'k?" *Arhument*, July 9, 2022, https://argumentua.com/novini/yak-chomu-pochali-zl -tati-v-pov-trya-zbroin-skladi-v-tilu-ros-iskikh-v-isk.

10. Illia Ponomarenko, "What would a Ukrainian counter-offensive in Kherson look like?" *Kyiv Independent*, July 19, 2022, https://kyivindependent.com/national/ what-would-a-ukrainian-counter-offensive-in-kherson-look-like; "Okupanty povi-domyly pro obstril Antonivs'koho mostu v Khersoni," *Tsenzor.net*, July 19, 2022, https://m.censor.net/ua/news/3355088/okupanty_povidomyly_pro_obstril_ antonivskogo_mostu_v_hersoni_udaru_zavdano_iz_himars_onovleno_video; "After Antonivskyi bridge explosion, occupiers may be left without ways to

retreat from Kherson," *Ukrainian News*, July 20, 2022, https://ukranews.com/en/news/870362-after-antonivskyi-bridge-explosion-occupiers-may-be-left-without-ways-to-retreat-from-kherson.

11. "Video from Antonivka Road Bridge in Kherson shows extensive damage," *Ukraïns'ka pravda, Yahoo!*, July 27, 2022, https://www.yahoo.com/video/video-antonivka-road-bridge-kherson-081127402.html; "'To consolidate the results': The Armed Forces of Ukraine report about new strikes on the main bridges of the Kherson region," *Ukraïns'ka pravda*, August 30, 2022, https://www.pravda.com.ua/eng/news/2022/08/30/7365397/.

12. "Kakhovs'kyi mist taky obvalyvsia," *24 kanal*, September 4, 2022, https://www.youtube.com/watch?v=5kRZBNf8KY8; "Okupanty zaiavyly pro obstril mostu cherez richku Inhulets' pid Khersonom," *Militarnyi*, July 23, 2022, https://mil.in.ua/uk/news/okupanty-zayavyly-pro-obstril-mostu-cherez-richku-ingulets-pid-hersonom/; David Axe, "The Bridge Battle in Southern Ukraine is Escalating," *Forbes*, July 31, 2022, https://www.forbes.com/sites/davidaxe/2022/07/31/the-bridge-battle-in-southern-ukraine-is-escalating/.

13. "Heneral Marchenko povernuvsia do Mykolaieva z novym zavdanniam," *Texty.org.ua*, July 27, 2022, https://texty.org.ua/fragments/107345/general-marchenko-povernuvsya-do-mykolayeva-z-novym-zavdannyam/; "Partyzany u Melitopoli pidirvaly zaliznychnyi mist," *TSN*, August 14, 2022, https://tsn.ua/ato/partizani-u-melitopoli-pidirvali-zaliznichniy-mist-okupanti-v-isterici-rozshukuyut-patriotiv-ukrayini–2134282.html; "U Melitopoli partyzany pidirvaly rosiis'ku viis'kovu bazu ta fsb-shnykiv za vechereiu," *Ukrainform*, August 30, 2022, https://www.ukrinform.ua/rubric-ato/3561283-u-melitopoli-partizani-pidirvali-rosijsku-vijskovu-bazu-ta-fsbsnikiv-za-vecereu-fedorov.html.

14. "Rozstrilialy z pistoleta. Khalan' rozpoviv pro smert' hauliaitera Novoï Kakhovky," *24 kanal*, August 24, 2022, https://24tv.ua/zastupnik-gaulyaytera-novoyi-kahovki-pomer-pislya-poranennya_n2119352; "Likvidatsiia kolaboranta kovaliova," *24 kanal*, August 29, 2022, https://24tv.ua/vbivstvo-oleksiya-kovalova-yaka-versiya-vbivstva-kolaboranta_n2146302; "Rozirvalo vid liubovi do Rosiï," *TSN*, August 24, 2022, https://tsn.ua/ukrayina/rozirvalo-vid-lyubovi-do-rosiyi-na-zaporizhzhi-partizani-visadili-v-povitrya-gaulyaytera-mihaylivki–2141695.html; "Partyzany pid Melitopolem 'pidrizaly' chleniv 'komisiï z pidhotovky referendum,'" *TSN*, August 9, 2022, https://tsn.ua/ato/partizani-pid-melitopolem-pidrizali-chleniv-komisiyi-z-pidgotovki-referendumu-zmi–2130334.html.

15. "Medvedev zaiavil, chto dlia Ukrainy mozhet nastupit' sudnyi den'," *RIA Novosti*, July 17, 2022, https://ria.ru/20220717/medvedev–1803047917.html.

16. "Krymskii most. Kerch," Russia Travel, https://russia.travel/objects/330378/.

17. Tania Matiash, "Zelens'kyi vidpoviv na pohrozy Miedviedieva 'sudnym dnem': 'ne duzhe tvereza zaiava,'" *Livyi Bereh*, July 18, 2022, https://lb.ua/society/2022/07/18/523446_zelenskiy_vidpoviv_pogrozi.html; "Vzryvov net, no vy derzhites'," Reanimatsiinyi paket reform, August 19, 2022, https://rpr.org.ua/news/vzr-vov-net-no-v-derzhytes-yak-vybukhy-v-krymu-kontuzyly-pobiedobiesov-ta-vykryly-impotentsiiu-kremlia/; "Putin's circle tension and confrontation rise due to possible loss of the Russian president's capacities," Robert Lansing Institute, July 19, 2022, https://lansinginstitute.org/2022/07/19/putins-circle-tension-and-confrontation-rise-due-to-possible-loss-of-the-russian

-presidents-capacities/; " 'Priseli na stakan. Kto-to vtianulsia.' Iz-za voiny ros-siiskie chinovniki stali bol'she i chashche pit' alkogol,'" *Meduza*, September 15, 2022, https://meduza.io/feature/2022/09/15/priseli-na-stakan-kto-to -vtyanulsya?utm_source=twitter&utm_medium=main/.

18. "Ukraine claims responsibility for Crimea attacks," *Aljazeera*, September 7, 2022, https://www.aljazeera.com/news/2022/9/7/ukraine-military-chief-claims -responsibility-for-strikes-in-crime.

19. "ZSU zavdaly udariv dronom-kamikadze po pozytsiiakh RF bilia Zaporiz'koi AES," *Fokus*, July 22, 2022, https://focus.ua/uk/voennye-novosti/523089-vsu -nanesli-udary-dronom-kamikadze-po-poziciyam-rf-vozle-zaporozhskyy -aes-video; Mark Santora, "Shelling at the Zaporizhzhia Nuclear Power Plant Is Raising Fears of an Accident. Here's a Look at the Risks," *New York Times*, August 12, 2022, https://www.nytimes.com/2022/08/12/world/europe/ukraine -zaporizhzhia-nuclear-plant.html.

20. "Arestovich skazal zachem Putinu iadernyi shantazh s Zaporozhskoi AES," Fei-gin Live, August 8, 2022, https://www.youtube.com/watch?v=_dQMoCRGAU8; Isabele Coles and Bojan Pancevski, "Ukraine Accuses Russia of Using Nuclear Plant to Blackmail West," *Wall Street Journal*, August 14, 2022, https://www.wsj .com/articles/ukraine-accuses-russia-of-using-nuclear-plant-to-blackmail-west– 11660478537; Vasco Cotovio and Tara John, " 'We are playing with fire,' IAEA chief warns as nuclear watchdog calls for 'safety zone' at Russian-occupied plant in Ukraine," *CNN*, September 6, 2022, https://www.cnn.com/2022/09/06/europe/ iaea-report-ukraine-nuclear-plant-intl/index.html; Gillian Duncan, "Russia ques-tions UN nuclear report calling for demilitarised zone at Zaporizhzhia," *N World*, September 7, 2022, https://www.thenationalnews.com/world/europe/2022/09/07/ russia-questions-un-nuclear-report-calling-for-demilitarised-zone-at-zaporizhzhia/.

21. Karl Ritter, "Last reactor at Ukraine's Zaporizhzhia nuclear plant stopped," AP News, September 11, 2022, https://apnews.com/article/russia-ukraine–8838067037a852 1e3bc764435144d8b7; https://www.epravda.com.ua/news/2022/09/12/691405/; "U Putina kazhut', shcho Rosiia ne planuie vyvodyty svoï viis'ka iz terytoriï ZAES," *Ekonomichna pravda*, September 12, 2022, https://www.reuters.com/ world/europe/iaea-board-passes-resolution-calling-russia-leave-zaporizhzhia– 2022-09-15/.

22. Benjamin Harvey, Daryna Krasnolutska, Kateryna Choursina, Alberto Nardelli, Alex Wickham, and Gina Turner, "Ukraine Strategy Targets Rus-sian Army's Lifelines in Kherson," Bloomberg, August 17, 2022, https:// www.bloomberg.com/news/articles/2022-08-17/ukraine-strategy-targets-russian-army -s-lifelines-in-kherson?leadSource=uverify%20wall; "Arestovich: The invaders gathered about 30 BTGs in the south for an attack on Kryvyi Rih and Myko-laiv," *Odessa Journal*, August 2, 2022, https://odessa-journal.com/arestovich -the-invaders-gathered-about–30-btgs-in-the-south-for-an-attack-on-kryvyi-rih -and-mykolaiv/.

23. "Na Khersons'komu napriamku pochavsia 'duzhe potuzhnyi' rukh viis'k RF— Danilov," *Radio Svoboda*, July 22, 2022, https://www.radiosvoboda.org/a/news -khersonskyy-napryam-viyska-rf-danilov/31962539.html.

24. Karolina Hird, Kateryna Stepanenko, Grace Mappes, George Barros, and Frederick W. Kagan, "Russian Offensive Campaign Assessment, August 23,"

Critical Threats, August 23, 2022, https://www.criticalthreats.org/analysis/russian-offensive-campaign-assessment-august-23; "Russia makes gains near Blahodatne—General Staff report," *Ukraïns'ka pravda*, August, 22, 2022, https://www.pravda.com.ua/eng/news/2022/08/22/7364254/.

25. "Ukrainian Counteroffensive Underway in Kherson Region," *Kyiv Post*, August 29, 2022, https://www.kyivpost.com/russias-war/ukrainian-counteroffensive-underway-in-kherson-region.html.

26. "Shoigu zaiavil o popytkakh nastupleniia VSU na Nikolaevo-Krivorozhskom i drugikh napravleniiakh," *Interfax*, September 2, 2022, https://www.interfax.ru/world/860425; Oleksii Iarmolenko and Tetiana Lohvynenko, "ZSU vpershe z 24 liutoho pishly u povnotsinnyi kontrnastup. Pro rezul'taty poky movchat', ale vony zminiat' khod viiny," *Babel'*, September 1, 2022, https://babel.ua/texts/83738-zsu-vpershe-z-24-lyutogo-pishli-u-povnocinniy-kontrnastup-pro-rezultati-poki-movchat-ale-voni-zminyat-hid-viyni-analizuyemo-situaciyu-na-fronti-na-180-y-den-povnomasshtabnogo-vtorgnennya-mapi-babelya.

27. "Vysokopillia na Khersonshchyni pid ukraïns'kym praporom. Shcho tam vidbuvaiet'sia?," *Radio Svoboda*, September 6, 2022, https://www.radiosvoboda.org/a/novyny-pryazovya-khersonshchyna-deokupatsiya-vysokopillya/32019601.html; Asami Terajima, "Ukraine war latest: Ukraine liberates villages in south and east," *Kyiv Independent*, September 4, 2022, https://kyivindependent.com/national/ukraine-war-latest-ukraine-liberates-villages-in-south-and-east.

28. "Arestovych pro Vysokopillia: sytuatsiia uskladnylasia, rosiiany perekynuly tekhniku," *RBK Ukraïna*, July 25, 2022, https://www.rbc.ua/ukr/news/arestovich-vysokopole-situatsiya-uslozhnilas-1658778302.html.

29. "Spetsoperatsiia 7 sentiabria: Minoborony soobshchilo o vziatii Kodemy," *RIA Novosti*, September 7, 2022, https://ria.ru/20220907/spetsoperatsiya-1815272570.html.

30. Isobel Koshiw, Lorenzo Tondo, and Artem Mazhulin, "Ukraine's southern offensive 'was designed to trick Russia,'" *Guardian*, September 10, 2022, https://www.theguardian.com/world/2022/sep/10/ukraines-publicised-southern-offensive-was-disinformation-campaign.

31. "ZSU pochaly zvil'niaty Balakliiu? Vse, shcho vidomo," *BBC News*, Ukraïna, September 6, 2022, https://www.bbc.com/ukrainian/features-62811889.

32. Karolina Hird, George Barros, Layne Philipson, and Frederick W. Kagan, "Russian Offensive Campaign Assessment," *Institute for the Study of War*, September 6, 2022, https://www.understandingwar.org/backgrounder/russian-offensive-campaign-assessment-september-6.

33. Oleh Verlan, "Za Balakliis'ku operatsiiu vidpovidav heneral-polkovnyk Syrs'kyi," *Na Paryzhi*, September 10, 2022, https://naparise.com/posts/za-balakliisku-operatsiiu-vidpovidav-heneral-polkovnyk-syrskyi; "Maiemo khoroshi novyny z Kharkivshchyny": Zelens'kyi skazav slova podiaky p'iat'om bryhadam," *Novynarnia*, September 8, 2022, https://novynarnia.com/2022/09/08/mayemo-horoshi-novyny-z-harkivshhyny-zelenskyj-skazav-slova-podyaky-pyatom-brygadam/.

34. "Expert: Cascading Collapse of Russian Front," *Khartyia 97*, September 12, 2022, https://charter97.org/en/news/2022/9/12/515297/.

35. Andrew E. Kramer and Jeffrey Gettleman, "In Reclaimed Towns, Ukraini-

ans Recount a Frantic Russian Retreat," *New York Times*, September 13, 2022, https://www.nytimes.com/2022/09/13/world/europe/ukraine-russia-retreat -morale.html.

36. "'My vyzhili': Boitsy SOBRa, derzhavshie oboronu v Balaklee, zapisali video," *Eurasia Daily*, September 10, 2022, https://eadaily.com/ru/news/2022/09/10/ my-vyzhili-boycy-sobra-derzhavshie-oboronu-v-balaklee-zapisali-video.

37. "Representative of General Staff of Armed Forces of Ukraine says over 20 settle-ments were liberated in Kharkiv region," *News Live*, September 8, 2022, https:// liveuamap.com/en/2022/8-september-representative-of-general-staff-of-armed -forces.

38. "Poiavilis' kadry perebroski kolonny gruppy 'otvazhnye' v Kupiansk pod Khar'kovom," *Novorossiia*, September 10, 2022, https://iz.ru/1393435/2022 -09-10/poiavilis-kadry-perebroski-kolonny-gruppy-otvazhnykh-v-kupiansk -pod-kharkovom; "ZSU zaishly v Kup'ians'k i vstanovyly prapor Ukraïny," *Hlavred*, September 10, 2022, https://glavred.net/ukraine/vsu-zashli-v-kupyansk-i-ustanovili -flag-ukrainy-sovetnica-glavy-harkovskogo-oblsoveta–10408007.html.

39. Kateryna Stepanenko, Grace Mappes, George Barros, Angela Howard, and Mason Clark, "Russian Offensive Campaign Assessment," *Institute for the Study of War*, September 10, 2022, https://www.understandingwar.org/backgrounder/ russian-offensive-campaign-assessment-september–10.

40. "Okupanty pokynuly Izium: ukraïns'ki viis'ka vvishly u misto," *DSNews.ua*, Sep-tember 10, 2022, https://www.dsnews.ua/ukr/politics/okupanti-pokinuli-izyum -ukrajinski-viyska-vvishli-u-misto-video–10092022–465867; Ievheniia Lut-senko, "Ukraïns'ki viis'kovi uviishly do Vovchans'ka, shcho na kordoni z rosi-ieiu," *Hromads'ke*, September 13, 2022, https://hromadske.ua/posts/ukrayinski -vijskovi-uvijshli-u-vovchansk-sho-na-kordoni-z-rosiyeyu; "U Minoboroni utoch-nyly dani pro zvil'neni terytoriï Kharkivshchyny—388 naselenykh punktiv," *Ukrinform*, September 14, 2022, https://www.ukrinform.ua/rubric-ato/3571524 -u-minoboroni-utocnili-dani-pro-zvilneni-teritorii-harkivsini–388-naselenih -punktiv.html.

41. "Mass grave of more than 440 bodies found in Izium, Ukraine, police say," Reuters, September 15, 2022, https://www.reuters.com/article/ukraine-crisis -zelenskiy-grave/ukraine-finds-a-mass-grave-in-recaptured-city-of-izium -zelenskiy-idUSKBN2QG248.

42. Andrew Stanton, "Counteroffensive Has Only 6 Percent of Kharkiv Left to Lib-erate: Ukraine," *Newsweek*, September 27, 2022, https://www.newsweek.com/ counteroffensive-has-only–6-percent-kharkiv-left-liberate-ukraine–1746750; "Ukraine tells Russia to appeal to Kyiv if it wants encircled troops freed," Reuters, September 30, 2022, https://www.reuters.com/world/europe/ukraine-tells-russia -appeal-kyiv-if-it-wants-encircled-troops-freed–2022-09-30/.

43. "Ukraine seizes the initiative in the east," *Economist*, September 9, 2022, https://www.economist.com/europe/2022/09/09/ukraine-seizes-the-initiative -in-the-east; Henry Foy, "Ukraine's advance boosts calls for more western weapons," *Financial Times*, September 12, 2022, https://www.ft.com/content/ bab05be8–8200–4804-b45f-00dcd65cd044; Marta Hychko, "'Protivnik uzhe vyigral': Girkin ustroil paniku iz-za porazheniia RF na Khar'kovshchine," *UNIAN*, September 10, 2022, https://www.unian.net/war/protivnik-uzhe

-vyigral-girkin-ustroil-paniku-iz-za-porazheniy-rf-na-harkovshchine–11973678
.html; "Dlia RF kartina ne radostnaia, u VSU prevoskhodstvo na vsem fronte—
Strelkov (Girkin)," UNIAN, September 17, 2022, https://www.youtube.com/
watch?app=desktop&v=4e6RqcpwmUQ.

44. Julian E. Barnes, Eric Schmitt, and Helene Cooper, "The Critical Moment
Behind Ukraine's Rapid Advance," *New York Times*, September 13, 2022, https://
www.nytimes.com/2022/09/13/us/politics/ukraine-russia-pentagon.html.

45. Foy, "Ukraine's advance boosts calls for more western weapons"; Adrienne Vogt,
"Russia's war in Ukraine: September 10, 2022," *CNN*, September 10, 2022,
https://www.cnn.com/europe/live-news/russia-ukraine-war-news-09–10–22/h_
a14d999bfb238edc6542eaaa671e314c.

46. "Putin shown in tense encounter with chief of staff at Far East war games,"
Reuters, September 6, 2022, https://www.reuters.com/world/europe/smiling
-putin-inspects-big-far-east-military-drills–
2022-09-06/; Sophia Ankel, "As Russia was forced to retreat in Ukraine,
Putin was opening a giant Ferris wheel—but it broke down and people had to
be refunded," *Insider*, September 14, 2022, https://www.businessinsider.com/
amid-ukraine-offensive-putin-opened-ferris-wheel-but-it-broke–2022–9; Tara
Subramaniam, Ivana Kottasová, Eliza Mackintosh, Adrienne Vogt, and Aditi
Sangal, "September 13, 2022 Russia-Ukraine news," *CNN*, September 13, 2022,
https://edition.cnn.com/europe/live-news/russia-ukraine-war-news-09–13–22/h_
b439762c2fb1cc0a92457f4214601e58; "Izmena na urovne Putina! Igor' Strelkov
(Girkin)," September 16, 2022, https://www.youtube.com/watch?v=gpahjt8zaNM.

47. Kateryna Stepanenko, Katherine Lawlor, Grace Mappes, George Barros, and
Frederick W. Kagan, "Russian Offensive Campaign Assessment," *Institute
for the Study of War*, September 15, 2022, https://www.understandingwar.org/
backgrounder/russian-offensive-campaign-assessment-september–15.

48. "Prigozhin verbuet zakliuchennykh rf: kommentarii Feigina i Arestovicha," *Feigin
Live*, September 14, 2022, https://www.youtube.com/watch?v=vvUMsmbChV4;
"Prigozhin—o verbovke zakliuchennykh na voinu: 'Libo zeki, libo vashi deti,'"
Radio Svoboda, September 15, 2022, https://www.svoboda.org/a/prigozhin—o
-verbovke-zaklyuchyonnyh-na-voynu-libo-zeki-libo-vashi-deti-/32035673.html;
"Ukraine Live Updates: Putin Calls Up More Troops as His War Effort Falters,"
New York Times, September 21, 2022; "Putin says Russia's mobilisation mistakes
must be 'corrected,'" *Aljazeera*, September 29, 2022, https://www.aljazeera
.com/news/2022/9/29/putin-says-russias-mobilisation-mistakes-must-be
-corrected.

49. Andrew E. Kramer, "Russia-Ukraine War: Armed Russian Soldiers Over-
see Referendum Voting," *New York Times*, September 24, 2022, https://
www.nytimes.com/live/2022/09/24/world/russia-ukraine-putin-news; Antony
Blinken, Secretary of State, "Russia's Sham Referenda in Ukraine," Press Statement, U.S. Department of State, September 29, 2022, https://www.state.gov/
russias-sham-referenda-in-ukraine/; Joshua Berlinger, Anna Chernova, and Tim
Lister, "Putin announces annexation of Ukrainian regions in defiance of international law," *CNN*, September 30, 2022, https://www.cnn.com/2022/09/30/
europe/putin-russia-ukraine-annexation-intl.

50. "Signing of treaties on accession of Donetsk and Lugansk people's republics and

Zaporozhye and Kherson regions to Russia," *President of Russia*, September 30, 2022, http://en.kremlin.ru/events/president/news/69465.

51. Thomas Gibbons-Neff, "Russia's withdrawal from Lyman comes a day after Putin said he was annexing the region." *New York Times*, October 1, 2022, https://www.nytimes.com/live/2022/10/01/world/russia-ukraine-war-news#ukraine-moves-to-encircle-lyman-a-strategic-eastern-rail-hub; "Official: Ukraine's military has liberated over 2,400 square kilometers in Kherson Oblast," *Kyiv Independent*, October 7, 2022, https://kyivindependent.com/news-feed/official-ukraines-military-has-liberated-over-2–400-square-kilometers-in-kherson-oblast; Michael Schwirtz and Andrew E. Kramer, "Blast on Crimean Bridge Deals Blow to Russian War Effort in Ukraine," *New York Times*, October 8, 2022, https://www.nytimes.com/2022/10/08/world/europe/ukraine-crimea-bridge-explosion.html; Karen DeYoung, "Ukraine war at a turning point with rapid escalation of conflict," *Washington Post*, October 10, 2022, https://www.washingtonpost.com/national-security/2022/10/10/russia-ukraine-war-turning-point/.

52. "Russian General Surovikin: "The Situation in Kherson is Tense, We Do Not Rule Out Difficult Decisions," *Nova.News*, October 19, 2022, https://www.agenzianova.com/en/news/il-generale-russo-surovkin-la-situazione-a-kherson-e-tesa-non-escludiamo-decisioni-difficili/; Anna Chernova and Rob Picheta, "Russia removes bones of 18th-century commander revered by Putin from occupied Ukrainian city," *CNN*, October 28, 2022, https://www.cnn.com/2022/10/28/europe/potemkin-remains-removed-kherson-ukraine-russia-intl; "Russian Defense Minister Orders Major Retreat From Kherson," *Radio Free Europe*, November 9, 2022 https://www.rferl.org/a/russia-kherson-retreat-shoigu-ukraine/32122802.html; "Strashnyi son rosiian. Chomu RF zaiavyla pro vidvid viisk z Khersona i naskilky tse mozhe zatiahnutysia," *Ukrainska pravda*, November 9, 2022 https://www.pravda.com.ua/articles/2022/11/9/7375683/.

53. Max Hunder and Tom Balmforth, "Exclusive: Russia needs time to pull back from Kherson, fighting to slow in winter -Kyiv," Reuters, November 10, 2022, https://www.reuters.com/world/europe/exclusive-russian-withdrawal-kherson-take-least-week-kyiv-2022-11-10/; Olga Pilipenko, "Rabotaiut po metodichke: rossiiskie SMI o potere Khersona," *Dialog.ua*, November 12, 2022, https://www.dialog.ua/russia/262355_1668198752; Mick Krever, Anna Chernova, Teele Rebane, Gianluca Mezzofiore, Tim Lister, and Sophie Tanno, "Ukrainian troops sweep into key city of Kherson after Russian forces retreat, dealing blow to Putin," *CNN*, November 11, 2022, https://www.cnn.com/2022/11/11/europe/russian-troops-leave-kherson-region-intl.

54. "General Hodges makes forecast for liberation of Mariupol, Melitopol, Crimea," *Ukrinform*, November 12, 2022, https://www.ukrinform.net/rubric-ato/3613120-general-hodges-makes-forecast-for-liberation-of-mariupol-melitopol-crimea.html; "Zelensky visits newly-retaken Kherson city, says "we are going forward," *CNN*, November 14, 2022, https://www.cnn.com/europe/live-news/russia-ukraine-war-news-11-14-22/h_8ddf7d7da8420737ed7008cdfoe 76fad.

55. Jack Watling, "Russia's Loss of Kherson Signals Change in Putin's Strategy," *The Guardian*, November 13, 2022, https://www.theguardian.com/world/2022/nov/13/russias-loss-of-kherson-signals-change-in-putins-strategy-ukraine;

Clare Mills, "Military Assistance to Ukraine since the Russian Invasion," Research Briefing, House of Commons Library, November 11, 2022, chrome-extension://efaidnbmnnnibpcajpcglclefindmkaj/https://researchbriefings .files.parliament.uk/documents/CBP-9477/CBP-9477.pdf.

12. The Return of the West

1. Cara Anna, "Rocket attacks hit Ukraine's Lviv as Biden visits Poland," *AP*, March 26, 2022, https://apnews.com/article/explosions-in-lviv-ukraine -russia-war-d19574a99afeb4bf964be7c3276c084c; "Biden gives speech in Poland," *Washington Post*, March 26, 2022, https://www.youtube.com/ watch?v=brIm2OmxuuM; J. Oliver Conroy, "Vladimir Putin 'cannot remain in power,' Joe Biden says in Warsaw speech," *Guardian*, March 26, 2022, https://www.theguardian.com/world/2022/mar/26/biden-tells-west-to -prepare-for-long-fight-ahead-in-warsaw-speech; Michael D. Shear and David E. Sanger, "Biden's Barbed Remark About Putin: A Slip or a Veiled Threat?" *New York Times*, March 26, 2022, https://www.nytimes.com/2022/03/26/ world/europe/biden-ukraine-poland-speech.html.

2. "Remarks by President Biden on the United Efforts of the Free World to Support the People of Ukraine," The White House, March 26, 2022, https:// www.whitehouse.gov/briefing-room/speeches-remarks/2022/03/26/ remarks-by-president-biden-on-the-united-efforts-of-the-free-world-to-support-the-people-of-ukraine/; J. Oliver Conroy and Philip Oltermann, "Vladimir Putin 'cannot remain in power' Joe Biden says in Warsaw speech," *Guardian*, March 26, 2022, https://www.theguardian.com/world/2022/mar/26/biden-tells-west-to -prepare-for-long-fight-ahead-in-warsaw-speech.

3. "Remarks by President Biden on the United Efforts of the Free World to Support the People of Ukraine."

4. "Remarks by President Biden on the United Efforts of the Free World to Support the People of Ukraine."

5. Michael D. Shear, "After meeting with Ukraine refugees, Biden calls Putin 'a butcher,'" *New York Times*, March 26, 2022.

6. Christopher Cadelago and Craig Howie, "Biden, off the cuff, says Putin 'cannot remain in power,'" *Politico*, March 26, 2022, https:// www.politico.com/news/2022/03/26/biden-putin-poland-speech-00020671; Daniel Boffey, Shaun Walker, and Philip Oltermann, "Biden: 'butcher' Putin cannot be allowed to stay in power," *Guardian*, March 27, 2022, https:// www.theguardian.com/us-news/2022/mar/26/biden-butcher-putin-cannot-be -allowed-to-stay-in-power; Winston Churchill—The Greatest Briton, UK Parliament, Appendix 2: Full transcript of a speech by Winston Churchill broadcast on 'The Home Service Programme' (BBC radio), 9 pm, Sunday, June 22, 1941 (BBK/C/87), https://www.parliament.uk › parliamentary-archives.

7. "Remarks by President Biden on the United Efforts of the Free World to Support the People of Ukraine."

8. Chad P. Bown, "Russia's war on Ukraine: A sanctions timeline," Peterson Institute for International Economics, https://www.piie.com/blogs/ realtime-economic-issues-watch/russias-war-ukraine-sanctions-timeline.

9. Michael D. Shear, Richard Pérez-Peña, Zolan Kanno-Youngs, and Anton

Troianovski, "U.S. and Allies Impose Sanctions on Russia as Biden Condemns 'Invasion' of Ukraine," *New York Times*, February 22, 2022, https://www.nytimes.com/2022/02/22/us/politics/us-russia-ukraine-sanctions.html; "Nord Stream 1: Why is Russia cutting gas supplies to Europe?" *BBC News*, July 27, 2022, https://www.bbc.com/news/world-europe-60131520; "Blocking Property of Certain Persons and Prohibiting Certain Transactions with Respect to Continued Russian Efforts to Undermine the Sovereignty and Territorial Integrity of Ukraine," *Federal Register*, A Presidential Document by the Executive Office of the President on 02/23/2022, https://www.federalregister.gov/documents/2022/02/23/2022-04020/blocking-property-of-certain-persons-and-prohibiting-certain-transactions-with-respect-to-continued.

10. Shear, Pérez-Peña, and Troianovski, "U.S. and Allies Impose Sanctions on Russia"; Bown, "Russia's war on Ukraine: A sanctions timeline"; Kate Davidson and Aubree Eliza Weaver, "The West declares economic war on Russia," *Politico*, February 28, 2022, https://www.politico.com/newsletters/morning-money/2022/02/28/the-west-declares-economic-war-on-russia-00012208.

11. Bown, "Russia's war on Ukraine: A sanctions timeline"; Erik de Bie, "EU Sanctions Russia with 'Maintenance and Alignment' Package of Restrictive Measures," *National Law Review* 12, no. 210 (July 29, 2022), https://www.natlawreview.com/article/eu-sanctions-russia-maintenance-and-alignment-package-restrictive-measures; Catherine Belton and Robyn Dixon, "Western sanctions catch up with Russia's wartime economy," *Washington Post*, November 26, 2022, https://www.washingtonpost.com/world/2022/11/26/russia-war-economy-military-supply/; Emily Rauhala, Karen DeYoung, and Beatriz Rios, "Western allies move to cap price of Russian oil at $60 a barrel," *Washington Post*, December 2, 2022, https://www.washingtonpost.com/world/2022/12/02/russian-oil-price-cap/; "EU agrees 9th sanctions package against Russia—diplomats," Reuters, December 15, 2022, https://www.reuters.com/world/europe/eu-agrees-9th-sanctions-package-against-russia-diplomats-2022-12-15/.

12. "Ukraine received 1,300 tons of US military aid in 2022," *UATV*, February 11, 2022, https://uatv.ua/en/ukraine-received-1-300-tons-of-us-military-aid-in-2022/.

13. Shane Harris, "Russia planning massive military offensive against Ukraine, involving 150,000 troops, US Intelligence Warns," *Washington Post*, December 3, 2021, https://www.washingtonpost.com/national-security/russia-ukraine-invasion/2021/12/03/98a3760e-546b-11ec-8769-2f4ecdf7a2ad_story.html; David E. Sanger, Eric Schmitt, Helene Cooper, Julian E. Barnes, and Kenneth P. Vogel, "Arming Ukraine: 17,000 Anti-Tank Weapons in 6 Days and a Clandestine Cybercorps," *New York Times*, March 6, 2022, https://www.nytimes.com/2022/03/06/us/politics/us-ukraine-weapons.html; Mark Gollom, "How successive U.S. administrations resisted arming Ukraine," *CBC News*, March 5, 2022, https://www.cbc.ca/news/world/obama-trump-biden-ukraine-military-aid-$26371378; Natasha Bertrand, "White House reiterates that US is ready to act if Russia invades Ukraine," *CNN*, December 24, 2021, https://edition.cnn.com/2021/12/23/politics/us-warning-russia-ukraine/index.html.

14. Sanger, Schmitt, Cooper, Barnes, and Vogel, "Arming Ukraine."

15. "Fact Sheet on U.S. Security Assistance for Ukraine," The White House, March 16, 2022, https://www.whitehouse.gov/briefing-room/statements-releases/2022/03/16/

fact-sheet-on-u-s-security-assistance-for-ukraine/; Bernd Debusmann Jr., "What weapons has the US given Ukraine—and how much do they help?" *BBC News*, April 21, 2022, https://www.bbc.com/news/world-us-canada–60774098.

16. "The Lend-Lease Act of 1941, March 11, 1941," History, Arts & Archives. United States House of Representatives, https://history.house.gov/Historical -Highlights/1901–1950/The-Lend-Lease-Act-of–1941/#:~:text=On%20this%20 date%2C%20the%20House,vital%20to%20American%20national%20 security; Michele Kelemen, "U.S. war aims shift in Ukraine—and bring additional risks," NPR, April 27, 2022, https://www.npr.org/2022/04/27/1094970683/u-s -war-aims-shift-in-ukraine-and-bring-additional-risks; Patricia Zengerle, "U.S. Congress revives World War Two-era 'Lend-Lease' program for Ukraine," Reuters, April 28, 2022, https://www.reuters.com/world/us-congress-revives-world-war -two-era-lend-lease-program-ukraine–2022-04–28/; David Vergun, "Biden Signs Lend-Lease Act to Supply More Security Assistance to Ukraine," U.S. Department of Defense, May 9, 2022, https://www.defense.gov/News/News-Stories/Article/ Article/3025302/biden-signs-lend-lease-act-to-supply-more-security-assistance -to-ukraine/.

17. John Ismay, "Allies will 'keep moving heaven and earth' to supply Ukraine, the U.S. defense chief says," *New York Times*, April 26, 2022, https://www.nytimes .com/live/2022/04/26/world/ukraine-russia-war-news#allies-will-keep-moving -heaven-and-earth-to-supply-ukraine-the-us-defense-chief-says; Ismay, "A new U.S.-led international group will meet monthly to focus on aiding Ukraine," *New York Times*, April 26, 2022, https://www.nytimes.com/2022/04/26/world/europe/ lloyd-austin-ukraine-contact-group.html.

18. "Winter is coming to Ukraine, warns NATO chief at Ramstein summit," *DW*, September 8, 2022, https://www.dw.com/en/winter-is-coming-to-ukraine-warns -nato-chief-at-ramstein-summit/a–63061788.

19. Volodymyr Landa and Kostiantyn Hennyi, "Reitynh druziv Ukraïny. 20 kraïn, iaki naibil'she dopomohly Ukraïni z momentu rosiis'koho vtorhnennia," *Forbes*, Voiennyi nomer, https://forbes.ua/inside/reyting-druziv-ukraini–20 -krain-yaki-naybilshe-dopomogli-ukraini-z-momentu-rosiyskogo-vtorgnennya -reyting-forbes–31052022–6292.

20. Kaja Kallas, "Our neighbor's problem today will be our problem tomor- row," ERR News, April 26, 2022, https://news.err.ee/1608578038/kaja-kallas -our-neighbor-s-problem-today-will-be-our-problem-tomorrow.

21. "Ukrainian refugees arrive in Poland," https://news.un.org/en/story/2022 /05/1119172; Jarosław Kuisz and Karolina Wigura, "The EU and the War in Ukraine (I): The Curse of Being Important. A View from Poland," *Internationale Politik Quarterly*, June 30, 2022, https://ip-quarterly.com/en/eu-and-war-ukraine -i-curse-being-important-view-poland; Giorgio Cafiero, "Analysis: Ukraine war has both blindsided and empowered Orban," *Aljazeera*, June 27, 2022, https:// www.aljazeera.com/news/2022/6/27/analysis-ukraine-war-has-both-blindsided -and-empowered-hungarys-orban.

22. Landa and Hennyi, "Reitynh druziv Ukraïny."

23. "Boris Johnson walks on the streets of war-hit Kyiv along with Zelensky; Pledges more aid to Ukraine," *Hindustan Times*, April 10, 2022, https:// www.youtube.com/watch?v=4LcCdf8hMTY; Roman Kravets and Roman Roma-

niuk, "Do i pislia kontrnastupu. Chy ie perspektyvy u myrnykh perehovo-riv z Rosiieiu," *Ukraïns'ka pravda*, July 28, 2022, https://www.pravda.com.ua/articles/2022/07/28/7360566/.

24. "Ukraine has shown the world it will prevail in its battle for freedom," Foreign, Commonwealth & Development Office and The Rt Hon Elizabeth Truss MP, June 3, 2022, https://www.gov.uk/government/news/ukraine-has-shown-the-world-it-will-prevail-in-its-battle-for-freedom; Pankaj Mishra, "Ukraine Should Beware of Brits Bearing Gifts," Bloomberg, May 19, 2022, https://www.bloomberg.com/opinion/articles/2022-05-19/is-boris-johnson-dragging-out-the-ukraine-war; Tim Adams, "Butler to the World by Oliver Bullough review—bent Britain at your service," *Guardian*, March 21, 2022, https://www.theguardian.com/books/2022/mar/21/butler-to-the-world-by-oliver-bullough-review-bent-britain-at-your-service.

25. Simon Tisdall, "Boris Johnson is using Ukraine crisis to launch a British comeback in Europe," *Guardian*, May 15, 2022, https://www.theguardian.com/commentisfree/2022/may/15/boris-johnson-ukraine-crisis-british-comeback-europe.

26. Tisdall, "Boris Johnson is using Ukraine crisis to launch a British come-back in Europe"; Sean Monaghan, "The Joint Expeditionary Force: Global Britain in Northern Europe?" Center for Strategic and International Stud-ies, March 25, 2022, https://www.csis.org/analysis/joint-expeditionary-force-global-britain-northern-europe; "Now it's official: Ukraine, UK, Poland form security alliance," Euromaidan Press, February 17, 2022, https://euromaidanpress.com/2022/02/17/now-its-official-ukraine-uk-poland-form-security-alliance/.

27. Philip Oltermann, "Germany agonises over Merkel's legacy: did she hand too much power to Putin?" *Guardian*, March 5, 2022.

28. "War in Ukraine: Is Germany losing its EU leadership role?" *DW*, May 25, 2022, https://www.dw.com/en/war-in-ukraine-is-germany-losing-its-eu-leadership-role/a-61879431; "German navy chief Schönbach resigns over comments on Putin, Crimea," *DW*, January 22, 2022, https://www.dw.com/en/german-navy-chief-sch%C3%B6nbach-resigns-over-comments-on-putin-crimea/a-60525709.

29. "Take joint action and do whatever is necessary," The Federal Government, G7 Germany, February 7, 2022, https://www.bundesregierung.de/breg-en/news/federal-chancellor-scholz-trip-washington-2003710; "Ex-German chancellor Schroeder's Russia ties cast a shadow over Scholz's trip to Moscow," *France24*, February 15, 2022, https://www.france24.com/en/europe/20220215-ex-german-chancellor-schroeder-s-russia-ties-cast-a-shadow-over-scholz-s-trip-to-moscow; Carlotta Vorbrüggen, "Scholz, Biden, Macron und Johnson fordern rasche Ins-pektion des AKW Saporischschja," *Welt*, August 21, 2022, https://www.welt.de/politik/ausland/article240586497/Ukraine-Krieg-Scholz-Biden-Macron-und-Johnson-fordern-Inspektion-des-AKW-Saporischschja.html.

30. "War in Ukraine: Is Germany losing its EU leadership role?"; Peter Dickinson, "Not just Putin: Most Russians support the war in Ukraine," Atlantic Council, March 10, 2022, https://www.atlanticcouncil.org/blogs/ukrainealert/not-just-putin-most-russians-support-the-war-in-ukraine/; Birgit Jennen and Michael Nienaber, "Scholz Touts Latest Ukraine Arms Delivery After Criticism," Bloom-

berg, June 1, 2022, https://www.bloomberg.com/news/articles/2022-06-01/scholz-touts-latest-ukraine-arms-delivery-as-criticism-persists#xj4y7vzkg; Mariia Koval-Honchar, "Krashche pizno nizh nikoly: iak Nimechchyna zminiuie svoiu pozytsiiu shchodo zbroï dlia Ukraïny," *Ievropeis'ka pravda*, June 6, 2022, https://www.eurointegration.com.ua/articles/2022/06/6/7140672/.

31. "War in Ukraine: What is Germany's strategy?" *DW*, May 30, 2022, https://www.dw.com/en/war-in-ukraine-what-is-germanys-strategy/a-61977500.

32. "Address by President of Ukraine Volodymyr Zelenskyy to the Bundestag," President of Ukraine, March 17, 2022, https://www.president.gov.ua/en/news/promova-prezidenta-ukrayini-volodimira-zelenskogo-u-bundesta-73621.

33. "Zelensky invites Merkel, Sarkozy to Bucha to look at results of concessions to Russia," *Ukrinform*, April 3, 2022, https://www.ukrinform.net/rubric-polytics/3447795-zelensky-invites-merkel-sarkozy-to-bucha-to-look-at-results-of-concessions-to-russia.html.

34. Bojan Pancevski, "German President Is Told He Isn't Welcome in Ukraine," *Wall Street Journal*, April 12, 2022, https://www.wsj.com/livecoverage/russia-ukraine-latest-news-2022-04-12/card/german-president-is-told-he-isn-t-welcome-in-ukraine-frQQduYTCR8yY5uvaQtl.

35. Melanie Amann, Markus Becker, Markus Feldenkirchen, Florian Gathmann, Matthias Gebauer, Serafin Reiber, Jonas Schaible, Christoph Schult, and Severin Weiland, "Why Has Germany Been So Slow to Deliver Weapons?" *Spiegel International*, June 3, 2022, https://www.spiegel.de/international/germany/olaf-scholz-and-ukraine-why-has-germany-been-so-slow-to-deliver-weapons-a-7cc8397b-2448-49e6-afa5-00311c8fedce.

36. "How heavily does Germany rely on Russian energy?" *Economist*, May 4, 2022, https://www.economist.com/the-economist-explains/2022/05/04/how-heavily-does-germany-rely-on-russian-energy; Melanie Amann et al., "Why Has Germany Been So Slow to Deliver Weapons?"

37. "Macron welcomes Putin, Zelensky for Ukraine peace talks in Paris," *France24*, December 8, 2019, https://www.france24.com/en/20191208-france-macron-ukraine-crimea-zelensky-putin-peace-paris-summit-%C3%A9lys%C3%A9e-palace-russia-ukraine-germany-merkel-eu-european-union-annex; Roger Cohen, Ivan Nechepurenko, Aurelien Breeden, Shashank Bengali, and Anton Troianovski, "Macron meets Putin in Moscow, aiming for a de-escalation," *New York Times*, February 7, 2022, https://www.nytimes.com/2022/02/07/world/europe/macron-heads-to-moscow-aiming-for-a-de-escalation.html.

38. Stephane Faure, "Ukraine crisis: Why is Macron taking on the role of mediator?" *Aljazeera*, February 23, 2022, https://www.aljazeera.com/news/2022/2/23/ukraine-crisis-macron-the-mediator-in-chief.

39. "Macron and Germany's Scholz urge Putin to hold 'direct negotiations' with Zelensky," *France24*, May 28, 2022, https://www.france24.com/en/europe/20220528-live-ukraine-says-everything-being-done-to-defend-donbas-from-russian-onslaught; "Vladimir Putin made 'historic' error in Ukraine: France," *Aljazeera*, June 3, 2022, https://www.aljazeera.com/news/2022/6/3/vladimir-putin-made-historic-error-in-ukraine-france.

40. John Irish and Max Hunder, "Ukraine says Macron remarks on Russia 'can only humiliate France,'" Reuters, June 4, 2022.

41. Faure, "Ukraine crisis: Why is Macron taking on the role of mediator?"; "Vladimir Putin made 'historic' error in Ukraine: France"; Philippe Ricard, "War in Ukraine: Macron and Zelensky at odds," *Le Monde*, May 20, 2022, https://www .lemonde.fr/en/international/article/2022/05/20/war-in-ukraine-emmanuel -macron-and-volodymyr-zelenskyy-at-odds_5984097_4.html; "Ukraine bid to join EU will take decades says Macron," *BBC News*, May 10, 2022, https://www .bbc.com/news/world-europe–61383632.

42. Nichola Farrell, "Roman Myths. Italy's growing opposition to NATO," *Spectator*, May 21, 2022, 20–21; Anurag Roushan, "US Supports Italy's Four-point Peace Plan For Ukraine Amid Ongoing Russian Invasion," *Republicworld.com*, June 1, 2022, https://www.republicworld.com/world-news/russia-ukraine-crisis/ us-supports-italys-four-point-peace-plan-for-ukraine-amid-ongoing-russian -invasion-articleshow.html.

43. "Ukraine confirms Italy proposed plan to end war," *Kyiv Independent*, May 20, 2022, https://kyivindependent.com/news-feed/ukraine-confirms-italy-proposed -plan-to-end-war/.

44. Jules Darmanin, Clea Caulcutt, and Christopher Miller, "Macron, Scholz and Draghi meet Zelenskyy in Kyiv during historic visit," *Politico*, June 16, 2022, https://www.politico.eu/article/macron-scholz-draghi-kyiv-visit-zelenskyy -ukraine/; Kate Bennett, "First lady Jill Biden makes unannounced trip to Ukraine," *CNN*, May 8, 2022, https://www.cnn.com/2022/05/08/politics/jill -biden-ukraine-visit/index.html.

45. Darmanin, Caulcutt, and Miller, "Macron, Scholz and Draghi meet Zelenskyy in Kyiv during historic visit"; "Macron, Zelensky turn page on Russia 'humiliation' spat," *France24*, June 17, 2022, https://www.france24.com/en/live-news/20220617 -macron-zelensky-turn-page-on-russia-humiliation-spat.

46. Jessica Parker, Joe Inwood, and Steve Rosenberg, "EU awards Ukraine and Moldova candidate status," *BBC News*, June 23, 2022, https://www.bbc.com/news/ world-europe–61891467; "Grant EU candidate status to Ukraine and Moldova without delay, MEPs demand," News. European parliament, June 23, 2022, https://www.europarl.europa.eu/news/en/press-room/20220616IPR33216/ grant-eu-candidate-status-to-ukraine-and-moldova-without-delay-meps -demand; Andrew Gray, "Big deal: What does EU candidate status actually mean for Ukraine?" *Politico*, June 18, 2022, https://www.politico.eu/article/why-eu -membership-candidate-status-matters-for-ukraine/.

47. "NATO formally invites Sweden, Finland to join the alliance," *France24*, June 29, 2022, https://www.france24.com/en/europe/20220629-alliance-faces-biggest-challenge -since-world-war-ii-says-nato-chief; Amanda Macias, "NATO reaches a deal with Turkey to admit Sweden and Finland, secretary-general says," *CNBC*, June 28, 2022, https://www.cnbc.com/2022/06/28/nato-reaches-deal-with-turkey-to-admit -sweden-and-finland-secretary-general-says.html; Owen Greene, "Sweden: a history of neutrality ends after 200 years," *The Conversation*, May 26, 2022, https:// theconversation.com/sweden-a-history-of-neutrality-ends-after–200-years–183583.

48. "Madrid Summit Declaration Issued by NATO Heads of State and Government participating in the meeting of the North Atlantic Council in Madrid, June 29, 2022," North Atlantic Treaty Organization, https://www.nato.int/cps/en/natohq/ official_texts_196951.htm.

49. Zachary Snowdon Smith, "Putin 'Calm and Cool' After Learning Finland Will Apply To Join NATO, Finnish President Says," *Forbes*, May 15, 2022, https://www.forbes.com/sites/zacharysmith/2022/05/15/putin-calm-and-cool-after-learning-finland-will-apply-to-join-nato-finnish-president-says/?sh=1bbbb3d26823; Elena Teslova, "Putin explains how Finland, Sweden membership in NATO different from Ukraine's. Russian president says Moscow views Scandinavian nations' accession to NATO differently, unlike Ukraine, since it has no territorial disputes," Anadolu Agency, June 3, 2022, https://www.aa.com.tr/en/russia-ukraine-war/putin-explains-how-finland-sweden-membership-in-nato-different-from-ukraines/2627019.

50. Simon Tisdall, "Behind Nato's defensive 'shield' lies weakness and division. Ukraine will pay the price," *Guardian*, June 12, 2022, https://www.theguardian.com/world/2022/jun/12/behind-natos-defensive-shield-lies-weakness-and-division-ukraine-will-pay-the-price; Jim Garamon, "Then and Now: The Changes Between 2 NATO Madrid Summits," U.S. Department of Defense, June 29, 2022, https://www.defense.gov/News/News-Stories/Article/Article/3078638/then-and-now-the-changes-between-2-nato-madrid-summits/.

13. The Pivot to Asia

1. Jack Lau, "Pelosi Taiwan visit: region 'tense' as Chinese navy watches US warships, holds drills in South China Sea," *South China Morning Post*, July 29, 2022, https://www.scmp.com/news/china/military/article/3187091/pelosi-taiwan-visit-region-tense-chinese-navy-watches-us; "China announces military exercise opposite Taiwan after warning Pelosi to scrap plans to visit," *CNBC*, July 30, 2022, https://www.cnbc.com/2022/07/30/china-announces-military-exercise-opposite-taiwan-after-warning-pelosi-to-scrap-plans-to-visit.html.

2. Zolan Kanno-Youngs and Peter Baker, "Biden Pledges to Defend Taiwan if It Faces a Chinese Attack," *New York Times*, May 23, 2022, https://www.nytimes.com/2022/05/23/world/asia/biden-taiwan-china.html; Aila Slisco, "No, China Didn't Threaten to Shoot Down Pelosi's Plane Over Taiwan Visit," *Newsweek*, July 29, 2022.

3. Daniel E. Slotnik and Matthew Cullen, "Your Friday Briefing: Biden and Xi's Fraught Phone Call," *New York Times*, July 28, 2022, https://www.nytimes.com/2022/07/28/briefing/biden-xi-china-us-gdp-australia.html.

4. David Molloy, "Taiwan: Nancy Pelosi trip labelled as 'extremely dangerous' by Beijing,' *BBC News*, August 2, 2022, https://www.bbc.com/news/world-asia-62398029; Paul Mozur, Amy Chang Chien, and Michael D. Shear, *New York Times*, August 2, 2022, https://www.nytimes.com/live/2022/08/02/world/pelosi-taiwan.

5. Seung Min Kim, "Nancy Pelosi's Proposed Taiwan Trip Is 'Not a Good Idea,' Says Joe Biden, Quoting U.S. Military Opinion," *Time*, July 21, 2022, https://time.com/6199197/nancy-pelosi-taiwan-biden-us-china/; Thomas L. Friedman, "Why Pelosi's Visit to Taiwan Is Utterly Reckless," *New York Times*, August 1, 2022.

6. Antony J. Blinken, "The Administration's Approach to the People's Republic of China," The George Washington University, Washington, DC, May 26, 2022, U.S. Department of State, https://www.state.gov/the-administrations-approach-to-the-peoples-republic-of-china/.

7. Blinken, "The Administration's Approach to the People's Republic of China."

8. "China criticizes US as tensions rise in South Pacific," AP News, May 27, 2022, https://apnews.com/article/russia-ukraine-biden-foreign-policy-antony-blinken-eed7c0b393ad18d4278291b8638f0e7d; "China rejects Blinken speech as 'smear,'" DW, May 27, 2022, https://www.dw.com/en/china-rejects-blinken-speech-as-smear/a-61955836.

9. Frederick Kempe, "A new world order is emerging—and the world is not ready for it," CNBC, April 3, 2022, https://www.cnbc.com/2022/04/03/a-new-world-order-is-emerging-and-the-world-is-not-ready-for-it.html; Christine Huang, Laura Silver, and Laura Clancy, "China's Partnership With Russia Seen as Serious Problem for the U.S.," Pew Research Center, April 28, 2022, https://www.pewresearch.org/global/2022/04/28/chinas-partnership-with-russia-seen-as-serious-problem-for-the-us/; Robert A. Manning, "Locking China Out of the Global Order Could Backfire," Foreign Policy, May 9, 2022, https://foreignpolicy.com/2022/05/09/china-global-order-decoupling-xi-beijing-reforms/.

10. Michael Nelson, "Barack Obama: Foreign Affairs," Miller Center, University of Virginia, https://millercenter.org/president/obama/foreign-affairs.

11. Graham Allison, Destined for War: Can America and China Escape Thucydides's Trap? (New York, 2018), 6–9.

12. Mark Landler, "Lost in Translation: A U.S. Gift to Russia," New York Times, March 6, 2009, https://www.nytimes.com/2009/03/07/world/europe/07diplo.html.

13. Simon Shuster, "U.S.-Russia Relations: In Need of a New Reset," Time, March 16, 2010, http://content.time.com/time/world/article/0,8599,1971651,00.html; Joseph R. Biden Jr., "Remarks by the Vice President at the Munich Security Conference," The White House, Office of the Vice President, February 7, 2015, https://obamawhitehouse.archives.gov/the-press-office/2015/02/07/remarks-vice-president-munich-security-conference.

14. Michael Crowley and Julia Ioffe, "Why Putin hates Hillary," Politico, July 25, 2016, https://www.politico.com/story/2016/07/clinton-putin-226153.

15. Crowley and Ioffe, "Why Putin hates Hillary"; Brian Ross, Rhonda Schwartz, and James Gordon Meek, "Officials: Master Spy Vladimir Putin Now Directly Linked to US Hacking," ABC News, December 15, 2016, https://abcnews.go.com/International/officials-master-spy-vladimir-putin-now-directly-linked/story?id=44210901; Alex Ward, "4 main takeaways from new reports on Russia's 2016 election interference," Vox, December 17, 2018, https://www.vox.com/world/2018/12/17/18144523/russia-senate-report-african-american-ira-clinton-instagram.

16. Charles Riley, "Trump's decision to kill TPP leaves door open for China," CNN Business, January 24, 2017, https://money.cnn.com/2017/01/23/news/economy/tpp-trump-china/; Bethany Allen-Ebrahimian, "Special report: Trump's U.S.-China transformation," Axios, January 19, 2021, https://www.axios.com/2021/01/19/trump-china-policy-special-report; Ben Westcott, "China looms as Biden's biggest foreign policy challenge. Here's where he stands," CNN, November 17, 2020, https://edition.cnn.com/2020/11/15/asia/biden-china-policy-trump-us-intl-hnk/index.html.

17. "Trump Hails 'Very, Very Good Relationship' In Talks With Vladimir Putin," NDTV, June 28, 2019, https://www.ndtv.com/world-news/donald-trump-hails

-very-very-good-relationship-in-talks-with-vladimir-putin–2060714; Mark Gollom, "How successive U.S. administrations resisted arming Ukraine," *CBC News*, March 2, 2022, https://www.cbc.ca/news/world/obama-trump-biden-ukraine-military-aid–\$26371378; Nicholas Fandos and Michael D. Shear, "Trump Impeached for Abuse of Power and Obstruction of Congress," *New York Times*, December 18, 2019, https://www.nytimes.com/2019/12/18/us/politics/trump-impeached.html.

18. James Dobbins, Howard J. Shatz, and Ali Wyne, "Russia Is a Rogue, Not a Peer; China Is a Peer, Not a Rogue. Different Challenges, Different Responses," RAND Corporation, October 2018, https://www.rand.org/pubs/perspectives/PE310.html; Paul Haenle and Sam Bresnick, "Why U.S.-China Relations Are Locked in a Stalemate," Carnegie Endowment for International Peace, February 21, 2022, https://carnegieendowment.org/2022/02/21/why-u.s.-china-relations-are-locked-in-stalemate-pub-86478; Brahma Chellaney, "America Is Focusing on the Wrong Enemy," *Project Syndicate*, February 14, 2022, https://www.project-syndicate.org/commentary/the-threat-to-us-global-leadership-is-china-not-russia-by-brahma-chellaney–2022-02?barrier=accesspaylog; Franco Ordonez, "The White House wants to focus on China, but Russia continues to be a distraction," NPR, December 21, 2021, https://www.npr.org/2021/12/21/1066181618/the-white-house-wants-to-focus-on-china-but-russia-continues-to-be-a-distraction.

19. Andrew Roth and Vincent Ni, "Xi and Putin urge Nato to rule out expansion as Ukraine tensions rise," *Guardian*, February 4, 2022, https://www.theguardian.com/world/2022/feb/04/xi-jinping-meets-vladimir-putin-china-russia-tensions-grow-west; Allison, *Destined for War*, 109–13.

20. Edward Wong and Julian E. Barnes, "China Asked Russia to Delay Ukraine War Until After Olympics, U.S. Officials Say," *New York Times*, March 2, 2022, https://www.nytimes.com/2022/03/02/us/politics/russia-ukraine-china.html; Chen Qingqing, "Chinese nationals' evacuation in Ukraine complete! All safe: embassy," *Global Times*, March 9, 2022, https://www.globaltimes.cn/page/202203/1254447.shtml.

21. "President Xi Jinping Speaks with Russian President Vladimir Putin on the Phone," Ministry of Foreign Affairs of the People's Republic of China, February 25, 2022, https://www.fmprc.gov.cn/eng/zxxx_662805/202202/t20220225_10645701.html.

22. Bobo Lo, "Friendship with Limits: Putin's War and the China-Russia Partnership," George W. Bush Institute, *The Catalyst* 23 (Spring 2022), https://www.bushcenter.org/catalyst/ukraine/lo-friendship-with-limits-china-russia.html.

23. Lo, "Friendship with Limits"; Jia Deng, "China treads a fine line on the Russia-Ukraine war," *East Asia Forum*, May 20, 2022, https://www.eastasiaforum.org/2022/05/20/china-treads-a-fine-line-on-the-russia-ukraine-war/; Evelyn C. Cheng, "China watches warily as Ukraine makes U.S., EU and Japan strengthen their alliance," *CNBC*, March 8, 2022, https://www.cnbc.com/2022/03/09/china-watches-as-ukraine-war-makes-us-eu-and-japan-show-unity.html.

24. John Feng, "China Refuses to Call Russia's War on Ukraine an 'Invasion,'" *Newsweek*, February 24, 2022, https://www.newsweek.com/china-refuses-call-russia-war-ukraine-invasion–1682140; Lo, "Friendship with Limits"; Reid Standish, "China's Messaging On The Ukraine War Is Evolving, But In Which Way?" *Radio*

Free Europe/Radio Liberty, May 3, 2022, https://www.rferl.org/a/china-ukraine-war-messaging-standish/31832716.html.

25. Wong and Barnes, "Russia Asked China for Military and Economic Aid for Ukraine War, U.S. Officials Say"; "China says it does not want to be impacted by Russia sanctions," *Aljazeera*, March 15, 2022, https://www.aljazeera.com/news/2022/3/15/china-does-not-want-to-be-impacted-by-russia-sanctions-fm; Allison, *Destined for War*, 110.

26. "Readout of President Joseph R. Biden Jr. Call with President Xi Jinping of the People's Republic of China," The White House, March 18, 2022, https://www.whitehouse.gov/briefing-room/statements-releases/2022/03/18/readout-of-president-joseph-r-biden-jr-call-with-president-xi-jinping-of-the-peoples-republic-of-china–2/; Cate Cadell and Ellen Nakashima, "Beijing chafes at Moscow's requests for support, Chinese officials say," *Washington Post*, June 2, 2022, https://www.washingtonpost.com/national-security/2022/06/02/china-support-russia-ukraine/.

27. "Putin Visits 'Friendly' Central Asia on First Trip During War," Bloomberg, June 28, 2022, https://www.bloomberg.com/news/articles/2022-06-28/putin-visits-friendly-central-asia-on-first-trip-during-war#xj4y7vzkg.

28. Marcel Plichta, "What Putin Can Do with His New, Deadly Gift From Iran," *Daily Beast*, July 22, 2022, https://www.thedailybeast.com/what-vladimir-putin-can-do-with-his-new-deadly-drones-from-iran.

29. Joyce Karam@Joyce_Karam Twitter, https://twitter.com/Joyce_Karam/status/1549487286966009858; Brendan Cole, "Video of Putin Being Kept Waiting by Erdogan Goes Viral: 'Sweet Payback,'" *Newsweek*, July 20, 2022, https://www.newsweek.com/putin-erdogan-waiting-video-tehran–1726241.

30. Cengiz Candar, "Erdogan's dance with Putin: Humiliating, but face-saving," *Al-Monitor*, March 6, 2022, https://www.al-monitor.com/originals/2020/03/turkey-russia-syria-idlib-deal-erdogan-accepts-regimes-gains.html; "Of course it's coincidence: Kremlin spokesman denies trolling Erdogan with bronzework of Russo-Turkish war," *RT*, March 6, 2020, https://www.rt.com/russia/482509-putin-erdogan-clock-trolling/.

31. "Of course it's coincidence"; "What is the significance of Putin making Erdoğan wait?" *Duvar English*, March 10, 2022, https://www.duvarenglish.com/diplomacy/2020/03/10/what-is-the-significance-of-putin-making-erdogan-wait; "Turkey's Baykar drone company 'will never' supply Russia: CEO," *Aljazeera*, July 19, 2022, https://www.aljazeera.com/news/2022/7/19/turkish-firm-wont-supply-uavs-widely-used-by-ukraine-to-russia; Joshua Keating, "How Turkey is turning the war in Ukraine to its own advantage," *Grid*, June 8, 2022, https://www.grid.news/story/global/2022/06/08/how-turkey-is-turning-the-war-in-ukraine-to-its-own-advantage/.

32. Isabel de Madariaga, *Ivan the Terrible: First Tsar of Russia* (New Haven, CT, 2005), 264–67; Brian Davies, *Warfare, State and Society on the Black Sea Steppe, 1500–1700* (London and New York, 2007), 158–70; Orlando Figes, *The Crimean War: A History* (New York, 2011).

33. "'Turkey to stand by Crimean Tatars to ensure their welfare,'" *Daily Sabah*, May 18, 2022, https://www.dailysabah.com/politics/diplomacy/turkey-to-stand-by-crimean-tatars-to-ensure-their-welfare; Alexander Gabuev, "Viewpoint: Russia

and Turkey—unlikely victors of Karabakh conflict," *BBC News*, November 12, 2020, https://www.bbc.com/news/world-europe–54903869.

34. Oliya Kusa, "Turkey's Goals in the Russia-Ukraine War," *Focus Ukraine*, The Wilson Center, June 13, 2022, https://www.wilsoncenter.org/blog-post/turkeys -goals-russia-ukraine-war.

35. Kusa, "Turkey's Goals in the Russia-Ukraine War."

36. Dorian Jones, Ukrainian, Russian Delegations Send Positive Messages After Istanbul Talks," *Voice of America*, March 29, 2022, https://www.voanews .com/a/ukrainian-russian-delegations-send-positive-messages-after-istanbul -talks/6506651.html.

37. Amberin Zamar, "Russia-Ukraine talks in Turkey yield respite but no ceasefire," *Al-Monitor*, March 29, 2022, https://www.al-monitor.com/originals/2022/03/ russia-ukraine-talks-turkey-yield-respite-no-ceasefire.

38. Firat Kozok and Selcan Hacaoglu, "Ukraine Cautious as Turkey, Russia Push Black Sea Grain Deal," Bloomberg, June 6, 2022, https://www.bloomberg.com/ news/articles/2022-06-06/ukraine-cautious-as-turkey-russia-push-black-sea -grain-deal?sref=C3P1bRLC#xj4y7vzkg; "Turkish inflation seen nearing 81% in July, falling to 70% by end–2022: Reuters poll," Reuters, July 29, 2022, https://www.reuters.com/world/middle-east/turkish-inflation-seen-nearing– 81-july-falling–70-by-end–2022-2022-07-29/; "Ukraine Says Russian Missiles Hit Odesa Port, Key To Grain Export Deal," *Radio Free Europe/Radio Liberty*, July 23, 2022, https://www.rferl.org/a/ukraine-odesa-russian-missiles -grain-export/31956567.html; Ievheniia Haber and Ol'ha Palii, "Shcho treba znaty dlia rozuminnia polityky Turechchyny pid chas viiny Ukraïny z rosiieiu," *Informator*, June 14, 2022, https://informator.ua/uk/shcho-treba-znati-dlya -rozuminnya-politiki-turechchini-pid-chas-viyni-ukrajini-z-rosiyeyu.

39. "U Chorne more razom iz dvoma turets'kymy fregatamy zaishov i pidvodnyi cho- ven," *Ukrinform*, July 28, 2022, https://www.ukrinform.ua/rubric-crimea/3538569 -u-corne-more-zajsli-dva-turecki-fregati-ta-pidvodnij-coven.html; Rhoda Kwan and Yuliya Talmazan, "1st grain shipment leaves Ukraine after months of Russian blockade," *NBC News*, August 1, 2022, https://www.nbcnews.com/news/world/1st -grain-shipment-leaves-ukraine-odesa-port-russian-blockade-rcna40581; Alexan- dra Prokopenko, "Russia's Return to Grain Deal is a Sign of Turkey's Growing Influence," Carnegie Endowment for International Peace, November 8, 2022, https://carnegieendowment.org/politika/88349.

40. "Medvedev: situatsiia vokrug Ukrainy uluchshat'sia ne budet, nuzhno priznavat' DNR i LNR," *TASS*, February 21, 2022, https://tass.ru/politika/13786995?utm_ source=google.com&utm_medium=organic&utm_campaign=google .com&utm_referrer=google.com.

41. "What are the sanctions on Russia and are they hurting its economy?" *BBC News*, June 27, 2022, https://www.bbc.com/news/world-europe–60125659; "EU sanctions against Russia explained," European Council, Council of European Union, https:// www.consilium.europa.eu/en/policies/sanctions/restrictive-measures-against -russia-over-ukraine/sanctions-against-russia-explained/; "EU's latest package of Russia sanctions will need to include oil embargo," *Reuters*, May 30, 2022, https:// www.reuters.com/business/energy/eus-latest-package-russia-sanctions-will-need -include-oil-embargo–2022-05-30/; Jack Guy, "Europe has bought $46 billion

worth of Russian energy since the Ukraine war began," *CNN Business*, April 28, 2022, https://edition.cnn.com/2022/04/28/business/eu-fossil-fuel-exports-russia-ukraine-energy-intl/index.html; David Wallace-Wells, "Considering Ukraine as a climate and energy war," *New York Times*, International edition, June 4–5, 2022.

42. Zeynep Beyza Kilic, "Natural gas prices hit record levels as Russia-Ukraine war rages," *Anadolu Agency*, March 3, 2022, https://www.aa.com.tr/en/energy/natural-gas/natural-gas-prices-hit-record-levels-as-russia-ukraine-war-rages/34766; Fareed Zakaria, "The only possible path to keep the pressure on Russia," *Washington Post*, April 21, 2022, https://www.washingtonpost.com/opinions/2022/04/21/russia-ukraine-oil-production-saudi-arabia-uae-gulf-states-security/.

43. "Russia's War on Ukraine: The Economic Impact of Sanctions," Congressional Research Service, May 3, 2022, https://crsreports.congress.gov/product/pdf/IF/IF12092#:~:text=Sanctions%20that%20isolate%20Russia%20are,slowdown%20in%20global%20economic%20growth; "Russia cuts off Finland gas flows over payment dispute," *Aljazeera*, May 21, 2022, https://www.aljazeera.com/news/2022/5/21/russia-cuts-off-finland-gas-flows-over-payment-dispute; Graeme Wearden, "Oil plunges to 10-month low as Saudi Arabia 'considers Opec+ production increase' – as it happened," *Guardian*, November 21, 2022, https://www.theguardian.com/business/live/2022/nov/21/cbi-uk-economy-growth-jeremy-hunt-ftse-oil-covid-business-live.

44. Alex Lawson, "Oil price rises after Joe Biden fails to secure Saudi output increase," *Guardian*, July 18, 2022, https://www.theguardian.com/business/2022/jul/18/oil-price-rises-joe-biden-saudi-output-petrol-diesel-prices.

45. "Over 1,000 Companies Have Curtailed Operations in Russia—But Some Remain," Chief Executive Leadership Institute, Yale University, July 31, 2022, https://som.yale.edu/story/2022/over-1000-companies-have-curtailed-operations-russia-some-remain; Joshua Askew, "Sanctions 'catastrophically crippling' Russian economy, study finds," *Euronews*, July 29, 2022, https://www.euronews.com/2022/07/28/sanctions-catastrophically-crippling-russian-economy-study-finds?utm_source=Facebook&utm_medium=Social&fbclid=IwAR2bjSn97eypqYuR3mpfBTKYz4aL2NguxqgbuY9QP-JFhZMgTsvNfn-k5t4.

46. "Russia's War on Ukraine: The Economic Impact of Sanctions"; "West's tech becomes a vulnerability for Russia," *New York Times*, International edition, June 4–5, 2022; Catherine Belton and Robyn Dixon, "Western sanctions catch up with Russia's wartime economy"; Agathe Demarais, "Sanctions on Russia Are Working. Here's Why," *Foreign Policy*, December 1, 2022, https://foreignpolicy.com/2022/12/01/ukraine-russia-sanctions-economy-war-putin-embargo-technology-financial-energy/.

47. Nikolaus J. Kurmayer, "Germany's Habeck: 'We have to try the unrealistic' to break free from Russian gas," *Euractiv*, April 28, 2022, https://www.euractiv.com/section/energy/news/germanys-habeck-we-have-to-try-the-unrealistic-to-break-free-from-russian-gas/; Anna Shirayevskaya, "For the First Time, US Is Sending More Gas to Europe Than Russia," Bloomberg, July 1, 2022, https://www.bloomberg.com/news/articles/2022-07-01/us-lng-supplies-to-europe-overtake-russian-gas-iea-says; Askew, "Sanctions 'catastrophically crippling' Russian economy."

48. "Putin nazval 'ėkonomicheskim samoubiistvom' politiku Evropy v ėnergeticheskoi

sfere," *Vedomosti*, May 17, 2022, https://www.vedomosti.ru/economics/news/2022/05/17/922394-putin-nazval-ekonomicheskim-samoubiistvom-politiku-evropi; Vladimir Soldatkin and Chen Aizhu, "Putin hails $117.5 bln of China deals as Russia squares off with West," Reuters, February 4, 2022, https://www.reuters.com/world/putin-tells-xi-new-deal-that-could-sell-more-russian-gas-china-2022-02-04/.

49. Ashley J. Tellis, "'What Is in Our Interest': India and the Ukraine War," Carnegie Endowment for International Peace, April 25, 2022, https://carnegieendowment.org/2022/04/25/what-is-in-our-interest-india-and-ukraine-war-pub-86961.

50. Anna Shirayevskaya, "Russian Gas Pivot Toward China Will Ease Europe's Energy Crunch," Bloomberg, July 29, 2022, https://www.bloomberg.com/news/articles/2022-07-29/russian-gas-pivot-toward-china-will-ease-europe-s-energy-crunch#xj4y7vzkg; Clifford Krauss, Alexandra Stevenson, and Emily Schmall, "In Russia's War, China and India Emerge as Financiers," *New York Times*, June 24, 2022, https://www.nytimes.com/2022/06/24/business/russia-oil-china-india-ukraine-war.html; Thomas Duesterberg, "Historic Shifts In Russian Energy Flows Bolstering China," *Forbes*, July 7, 2022, https://www.forbes.com/sites/thomasduesterberg/2022/07/07/historic-shifts-in-russian-energy-flows-bolstering-china/?sh=24165f9f2423; Xiao Zibang, "Russia Overtakes Saudi Arabia as China's Top Oil Supplier," Bloomberg, June 7, 2022, https://www.bloomberg.com/news/articles/2022-06-20/china-buys-7-5-billion-of-russian-energy-with-oil-at-record#xj4y7vzkg.

51. Muyu Xu and Chen Aizhu, "China refiners slow down Russian oil purchases as sanctions near trade," Reuters, November 14, 2022, https://www.reuters.com/business/energy/china-refiners-slow-down-russian-oil-purchases-sanctions-near-trade-2022-11-14/; "Value of Russia-China energy trade up 64%, deputy PM says," Reuters, November 18, 2022, https://www.reuters.com/business/energy/value-russia-china-energy-trade-up-64-deputy-pm-says-2022-11-18/; Sean Golden, "The US and China in the new global order," Barcelona Center for International Affairs, January 2020, https://www.cidob.org/en/publications/publication_series/opinion/seguridad_y_politica_mundial/the_us_and_china_in_the_new_global_order; Yvonne Lau, "Why China buying more Russian oil than ever doesn't mean that Putin has a blank check," *Fortune*, July 13, 2022, https://fortune.com/2022/07/13/china-buying-russian-oil-putin-xi-sanctions/.

52. Seth Cropsey, "SCO summit did not show what you think it showed," *Asia Times*, September 21, 2022, https://asiatimes.com/2022/09/sco-summit-did-not-show-what-you-think-it-showed/; Pavel K. Baev, "Eurasian Summit of Hidden Tensions and Thin Pretenses," *Eurasia Daily Monitor*, 19, no. 136 (September 19, 2022), https://jamestown.org/program/eurasian-summit-of-hidden-tensions-and-thin-pretenses/.

53. Michael Howle, "Rishi Sunak brands Russia a 'pariah state' ahead of G20 summit encounter with Putin's foreign minister," *Evening Standard*, November 14, 2022, https://www.standard.co.uk/news/politics/rishi-sunak-g20-bali-russia-ukraine-lavrov-pariah-state-putin-biden-b1039848.html; Emily Febg," 4 takeaways from President Biden's 'very blunt' meeting with China's Xi Jinping," NPR, November 14, 2022, https://www.npr.org/2022/11/14/1136459450/biden-xi-meeting.

54. Stuart Lau, "China's new vassal: Vladimir Putin," *Politico*, June 6, 2022, https://www.politico.eu/article/china-new-vassal-vladimir-putin/.

INDEX

Abkhazia, 89–90
Afghanistan
  Islamic Republic of
    Afghanistan, 52, 54
  Soviet invasion of xviii,
    111, 145, 290
  US war in, 81–82,
    272–73, 300
Africa, 29–30, 239, 263, 285
Akayev, Askar, 84
Aksakov, Konstantin, 102
Aksenov, Sergei, 111–13, 115
al-Assad, Bashar, 282
Albania, 31, 89
Algeria, 29
Al Qaeda, 81, 272
Amanpour, Christiane, 227
Angolan Civil War, 30
annexation
  in eastern Ukraine,
    238–40
  Putin's annexation play-
    book, 214–18
  Russia's annexation of
    the Crimea, 100–117,
    118–26, 242, 246, 257,
    275, 279, 283, 300
  during WWII, 25, 26, 82
Anschluss of Austria, xv,
    116–17
anti-aircraft systems
  Russian, 128, 225
  Stingers, 145, 163, 177,
    249–50
Anti-Ballistic Missile Treaty,
    82
anti-tank systems (Javelins),
    144–45, 161, 163,
    249–50, 276

"anti-terrorism," 55, 127
Antonivka Bridge, 204–5,
    207, 211, 217, 221–24,
    228
Arestovych, Oleksii, 226,
    228, 230
Armenia, 18, 25, 93, 284, 302
Ashton, Catherine, 96
Asia
  countries supporting
    sanctions against Rus-
    sia, 247
  financial crisis of 1997,
    50, 57
  US policy in, 273–75, 277
Astrakhan, 6
Austin, Lloyd, 251, 254
Austria, 10
  Anschluss of, xv, 116–17
  Serbia and, 14
  Ukrainians in Galicia,
    12–16
Austria-Hungary, 12–13, 14,
    16, 30, 137
autocracy, 10, 36–37, 56,
    83–84, 98–99, 244–45
Avakov, Arsen, 110
Axe, David, 223
Azarov, Mykola, 97
Azerbaijan, 18, 24, 93
Azov regiment, 127, 182–89
Azov, Sea of, 153, 190, 201,
    202, 209, 263

Baerbock, Annalena, 258
Bakanov, Ivan, 207–8
Baker, James, 75–76
Bakhmut, 230
Balakliia, 231, 233–34

Balkan peninsula, 14, 30,
    31, 284
Baltic states, 6, 8
  Bolshevik revolution in
    the, 15
  fall of the Soviet Union
    and, 24–26
  NATO and, 82–83, 143,
    255–56
  in the 1990s, 31
  "Popular Fronts" of the,
    25, 37
  Russia's invasion of Geor-
    gia, 90
  during the Russo-Ukrai-
    nian War, 253, 255–56
Bandera, Stepan, 20
Banderites, 20, 162
Baraniuk, Volodymyr, 184,
    185
Battalion Tactical Groups
    (BTGs), 189
Baykar company, 283
Bayraktar TB2 drones,
    282–83, 284
Belarus
  as the Belarusian Soviet
    Socialist Republic,
    17–18
  border with Ukraine, 153,
    178–79
  Chernobyl and, 159, 161,
    171
  dissidents in, 152
  fall of the Soviet Union
    and, 3, 26–27, 48
  NATO and, 86
  as a non-nuclear state,
    71, 72

Belarus (*continued*)
  Russian Federation and,
    91–92
  Russian troops posi-
    tioned in, 224, 301
  Slavic identity and
    nationalism, 4–12, 15,
    17, 102–5, 119, 294
  during WWII, 19, 261
Belavezha agreements
  (1991), 3, 27, 48
Belgium, 30, 31
Berdiaev, Nikolai, 194
Berdiansk, 183, 209, 217
Berezovets, Taras, 231
Berezovsky, Boris, 83
Bernes, Mark, 193–94
Beryslav, 220, 221, 223, 231,
  234, 236
Beseda, Sergei, 166
Beslan school attack (2004),
  84
Bessarabia. *See* Moldova
Biden, Hunter, 276
Biden, Jill, 265
Biden, Joe
  assurances to Zelensky,
    142, 157
  China and, 269–71, 276,
    280, 292
  energy security and, 288
  meeting with Putin in
    Geneva (2021), 142–43
  military aid to Ukraine,
    249–52
  Nord Stream II, 257–58
  remarks in Warsaw,
    244–46, 252
  on Russian war crimes as
    genocidal, 171–72
  sanctions on Russia,
    246–47
  Ukraine's NATO mem-
    bership and, 142–46
  as vice president, 273–74
Biletsky, Andrii, 183
Bilohorivka village, 190
Black Sea, 199–218. *See also*
  Black Sea Fleet *under*
  Russian military
Blahodatne village, 229
Blinken, Antony, 146, 251,
  254, 271–72
Bogoiavlensky, Vladimir,
  Metropolitan of Kyiv,
  16
Boichenko, Vadym, 185
Bolshevik revolution, 15–17

national identities and
  the, 17–18, 102, 105,
  123, 137
in parts of Ukraine, 125
Putin on the, 137, 151
See also Soviet Union
Borodai, Aleksandr, 125,
  128, 131
Bosnia, 31
Brexit, 255, 256
Brezhnev, Leonid, 22, 23–24
Britain. *See* United King-
  dom
Brussels Summit (2022),
  243
Brzezinski, Zbigniew, 4
Bucha, 168–74, 194, 235,
  250, 254, 260, 265,
  285
Bucharest Summit (2008),
  86–91, 141, 260
Budapest memorandum
  (1994), 70–74, 98, 114,
  120, 147–48
Buk TELAR surface-to-air
  missile launcher, 128
Bulgaria, 14, 284, 287
Bullough, Oliver, 254
Bunin, Ivan, 194
Burbulis, Gennadii, 27
Burns, William, 143, 146,
  160
Bush, George H. W., 27, 32,
  71, 76, 82, 273
Bush, George W., 81–84, 88,
  272–74
Bychok, Vitalii, 233
Byzantine Empire, 6, 8

Canada, 29
Catherine the Great (Cath-
  erine II), 9, 122–23
Catholicism, 6, 8
Caucasus, 24, 26, 284
Central Asia, 3, 24, 26–27,
  31, 82, 91, 291, 303
Central Intelligence Agency
  (CIA), 143, 146, 160
Chamberlain, Neville, 146
Charap, Samuel, 276–77
Charles XII of Sweden, 8
"Charter on Distinctive
  Partnership," 78
Chechnya
  Beslan hostage crisis, 84
  under Gorbachev, 32
  Putin's early experience
    in, 52–55

refugee crisis, 54
Russian Federation's
  wars in, xviii, 41,
  51–56, 101
  during the Russo-Ukrai-
    nian War, 160, 183,
    238, 239
  US intelligence sharing
    on, 82
  under Yeltsin, 32, 51–56
Cherniaev, Anatolii, 3, 28
Chernihiv, 161, 171, 172,
  194–96
Chernobyl, xvii–xviii, 64,
  158–59, 161, 167, 171,
  201, 299
China
  Beijing Olympics, 277–78
  communism in, 300
  GDP of, 273, 288, 289
  NATO and, 79, 114, 277,
    278, 302
  Putin and, 92, 93, 271,
    277–80, 302–3
  Russo-Chinese relations
    and, 272, 292, 302–3
  during the Russo-
    Ukrainian War, 227,
    277–80, 290–92, 301–2
  Sino-Soviet split, 272
  Taiwan and, 269–71
  Ukraine in the 1990s, 72
  US-China relations and,
    269–77, 300, 302–3
Chornobaivka village, 205,
  212
Chornovil, Viacheslav, 57
Christian Democratic
  Union (Germany), 261
Christianity. *See* Orthodox
  Church of Ukraine
  (OCU); Russian
  Orthodox Church
Christopher, Warren, 76
Chubais, Anatolii, 49
Churchill, Winston, xviii,
  225, 244, 245, 255
Church of St. Catherine,
  196
Church of St. Elijah, 195
Churkin, Vitalii, 115
Chychenina, Lena, 168–69,
  170
Clinton, Bill, 39, 71–79
Clinton, Hillary, 274–75
Cold War
  continuity with the, 244,
    245, 295, 302–4

end of the, xx, 41–42, 76, 83
NATO and the, 76
primacy of the US and, 273
Russo-Chinese relations during the, 272, 292, 302–3
US-China relations during the, 270–71, 272, 303
Collective Security Treaty Organization (CSTO), 302
Commonwealth of Independent States (CIS), 3, 27–28, 41, 65, 66, 91
communism
in China, 300
in Russia, 1, 18, 40, 43, 48–50, 56, 69–70, 84, 101
in Ukraine, 19, 26, 46–47, 57–58, 132–33
Congress of Berlin (1878), 14
Congress of People's Deputies, 37, 38
Constantinople, Patriarch of, 134, 149, 196, 197
Convention on Cluster Munitions (2008), 179
Cooper, Laura, 249
Cossacks, 6–9, 11, 22, 68, 178, 195, 232, 283
COVID-19, 136, 148, 169, 254, 276, 279
Crimea, 65–70
annexation of, 100–117, 118–26, 242, 246, 257, 275, 279, 283, 300
elections, 112, 116, 130–31
referendum on Crimean independence, 68–70, 112, 116, 118, 120, 121, 125, 189, 218, 224
sovereignty as pretext for invasion, 67–68, 108, 118–19
during WWII, 121
Crimean Khanate, 7
Crimean Tatars, 9, 22, 66–67, 112, 128, 283–84
Croatia, 31, 89
Cuba, 145
culture. See nationalism; Slavic identity
"Cyborgs," 130, 211

Czechoslovakia, xvii, 20, 75–76, 78–79, 85, 173, 253
Czech Republic, 74, 75–76, 116, 145, 290

Dagestan, 52–54, 239
Danilov, Oleksii, 147, 156, 164, 228
Debaltseve, 130
de Hoop Scheffer, Jaap, 87
democracy, xviii
in Eastern Europe, 83–86
in the Balkans, 80
"managed" or "sovereign," 48, 275
in the Russian Empire, 5
in the Russian Federation, 35–36, 36–40, 48–53, 56, 83–84, 87, 92
in Taiwan, 270–72
in Ukraine, 36, 41–48, 56–62, 70, 83, 87, 94, 138
in US foreign policy, 82–83, 244, 270–72, 275
See also elections/referendums
Democratic Party (US), 270, 275
"denazification," 152–54, 162–63, 166–67, 183, 187–88, 244
Denikin, Anton, 103, 151
Denmark, 6, 256
Diachenko, Tatiana, 49
Di Maio, Luigi, 264
Dnieper (Dnipro) River, 2
during the Russian Empire, 7
during the Russo-Ukrainian War, 201–5, 217, 220, 221–24, 226, 228–29, 234, 236, 240–42
in Ukrainian and Russian culture, 2, 197
Dnipropetrovsk (Dnipro), 22, 26, 123, 126, 182
Donbas region (Donets Basin)
during the Bolshevik Revolution, 16
at the end of the Cold War, 28

industry in, 16, 45
Russian interests in the, 66–67, 95, 104
during Russia's annexation of the Crimea, 123–31, 132, 138, 140–41
during the Russo-Ukrainian War, xix, 150–52, 156–58, 176–78, 183, 188–92, 216–18
Ukrainian counteroffensive in the, 228, 230–31, 235, 246
vote for Ukrainian independence in the, 2
the Western coalition and the, 246–47, 256–57, 264, 275, 300
during WWII, 26
See also Donetsk; Luhansk
Donetsk
Minsk I and Minsk II agreements, xix, 126–31, 132, 139–40, 150, 247, 256–57, 261, 278, 286
in "New Russia," 122–27
during Russia's annexation of the Crimea, 127, 130, 131
during the Russo-Ukrainian War, 157, 176, 189–91, 197, 211, 216, 218
Ukrainian counteroffensive in, 221, 224, 229–31, 238, 240
vote for Ukrainian independence, 67
Yanukovych and, 60, 108
Donetsk People's Republic, 123, 125, 127, 150, 151–52, 157, 197, 229
Dormition Cathedral, 195
Draghi, Mario, 264, 265, 266
drone warfare, 213, 225, 226, 281, 282–83
Duda, Andrzej, 157, 265
Dudaev, Dzhokhar, 53–54
Dugin, Aleksandr, 102, 125
Dunaevsky, Isaak, 194
Dutch empire, 29, 298
Dzhankoi, 225

Eastern Europe
  fall of the Soviet Union
    and, 25, 41, 83
  missile defense systems
    in, 274
  NATO and, 75–80, 82–83,
    89, 250, 252–53,
    255–56, 258
  refugees in "Fortress
    Europe," 174–75
  in Russia's sphere of
    influence, 300
elections/referendums
  election of Kuchma,
    45–46, 57, 60, 70
  election of Poroshenko,
    126–27, 132
  election of Putin as presi-
    dent, 51–53, 55–56,
    92–93
  election of Trump, 275
  election of Yanukovych,
    60–61, 90, 94, 97, 107
  election of Yeltsin, 37, 46,
    48–51
  election of Zelensky,
    138–40
  referendum on Crimean
    independence, 68–70,
    112, 116, 118, 120, 121,
    125, 189, 218, 224
  referendum on presiden-
    tial power in Ukraine,
    42, 45, 58, 61
  referendum on the Rus-
    sian constitution, 35,
    37–38, 42
  referendum on the
    Ukrainian constitu-
    tion, 46–47
  referendum on Ukrai-
    nian independence,
    3–4, 45
  Russian parliamentary
    elections, 38–40,
    48–49, 69, 84, 274–75
  Ukrainian parliamentary
    elections, 46, 57
  See also Orange Revolu-
    tion
energy security
  China and, 290–91
  France and, 86
  "gas wars," 86
  Gazprom, 290
  Germany and, 247,
    257–58, 261, 287, 289,
    291

Nord Stream II, 247,
    257–58
OPEC, 288
Russian oil and gas, 41,
    69, 71, 74, 86, 248,
    284, 287–91
  sanctions and, 286–89
  Soviet oil and gas, 22–23,
    26–27
  of Ukraine, 41, 69, 71, 74,
    86, 94–95, 260
  See also nuclear power
Enerhodar, 206, 226
England. See United King-
    dom
Erdogan, Recep Tayyip, 186,
    281–86
Estonia, 25, 53, 252, 253, 258
Euromaidan protests, 61,
    95–99, 106–11, 115,
    121, 124, 127, 132, 134
European Parliament, 266
European Union (EU),
    83–85
  Baltic states and the,
    252–53
  China and the, 291, 302
  former East European
    satellites in the, 253
  France and the, 262–63,
    266
  during the "gas wars," 86
  Germany and the, 260
  Malaysian Airlines Flight
    MH 17, 128
  refugees and, 173
  Russia and the, 92–93,
    131, 248, 287–89, 291
  during the Russo-Ukrai-
    nian War, 243, 246–48
  Turkey and the, 281, 285
  Ukraine and the, 84–85,
    92–96, 98, 106, 111,
    121, 124, 131, 134,
    164–65, 266, 267
  United Kingdom and the,
    253, 255–56
  Vilnius Summit (2013),
    95

Facebook, 151, 159, 180, 248
Federal Security Service
    (FSB) of Russia, 54–55,
    131, 163, 166
Fedorov, Ivan, 208
Fedoruk, Anatolii, 168,
    170, 171
Filatiev, Pavel, 205–6

Filenko, Volodymyr, 64
Finland, 15, 184, 255–56,
    266–68, 284, 287, 301
Finno-Ugric peoples, 215
"Fortress Europe," 174
France
  energy politics of, 86
  the EU and, 262–63, 266
  imperial history of, 29,
    239
  NATO and, 89, 262
  Russia's annexation of
    the Crimea, 114, 130,
    139, 140
  Russia's invasion of Geor-
    gia, 90
  during the Russo-Ukrai-
    nian War, 186, 252,
    253, 256, 262–65,
    301
  during WWII, 29
Francis (pope), 186
Freedman, Lawrence, 216
Friendship Treaty (1997),
    74, 120
Fukuyama, Francis, xviii

G-20 Bali Conference,
    291–92
G7 and G8 group, 79, 264
Gaidar, Yegor, 28, 37, 40
Galicia, 4, 12–14
Gazprom, 290
Gellner, Ernest, 101, 103
genocide, 30, 31, 79, 151,
    171–72, 216
Georgia, 18, 84, 88–90,
    93, 104, 108–9, 114,
    273–74, 284, 300
Gerasimov, Valerii, 237
Germany
  Christian Democratic
    Union of, 261
  at the end of the Cold
    War, 75
  energy politics of, 247,
    257–58, 287, 289, 291
  the EU and, 260
  "Greater Germany," 116
  nationalism and, 10,
    14–15, 21
  NATO and, 75–76, 87,
    89, 257–60
  Nazi Germany, 19–21, 25,
    29, 121, 145–46, 193,
    209, 223
  Putin and, 257–60
  Russian Empire and, 12

Russia's annexation of the Crimea and, 115, 116–17, 130
during the Russo-Ukrainian War, 139–40, 173, 252, 253, 256–62, 263–64
Social Democratic Party of, 257
US military bases in, 149, 251
during WWI, 14–16
Zelensky and, 139, 258, 260–61
Girkin, Igor "Strelkov," 125, 127–28, 131, 236, 238–39
Glazev, Sergei, 112
global financial crisis of 1997, 50, 57, 79
Gogol, Nikolai, 221
Gongadze, Heorhii, 58–59
Gorbachev, Mikhail, 1–4, 24–27, 28, 31–33, 35–36, 43, 53, 66, 75–76, 244
Gorodilov, Artyom, 172
Grachev, Pavel, 39
Grand Duchy of Lithuania, 6, 7
Grandi, Filippo, 175
"Greater Germany," 116
"Greater Russia," 105, 111, 116–17, 120, 136, 216
"Greater Serbia," 30, 101
Great Patriotic War, 152. See also World War II
Greece, 14
gross domestic product (GDP)
of China, 273, 288, 289
military assistance as share of, 252, 258
of Russia, 37, 44, 288–89
of Ukraine, 73, 182
Grossi, Mario, 206–7, 226–27
Grossi, Rafael Mariano, 206, 226–27
Grozev, Christo, 150
Grozny, 53–55
Guterres, Antonio, 186

Habsburg monarchy, 9–13
Haines, Avril, 163
Harris, Kamala, 246
Havel, Vaclav, 75
Helsinki Accords, 24, 259

Helsinki Group, 24
Herashchenko, Anton, 159
Herder, Johann Gottfried von, 10, 11
Herzegovina, 14
High Mobility Rocket Systems (HIMARS), 192, 217, 222, 229, 240, 281
Hirske village, 190
Hitler, Adolf, 245
Anschluss of Austria, xv, 116–17
attack on the Soviet Union, 19, 245
invasion of Czechoslovakia, xvii, 145
Ukrainian nationalism and, 142
WWII as "Hitler's war," 259, 261
See also Nazism; World War II
Hollande, François, 130
Holocaust, 20–21, 75, 245
Holodomor, 19, 21
Holy Savior Cathedral, 195, 196
Hostomel, 146, 159–61, 162, 165, 167–68, 170
Hrushevsky, Mykhailo, 13, 16
Hrybov, Roman, 200–201
Hua Chunying, 292
Hul, Vitalii, 223
Hungary, 75–76, 78, 79, 85, 86, 121, 173, 174, 253, 290
Hussein, Saddam, 272–73

Iceland, 256
Ilovaisk, 129–31
Ilyin, Ivan, 103, 104, 239
imperialism, 5–6, 29–30.
See also Russian Empire; other imperial powers
India, 29, 239, 290, 303
Indochina, 29
Indonesia, 30, 273, 292
International Atomic Energy Agency (IAEA), xvi, 159, 206, 226–27, 231
International Monetary Fund (IMF), 57
Iran, 82, 274, 281, 282, 288, 302

Iraq, xviii, 82, 87, 162, 272–73, 290, 300
Irpin, 169, 265
Islam, 27, 54, 79, 81–82, 283, 286, 300
Islamic Republic of Afghanistan, 52, 54
Islamic State of Iraq and the Levant, 300
Israel, 186, 251, 283
Italy, 86, 252, 253, 264, 302
Ivan III, 5–6
Ivan I of Moscow, 5
Ivanivka (Skovorodynivka) village, 195
Ivan the Terrible (Ivan IV), 6
Ivashov, Leonid, 149
Izium, 190, 234–36, 237–38

Japan, 29, 251, 273
Javelin anti-tank systems, 144–45, 161, 163, 249–50, 276
Jewish people, 7, 20, 139, 167, 194, 245
John Paul II (pope), 244
Johnson, Boris, 157, 254–56, 260, 265

KA52 attack helicopters, 160
Kadyrov, Ramzan, 160, 183, 238
Kakhovka Dam, 201, 202, 205, 221, 222. See also Nova Kakhovka
Kakhovka Operational Group, 229
Kallas, Kaja, 253
Karam, Joyce, 281
Kasatonov, Igor, 67
Katkov, Mikhail, 12
Kazakhstan, 24, 26, 66, 71, 72, 91–92, 103, 291, 302
Kazan, 6
Kennan, George, xvii, 28–29
Kerch, 112
Kerch Strait, 224–26, 240
KGB, 51, 110
Khamenei, Ayatollah Ali, 281
Kharkiv, 177–82
as alternative capital, 108
Russian claims to, 122–23

Kharkiv (*continued*)
during the Russo-
Ukrainian War, 123,
153, 174–82, 193–95,
231–32, 235, 236–37,
291
Khasbulatov, Ruslan, 34, 35,
39, 49
Khashoggi, Jamal, 288
Kherson
liberation of, 236–42
Russian attack and Ukrai-
nian counteroffensive
in, 153, 202, 205–12,
217–18, 220, 221–22,
228, 230–31, 234
Russian claims to, 104,
122
Khlebnikov, Velimir, 194
Khmelnytsky, Bohdan, 7, 68
Khomiakov, Aleksei, 102
Khrushchev, Nikita, 21–23,
135–36
Kim, Vitalii, 211, 212
Kirby, John, 166, 218
Kirienko, Sergei, 218
Kirievsky, Ivan, 102
Kisel, Sergei, 182
Kizilova, Svetlana, 169
Kliuchevsky, Vasilii, 6–7
Kliuiev, Andrii, 110
Klychko, Vitalii, 258
Kodema village, 230
Kolbin, Gennadii, 24
Kolomoisky, Ihor, 126
Kolykhaev, Igor, 209
Konstantinov, Vladimir,
112, 113
Korzhakov, Aleksandr, 49
Kosovo, 31, 79, 80, 119
Kostenko, Lina, 24
Kostomarov, Mykola, 11
Kovaliov, Oleksii, 223
Kozak, Dmitrii, 147, 156
Kozatsky, Dmytro, 187–88
Krasniashchikh, Andrei,
193–94
Krasylnykov, Dmytro,
157–58, 161
Kravchenko, Yurii, 59
Kravchuk, Leonid, 3, 42–43,
45–46, 68, 69, 71,
74, 78
Kroenig, Matthew, 292
Kronau (Vysokopillia), 230
Kryvoruchko, Serhii, 207
Kryvyi Rih, 125, 220, 228

Kuchma, Leonid, 45–47,
56–62, 70, 72–74, 79,
84, 91, 106
Kuleba, Dmytro, 146, 243,
256, 261, 263, 280
Kulinich, Oleh, 208
Kulman, Tamara, 174
Kunaev, Dinmukhamed, 24
Kupiansk, 234–35, 236, 237
Kyiv, 4–11
Bolshevik Revolution
in, 16
legendary founders of,
151
Maidan protests, 61,
95–99, 106–11, 115,
121, 124, 127, 132, 134
monuments in, 193–95
official visits of Western
allies to, 251, 254,
256, 258, 260, 262,
265–66
protests in, 45, 59
Putin's 2013 visit to, 149
during Russo-Ukrainian
War, 146, 153–54, 157–
72, 176, 189, 193–98,
216, 220, 240, 250
Soviet Union and, 22
Kyivan Chronicle, 195, 198
Kyivan Rus, 4–11, 136–37,
195, 196
Kyrgyzstan, 82, 84, 302

Landsbergis, Vytautas, 26
Latvia, 216, 252
Lavrov, Sergei, 150, 189, 221,
247, 264, 274
Lebed, Aleksandr, 50, 54
Lebedev, Yevgenii, 255
Lend-Lease, 250–51
Lenin, Vladimir, 15–16,
17–18, 103, 104, 132,
137, 151
Lepiavko, Serhii, 196
Levchenko, Ihor, 233
Liberal Democratic Party
(Russia), 40, 121
Liga group, 239
liquefied natural gas (LNG),
289, 291
Lisbon Protocol (1992),
71–72
Lithuania, 6–10, 25–26
Little Russian Collegium, 9
Liubomirsky, Vitalii, 185
Livonian War (1558–83), 6, 7

Luhansk
Minsk I and Minsk
II agreements, xix,
126–31, 132, 139–40,
150, 247, 256–57, 261,
278, 286
Russian occupation of,
122–25, 130–31
during the Russo-Ukrai-
nian War, 157, 176,
189–91, 197, 216, 218,
221, 233, 238
Ukrainian independence
vote in, 67
Luhansk People's Republic,
125, 150, 157, 191
Lukashenka, Aliaksandr,
301
Lukin, Vladimir, 67–68,
97–98
Luzhkov, Yurii, 55–56
Lviv, 13, 20, 243
Lyman, 236, 240
Lysychansk, 190–91, 236

Macedonia, 31, 80
Macron, Emmanuel, 139,
262–64, 265–66, 285
Madrid Summit (1997), 78,
266–68
Maidan protests, 61, 95–99,
106–11, 115, 121, 124,
127, 132, 134
Malaysian Airlines Flight
MH 17, 128
Malorussia. *See* Ukraine
Marchenko, Dmytro, 211,
223
Mariupol, 127, 174, 182–87,
188–90, 237, 242
Markov, Sergei, 148, 149,
154, 158
Marxism, 80
Mashkadov, Aslan, 54, 55
Massandra Accords (1993),
69
Matlock, Jack F., 28
Mazepa, Ivan, 8
McCain, John, 87
Mearsheimer, John, 71–72
Medvedchuk, Viktor, 132,
141, 188
Medvedev, Dmitrii, 92,
224–26, 274, 286
Melitopol, 104, 204,
208–9, 210, 217, 221,
222, 223

Melnychenko, Mykola, 59, 84, 91
Melnyk, Andrii, 20
Merkel, Merkel, 130, 139–40, 256–58, 260, 261
Meshkov, Yurii, 69
Mexico, 290
Mezhyhiria, 98
military materiel
  anti-aircraft systems, 128, 145, 163, 177, 225, 249–50
  anti-tank systems (Javelins), 144–45, 161, 163, 249–50, 276
  drone warfare, 213, 225, 226, 281, 282–83
  High Mobility Rocket Systems (HIMARS), 192, 217, 222, 229, 240, 281
  KA52 attack helicopters, 160
  MI8 transport helicopters, 160, 185
  military assistance as share of GDP, 252, 258
  Neptune anti-ship missiles, 213
  Skif and Stuhna anti-tank guided missiles, 163
  Strela (Arrow) anti-aircraft missile complex, 214
  T-80 tanks, 34
  See also nuclear weapons
Miller, Alexey, 103
Milley, Mark A., 143, 192, 251
Minsk I and Minsk II agreements, xix, 126–31, 132, 139–40, 150, 247, 256–57, 261, 278, 286
missile defense systems, 82, 274, 277
Mitiaev, Oleg, 184
Mitterrand, François, 262
Mizintsev, Mikhail, 183–84
Mogilev, Anatolii, 111
Moldova, 15, 26, 69, 70, 93, 122, 125, 173, 174, 220, 266
Molotov-Ribbentrop Pact (1939), 19, 25, 26, 121
Mongols, 4–7, 11, 137
Montenegro, 14, 31, 79

Montreux Convention (1936), 284
Moore, Richard, 191–92
Morocco, 251
Moroz, Oleksandr, 58–59
Moshchun village, 161
Moskva cruiser, 67, 200, 213–14
Moskva River, 34, 39
Motyzhyn village, 167
Munich Conference (1938), 146
Munich Security Conference (2022), 147–48, 246
Munich Security Forum (2007), 86–87
Muraviev, Mikhail, 16
Musiienko, Svitlana, 167, 169
Muzyka, Konrad, 236
Mykhailivka village, 224
Mykolaiv, 122, 153, 204, 205, 211–13, 217, 220, 221, 228–30
Mylove, 156

Nagorno-Karabakh, 24, 284
Nalyvaichenko, Valentyn, 110, 113, 115
Naryshkin, Sergei, 102, 114, 150, 151
"Nashi" ("Ours") youth group, 84
nationalism
  in Crimea, 67–70, 106, 109, 120, 121, 123–25, 131
  defining the "nation," 101, 103
  "New Russia," 104, 120–26, 131–32, 210, 239
  in the Ottoman Empire, 13–14
  Polish, 10
  populist, xii
  in Russia, 25–26, 37, 40, 50, 119–20, 152, 163
  in the Russian Empire, 9–13
  Serbian, 79–80
  Solzhenitsyn and, 21, 66, 100–105, 123, 136, 151
  Ukrainian, 10–13, 20–21, 26, 41–42, 47, 109, 183
  during WWII, 19

National Security and Defense Council, 126, 141, 156
NATO-Russia Council, 82
"NATO-Russia Founding Act," 78–79
Naumov, Andrii, 207–8
Nazarbaev, Nursultan, 24
Nazism
  "de-Nazification" as Russian pretext, 152, 154, 162–63, 166–67, 183, 187–88, 244
  Nazi Germany, 19–21, 25, 29, 121, 145–46, 193, 209, 223
  neo-Nazis in Russia, 125
Neptune anti-ship missiles, 213
Netherlands, 29–30, 148, 220, 256, 258, 293
"New Russia," 104, 120–26, 131–32, 210, 239
New Zealand, 29
Nicholas I, 10
Nigeria, 290
9/11 attack, 81–82, 272–73
Nikopol, 226
Nizhnii Novgorod, 4–5, 215
Nizhyn, 194
non-governmental organization (NGOs), 84, 96
Nord Stream II, 247, 257–58
North Atlantic Treaty Organization (NATO)
  and the Baltic states, 82–83, 143, 255–56
  Brussels Summit (2022), 243
  Bucharest Summit (2008), 86–91, 141, 260
  China and, 79, 114, 277, 278, 302
  Eastern European countries in, 75–80, 82–83, 89, 250, 252–53, 255–56, 258
  expansion in the 1990s, 75–80
  Expeditionary Force, 256
  Finland and Sweden in, 255–56, 266–67, 287, 301
  in the former Yugoslavia, 30, 79–80, 118–19
  France and, 262

North Atlantic Treaty
Organization (NATO)
(*continued*)
Georgia and, 88–90, 224,
273–74
Germany and, 75–76, 87,
89, 257–60
Kuchma on Ukraine
in, 59
Madrid Summit (1997),
78, 266–68
Membership Action Plan
(MAP), 85–87, 89, 114,
122, 141
military assistance as
share of GDP, 252, 258
NATO-Russia Council,
82
"NATO-Russia Founding
Act," 78–79
9/11 and, 81–82
Partnership for Peace
Program, 78
polls in Ukraine on
membership in,
164–65
postponing Ukraine's
membership, 89
Russian objections to
expansion, 76–77,
86–88, 143–47, 152
Russian partnership
with, 78–79, 82, 85
during Russia's annexa-
tion of the Crimea,
114–15, 118–19
and Russia's invasion of
Ukraine, 143–47, 152
support for Ukraine's
membership in, 85–86
Turchynov on Ukraine
in, 113–14
Turkey and, 284, 285
Ukraine after the Revolu-
tion of Dignity, 134
Ukrainian military and,
158, 232
Ukraine's Friendship
Treaty with Russia
and, 74
Western arms to
Ukraine, 191
Yanukovych on Ukraine
in, 93
Yushchenko on Ukraine
in, 59, 90
Zelensky on Ukraine in,
139–42, 156

North Crimean Canal,
202–4
Northern War (1721), 8, 215
Norway, 256
Novak, Kateryna, 180–82,
186
Novgorodian republic
(Great Novgorod),
4–5, 215
Novinsky, Vadim, 156
Novorossiia. *See* "New
Russia"
Novorossiysk, 67, 122
Novoukrainsk, 221
Nuclear Nonproliferation
Treaty (NPT), 71, 72
nuclear power, xvii–xviii,
211, 221
Chernobyl, 64, 158–59,
161, 167, 171, 201, 299
International Atomic
Energy Agency
(IAEA), xvi, 159, 206,
226–27, 231
Zaporizhia nuclear power
plants, 206, 226–27,
231, 299
nuclear weapons, xviii, xx,
63–65, 71–73, 74
Anti-Ballistic Missile
Treaty, 82
Budapest Memorandum
of 1994, 70–74, 98,
114, 120, 147–48
NATO and, 76–78, 90,
114–15, 143
Nuclear Nonproliferation
Treaty (NPT), 71, 72
START-1 and START-2
treaties, 71, 73, 82,
274
threat of use by Russia,
226, 292
Nuland, Victoria, 96

Obama, Barack, 90, 107,
273–77
O'Brien, Phillips, 231
Obukhovychi village, 167
Odesa, 104, 122, 123–25
during the Russo-Ukrai-
nian War, 153, 201,
204, 210–14, 220, 266
as strategic port, 263,
282–86
Olenivka, 188
Olympic Games, 110–11,
276, 277–78

Onuphry, Metropolitan of
Kyiv, 196–97
Operation "Successor," 51
Orange Revolution, 36,
56–62, 83–85, 91
Orban, Viktor, 253
Organization for Security
and Cooperation in
Europe (OSCE), 129,
145
Organization of the Petro-
leum Exporting Coun-
tries (OPEC), 288
Organization of Ukrainian
Nationalists (OUN),
20–21
Orlov, Dmytro, 206
Orthodox Church of
Ukraine (OCU),
133–34, 196–97
Oskil River, 234–36
Ottoman Empire, 13–14,
30–31, 80, 282, 282,
298

Pakistan, 290
Palchenko, Yevhen, 204–5
Pan-Russianism, 104, 111,
136, 149
Pan-Slavism, 14, 80
Partnership for Peace, 78
Pavlovsky, Gleb, 83
Pelosi, Nancy, 269–70
People's Democratic Party
(Ukraine), 57
Pereiaslav, 8, 193
Pereiaslav Agreement
(1654), 22, 68
Peskov, Dmitrii, 136, 217
Peter the Great (Peter I),
214–15
Philippines, 269
Pivdennoukrainsk, 211
Podoliak, Mykhailo, 216
Poland, 6–15
during the Bolshevik
Revolution, 15
economy of, 252
nationalism in, 10–15, 137
NATO and, 74, 75–79,
85, 143
religion in, 11
Russian nationalism and,
104, 137
during Russia's annexa-
tion of Crimea, 121–22
during Russia's invasion
of Georgia, 90

during Russia's invasion of Ukraine, 157, 173–74, 243–44, 249, 251, 253, 255–56, 265, 287, 301
Solidarity movement, 75
during WWII, 19–21
Polish-Lithuanian Commonwealth, 6–10
Poltava, Battle of (1709), 8
Pontic steppes, 122–23, 200, 219
Poroshenko, Petro, 126–27, 129–30, 132, 134, 138–41, 164
Portuguese empire, 30, 31, 293
Potemkin, Grigorii, 122, 210, 241
Potter, Carole Grimaud, 262
Prigozhin, Yevgenii, 238–39
Primakov, Yevgenii, 56, 79–80
prisoners of war (POWs), 129, 140, 186–88, 201, 208
Prokopenko, Denys, 184, 185, 186, 188
Prokopenko, Kateryna, 186
Prylypko, Yurii, 167
Pushkin, Aleksandr, 104, 210
Putin, Vladimir, xvii, 51–52
annexation playbook of, 214–18
Beslan hostage crisis, 84
Biden and, 142–46, 244–45, 250
on the Bolsheviks Revolution, 15, 137, 151
Chechnya operations in 1999, 52–55
China and, 92, 93, 271, 277–80, 289–92
election as president, 51–53, 55–56, 92–93
Erdogan and, 281–86
Eurasian (re)integration and Russian imperial ambition, 66, 91–95, 100, 102–5, 120–26, 131, 135–38, 149, 215–17
George W. Bush and, 81–83
Georgian war (2008), 89–90
Germany and, 257–60
health rumors, 148

Hillary Clinton and, 274–75
Iran, 281
in the KGB, 51, 110
Kuchma and, 59, 74
launching the "special military operation" in Ukraine, 148–66
Macron and, 262–63
Medvedev and, 224–25
Munich Security Forum (2007), 86–87
on NATO expansion, 76, 86–90, 142–46, 267–68
nuclear weapons treaties and, 82
Obama and, 107
opposition to, 238
Orban and, 253
Poland and, 122
Poroshenko and, 126
prisoner exchanges, 188
rise to power of, 55–56, 83–84, 92
sanctions on, 247
Trump and, 275–76
Turchynov and, 126
Ukrainian counteroffensive and, 237–38
on Ukrainian protests, 63, 96–98, 106–8
Ukrainian supporters of, 132
United Nations and, 186
united reaction of the West to, 286–87, 289–90
using Ukrainian refugees, 175
US withdrawal from Afghanistan, 301
vision of a "New Russia," 104, 120–26, 131–32, 210, 239
Yanukovych and, 84, 93–95, 96–98, 106–11, 115
Zelensky and, 139–41

Qatar, 251

Ramstein air base, 251–52
RAND Corporation, 276
Reagan, Ronald, 244
refugees, xvii, 54, 172–75, 243–46, 253, 255, 285
Remchukov, Konstantin, 107

Republican Party, 87, 270, 275
Revolution of Dignity, 95–99, 113, 115, 124, 126–27, 134, 183
Revolution of Roses, 84, 88
Rezantsev, Yakov, 204, 212
Reznikov, Oleksii, 147, 217, 219–22, 241, 243, 248, 251
Rhodes, Ben, 107
RIA Novosti, 210, 217
Riazan, 54
Rizak, Mykola, 202
Rogozin, Dmitrii, 88
Romania, 14, 15, 19–20, 88, 121, 173, 174, 284
Romanov dynasty, 11, 15, 68, 135, 178
Romanticism, 178
Roosevelt, Franklin D., 225, 251, 300
Royal United Services Institute, 192, 242
RSFSR. See Russian Federation
Rubizhne, 189
Rukh, 57
Runov, Sergey, 131
Russia
autocracy in, 10, 36–37, 56, 83–84, 98–99, 244–45
"Greater Russia," 105, 111, 116–17, 120, 136, 216
nationalism in, 25–26, 37, 40, 50, 119–20, 152, 163
road to autocracy, 36–40
See also Russian Empire; Russian Federation; Soviet Union
Russian Central Bank, 247, 287, 289
Russian Empire
fall of the, 13–17
nationalism and, 9–11
Ukraine in the, 9–13
Russian Exhibition of Achievements of the National Economy (VDNKh), 214–15
Russian Federation
annexation playbook of the, 214–18
autocracy in the, 10, 36–37, 56, 83–84, 244–45

Russian Federation (*con-
tinued*)
  constitution of the, 35,
    37–40, 48–49, 51, 65,
    92, 108, 120
  democracy in the, 35–36,
    36–40, 48–53, 56,
    83–84, 87, 92
  Duma, 48, 49, 51, 69, 71,
    84, 114
  economy of the 1980s
    and 1990s, 41
  elections of the 1990s,
    48–53
  the EU and the, 92–93,
    131, 248, 287–89, 291
  Eurasianism and the
    Slavic people, 100–105
  GDP of the, 37, 44,
    288–89
  Liberal Democratic Party,
    40, 121
  objections to NATO
    expansion, 76–77,
    86–88, 143–47, 152
  October 1993 coup,
    34–35, 38–39
  oil and gas, 41, 69, 71, 74,
    86, 248, 284, 287–91
  preparations for invading
    Ukraine, 141–42
  Turkey and, 281–86
  Ukraine in the 1990s,
    28–33, 36
  under Yeltsin, 25–26
  See also Chechnya; Putin,
    Vladimir
Russian military
  Battalion Tactical Groups
    (BTGs), 189
  Black Sea Fleet, 2, 67–70,
    70–71, 74, 90, 200,
    213–14, 225
  Buk-Telar surface-to-air
    missile launcher, 128
  Moskva cruiser, 67, 200,
    213–14
  Russian Air Force, 159,
    172
  Russian Navy, 67, 225
Russian Orthodox Church,
    11, 133–34, 135, 149,
    196–98
Russophile movement,
    13, 14
Russo-Ukrainian War, xv–
    xx, 135–54, 293–99

Baltic states during, 253,
    255–56
  in the Black Sea region,
    199–218
  China and, 227, 277–80,
    290–92, 302–4
  death of shared identity,
    193–98
  declaration of war,
    148–52
  "denazification" as Rus-
    sian pretext, 152–54,
    162–63, 166–67, 183,
    187–88, 244
  on the eastern front,
    176–98
  first phase of, 155–72
  as fratricidal, 197
  invasion and annexation
    of Crimea, 100–117,
    118–26, 128–31, 132–34
  invasion of Ukraine,
    153–55, 155–57
  loyalty and betrayal dur-
    ing, 207–10
  preparing for Russia's
    invasion of Ukraine,
    142–48
  refugees of the, xvii,
    172–75, 243–46, 253,
    255, 285
  the response of the West,
    243–68
  Snake Island, 199–201
  Ukrainian counteroffen-
    sive, 219–42
  the uncertain end of the,
    293–99
  villages under occupa-
    tion, 166–67
  war in the Donbas and
    the Minsk Agree-
    ments, 126–31
  See also military materiel;
    Russian military;
    sanctions; Ukrainian
    military; *specific cities
    and theatres of war*
Ruthenians/Rusyn, 12–13
Rutskoi, Aleksandr, 34–35,
    38, 49, 68
Rutte, Mark, 220

Saakashvili, Mikheil, 84,
    89–90
Sadokhin, Ihor, 207
Saki, 225

Salman, Mohammed bin,
    288
Samara, 233
Samarkand, 291, 292
Samoilenko, Oleksandr, 230
sanctions, 128, 144, 145,
    246–48
  China and, 276, 280
  energy security and,
    286–89
  by European powers,
    253–55, 257–58
  against Iran, 274
  Turkey and, 281, 284–85
  the US and, 275–76,
    300–2
Sarkozy, Nicolas, 90, 260
satellite imagery, 222, 231
Saudi Arabia, 288, 290
Savitsky, Petr, 101–2
Schlegel, Karl Wilhelm
    Friedrich, 10
Scholz, Olaf, 257–66, 285
Schönbach, Kay-Achim, 257
Schröder, Gerhard, 261
Security Service of Ukraine
    (SBU), 207–8
Serbia, 14, 30–31, 79–80,
    101, 119
Sergeitsev, Timofei, 210
Servant of the People party,
    140, 223
Servant of the People (TV
    show), 138
Sevastopol, 2
  annexation of Crimea
    and, 118–20, 152
  Russian claims on, 63,
    67–71, 74, 90, 93, 110,
    112–13
  during the Russo-Ukrai-
    nian War, 213–14, 225
Shahed 129 drones, 281
Shanghai Cooperation
    Organization, 291
Shcherbytsky, Volodymyr,
    26
Shelest, Petro, 23
Shelon, Battle of (1471), 5
Shevchenko, Taras, 231
Shleha, Denys, 184
Shmelev, Ivan, 104
Shoigu, Sergei, 188–89,
    191–92, 229, 237, 241,
    285
Shulzhenko, Klavdiia, 194
Shushkevich, Stanislav, 3

Siberia, 303
Sikorski, Radosław, 106–7, 122–23
Simferopol, 111, 112–13
Sino-Soviet split, 272
Sirko, Ivan, 232, 234, 235
Siverodonetsk, 190–91, 236
Skif and Stuhna anti-tank guided missiles, 163
Skoropadsky, Pavlo, 16
Skovoroda, Hryhorii, 194
Skovorodynivka village, 195
Skuratov, Yurii, 52
Slavic identity, 10–12, 14, 104–5, 119, 149, 215
fall of the Soviet Union and, 26–27
language, 4–5, 10–15, 133, 137
national identities and the Bolshevik revolution, 17–18, 102, 105, 123, 137
in the Ottoman Empire, 80
Pan-Slavism, 14, 80
Russification of culture, 18, 24
Russophile movement, 13, 14
Serbia and, 30, 80
shared, 4–11, 136–37, 193–98
during WWII, 20
Slavophiles, 102–3
Slobodan, Milošević, 30, 79–80, 101
Sloboda Ukraine, 178
Slovakia, 85, 173, 174
Slovenia, 30–31, 253
Sloviansk, 125–27
Slutsky, Leonid, 153
Smerch (Tornado) multiple rocket launchers, 179
Snake Island, 200–201, 213–14
Sobchak, Anatolii, 51, 67
Sobolevsky, Yurii, 222
Social Democratic Party (Germany), 257
Socialist Party (Ukraine), 58–59
Solidarity movement, 75
Soloviev, Vladimir, 194
Solzhenitsyn, Aleksandr, 21, 66, 100–105, 123, 136, 151

South Korea, 247
South Ossetia, 89–90, 108–9
sovereignty
assurances of Ukraine's territorial integrity and, 72–73, 74, 85–86, 112, 172, 259, 266–67, 271, 285, 298
China and Ukraine's 278–79, 291
Crimean sovereignty as pretext for invasion, 67–68, 108, 118–19
denuclearization and Ukrainian sovereignty, 72, 74
fall of the Soviet Union and, 25–28, 48
"managed" or "sovereign" democracy, 48, 275
Russian challenges to Ukraine's territorial integrity and, 65–66, 115, 197
during the Russian Empire, 8, 10
Westphalian principles of state sovereignty, 300
Soviet Union
under Brezhnev, 23–24
Central Committee of the Communist Party, 21, 43
communism in, 1, 18, 40, 43, 48–50, 56, 69–70, 84, 101
fall of the, 2–4, 25–28
under Gorbachev, 23–25
invasion of Afghanistan, xviii, 111, 145, 290
under Khrushchev, 21–22
under Lenin, 17–19
nationalism and Soviet nationality policy, 17–21
oil and gas, 22–23, 26–27
political prisoners in, 21
Red Army, 20, 103, 110, 238
Russo-Chinese relations and, 272, 292, 302–3
Sino-Soviet split, 272
under Stalin, 19
during WWII, 19–20
See also Bolshevik Revolution

Spain, 287, 293
Stalin, Joseph, 17–24, 80, 103, 152, 238, 246, 267, 300
Stankevich, Sergei, 68
Starovoitova, Galina, 2
START-1 and START-2 treaties, 71, 73, 82, 274
State Inspectorate for Nuclear Regulation, 159
Stefanchuk, Ruslan, 155
Steinmeier, Frank-Walter, 260–61
Stepashin, Sergei, 51, 52
Stinger anti-aircraft missiles, 145, 163, 177, 249–50
Strela (Arrow) anti-aircraft missile complex, 214
Sukhenko, Olha, 167
Sukhoi SU-30 fighter jets, 270
Sumy region, 161, 171
Sunak, Rishi, 292
Suriname, 30
Surkov, Vladislav, 140
Surovikin, Sergei, 240, 241
Sushko, Ivan, 224
Suvorov, Aleksandr, 210, 282
Sverdlovsk oblast, 43
Sweden, 6, 8, 215, 256, 266–67, 284, 301
SWIFT messaging service, 248
Switchblade drones, 250
Switzerland, 148, 186–87
Symonenko, Petro, 57
Syrian, 174–75, 179, 183, 282, 283
Syrsky, Oleksandr, 158, 232, 235

T-80 tanks, 34
Tactical Unmanned Aerial Systems. See drone warfare
Taiwan, 247, 269–72, 277, 279
Tajikistan, 302
Talbott, Strobe, 77–78
Taliban, 81, 82
Taran, Andrii, 141
Tarasiuk, Borys, 77
Tatar people, 5, 9, 22, 66–67, 112, 283–84

Tatarstan, 70
Taurida, 201
Tavriysk, 202
Teniukh, Ihor, 113
Terekhov, Ihor, 182
Thomas-Greenfield, Linda, 207
Tikhon, Patriarch of Moscow, 104
Tkachenko, Oleksandr, 195
Transcarpathia, 12
Transcaucasian Federative Socialist Republic, 17–18
Transnistria, 69, 122, 191, 266
Trans-Pacific Trade Agreement, 275
Trenin, Dmitri, 122
Trubetzkoy, Nikolay, 101–2
Trump, Donald J., 275–76
Truss, Liz, 254–55
"Tulip Revolution," 84
Turchynov, Oleksandr, 98, 112–14, 126
Turkey
    drones from, 281–83, 284
    Russo-Turkish wars, 9, 14
    during the Russo-Ukrainian War, 172, 186–87, 266, 281–86
    during WWI, 30
Twitter, 187, 231, 264
Tymoshenko, Yulia, 57–59, 94, 114

UAVs (unmanned aerial vehicles). See drone warfare
Ufa, 233
Ukraine
    Africa's reliance on, 263, 285
    Bolshevik revolution in, 15–17
    Central Rada, 15–16
    communism in, 19, 26, 46–47, 57–58, 132–33
    constitution of, 45–48, 56, 58–61, 93, 97, 120–21, 130–31, 134, 140
    Cossacks and the history of, 6–9, 11, 22, 68, 178, 195, 232, 283
    Crimea and Ukrainian territorial integrity, 65–70

democracy in, 36, 41–48, 56–62, 70, 83, 87, 94, 138
economy of the 1980s and 1990s, 41–45
energy security of, 41, 69, 71, 74, 86, 94–95, 260
the EU and, 84–85, 92–96, 98, 106, 111, 121, 124, 131, 134, 164–65, 266, 267
Euromaidan protests, 61, 95–99, 106–11, 115, 121, 124, 127, 132, 134
fall of the Soviet Union and, 25–28
Galicia, 4, 12–14
GDP of, 73, 182
gross domestic product (GDP) of, 73, 182
language law, 106, 133–34
nationalism in, 10–13, 20–21, 26, 41–42, 47, 109, 183
nuclear weapons and nuclear power in, 63–65
Orange Revolution, 36, 56–62, 83–85, 91
Orthodox Church of Ukraine, 133–34, 196–97
People's Democratic Party of, 57
political identity of, 132–34
political prisoners in, 94
referendum on independence, 2–4, 26–27
Revolution of Dignity, 95–99, 113, 115, 124, 126–27, 134, 183
during the Russian Empire, 11–13
Servant of the People party, 140, 223
shared history with Russia, 4–9
symbolic importance of, 22
Verkhovna Rada, 42
during WWII, 19–20, 167, 190, 223
See also sovereignty; Ukrainian People's Republic; Zelensky, Volodymyr

"Ukraine Defense Consultative Group," 252
Ukrainian military
    Azov regiment, 127, 182–89
    "Cyborgs," 130, 211
    National Guard of Ukraine, 127, 160, 183, 184
    National Security and Defense Council, 126, 141, 156
    Security Service of Ukraine (SBU), 207–8
    Sicheslav Brigade, 232, 235
    Ukrainian Armed Forces, 154, 158, 229–30, 248
    Western arms and, 248–52
    See also military materiel
Ukrainian People's Republic, 16
    under Brezhnev, 23–24
    under Gorbachev, 23–25
    Holodomor, 19, 21
    under Khrushchev, 21–22
    under Lenin, 17–19
    under Stalin, 19
UNESCO, 193
Uniate Church, 11
United Kingdom, 252–56
    African colonies of, 29
    British Empire and World War II, 29–30
    the EU and the, 253, 255–56
United Nations
    charter of the, 271, 278
    Chechnya and, 55
    International Atomic Energy Agency (IAEA), xvi, 159, 206, 226–27, 231
    on refugees, 175
    Russia in the, 88, 114
    during the Russo-Ukrainian War, 115, 186–87, 175, 264
    Security Council, 73, 79, 114–15, 159, 207
    Turkey and, 285
United States
    China and, 269–77, 303
    military assistance as share of GDP, 252, 258

9/11 attack, 81–82,
    272–73
preparing for Russia's
    invasion of Ukraine,
    142–48
during the Russo-Ukrai-
    nian War, 272–77
sanctions and, 275–76,
    300–304
war in Afghanistan,
    81–82, 272–73, 300
See also specific presidents
    and agencies/depart-
    ments
US Congress, 145, 163, 250,
    270, 276
US Department of Defense,
    251
US Department of State,
    146
US Holocaust Memorial
    Museum, 75
US Joint Chiefs of Staff, 143,
    192, 251
USSR. See Soviet Union
USS Ronald Reagan,
    269–70
Ustrialov, Nikolai, 136–37
Uvarov, Sergei, 10–11, 136
Uzbekistan, 82, 84, 291,
    302

Vasylkiv airport, 161
VDNKh (Russian Exhibition
    of Achievements of the
    National Economy),
    214–15
Venediktov, Aleksei, 135
Venezuela, 145, 288
Verbivka village, 233
Vereshchuk, Iryna, 219–20
Verkhovna Rada, 42
Verstiuk, Vladyslav, 170–71
Vilnius Summit (2013), 95
Visegrad Group, 75
Voshchanov, Pavel, 64,
    65–66
Vovchansk, 234–35
Voznesensk, 211
Vukovar, 31
Vysokopillia village, 230

Wadephul, Johann, 261
Wagner Group, 239
Wałęsa, Lech, 75, 77–78
Wall, 260, 299, 302
Wang Wenbin, 272
Wang Yi, 280

Watling, Jack, 242
Way, Lucan, 42
Westernizers, 102
Westphalian principles of
    state sovereignty, 300
World War I, 14, 17, 29, 30
World War II, xviii–xix,
    19–20, 299
Anschluss of Austria,
    xv, 116–17
appeasement of Hitler
    and, 146
British Empire and,
    29–30
Crimea during, 121
Germany after, 259, 261
Holocaust, 20–21, 75,
    245
nationalism at the end of,
    20, 25, 30
refugee crisis of, xvii, 172
Russia during, 19, 25
Ukraine during, 19–20,
    167, 190, 223
Yalta Conference, 25,
    225, 300

Xi Jinping, 270, 277–80,
    291–92

Yakovlivka village, 181
Yalta Conference, 25, 225,
    300
Yanukovych, Viktor, 36,
    60–61, 90–91, 93–99
election of, 60–61, 90,
    94, 97, 107
EU and, 93–95
Euromaidan protests,
    95–99, 106–11, 124,
    127
NATO and, 90–91
during the Orange Revo-
    lution, 83–84
Putin and, 60–61, 84
Russia's annexation of
    the Crimea, 111–15,
    120–21
Yatseniuk, Arsenii, 98, 114
Yavlinsky, Grigorii, 56
Yelets Monastery, 195
Yeltsin, Boris, 2–4, 25–28,
    31–33, 34–40, 44–45,
    48–49, 55–56, 100–102
Chechnya and, 53–54
Commonwealth of Inde-
    pendent States (CIS)
    and, 91

on the Crimea, 67–71
election of, 37, 46,
    48–51
Kravchuk compared to,
    42–45
Kuchma compared to,
    46, 57–58, 60–61
on NATO expansion,
    77–79, 82
nuclear disarmament
    under, 74, 82
opponents of, 32, 34–35
Putin and, 51–53, 106
Serbia and, 31, 79,
    100–102
Ukrainian independence
    and, 64–66
Yermak, Andrii, 147, 156
Yugoslavia, xviii, 30–31,
    79–80
"Yugoslavia with nukes," 32,
    63, 79
Yumashev, Valentin,
    51–52
Yushchenko, Viktor, 36,
    57–61, 83–86, 87–88,
    90, 91, 93

Zaluzhny, Valerii, 158
Zaporizhia, xvi
counteroffensive in,
    217–18, 219–20, 221,
    226–27
nuclear power station
    in, xvii–xviii, 206,
    226–27, 231, 299
Russian annexation
    attempts, 218, 224,
    238, 239
during the Russian
    empire, 9
Russian-financed revolt
    in, 123
Zelensky, Olena, 155
Zelensky, Volodymyr,
    138–42
on attack on Chernobyl,
    159, 206–7, 226
China and, 292
counteroffensive by, 217,
    220, 224–25,
    229–31
election of Zelensky,
    138–40
Germany and, 139, 258,
    260–61
Jewish ancestry of, 245
Johnson and, 254, 256

Zelensky, Volodymyr (*continued*)
  leading up to Russia's invasion, 146–48, 155–58
  Macron and, 139, 262–63
  negotiations to broker peace, 186–87, 265–66
  Paris meeting with Putin, 140
  personnel changes under, 207–8
  popularity of, 164–65
  Putin's attacks on, 138, 143, 155–56
  refusal to flee, 146, 148, 157, 163–65
  remarks at the Munich Security Conference (2022), 147–48
  among the troops, 232, 235, 242
  Trump and, 276

US intelligence sharing with, 143, 146–47
Zhadan, Serhii, 178
Zhirinovsky, Vladimir, 40, 121–22
Zhuravlev, Aleksandr, 179–80
Zhytomyr, 153, 174
Ziuganov, Gennadii, 49, 50, 56
Zolote village, 190
Zubov, Andrei, 116